SAGE was founded in 1965 by Sara Miller McCune to support the dissemination of usable knowledge by publishing innovative and high-quality research and teaching content. Today, we publish over 900 journals, including those of more than 400 learned societies, more than 800 new books per year, and a growing range of library products including archives, data, case studies, reports, and video. SAGE remains majority-owned by our founder, and after Sara's lifetime will become owned by a charitable trust that secures our continued independence.

Los Angeles | London | New Delhi | Singapore | Washington DC | Melbourne

Business Laws

Business Laws

Text and Problems

Inderjeet Dagar

Principal, College of Vocational Studies, University of Delhi, New Delhi

Anurag Agnihotri

Faculty, College of Vocational Studies, University of Delhi, New Delhi

SAGE | TEXTS

Los Angeles | London | New Delhi
Singapore | Washington DC | Melbourne

First published in 2020 by

SAGE | TEXTS

SAGE Publications India Pvt Ltd
B1/I-1 Mohan Cooperative Industrial Area
Mathura Road, New Delhi 110 044, India
www.sagepub.in

SAGE Publications Inc
2455 Teller Road
Thousand Oaks, California 91320, USA

SAGE Publications Ltd
1 Oliver's Yard, 55 City Road
London EC1Y 1SP, United Kingdom

SAGE Publications Asia-Pacific Pte Ltd
18 Cross Street #10-10/11/12
China Square Central
Singapore 048423

Published by Vivek Mehra for SAGE Publications India Pvt Ltd. Typeset in 9.5/11.5 pt ITC Stone Serif by AG Infographics, Delhi.

Library of Congress Cataloging-in-Publication Data Available

ISBN: 978-93-5328-751-1 (PB)

SAGE Team: Indrani Dutta, Ritesh Ranjan, Syeda Aina Rahat Ali, Sonam Rana, Ankit Verma and Kanika Mathur

Contents

Unit III. The Sale of Goods Act, 1930

Unit IV. The Limited Liability Partnership Act, 2008

Unit V. The Information Technology Act, 2000

Unit VI. The Negotiable Instruments Act, 1881

Detailed Contents

Unit III. The Sale of Goods Act, 1930

List of Abbreviations

B2B	Business-to-business
B2C	Business-to-customer
CBIS	Computer Based Information System
CCA	Controller of Certifying Authorities
CLB	Company Law Board
DPIN	Designated partner identification number
EDI	Electronic data interchange
EMPI	Entrepreneurship and Management Processes International
HUF	Hindu undivided family
IPC	Indian Penal Code
IT	Information technology
KYC	Know Your Customer
LLP	Limited liability partnership
ODI	Outward direct investment
RoC	Registrar of companies/Registrar of company
SCERT	State Council of Educational Research and Training
STC	State Trading Corporation
USMS	University School of Management Studies
VRS	Voluntary retirement scheme
VS	Vocational studies

Preface

Any business or commercial transaction is governed and regulated by law. One of the problems faced by any person or student studying business law is that business takes place within a wide-ranging legal environment and system. Therefore, students are required to have knowledge of the legal rules and procedures impacting business activities, which is more than what is required for just passing the examination. The difficulty is in acquiring an adequate knowledge of the wide-ranging areas that govern the business and commercial activities. The learners of business law are expected to focus their attention and energy on reading and understanding between the lines.

For the authors of a textbook on business law, the aim should be to provide the materials in simple language and words, which is considered sufficient, without compromising the quality of the content required to understand law and equip the students to pass the exams. To achieve this goal, the text must not be too specialized, nor should it provide the students with no more than a superficial general knowledge of most of the possible interfaces between law and business enterprise.

The object of this book titled *Business Laws: Text and Problems* is to set out the basic principles of business law in simple and clear terms. An attempt has been made to present the concepts as briefly and concisely as possible without sacrificing essential features and contents.

In this book, the authors have not attempted to cover all the areas within the scope of business law, since the book has been designed to cover the syllabus of business law paper of the BCom (Hons) and BCom, BBE (Hons), BMS and BA (VS) courses of the University of Delhi and Guru Gobind Singh Indraprastha University (GGSIPU). The book fully covers the syllabus with the help of examples and leading cases. Authors sincerely hope that the book will serve the requirements of the students of these courses.

Acknowledgements

First and foremost, we would like to express our gratitude and thanks to God for giving us wisdom and the urge to author this book. Writing a book is a journey in which one experiences the support and guidance of various persons such as parents, teachers, friends, colleagues, authors of books studied, publisher and students. The guidance, reviews and support make the journey easy, productive, fruitful and effective. The journey started when we entered the school and then went to college to gain knowledge. We are indebted to all our teachers who taught us in schools and colleges in general and to Dr M. C. Kuchhal, Professor B. P. Singh, Professor R. A. Sharma, Professor D. P. S. Verma and Professor B. M. L. Nigam in particular. Our parents have always been the sources of inspiration, and we are deeply indebted to them. This book would not have been possible without the support of our family members. We express our thanks to our family members for their patience and sacrifice and for bearing with us which helped in successful completion of the book.

During our careers as teachers, we have learnt a lot either directly or indirectly through interactions with our peers and students. It is difficult to name all of them, and we express our sincere thanks and gratitude to all of them. We would like to acknowledge the direct and indirect support of a large number of friends, colleagues and faculties in different colleges and departments of the University of Delhi and other universities. Mention may be made of Professor R. K. Singh, Professor Madan Lal and Dr Amit Singh from the Department of Commerce and Business, University of Delhi and Principal colleagues, Dr P. K. Khurana (Shaheed Bhagat Singh College), Dr S. P. Agarwal (Ramanujan College), Dr G. K. Arora (Dr Bhim Rao Ambedkar College), Dr Pawan Kumar Sharma (Dyal Singh College), Dr Vipin Agrawal (Sri Aurobindo College) and Dr P. V. Khatri (Swami Shraddhanand College).

Our thanks are due to all our colleagues in the College of Vocational Studies (CVS) for helping in college administration so that we could find time for writing this book. Mention may be made of Mr S. K. Bhatia, Dr Surender Singh, Dr Anjana Arora, Dr Ratnavali Kaushik, Ms Anu Singh, Dr Shalini Singhal, Dr M. Geetha, Dr Anu Satyal, Dr Kuldeep Ahuja, Ms Anuradha Bawa Singh, Mrs Neerja Arya, Mrs Deepa Sahai Garg, Dr Meenakshi Aggarwal, Dr Sunil and Dr Bhupinder Singh.

Our thanks are due to all our colleagues, friends, well-wishers and faculties in other colleges of the University of Delhi and other universities. Mention may be made of Dr Anil Kumar (Shri Ram College of Commerce); Dr Arun Atree, Dr Anil Sardana, Dr Desh Raj Saklani (Shaheed Bhagat Singh College); Dr Surender Kumar (Pannalal Girdharlal Dayanand Anglo Vedic College); Dr Anil Kumar Singh (Sri Aurobindo College, Evening); Dr Divya Sharma (Bharti College); Dr Rajender Kumar (Rajdhani College); Professor R. B. Solanki (Chaudhary Ranbir Singh University [CRSU]); Professor P. K. Gupta (Jamia Millia Islamia); Professor M. B. Shukla and

Professor Ajeet Kumar Shukla (Mahatma Gandhi Kashi Vidyapith); Professor Naval Kishore and Professor Sunil Gupta (University School of Management Studies [USMS], Indira Gandhi National Open University [IGNOU]); Professor Sanjeev Mittal (USMS, GGSIPU); Dr Jagbeer Ahelawat, Dr Pranveer and Dr Rajiv Dahiya (Maharaja Surajmal Institute, GGSIPU); Professor Narender Garg (Maharshi Dayanand University); Professor Anand Sharma (Department of Commerce, Central University of Haryana); Professor R. K. Sharma (Bharati Vidyapeeth Institute of Management & Research [BVIMR]); and Professor N. Ravichandran (School of Management & Business Studies, Jamia Hamdard University). Special thanks are due to Dr T. N. Chabra, our ex-colleague in CVS.

We also express our sincere thanks and gratitude to our publisher and the editorial team of SAGE for their cooperation, dedication and sincere efforts for publishing this book.

The publication of this book is a beginning, and we do not claim it to be complete and perfect. There is a lot of scope for improvement based on your suggestions and feedback. Suggestions and feedback from faculties, students and all others are welcome and will be highly appreciated.

About the Authors

CMA (Dr) Inderjeet Dagar has been working as Principal, CVS, University of Delhi, since December 2005. He started teaching in 1983 in CVS, University of Delhi. He has been the Director-cum-Professor of a college affiliated to GGSIPU. He has also worked as a training manager in Salalah Port Services Company, Sultanate of Oman. He has also been the coordinator for an IGNOU study centre for MBA, MTM and MCom courses. He did his BCom (Hons) from Shri Ram College of Commerce, MCom and MPhil (Management) from the University of Delhi, and PhD from Jamia Millia Islamia. He is a fellow member (FCMA) of the Institute of Costs and Management Accountants of India. He is a life member of Indian Commerce Association (ICA), Indian Accounting Association (IAA) and All India Management Association (AIMA).

He has authored books on business laws and corporate laws and many articles in the field of management. He has completed two UGC Major Research Projects. He has also been involved in curriculum framing at university and UGC levels, that is, he has been associated with Course Revision Committee as a convener/member for UGC; Choice Based Credit System Course Subcommittee for BA (Vocational Studies); Bachelor with Honours in Management Studies, University of Delhi; BA (Vocational Studies [VS]), University of Delhi; BCom, University of Delhi; BBA (Tour and Travel Management), GGSIPU; and CRSU and so on.

He has been a member of the University Court, Executive Council and Academic Council of the University of Delhi. He was visitor's nominee in IGNOU. He has also been on some committees of UGC and AICTE. He has been a member of Board of Studies, School of Vocational Education and Training, IGNOU, Delhi.

He has been honoured with several awards such as 50 Most Influential Principals of India by World Education Congress, Dr Radhakrishnan Memorial Award 2006, Alumni Excellence Award by Shri Ram College of Commerce Alumni Association, Amity Excellence Award for outstanding contribution in the field of education, a certificate for Exemplary Contribution towards education by Career Launcher and so on.

Dr Anurag Agnihotri has been working as Assistant Professor in CVS, University of Delhi, since July 2007. He started teaching in 2003 in Delhi College of Advance Studies, affiliated to GGSIPU. He is graduate in commerce from Kakatiya University, Warangal, and postgraduate in commerce from Chhatrapati Shahu Ji Maharaj University, Kanpur. He holds an LLB degree from Dayanand College of Law, Kanpur, and MPhil from Madurai Kamaraj University, Madurai. He is also UGC-NET qualified. He has his doctorate in risk management from Mahatma Gandhi Kashi Vidyapith. He also has several National Institute of Securities Markets (NISM) certifications.

He has authored books on business laws, company law and economic laws. He has authored many research papers on finance, corporate governance and risk management which have been published in many national and international journals in India and abroad. He has presented his research papers in national and international conferences. His work on demonetization and outward direct investment (ODI) is appreciated by the Ministry of Finance, Government of India.

He is visiting faculty to many reputed B-schools in Delhi and NCR such as USMS (GGSIPU), BVIMR, Entrepreneurship and Management Processes International (EMPI), Bharatiya Vidya Bhavan's Usha and Lakshmi Mittal Institute of Management (BULMIM), Jamia Millia Islamia and Jamia Hamdard. He is a member of Student Research Advisory Committee of Jamia Hamdard. He is Accredited Management Teacher by AIMA in finance. He was a member of the subcommittee of the syllabus for marketing management and insurance (MMI; BA [VS]), marketing management and retail business (MMRB; BA [VS]) of the University of Delhi. He was convener and member of subcommittee of syllabus for BBE.

He is a life member of ICA, IAA and AIMA. He is a steering committee member of The Professional Risk Managers' International Association (PRIMA and Secretary, Northern Region [NIRC]), Indian Council for Business Education.

He is Resource Faculty for INSET Programme of PGT (Commerce), State Council of Educational Research and Training (SCERT), Delhi, and Kendriya Vidyalaya Sangathan. He has prepared online modules for AIMA and IACM. He has acted as a resource person for management development programme (MDP) in Gujarat Narmada Valley Fertilizers & Chemicals (GNFC), (n)Code Solutions, Dalmia Industries, National Small Industries Corporation (NSIC) and so on. He is involved in corporate consultancy, which includes companies such as IST Limited, Gurgaon Infospace Limited, IST Steel and Power Limited, Riqueza Capital, Standard Securities, NSIC and so on.

He has worked as the member interview panel for public sector undertakings such as Food Corporation of India (FCI), Coal India Limited (CIL), State Trading Corporation (STC), Container Corporation of India, CRWAI and Central Warehousing Corporation.

About the Book

This book aims to equip the learners with knowledge and understanding of the fundamental concepts of business law as they relate to business. It has been designed to cover the syllabus of business law paper of the BCom (Hons) and BCom, BBE (Hons), BMS and BA (VS) courses of the University of Delhi and GGSIPU. It fully covers the syllabus with the help of examples and leading cases. It is divided into 6 units with 27 chapters and 1 appendix. The six units are as follows:

Unit I. The Indian Contract Act, 1872
Unit II. The Indian Contract Act, 1872: Special Contract
Unit III. The Sale of Goods Act, 1930
Unit IV. The Limited Liability Partnership Act, 2008
Unit V. The Information Technology Act, 2000
Unit VI. The Negotiable Instruments Act, 1881

Unit I: This unit covers the basic features of a contract, its types and essentials of a valid contract. It explains the contractual capacity of parties, consideration, free consent, legality of objects and void agreements. It also explains discharge of contract, modes of discharge including breach and remedies for breach of contract.

Unit II: This unit explains various special contracts provided in the Contract Act such as a quasi-contract, contract of indemnity and guarantee, contract of bailment and pledge, and contract of agency.

Unit III: This unit explains various provisions of the Sale of Goods Act, 1930, such as a contract of sale, sale and agreement to sell, different conditions and warranties applicable in a contract of sale, and transfer of ownership in goods including sale by non-owners. It also explains the performance of a contract of sale and rights of an unpaid seller.

Unit IV: This unit covers the various provisions of the Limited Liability Partnership Act such as the nature of limited liability partnership (LLP), partners and designated partners, incorporation documents, incorporation process, registered office of LLP and change therein. It also explains the extent and limitation of liability of LLP and partners, whistle-blowing, taxation of LLP, conversion into LLP, winding up and dissolution of LLP.

Unit V: This unit explains the relevant provisions of the Information Technology Act, 2000, including digital signature, digital signatures' certificates, electronic governance, attribution, acknowledgement and dispatch of electronic records. It also covers the provisions related to regulation of certifying authorities, duties of subscribers, penalties, adjudication and various offences under the Act.

Unit VI: This unit is especially added in the book to cater to the needs of the students who are not from the University of Delhi. It explains negotiable instruments, their types, holder and holder in due course, endorsement, crossing of cheque and dishonour of negotiable instruments.

After covering the syllabus in 27 chapters, the book has one appendix which explains the keywords. It has been added for better understanding of the legal concepts with the help of legal cases-based problems and for better preparation for examination.

UNIT I

The Indian Contract Act, 1872

1

CHAPTER

Introduction of Contract and Kinds of Contracts

Learning Objectives

- To understand the meaning of law and business law
- To know about the sources of business law
- To understand the meaning of contract and agreement
- To understand the essential elements of a valid contract
- To know about the kinds of contracts
- To understand the difference between different kinds of contracts

The term 'law' denotes a set of rules and regulations which govern the social conduct and which can be enforced through the courts. 'Law' has been one of the most effective instruments for control of social relations and transactions from the ancient times. It is expected to deal with the new developments which create new problems in the society. It regulates the actions of persons in respect to one another and in respect to the entire social group. According to Austin, 'Law is a rule of conduct imposed and enforced by the sovereign.' Holmes says, 'Law is a statement of the circumstances in which the public force will be brought to bear upon men through courts. Again the prophecies of what the court will do in fact and nothing more pretentious are what I mean by law.' According to Salmond, 'Law is the body of principles recognized and applied by the state in the administration of justice.' From the above definitions of law, the following *essential characteristics* of law can be drawn:

1. Law presupposes a state
2. The state makes law as a rule relating to the actions of human beings
3. Law aims to regulate the external actions of human beings
4. Law is enforced by the state
5. Law is applied in the administration of justice
6. Law applies to all without discrimination, including the state, which itself is regulated by law
7. Law is always supreme

In simple words, rules of conduct enforced by the state to maintain peace and order in the society are called 'laws'. Laws are made effective by:

1. Preventing disobedience
2. Directing someone, who defaults, to complete his obligations
3. Imposing obligation to pay damages for an injury caused due to disobedience
4. Administering punitive action upon failure to comply the rule of law

Sources of Law

Sources of law denote the formal and material sources, from which the law derives its force and validity. The following are the main sources of law:

1. Statutes having their source in legislation made by the State
2. Customs and precedents, which over a period of time become as good as law
3. Common law, which though originated in the Great Britain has now been well absorbed into the Indian legal system
4. International treaties and agreements
5. Judicial decisions and precedents
6. Miscellaneous, for example, juristic writings, literary works and foreign decisions

Why to Study Law?

Law and society are closely related. No society can exist without law. *Ignorantia juris non excusat* is a familiar maxim, which means *ignorance of law is no excuse*. Thus, it is essential for every person to have knowledge of the law of the land. However, although it is not possible for a person to have the knowledge of every branch of law, it will be to the advantage of a person to know as much as possible. In fact, law and society are inseparable companions and have profound effect upon each other. Ignorantia juris non excusat, however, lays down exception that the ignorance of a foreign law is excused.

What Is Business Law?

Business law is a wide term and embraces all legal principles concerning business transactions. It is also known as 'commercial law', 'law of merchant' or 'mercantile law'. It consists of those legal rules which govern and regulate business activities, transactions and trade. It also encompasses the law relating to the regulation of business associations and other incidental matters. Business laws affect not only the business community but also the members of the society. Man, as a social being, comes into contact with people in different capacities. According to S. R. Davar, business law 'means that branch of law which is applicable to or concerned with trade and commerce in connection with various mercantile or business transactions'. As per Slater, 'The phrase Mercantile Law or Commercial Law is generally used to denote those portions of the law which deal with the rights and obligations arising out of transactions between mercantile persons.' It comprises a vast number of laws pertaining to business transactions, and these laws govern the relations of businessmen with the society. Business law cannot be regarded as a separate branch of law. It is only a part of the civil laws. Some of the legislations which are covered in the Indian business law are the Indian Contract Act, 1872; the Negotiable Instruments Act, 1881; the Sale of Goods Act, 1930; and corporate laws, that is, the Indian Companies Act, 2013; the Information Technology Act, 2000 and so on.

Sources of Business Law

Business law finds its origin in the customs and usages of merchants or traders in England, which eventually became a part of the common law of England. The main sources of business law are as follows:

1. **The Lex mercatoria,** that is, the Law Merchant, which emanated from the customs and usages which are binding on traders in their dealings with each other.
2. **The statute law**, which is derived from the legislation or enactments or the subordinate legislation made by the legislative bodies
3. **The common law**, which includes the principles of law evolved by the judges in making decisions on cases that are brought before them.
4. **The principles of equity**, which are neither the customs nor codified law but are imperative dictates of conscience and have been set forth and developed in the Court of Chancery.

Indian business laws are largely based upon the English business law. Prior to 1872, the personal laws of the parties to the suit resulted in 'mercantile transactions'. The first efforts to codify and establish uniform principles of business law were made in 1872 by the passing of the Indian Contract Act. Since then, various Acts have been codified to regulate transactions related to sale of goods, partnership, negotiable instruments, carriage of goods, insurance and so on.

Law of Contracts

The law of contracts forms the oldest branch of laws relating to business/commercial transactions. It enunciates the legal principles governing business transactions in India. Just as the safety of persons and property depends upon the rules of criminal law, the security and stability of the business world depend upon the law of contracts. The object and function of the law of contracts are to see that as far as possible, the expectations created by the promises of the parties and obligations prescribed by the agreement of the parties are enforced. Indeed, the bases of trade and commerce today are the promises or agreements and their enforceability by law.

The rules relating to contracts in India are contained in the Indian Contract Act, 1872. It enunciates legal principles, which govern business in India, but the Act is by no means extenuative. It does not deal with all branches of the law of contracts. Laws relating to partnership, sale of goods and negotiable instruments are not part of the Indian Contract Act. However, the Contract Act contains not only the general principles of contracts but also the rules governing special contracts. The Contract Act is of special importance to the businesspersons and others, as it enables them to plan with certainty that the promisor will perform whatever has been promised to them; otherwise, the promisor will be liable for the loss suffered by the promisee.

THE INDIAN CONTRACT ACT, 1872

The Contract Act neither affects nor overrides any usage or custom of business. It deals with movable properties and right *in personam*. It deals with the agreements which can be enforced through courts of law. It lays down a number of limiting principles subject to which the parties may create rights and obligations for themselves. The Indian Contract Act, 1872, is applicable to the whole of India, except the state of Jammu and Kashmir. It came into force on 1 September 1872. It has the following parts.

Contract

According to Salmond, 'A contract is an agreement creating and defining obligation between the parties.' Further, Sir William Anson says, 'A contract is an agreement enforceable by law, made between two or more persons, by which right[s] are acquired by one or more to acts or forbearance on the part of other or others.' Justice Pollock observed, 'Every agreement and promise enforceable at law is a contract.' The above definitions bring out two connected elements: obligation and agreement, enforceable by law. According to Section 2(h), 'An agreement enforceable by law is a contract.' As per the above definition, under Section 2(h), the two important features of a contract are as follows:

1. An agreement
2. Its enforceability by law

} Contract

An Agreement

According to Section 2(e), 'Every promise and every set of promises, forming the consideration for each other, is an agreement.' An agreement is preliminary to a contract. In other words, it is formed when one party makes the proposal and the other party accepts it. It establishes a relationship between the parties. Thus, it is an outcome of the offer and acceptance between parties, that is,

Offer + Acceptance = Agreement.

Example: A promises to sell his car to B for ₹5,000 and B accepts it. Now this is an agreement between A and B, which constitutes a legal obligation on A to sell (deliver) his car to B and on B to pay ₹5,000.

Consensus Ad Idem

An agreement is the outcome of consenting minds or *consensus ad idem*. This means meeting of minds of the parties to the contract on the subject matter of contract at the same time and in the same sense. It is an important condition for converting an agreement into a contract.

Example: A, who owns two cars, black and white, proposes to B to sell his black car for ₹50,000 and B accepts it. Now, here is consensus ad idem as both parties agree to the same subject matter as A wants to sell his black car and B wants to purchase it, so they agree on same facts. The acceptance has the same relationship with the offer as the matchstick has with the gunpowder.

Obligation

It is *vinculum juris*. It means a legal tie, bond or duty. It is defined as a legal tie, which imposes upon a person the necessity of doing or abstaining from doing a definite act or acts.

Essential Elements of a Valid Contract (Under Section 10)

A proposal (offer) can become a contract only when it has two features: there is an agreement and it is legally enforceable. When these two conditions exist, there will be a contract, which will be legally binding on the parties. Section 10 of the Indian Contract Act provides the following essential elements to make a valid contract:

1. **Agreement:** An agreement is the essence of any contract. It is the result of the offer and acceptance between two or more parties. The offer and acceptance should be lawful. They should relate to the same thing in the same sense. The acceptance must be unconditional and absolute. It should be given in the mode prescribed by the offeror.
   Example: A proposes to sell his house to B for ₹5 lakh, and B gives his consent to purchase it for the said amount. This is an agreement between A and B. An agreement is complete when an offer made is accepted. It is the acceptance which gives rise to the cause of action, and not merely making an offer. The Karnataka High Court has given a similar view in the case of Republic Medico Surgical Co. vs. UOI.
2. **Intention to create a legal relationship:** An agreement must create a legal relationship between the parties. The intention of both the parties entering into an agreement must be to create a legal relationship between them. If there is no intention on the part of the parties to create a legal relationship, there is no contract. The social and moral agreements between the parties cannot be a contract. For example, to invite a friend to dinner is not an agreement which creates a legal relationship. Hence, it cannot be a contract. An intention not to create a legal relationship was implied in the case of Balfour vs. Balfour. In this case, Mr Balfour, who was employed on a government job in Ceylon, went to England with his wife on leave. For health reason, his wife was not able to come back with him to Ceylon. Mr Balfour promised to pay $30 per month to his wife as maintenance for the period she lived apart. He failed to send the money to his wife, and she sued him to recover the amount. It was held by the court that there being no intention to create a legal relationship, the husband (Mr Balfour) was not liable to pay. In the case of S. V. R. Mudaliar vs. Rajababu, the Supreme Court held that even if an agreement is described as gentlemen's understanding, there is a clear agreement that the property which is being conveyed will be reconceived to the vendor, the agreement is binding and there was an intention to create a legal relationship because that is presumed in such cases. In commercial transactions, the presumption is that the parties intend to create a legal relationship.

3. **Free consent:** The consent of the parties to the agreement must be free and genuine. According to Section 14,

   Consent is said to be free when it is not caused by—
   (1) coercion, as defined in section 15, or
   (2) undue influence, as defined in section 16, or
   (3) fraud, as defined in section 17, or
   (4) misrepresentation, as defined in section 18, or
   (5) mistake, subject to the provisions of sections 20, 21 and 22.

   A consent is said to be so caused when it would not have been given but for the existence of such coercion, undue influence, fraud, misrepresentation or mistake. The party, whose consent is not free, can avoid the contract. In other words, when the consent of a party is not free, then the agreement is voidable at the option of the aggrieved party.
   Example: X at the gunpoint asks Y to sell his watch worth ₹9,000 for ₹900 only. Y accepts the offer to sell his watch. Y's consent is not free. The agreement, therefore, is voidable at the option of Y.
4. **Contractual capacity:** According to Sections 11 and 12, a person is said to have the contractual capacity if he has attained the age of majority, is of sound mind and is not disqualified from contracting by any other law. A person is minor if he is below the age of 18 years. An agreement with an incompetent person is void and is a nullity in the eyes of law and hence cannot be enforced in a court of law. In the case of Mohori Bibee vs. Dharmodas Ghose, the court held that a minor does not have the contractual capacity, and any contract with a minor will be void, which means that the court will not enforce such cases.

   Therefore, a minor cannot enter into a contract; similarly, law considers idiots as incompetent to contract.
5. **Lawful consideration:** Consideration is an essential element in a contract. An enforceable agreement should be supported by consideration. According to Section 25, 'An agreement made without consideration is void', subject to certain exceptions given in this section. Consideration means something in return, which implies that there must be something in contract for all the parties to the contract.
   Example: X promises to sell his car to Y for ₹50,000. In this agreement, there is consideration for both the parties; for X it is ₹50,000 and for Y it is the car.

   Consideration need not be in cash or kind. It may be an act, abstinence or promise to do or not to do something. It may be in past, present or future, but it must be lawful as provided under Section 23. It becomes unlawful if it is forbidden by law or it is opposed to public policy. A lawful consideration is essential for a contract.
6. **Lawful object:** Section 23 of the Act provides that the object or purpose of an agreement should be lawful. It must not be illegal or immoral or opposed to the public policy. It must not be forbidden by law. If it suffers from any defect, then it will not be enforceable by law.
   Example: X promises to give his car to Y for ₹50,000 if he beats Mr Sudhir. Here, the object of the contract is unlawful as law forbids the object of contract. Any agreement entered into by the parties for doing a crime or committing an offence is void and unenforceable.
7. **Certainty of terms:** Section 29 of the Act provided that the terms and conditions of an agreement must be precise and certain. They must not be vague, indefinite or uncertain. If they are so, the agreement is not enforceable.
   Example: A agrees to sell to B 50 tons of oil. There is nothing to show what kind of oil was intended. The agreement is uncertain and, therefore, void.

8. **Possibility of performance:** The agreement entered into by the parties must be capable of being performed. Any agreement to do an impossible act is void and cannot be enforced by law under Section 56(i).
   Example: A agrees to B to put life in the dead body of his brother. The agreement is void as it is impossible to be performed.
9. **Agreement should not be declared void:** An agreement must not have been expressly declared void by any law in force in the country. Under the Indian Contract Act, the following agreements are expressly declared to be void and not enforceable by law:
   - Agreements in restraint of marriage under Section 26
   - Agreements in restraint of trade (with some exceptions) under Section 27
   - Agreements in restraint of legal proceeding under Section 28
   - Uncertain agreements under Section 29
   - Wagering agreements under Section 30
   - Agreements to do an impossible act under Section 56
10. **Legal formalities:** According to the provision of Section 10, Para II, a contract may be made by words spoken or written. As regards the legal effects, there is no difference between a contract in writing and a contract made by words of mouth. There are other formalities also which have to be satisfied in order to make an agreement enforceable. The documents containing the agreement are to be stamped if it is needed to be stamped. The entire statutory requirement with regard to an agreement must be fulfilled when it is specified under any Act for the time being in force.

The elements mentioned above are essential and must be present. If any one of them is absent, the agreement does not become a contract. An agreement which fulfils all the essential elements is enforceable by law and is called a contract. From the above, it follows that every contract is an agreement but all agreements are not contracts.

It is further to be stated that with the improvement in the information technology and introduction of e-commerce and e-contract, the elements of Section 10 of the Contract Act should be present in the agreement which is entered into by two parties via the Internet.

Kinds of Contracts

Contracts which are entered into by the parties can be classified according to the following:

1. Validity or enforceability
2. Formation or aeration of contract
3. Performance of contract
4. Forms of contracts

Classification on the Basis of Validity of a Contract

Based upon the validity or enforceability, contracts may be as follows:

1. **Valid contract:** Section 2(h) of the Act provides that an agreement enforceable by law is a contract. In other words, it can be said that the presence of all the essential elements

that are provided under Section 10 of the Act will make it a valid contract. When any one or more of the essential elements are missing, then it will not be a valid contract. Rather, the contract will be void, voidable, illegal or unenforceable.

2. **Voidable contract:** Any contract which ceases to be enforceable at the option of the aggrieved party is known as a voidable contract. According to Section 2(i), 'An agreement which is enforceable by law at the option of one or more of the parties thereto, but not at the option of the other or others, is a voidable contract.' A contract becomes voidable in the following circumstances:
   a. When a contract contains reciprocal promises and any one party to the contract prevents the other party from performing his promise, the contract becomes voidable at the option of the party so prevented (under Section 53).
      Example: A and B contract that B shall execute certain work for A for ₹5,000. B is willing to execute the work accordingly, but A prevents him from doing so. The contract is voidable at the option of B and can claim damages.
   b. When a party to a contract promises to do certain thing at or before a specified time or certain things at or before specified times but fails to do so, the contract becomes voidable at the option of the promisee (under Section 55).
      Example: X enters into a contract with Y that X will make available some article within a specified time but fails to do so. The contract is voidable at the option of Y.
   c. If the consent given to the contract is not free, then also the contract will be voidable at the option of the party whose consent has been so obtained (under Section 14).
3. **Void contract:** According to Section 2(j), 'A contract becomes void when it ceases to be enforceable.' Further, Section 2(g) provides that an agreement not enforceable by law is said to be void. A void agreement does not give rise to any legal obligation between the parties. It is a nullity and void *ab initio*, which means that the contract is void from the very beginning.
   Example: Agreements in restraint of trade and marriage and wagering agreements are void.
4. **Illegal agreement:** An illegal agreement is one which is against the provisions of any law prevalent in India; that is, law forbids the very act which is contemplated in the agreement.
   Example: An agreement to commit a crime or a tort, an agreement which tends to corrupt public life or an agreement to defraud public revenue. It may be noted that an illegal agreement is wider than a void agreement. All the illegal agreements are void, but all void agreements are not illegal. For example, an agreement with a minor is void but not illegal.
5. **Unenforceable contract:** Certain contracts cannot be enforced in a court of law because of some technical defects such as lack of attestation and registration, non-fixing of certain amount of stamps, absence of writing or where the remedy has been barred by the lapse of time. Such contracts are called unenforceable contracts. However, if these technical defects are removed, then these contracts can be enforced.
   Example: If proper amount of stamps are fixed, then the defect of lack of stamps will be removed; hence, the contract can be enforced.

Classification on the Basis of Mode of Formation of a Contract

1. **Express contract:** When parties, in writing or by words of mouth, make a contract, it is called an express contract. In this, all the terms and conditions of the contract are

explained to other parties. According to Section 9 of the Act, when the proposal or acceptance is made in words either spoken or in writing, the promise is said to be express.

Example: If X makes a proposal to sell his car to Y for ₹75,000 and Y accepts the offer, then the contract entered into by X and Y is an express contract.

2. **Implied contract:** It comes into existence from the conduct or behaviour of the parties. Section 9 provides that in so far as the proposal or acceptance is made otherwise than in words, the promise is said to be implied. Contracts which are the outcome of any act or conduct of parties to the contract are called implied contracts. Following are the examples of implied contracts:
   a. X buys a ticket in a DTC bus and occupies the seat; this is an implied contract.
   b. A purchases a token for Delhi Metro for a destination. Now, here is an implied contract between A and Metro Rail Corporation.
   c. If someone enters a coffee shop and has a cup of coffee or tea, there is an implied contract that he will have to pay for that cup of coffee or tea.

   An implied promise results in an implied contract, whereas an express promise results in an express contract.
3. **Quasi-contract:** A quasi-contract is created by the law and is based on the principle that none should be allowed to enrich himself unjustly at the expense of another person. Under certain circumstances, the law creates and enforces legal rights and obligations where no express or implied contract exists. These obligations are known as quasi-contracts and are provided in the Contract Act under Sections 68–72, which specify the different obligations which may give rise to a contract between the parties.

   Example: A supplies to the wife and children of B, a lunatic, with necessaries suitable to their condition in life. A is entitled to be reimbursed from B's property. This way, quasi-contracts are nothing other than arrangements made by the law of equity to remove the inequity which creep up between the parties and due to circumstances of contract or change in that.

Classification on the Basis of Performance of a Contract

1. **Executed contract:** When both the parties to a contract fulfil their respective obligations, the contract is called an executed contract. A contract may be executed at the time it is made or in the future by its terms being carried out in a specified time period provided in the contract.

   Example: X agrees to sell his car to Y for ₹50,000 and Y accepts the proposal. Y pays ₹50,000 and X delivers the car. This is an executed contract.
2. **Executory contract:** When one or both the parties to a contract do not perform their obligations fully and something is still to be done, the contract is called an executory contract. It should be kept in mind that a contract is a contract from the beginning, not from the time of its performance. If both the parties are still to perform their obligations, then also it has no impact (effect) on the validity of the contract.

   Example: If X promises to sell his house to Y for ₹5 lakh and Y agrees to it, but neither of the two have performed their obligations, the contract between them is an executory contract.
3. **Partly executed and partly executory contract:** These contracts are the combination of executed and executory contracts, where parties to the contract have

partly performed a part of the contract and are yet to perform the other part. In such contracts, certain parties perform their obligations, while others have to perform their part of obligations.

Example: There is a contract entered into by X and Y to paint X's house for ₹5,000. X in consideration pays in full ₹5,000 to Y. Now, this contract is executed as regards X but executory on the part of Y.

4. **Unilateral contract:** A unilateral contract is one where one party performs his obligations either before the contract comes into existence or at the time when it comes into existence and the obligation of the other party remains to be fulfilled at the time of the formation of the contract.

   Example: A, a coolie, puts B's baggage into his vehicle. The contract comes into existence on A putting B's baggage into his vehicle. Now, B's obligation will complete when he pays the charges to A. These contracts are called unilateral contracts and can also be known as one-sided contracts or contracts with executed consideration.

5. **Bilateral contract:** A contract is said to be bilateral when obligations of both the parties remain outstanding at the time of the formation of contract. Bilateral contracts are very similar to executory contracts, and they are called contracts with executory consideration.

   Example: B promises to A that he will purchase A's house after six month, and A also promises to pay the value of B's house to B on a sale deed. This contract is bilateral as the performance of obligations of A and B, who are parties to the contract, are still outstanding at the time of the formation of the contract.

Classification on the Basis of the Form of a Contract

1. **Formal contract:** Formal contracts are of two types, that is, contracts under seal and contracts of records. Formal contracts are recognized under the English law but do not have any place in the Indian law. When the terms and obligations are written or printed on paper and are signed, sealed and delivered, the obligation constitutes under seal. Any obligation or duty imposed on any party by the judgment of a court or the decision of any other authority and entered into their record is known as a contract of record. These types of contracts are mainly used for future reference and as evidence in the court.
2. **Simple contract:** Indian Contract Act recognizes simple contracts, which are supported by the consideration except in the circumstances provided under the Act. These contracts may be oral or inferred from the parties' conduct in the absence of a statute requiring a writing. Sometimes, these contracts are also known as informal contracts.

Difference between Illegal and Void Agreements

Illegal agreements are those whose objective is unlawful; hence, these are punishable by law. Void agreements are those which are not enforceable by law due to any element given under Section 10 of the Act, but these are not punishable by law. In the case of Rajat Kumar Rath vs. Government of India, it was held that a distinction has to be drawn between void agreements and illegal agreements. Both types of agreements do not have any legal effect. On the basis of this case and other provisions of the Act, the difference between illegal and void agreements is as follows:

1. All the illegal agreements are void, but all void agreements are not illegal.
2. Illegal agreements are void ab initio, but a valid agreement may become void subsequently.
3. There is no punishment for the parties to a void agreement, but parties to illegal agreements are punishable by law.
4. All the agreements which are collateral to void agreements are valid, but agreements which are collateral to illegal agreements are void ab initio.
5. Void agreements are not illegal until they are proved to be so, but illegal agreements are illegal from the very beginning.
6. Void agreements can be void for various reasons as provided under the Contract Act, but illegal agreements can be void due to provisions of other Acts also.

Difference between Void Agreements and Voidable Contracts

Void and voidable contracts are defined under Sections 2(g) and 2(i) of the Act. They may be differentiated on the basis of the following:

1. An agreement not enforceable by the law is known as a void agreement (Section 2(g)), whereas a voidable contract is an agreement which is enforceable at the option of one or more of the parties thereto but not at the option of other or others (Section 2(i)).
2. A void agreement is not enforceable from the beginning itself and in no case it can be made enforceable by the party, whereas a voidable contract is void only at the option of the aggrieved party and who can rescind it; however, if the aggrieved party does not want to rescind it, then it remains valid and enforceable by law.
3. An agreement can be void if any of the essential elements of the agreement, as specified under Section 10 of the Act, is missing, whereas a voidable agreement can be voidable only due to absence of free consent of the parties.
4. In the case of a void agreement, no party to the contract can claim damages as law awards damages or compensation only when an agreement is valid. So in the case of a void agreement, there is no question of damages to be granted. However, in the case of a voidable agreement, the party who rescinds the contract can claim the compensation or damages for any loss which is suffered by the party for such rescind of the contract.
5. In the case of a void agreement, restitution is not allowed if parties to the contract were aware of the nature of the contract. However, in the case of a voidable contract, restitution is always possible.
6. A third party does not acquire any right under a void agreement, whereas in the case of a voidable agreement, a third party always acquires the right, provided the third party acquires the rights in good faith.
7. In the case of a void agreement, the lapse of reasonable time does not affect the validity of the contract. But in the case of a voidable contract, parties lose their right after the lapse of time.

Test Questions

1. Define 'law'. Why should one have the knowledge of law? What are the sources of law?
2. Explain the nature and scope of business law. Describe the main sources of Indian mercantile law.
3. 'An agreement to be a contract should be enforceable by law.' Discuss.
4. 'The law of contracts is not the whole law of agreements, nor is it the whole law of obligations.' Discuss. What tests would you apply to ascertain whether an agreement is a contract?
5. 'All contracts are agreements, but all agreements are not contracts.' Comment.
6. 'An agreement enforceable at law is a contract.' Discuss it, bringing out clearly the essentials of a valid contract.
7. Define a contract. State the essential elements of a valid contract.
8. 'A contract is a contract from the time it is made and not from the time its performance is due.' Comment.
9. Differentiate between the following:
   a. Executed and executory contracts
   b. Formal and informal contracts
   c. Void agreements and voidable contracts
   d. Void and illegal agreements
10. Write short notes on the following:
    a. Unilateral and bilateral contracts
    b. Quasi-contracts
    c. Illegal agreements

2

CHAPTER

Offer and Acceptance

Learning Objectives

- To understand the meaning of an offer and acceptance
- To understand the legal rules of an offer and acceptance
- To understand the essentials of acceptance
- To know about communication and revocation of an offer and acceptance

An agreement between parties is one of the most essential elements for the formation of a contract. An agreement arises from an offer or proposal by one or more parties and the acceptance of that offer by the other party/parties. Therefore, a proposal or an offer is the starting point of an agreement. In general terms, an offer is a statement by the offeror of what he will give in return for an act or promise by the offeree. Every contract is made by the process of a lawful offer by one party and the lawful acceptance by the other party.

Example: X asks Y, 'Will you buy my flat in Delhi for ₹50 lakh?' This is nothing but an offer made by X to Y. If Y agrees to buy it for the said amount, then the offer is said to be accepted by Y and an agreement is formed between X and Y.

OFFER

Section 2(a) defines a proposal or an offer as follows: 'When one person signifies to another his willingness to do or abstain from doing anything, with a view to obtaining the assent of that other to such act or abstinence, he is said to make a proposal.' An offer consists of two elements, that is, there is an expression of willingness by the offeror to do or abstain from doing something. Such expression of willingness is made to obtain the assent of the other person to such act or abstinence. The person making the offer is known as *offeror* and the person to whom the offer is made is known as the *offeree*.

Example: A says to B that he wants to sell his bike to him for ₹40,000. Here, A is the offeror and B is the offeree.

In Bank of India & Ors vs. O. P. Swarnakar, it was held by the court that a contract of employment is governed by the Contract Act and the announcement of voluntary retirement scheme (VRS) by a bank is not an offer. An employee asking for retirement is an offer, and the bank may or may not accept it. If it is accepted by the bank, then it becomes a contract. An employee offering the retirement can withdraw it at any time before the bank accepts it.

Essentials of a Valid Offer

The Indian Contract Act contains various requirements which an offer must satisfy in order to be a valid offer. These are as follows:

1. **An offer must create a legal relationship between the parties:** An offer should be able to create a legal relationship between the parties to create a valid contract. Sometimes, such offers are made which are social in nature. Such social offers do not make valid agreements because in these cases the intention is not to create a legal relationship. In the case of Balfour vs. Balfour, it was held that an informal kind of arrangement with no intention to create a legal relationship cannot make a valid agreement. Therefore, the law requires that the parties must intend a legal relationship.
2. **Terms of an offer must be clear, definite, certain and capable of being made certain:** An offer must be definite and certain. An indefinite or vague offer cannot be accepted because the courts in such cases cannot tell what the parties are to do. However, if it is possible to ascertain vague terms or terms of an agreement, such an agreement cannot be considered void on the ground of it being vague or indefinite.
   Example: X offers to sell to Y 250 litres of oil. It is a vague offer, as there is nothing to show what kind of oil is intended to be sold by X. However, if in the above example, X is a dealer in mustard oil only, it shall constitute a valid offer, as the nature of X's trade gives an indication as to which oil is being offered.
3. **An offer must be distinguished from a mere declaration of intention:** The preliminary discussion or an invitation by one party to the other to negotiate terms or simply express intentions will not be an offer. Such declarations merely indicate that an offer will be made in future. A person may also make a statement without the intention of creating contractual obligations. In such cases, no valid offer exists.
4. **An offer is different from an invitation to an offer:** An offeror should express his willingness to do or abstain from doing something with such finality that the only thing to be wanted is the assent of the other party. But where a party proposes certain terms on which he is willing to negotiate, he is not making an offer but only inviting others to make an offer on those terms. In the case of Harvey vs. Facey, Harvey telegraphed to defendant Facey, 'Will you sell us Bumper Hall Pen? Telegraph lowest cash price.' The defendant replied by a telegram, 'Lowest price for Bumper Hall Pen £900.' The plaintiff immediately sent his last telegram stating, 'We agree to buy Bumper Hall Pen for the sum of nine hundred pounds asked by you.' The defendant, however, refused to sell the Bumper Hall Pen at that price. The point raised by the plaintiff was that by quoting their minimum price in response to the enquiry, the defendant had made an offer to sell at that price. But the judicial committee pointed out that out of the two questions asked by the plaintiff in his first telegram, the defendant had only answered the second by giving lowest price but did not express their willingness to sell. Rather, the plaintiff's second telegram was an offer to buy, which was never accepted by the defendant. Similarly, it has been held that a shopkeeper's catalogue of prices, or display of goods in the shop window, is not an offer. It is an invitation to offer (Pharmaceutical Society of Great Britain vs. Boots Cash Chemists). Likewise, an advertisement for tenders and for sale of goods by auction, published timetable of a railway and prospectus of a company are merely invitations to offers.
5. **The offer should not include any term or terms, the non-compliance of which may be assumed to lead acceptance:** An offeror cannot say that if the

offeree does not communicate acceptance by a certain time, the offer would have been deemed to be accepted. The burden of communication, or rejection of offer, cannot be imposed on the offeree. If the offeree sends no reply, there is no contract.

6. **The offer must be communicated to the person to whom it is intended to be made:** The communication of an offer is important to conclude an agreement because the acceptance can be given only after one knows about the offer. The communication can be express or implied. Section 4 of the Act states that the communication of a proposal is complete when it comes to the knowledge of the person to whom it is made.
Example: In the case of Lalman Shukla vs. Gauri Dutt, Gauri sent Shukla, the *munim* (accountant) of his firm, in search of his missing nephew. After this, certain handbills were issued offering a reward of ₹501 to anyone who might find out the boy. Shukla traced the boy and informed Gauri. After about six months, when he was dismissed, Shukla asked for the reward. It was held in the case that he was not entitled for the reward. The court held that since there can be no acceptance unless there is knowledge of the offer, the contract had not concluded and so Shukla was not entitled for the reward.
According to Section 4 of the Act, the communication of a proposal is complete when it comes to the knowledge of the person to whom it is made.

Kinds of Offers

Offers can be classified on the basis of the following:

1. Form of the offer, that is, an offer may be either express or implied
2. To whom the offer is made, that is, an offer may be specific or general

Express Offer

An express offer is one which is made by words spoken (oral) or written. An oral offer can be made either in person or through a telephone. But a written offer can be made by a letter or telegram. An express offer explains all the terms and conditions to the offeree.

Example 1: A asks B, 'Will you purchase my bike for ₹35,000?'

Example 2: A writes a letter to B, 'I want to sell my car to you for ₹125,000.'

Implied Offer

An implied offer is one which is not made by words spoken or written. It is implied from the conduct of the parties or circumstances of the case. In this type of offer, the terms and conditions are pre-stipulated and the parties are supposed to act on those terms and conditions.

Example 1: DTC runs buses on a particular route. There is an implied proposal from DTC to carry passengers on the route who are prepared to pay the fare according to the rates fixed by DTC.

Example 2: DMRC is running metro on a particular route as per the specified terms including the fare and any person who board the metro will be said to have accepted the implied offer of DMRC.

Specific Offer

A specific offer is one which is made to a definite or a particular person. In this case, the offeror wants only a specific person to whom the offer is made to do what he has proposed. As a result, such an offer can be accepted only by that person and none else.

Example: A makes an offer to B to sell his car for ₹200,000. This is a specific offer which can be accepted only by B and none else.

In the case of Boulton vs. Jones, it was held by the court that a specific offer could be accepted by the person to whom the offer is made.

General Offer

A general offer is one which is made to the public in general. In this case, the offeror may not care by whom anything is done so long as it is done. But such an offer cannot form the foundation of a contract until it has been accepted by a certain person. In the case of Carlill vs. Carbolic Smoke Ball Co., Carbolic Smoke Ball Company, who were proprietors of a medicinal preparation called 'the Carbolic Smoke Ball', published an advertisement in a magazine and newspaper. The company offered to pay £100 reward to anyone who contracted the increasing epidemic influenza, cold or any disease caused by cold after having used the medicine according to the printed directions. A lady, Mrs Carlill, bought the Smoke Ball and used it as directed but she was attacked by influenza. She sued for the reward. One of the points raised by the advertiser was that it was only an offer made to the public and also that its terms were very vague. It was also said that one could not contract with anybody and everybody. But the court was of the opinion that although it was an offer made to the world at large, it was to ripen into a contract with anybody who came forward and performed the conditions. Therefore, in this case, Mrs Carlill was held entitled for the reward.

In the case of Har Bhajan Lal vs. Har Charan Lal, a young boy ran away from his father's home. The father issued a pamphlet offering a reward of ₹500 to anybody who would bring the boy home. The plaintiff saw the boy at a railway station and sent a telegram to the boy's father. It was held that the handbill was an offer open to the world at large and was capable of acceptance by any person who fulfilled the conditions contained in the offer. The plaintiff substantially performed the conditions and was entitled to the reward offered.

Printed or Standard Contracts and Court's View

An offeror can include any terms and conditions in his offer. Large size companies generally have printed forms of contracts such as banks, insurance companies, railway corporations and dry cleaners. In all such cases, courts hold that the party will be bound by the document even if he never read the terms and conditions. The rule of law in such cases is that if the document is signed by the offeree, he is bound by all the conditions of the document signed even if he has not read them. Courts assume that the party has read and then signed the document. This rule was laid down in L'Estrange vs. F. Graucob Ltd (1934). In all similar contracts, the individual dealing with LIC or a drycleaner or railways is bound by the terms and conditions once he signs the document. However, in some cases, courts have given some exceptions/rules/relief in order to protect the consumers, which are as follows:

1. **Reasonable notice:** It is the duty of the person delivering a document to give adequate notice to the offeree regarding all the printed terms and conditions of the contract.

Whenever it is not done, the acceptor will not be bound by the terms of the contract. In the case of Henderson vs. Stevenson, it was held that the passenger was entitled to recover his loss from the company in spite of exemption clauses, as sufficient communication of the terms and conditions was not there.

2. **The notice should be at the time of contract or before the time of the contract:** It is the duty of the offeror to give the notice to the offeree before or at the time of the contract. A subsequent notice will amount to a modification of the original contract and will not bind the other party unless he has assented thereto. In the case of Olley vs. Marlborough Court Ltd, it was held by the court that Mrs Olley was entitled to recover the damages for the lost articles because the notice excluding the liability of the offeror was held not to be a part of the contract as they had entered into the contract before seeing the condition given on the wall of the room.
3. **The terms and conditions must not exclude the liability for breach of a contract:** Where sufficient notice of the terms and conditions has been given, the party imposing the conditions may still be liable if he had committed a fundamental breach of contract. If one party fails to perform this fundamental obligation, he will be guilty of breach whether or not any exempting clause has been inserted or not. In Davis vs. Collins, the court observed that limitation clauses do not apply where the goods are lost not within the four corners of the contract but while something was being done which was outside the terms of the contract altogether, or when loss takes places in the course of some operation which was never contemplated by the contract at all.
4. **The terms and conditions should not be unreasonable:** Sometimes, the exemption clauses are so unreasonable that courts do not allow their operation even if the other party had notice of them. A term is said to be unreasonable where it would defeat the very purpose of the contract or is repugnant to public policy. In the case of Lilly White vs. R. Munuswami, the court held that the laundry could not rely on the term limiting the liability as it was unreasonable and was therefore held liable to pay full value of the sari.
5. **Liability in tort:** Even where an exemption clause is exhaustive enough to exclude all kinds of liabilities under a contract, it may not exclude the liability in tort. A tort is a civil wrong for which there is remedy in law. In White vs. John Warwick & Co. Ltd, it was held that although the clause exempted the company from their liability under the contract, it did not exempt them from liability of negligence (under law of torts).

Acceptance

Acceptance of an offer is very important for the formation of a contract, since it is a precondition for an agreement/contract. Acceptance is the consent given by a promisee or an offeree and has the effect of converting an offer into an agreement. An offer does not create a legal relationship unless the offer is accepted. Section 2(b) explains that acceptance is 'When the person to whom the proposal is made signifies his assent thereto, the proposal is said to be accepted. A proposal, when accepted, becomes a promise'.

Further, Section 2(e) states, 'Every promise and every set of promises, forming the consideration for each other, is an agreement.' According to Section 2(h), 'An agreement enforceable by law is a contract.' Thus, a contract emerges from the acceptance of an offer, and an acceptance is nothing but the expression of assent for the proposal by the acceptor or offeree of his willingness to be bound by the terms of the offer. Thus, to create a legal relationship between the parties, it is essential that the offer is accepted. Once accepted, it gives rise to a legal binding relationship. The offeree is not bound to accept the offer. He is free to reject it or make it to lapse by non-acceptance. A similar view was held by the Supreme Court in Patna Regional Development Authority vs. Rashtriya Pariyojana Nirman Nigam. It is on the offeree to accept or reject the offer made to him by the offeror. Under no condition an offeror can be compelled to accept the offer. Even the Parliament was of the same view, and that is why it included the provision of free consent under Sections 14–22 of the Contract Act.

WHO CAN ACCEPT AN OFFER?

Only the offeree can accept an offer. In other words, the person or persons to whom an offer is made can accept it. If anyone else attempts to accept it, then no contract will arise with that person. Section 2(b) makes it very clear, 'When the person to whom the proposal is made signifies his assent thereto, the proposal is said to be accepted.' So a specific offer can be accepted only by a person to whom it is made. But a general offer, not directed to a particular person but to the world at large, can be accepted by anyone having knowledge of the offer.

Modes of Acceptance

Acceptance can be in two ways/modes:

1. **Express acceptance:** An express acceptance is one which is given in words spoken or written.
   Example: Ram makes an offer to Shyam to sell his car for ₹225,000. Shyam accepts the same, and it will result in a contract. Once the proposal is accepted, it becomes a promise which is binding on both the parties to contract.
2. **Implied acceptance:** It means an acceptance which is given by performance of a particular act which is required to be done according to the terms of an offer which is to be gathered from the circumstances or the conduct of parties. Compliance with the terms of an offer may amount to acceptance. In the case of Carlill vs. Carbolic Smoke Ball Co., Mrs Carlill had consumed the tablets for influenza as per the terms of the offer (advertisement) and the court held that it was a valid acceptance.

Legal Rules Regarding Valid Acceptance or the Essentials of a Valid Acceptance

In order for the acceptance of an offer to result in an agreement, the acceptance must satisfy the following requirements:

1. **Acceptance must be absolute and unqualified:** In order to form a contract, acceptance must be absolute and according to the terms of the offer. Section 7(1) provides that in order to convert a proposal into a promise, the acceptance must be 'absolute and unconditional'; conditional acceptance is no acceptance and will not give rise to any contract unless there is an absolute and unqualified acceptance. The word absolute implies acceptance of the offer in total and not in parts. It should be of the

whole of the offer. The offeree cannot accept a part of its terms which are favourable to him and reject the rest. The acceptance should also be unconditional. This means that the acceptor should not attach any conditions to the acceptance. If acceptance is conditional, it is no acceptance. It will be a case of *counter-offer*, which may or may not be accepted by the original offeror. Any acceptance with a variation is no acceptance.
Example: A offered through a letter to sell certain goods to B at ₹700, but in turn B offered to buy it for ₹500 which A did not accept and then B agreed to pay ₹700. The court held that A was not bound by such acceptance.

2. **Acceptance must be in the mode prescribed or some usual and reasonable mode:** It provides that acceptance must be given in the mode prescribed in the offer, and if nothing is mentioned in the offer, then it should be in some usual and reasonable mode as per the circumstances or as per trade custom. Section 7(2) states,

   > The acceptance must be expressed in some usual and reasonable manner, unless the proposal prescribes the manner in which it is to be accepted. If the proposal prescribes a manner in which it is to be accepted, and the acceptance is not made in such manner, the proposer may, within a reasonable time after the acceptance is communicated to him, insist that his proposal shall be accepted in the prescribed manner, and not otherwise; but if he fails to do so, he accepts the acceptance.

   This section clearly states that the acceptance should be expressed in some usual and reasonable manner. What is usual and reasonable mode depends upon circumstances of the case. For example, a usual mode is a letter in reply to a letter.
   Example: A sends his employee B with a letter to P offering to sell certain goods and asks P to send the reply through B and P sends B away but decides to accept the offer by courier. It reaches A before B's return. In this case, A can refuse the acceptance, as it is not made in the mode prescribed. But this should be done within a reasonable time. If he fails to do so, he is deemed to have accepted the different mode adopted by P.

3. **Acceptance must be communicated within the time prescribed or within a reasonable time:** To make it legally binding, the acceptance should be given 'either within the period prescribed or, if no period is specified, within a reasonable period'. What is reasonable is in each case dependent upon circumstances. In Ramsgate Victoria Hotel Co. vs. Montefiore, Mr Montefiore applied for shares in a company on 8 June but the allotment of shares was made on 23 November. He refused to accept the shares. It was held that he could refuse to take shares because there was inordinate delay in acceptance. Six months could not be considered a reasonable period in any case. It clearly shows that if no time limit is specified, the acceptance must be given within a reasonable time. However, the concept of reasonable time will depend upon the circumstances.

4. **Acceptance must be given before the offer lapses or is revoked:** Acceptance should be received by the offeror before the offer lapses by the expiry of a fixed or reasonable period or before it is revoked by the offeror. Revocation can also occur in case of death or insanity of the proposer. Similarly, counter-offers put an end to the contract. So if R makes an offer to S on Monday to be accepted within a week and B accepts it after 10 days, such an acceptance is not valid. Thus, only those offers can be accepted which are valid and not revoked by the offeror or by the lapse of time.

5. **In no case acceptance can be before the offer:** There can be no acceptance of an offer which is not communicated. Similarly, performance of conditions of an offer in general offer without the knowledge of the offer is no acceptance. Acceptance can be given only for an offer which has been communicated. In Lalman Shukla vs. Gauri Dutt, the court decided that an acceptance cannot precede an offer, which means that nobody

can give one's acceptance in anticipation of an offer. He can give acceptance when he has received the offer from the offeror.

6. **Acceptance must be communicated to the offeror:** Acceptance should be made known to the offeror. Mere mental acceptance not evidenced by words or conduct is no acceptance in the eyes of law. Acceptance must come to the knowledge of the offeror. An acceptance of an offer must be communicated to the offeror in the same perceptible form so that a binding contract may be created. It can be express or implied. In Brogden vs. Metropolitan Railway Co., Brogden received a draft agreement relating to the supply of coal from Metropolitan Railway Co. He signed the draft and put the draft in the drawer assuming the approval having been signified; that is, the signed draft was not sent back to Metropolitan Railway Co. The court held that there was no contract because the Railway Co. had not been informed. It is true that the conduct of the company's agent in keeping the agreement in the drawer was an evidence of the fact that he had accepted it. But he had not communicated it.
7. **Silence cannot be a mode of acceptance:** Acceptance cannot be implied from silence. For example, X makes a proposal of selling his car to Y for ₹75,000 by writing a letter to him and writes further, 'If I do not hear anything from you regarding the purchase of my car for ₹75,000 within 15 days, I will assume that you have accepted my proposal.' In no case an offeror can impose a condition that the offeree's silence would be considered as acceptance. However, there are some exceptions to this rule, which are as follows:
   a. Where because of previous dealings the offeree has given the offeror a reason to understand that his silence amounts to acceptance.
   b. Where the offeror has dispensed with communication of acceptance. This can be inferred from the terms of the offer or circumstances of the case.
   c. Sometimes performance of all conditions of the offer without communication of acceptance is considered sufficient acceptance of the offer.
   d. Where the offeree takes the benefit of the offer, it will amount to acceptance.

Communication of Offer, Acceptance and Revocation

A proposal or an acceptance of a proposal and their revocation to be complete must be communicated. An offer, acceptance or revocation may be communicated to the offeree in various ways. Section 3 of the Act provides that the communication of a proposal and its acceptance and revocation of proposal are deemed to be made by any act or omission of the party proposing, accepting or revoking by which he intends to communicate such proposal acceptance or revocation or which has the effect of communicating it. No problem arises in cases where parties are face-to-face because in such cases, the communication of the offer and acceptance are instantaneous. If parties are negotiating over telephone, the agreement is concluded when the offeror has heard the acceptance.

Communication of an Offer

The communication of an offer is complete when it comes to the knowledge of the person to whom it is made.

Example: A proposes by a letter to sell a house to B at ₹25 lakh. The communication of the proposal will be complete when B receives the letter. In the case of communication by post, the rules given in Section 4 apply: 'The communication of a proposal is complete when it comes to the knowledge of the person to whom it is made.' From the above, it can be said that the acceptor cannot revoke the acceptance once it comes to the knowledge of the offeror.

Communication of Acceptance

The communication of an acceptance is complete as against the proposer when it is put in a course of transmission to him, and as against the acceptor when the letter of acceptance comes to the knowledge of the offeror. Section 4(2) states,

> The communication of an acceptance is complete,—as against the proposer, when it is put in course of transmission to him so as to be out of the power of the acceptor; as against the acceptor, when it comes to the knowledge of the proposer.

Example: If in the reply to the offer letter of X, Y sends an acceptance letter to X on 7 September 2015, which reaches X on 10 September 2015, the acceptance against X is complete when the letter of acceptance is posted by Y, that is, 7 September 2015, whereas against Y when it reaches X, that is, 10 September 2015.

Communication of Revocation

Revocation means withdrawal of an existing statement, offer or promise, and the communication of revocation is complete as against the person who makes the same when it is put in the course of transmission to the person to whom it is made, so as to be out of the power of the person who makes it, and as against the person to whom it is made when it comes to his knowledge. Revocation is complete at different times for the person making it and the person to whom it is made. An offer can be revoked at any time before the communication of its acceptance is complete as against the offeror but not afterwards, and the acceptance can be revoked at any time before its communication is complete as against the acceptor but not afterwards. Section 5 provides,

> A proposal may be revoked at any time before the communication of its acceptance is complete as against the proposer, but not afterwards. An acceptance may be revoked any time before the communication of the acceptance is complete as against the acceptor, but not afterwards.

CONTRACTS OVER TELEPHONE

The contracts by instantaneous communication such as telephone or telex are not treated in the same way as contracts by postal communications. Such contracts are treated on the basis of the same principles as in case of the contract negotiated by the parties in their actual presence. When the parties negotiate a contract face-to-face or over telephone, no question of revocation can possibly arise, since in such cases a definite offer is made and accepted at one and the same time. Sections 4 and 6 provide that either party negotiating the contract over telephone is precluded from changing his mind. Justice Denning in Entores Ltd vs. Miles Far East Corporation explained the following points regarding communication through telephone or telex:

1. A contract by telephone or telex has the same effect as an oral agreement entered into by the parties when they are face-to-face. A binding contract can arise only when the offeror has heard the acceptance. If it is not heard, no binding contract can arise.
2. If in the course of communication over telephone or telex the line goes dead when the acceptor is giving acceptance, no contract arises. The contract comes into existence only when the acceptor repeats the acceptance and it is heard by the offeror.
3. In such cases, the question of revocation does not arise and a definite offer is made and accepted at the same time.

In India also, in Kanhaiyalal vs. Dineshchandra, it was held that where a contract is made by telephone, the contract is not complete till the acceptance of the offer is clearly heard and understood by the offeror. The Supreme Court in the case of Bhagwandas Goverdhandas Kedia vs. Girdharilal Purshottamdas & Co. ruled by a majority bench judgment that the rules of communication by post are not applicable to contracts over telephone or telex. Such a contract will be complete when the acceptance has been communicated to the offeror. As regards the place where the contract is complete, the court held that the contract would come into existence at the place where the acceptance has been received.

Termination or Lapse of an Offer

An offer is made with a view to obtain the assent of the other party to it. If it is accepted, a valid agreement is made. But before being accepted, the offer may lapse, may be revoked or may be rejected by the offeree. In these cases, the offer comes to an end. Section 6 provides the following circumstances under which an offer will terminate or come to an end:

1. **By notice of revocation:** Section 6(1) provides that a proposal may be revoked by communication of notice of revocation by the proposer to the other party at any time before acceptance. Revocation of general offers must be made through the same channel by which the original offer was made.
2. **By lapse of time:** A proposal is revoked by the lapse of the time prescribed in the proposal for acceptance. If no time is prescribed, it is revoked by the lapse of a reasonable time, without communication of the acceptance. An offer, therefore, comes to an end if it is not accepted within a fixed or reasonable period. What is reasonable period will depend upon circumstances of each case.
3. **By failure of the acceptor to fulfil a condition precedent to acceptance:** A proposal is revoked by the failure of the acceptor to fulfil a condition precedent to acceptance. Sometimes, the offeror may ask the acceptor to fulfil certain conditions before acceptance. In such cases, the acceptance should be given by fulfilling the conditions. If the conditions are not fulfilled, then the offer will lapse.
4. **By death or insanity of the proposer:** It provides that a proposal can be revoked by death or insanity of the proposer, if the fact of his death or insanity comes to the

knowledge of the acceptor before acceptance. The death of the offeror revokes the proposal, and if the acceptance is made, it has no effect. The offer can be accepted only by an offeree and not by any other person; it cannot be accepted by offeree's executor also.

An offer can be revoked in the following circumstances:

a. **Counter-offer by the offeree:** A counter-offer means an offer in response to an offer. In such cases, where instead of accepting the offer the acceptor gives his own offer, the first offer lapses. But if this counter-offer is rejected by the offeror, the offeree cannot accept the first offer unless it is revived by the offeror.
   Example: A makes an offer to B to sell his car for ₹80,000. B in return offers to purchase it for ₹60,000. Here, B's offer terminates the original offer. So if after rejection, B again agrees to purchase it for ₹80,000, there is no contract.
b. **By not being accepted in the mode prescribed:** In the cases where the offeror has prescribed a mode of acceptance, it should be strictly followed by the offeree. If the offer is not accepted in the mode prescribed, the offeror can reject the acceptance by giving a notice to the offeree within a reasonable time that the offer should be accepted in the mode prescribed and not otherwise.
c. **Rejection of the offer by offeree:** An offer also comes to an end when the offeree does not accept it and an offer once rejected cannot be revived again by him unless the offeror revives it. An offer can be rejected by express words or by a counter-offer or conditional acceptance.

Test Questions

1. What is an offer? When is it complete? What are the legal rules of an offer?
2. What is an acceptance of offer? When is it complete? What are the legal rules of an acceptance?
3. What do you understand by communications of an offer and acceptance?
4. 'Acceptance is to an offer what a lighted match is to a train of gunpowder.' Comment.
5. State whether these are offers:
   a. Issue of a catalogue, price list or a prospectus
   b. Declaration to do something
   c. An offer made by joke or under great excitement
6. How does an offer lapse? Can an acceptance lapse?
7. State how a contract can be formed by communication of an offer and acceptance over the telephone? State the law relating to a contract by post.
8. Comment on the following statements:
   a. 'A mere mental acceptance, not evidenced by word or conduct, is in the eye of law no acceptance.'
   b. 'A contract is formed when the acceptor has done something to signify his intention to accept, not when he has made up his mind to do so.'
   c. 'An offer does not come into existence until it comes to the knowledge of the offeree, but acceptance, in some cases, may be held to be made even when it has not come to the knowledge of the offeror.'
   d. 'The offer and the acceptance bring the parties together, but the law requires some further evidence of their intention to create an obligation.'

PRACTICAL PROBLEMS

1. A agrees to sell B '100 tons of oil'. There is nothing whatever to show what kind of oil was intended. Is this agreement enforceable?
   Hint. The agreement is void since the terms of the offer are not certain or capable of being made certain. (Section 29)
2. A's nephew was missing. A sent his munim B in search of the missing boy. In the meanwhile, A issued handbills offering ₹50 to any person who would find out the missing boy. B could trace the boy and brought him home. B was not aware of the handbill. Later, he asked for ₹50. Will he succeed? Give reasons for your answer.
   Hint. No. He cannot accept the offer in ignorance of the same. (Lalman Shukla vs. Gauri Dutt)
3. A, by advertisement in a newspaper, offers a reward of ₹1,000 to anyone who got influenza after taking his medicine for the disease. B used it according to the directions and contracted influenza. Can B recover the reward? Give reasons.
   Hint. Yes. He performed the conditions of the proposal under Section 8.
4. Peter Feraro offered to pay ₹10,000 to any person who would swim 100 yards on Bombay's seacoast on the New Year's Day of 1983. A fisherman, without any information about the offer, claimed ₹10,000 on swimming the distance to save his life after he was accidentally thrown overboard by the rough sea waves. Can the fisherman claim the money?
   Hint. No. The fisherman cannot claim the money because he swam the required distance without knowing about the offer. The case of Lalman Shukla vs. Gauri Dutt can be quoted in support of the answer.
5. A lost his dog. He sent his servant to search the dog. When he did not hear about the lost dog, he advertised a reward of ₹100 to any person who found the lost dog and returned it to A. The servant found the lost dog and returned the dog to A. When the servant came to know about the reward of ₹100, he claimed the reward from A. Can he claim the reward? Give reasons.
   Hint. No. The servant cannot claim the reward. The rule is that the offer must be communicated to the acceptor. The facts of this problem are similar to the case of Lalman Shukla vs. Gauri Dutt.

3

CHAPTER

Consideration

Learning Objectives

- To understand the meaning of consideration
- To know about the legal rules regarding consideration
- To understand that an agreement without consideration is void, with exceptions
- To understand the doctrine of privity of contract

Three most important things which are required to form a contract are an offer, acceptance and consideration. An offer and acceptance to it lead to a promise, but there must be something to be assented to and agreed upon on each side. That something is consideration. Each party must give something in return for the other's promise. Consideration is one of the essential elements for the formation of a valid contract. A contract without consideration is normally void. According to Sir Pollock, 'Consideration is the price for which the promise of other party is bought.' Another most commonly accepted definition is given by Justice Lush in Currie vs. Misa case, 'A valuable consideration, in the sense of the law, may consist either in some right, interest profit or benefit accruing to one party, or some forbearance, detriment, loss or responsibility given, suffered or undertaken by the other.'

CONSIDERATION

Consideration is the price for which a promise is bought by the promisee. This may consist of some act or abstinence. Section 2(d) defines consideration as follows:

> When, at the desire of the promisor, the promisee or any other person has done or abstained from doing, or does or abstains from doing, or promises to do or to abstain from doing, something such act or abstinence or promise is called a consideration for the promise.

So consideration may be a benefit to one party or some detriment to the other. It may be an act or abstinence or promise. It requires the following:

1. The act or abstinence should be done at the desire of the promisor.
2. The act should be done by the promisee or any other person.

3. The act or abstinence may have been already executed or be in the process of being done or may still be executory; that is, it is promised to be done.

Further, Section 2(f) states, 'Promises which form the consideration or part of the consideration for each other are called reciprocal promises.' Thus, consideration implies some benefits to the promisor and some inconvenience or forbearance to the promisee. A few example of consideration are as follows:

1. X agrees to sell his car to Y for ₹50,000. Here, for X's promise, the consideration is the price for his car of ₹50,000, and for Y's promise, the consideration is X's car.
2. X took a loan of ₹50,000 from Y which he did not repay within the period specified. Y promises not to file a suit in the court of law against X, provided X repays the loan of ₹50,000 within 15 days along with ₹2,000 as interest. Here, the forbearance of Y is the consideration for X's repayment of loan.

The Need for Consideration

Consideration provides some guarantee of deliberation and a certain protection against hasty and ill-considered contracts. It helps in determining the enforceability of promises. It ensures reciprocity and mutuality of promises. Hence, it is very important for a contract. In the case of Sonia Bhatia vs. State of U.P. & Ors (AIR 1981, SC 1274), Hon'ble Supreme Court held,

> 'Consideration' means a reasonable equivalent or other valuable benefit passed on by the promisee to the promisee or by the transferor to the transferee. When the term consideration is qualified by the word 'adequate', it makes sufficient and valuable having regard to the facts, circumstances and necessities of the case.

In this case, the court not only explained consideration but also emphasized on its adequacy.

Section 25 of the Indian Contract Act states, 'An agreement made without consideration is void.' In the same section, certain exceptions are also given. Except under these cases, consideration is a must in all other cases which are explained later in this chapter.

Example: A agrees to sell his house to B for ₹10,000. Here, B's promise to pay the sum of ₹10,000 is the consideration for A's promise to sell the house, and A's promise to sell the house is the consideration for B's promise to pay ₹10,000.

Kinds of Consideration

Consideration may be of three kinds:

1. **Present consideration:** It is basically an act which is done in response to a positive promise. It is also called executed consideration. The words 'does or abstains from doing' in Section 2(d) indicate that consideration may be present also. So when a promisor receives consideration simultaneously with his promise, it is known as present consideration.

Example: X goes to Y's shop and asks for a television set. Y gives him the television set. X gives him the money. In this case, consideration and promise move simultaneously. It is present consideration.

2. **Past consideration:** It is something wholly done, forborne or suffered before the making of the agreement. Past consideration is indicated by the words 'has done or abstained from doing' in Section 2(d). This means that consideration may have already moved in the past. But this should be distinguished from the exception provided in Section 25(2) regarding a promise to compensate for voluntary service. Section 2(d) presupposes the request by the promisor. So for any services rendered in the past at the desire of the promisor, he may agree to give something now. The words used in Section 2(d) clearly indicate that an act done by X at Y's request without any contemporaneous promise from Y may be a consideration for a subsequent promise from Y to X.
3. **Future consideration:** The words 'promises to do or to abstain from doing something' in Section 2(d) indicate future consideration. When consideration is to move at a future date, it is called future consideration. It is the price promised by one party in return for the other party's promise. There may be a simple exchange of promises, and each promise is a consideration for the other. A contract is concluded as soon as the promises are exchanged.

   Example: X agrees to sell 150 bags of wheat after 2 weeks and Y agrees to pay for it on delivery. In this case, consideration is to move in future on both sides. It is future or executory consideration.

Legal Rules Regarding Consideration

Consideration is nothing but some act or forbearance or promise suffered or done or made by the promisor for the promise. Nothing is consideration unless it possesses certain essentials. Following are the legal rules regarding consideration:

1. **There must be some consideration in every contract:** According to Section 25 of the Indian Contract Act, an agreement without consideration is void. Hence, no valid contract can arise without consideration. According to Salmond, 'A promise without consideration is a gift; one made with consideration is a bargain.' Except for certain exceptions provided in Sections 25 and 185 of the Contract Act, the rule is 'no consideration, no contract'.
2. **Consideration should move at the desire of the promisor:** An act shall not be a good consideration for the promise unless it is done at the desire of the promisor. So the act or abstinence must be done or promised to be done at the desire of the promisor. It is not necessary that the promisor himself should be benefited by this act, but his desire is essential. In Durga Prasad vs. Baldeo, Durga Prasad on the order of the collector of a town built at his own expense certain shops in a bazaar. The shops were occupied by different shopkeepers who promised to pay Durga Prasad a commission on articles sold through their agency in the bazaar. In a suit filed by Durga Prasad to recover the commission, it was held that the promise was not supported by consideration, since the market was not constructed at the desire of the shopkeepers but the district collector. The act was not the result of the promise but of the collector's order.

In the case of Kedar Nath vs. Gorie Mohamed, for construction of a town hall at Howrah, the commissioner of the Howrah Municipality set out to obtain funds by public subscription. A trust was formed by commissioners including Kedar Nath who was the vice-chairman of the municipality; Gorie Mohamed was a subscriber for ₹100 and had signed his name in the subscription book. On the faith of this, Kedar Nath entered into contract with the contractor for building the hall. But Gorie Mohamed refused to pay on the ground that there was no consideration for his promise. But he was held liable as the act of Kedar Nath of entering into a contract with the contractor was done at the desire of Gorie Mohamed so as to constitute consideration within the meaning of Section 2(d).

3. **Consideration may move from any other person including the promisee:** This means that the promisee or any other person can give consideration. As long as there is consideration, it is not important who has given it. Therefore, a stranger to consideration can sue on a contract, provided he is not a stranger to the contract. This is known as the doctrine of constructive consideration. In Chinnaya vs. Ramayya, an old lady, by deed of gift, made over certain landed property to her daughter Ramayya with a condition that the daughter would pay annually to Chinnaya, who was the sister of the old woman, ₹653. Ramayya on the same day executed an agreement in favour of Chinnaya promising to give effect to the terms of the gift deed. But later on, Ramayya refused to pay. Chinnaya, therefore, sued Ramayya. Ramayya was held liable to pay since the old lady gave consideration of this promise to Chinnaya. However, one point should be noted in this connection. A third party can be stranger to consideration but not stranger to the contract. A stranger to consideration can sue if he is a party to the contract. But a stranger to a contract cannot sue upon it. This rule is called 'privity of contract'
4. **Consideration must have some value in the eyes of law:** A worthless act by the desire of the promisor will not make a good consideration. Consideration shall be 'something' which not only the parties regard but the law can also regard as having some value.
   Example: A promises to give his new car to B if he fetches it from the garage. It cannot be called a contract based on consideration. Fetching of car cannot be said to be implied as sufficient consideration by law.
5. **Consideration need not be adequate:** Section 25(3), Explanation 2 clearly provides, 'An agreement to which the consent of the promisor is freely given is not void merely because the consideration is inadequate.' This means that consideration is for the parties to decide at the time of making the contract, not for the court when it is sought to be enforced.
   Example: X agrees to sell a bike worth ₹20,000 for ₹200. X's consent to the agreement is free. The agreement is a contract notwithstanding the inadequacy of consideration.
   So long as the consent of the parties is free, inadequacy of consideration is immaterial. However, Explanation 2 to Section 25(3) provides, 'Inadequacy of the consideration may be taken into account by the court in determining the question whether the consent of the promisor was freely given.'
6. **Consideration may be an act to do or abstinence or forbearance of doing something:** According to Section 2(d), consideration may be a promise to do something or not to do something. So it may be either positive or negative. It need not always be doing some act. It can also be not doing an act.
   Example: X requested Y to sell and deliver certain goods on credit. Y agreed to do so, provided Z will guarantee the payment of the price of goods. Z guaranteed the payment

of the price. Here, selling of goods by Y to X is the consideration for Z's promise to guarantee the payment. This is positive consideration by Z.

7. **Consideration may be forbearance to sue:** A plaintiff has the right of action, but he refrains from filling a suit in return for a promise by the other party. This is regarded as a valid consideration.
   Example: X's wife Y was ready to sue X for maintenance allowance. X promised to pay her monthly allowance, provided she did not file a suit against him. Y agreed not to file a suit. In this case, Y's forbearance to sue is consideration for X's promise for payment of monthly allowance. But forbearance to sue is a good consideration only when there is bona fide claim and is immediately due.
8. **Consideration must be lawful:** According to Section 10, 'All agreements are contracts if they are made by the free consent of parties competent to contract, for a lawful consideration.' So consideration should be lawful; otherwise, the agreement is void. Section 23 states that consideration is unlawful if:
   a. Law forbids it.
   b. It is of such a nature that if allowed, it would defeat the provisions of any law.
   c. It is fraudulent.
   d. It involves injury to the person or property of another.
   e. Court regards it as immoral or opposed to public policy.

   Where a part of a single consideration or any part of several considerations is unlawful, the whole agreement is void unless the unlawful part can be separated from the lawful part.
   Example: X promises to supervise Y's business of manufacture of denim cloth and an illegal traffic in other article in return for Y's promise to pay him a salary of ₹40, 000 per month. In this case, as the consideration of Y's promise is partly unlawful, the whole agreement is void. But if the legal part can be separated from the illegal part, the legal part would be enforceable.
9. **Consideration must be real and not illusory or impossible:** Although the Indian Contract Act does not so require, consideration must be real and not illusory, whether adequate or not. So long as the consideration is not unreal, it is sufficient if it were of slight value only. It must not be illusory or impossible. Real consideration is one which is not physically or legally impossible. Illusory means that it may give the impression of a consideration which is not actually there. If it is something which the promise is already bound to do, there is no consideration.

In the following cases, consideration is not real because of legal or physical impossibility or uncertainty.

1. **Physical impossibility:** A promise to do something which is not physically possible, for example, to bring a dead man to life or search a treasure hidden under the sea, is not enforceable, as the consideration is physically impossible.
2. **Legal impossibility:** A promise must be for a consideration which is legally possible.
   Example: A's agreement to give his house on rent to a prostitute is not legally enforceable because consideration is legally impossible.
3. **Uncertain consideration:** The consideration should be certain; if it is vague or uncertain, it is not valid. So a promise to pay a reasonable sum for services is uncertain and therefore void.

'An Agreement without Consideration Is Void' or 'No Consideration, No Contract'

Consideration is one of the most important conditions of a valid contract. A contract without consideration is void. According to Salmond and Winfield, 'A promise without consideration is a gift and one made by consideration is a bargain.' Section 25 declares, 'An agreement made without consideration is void.' This means that consideration is a must in all cases. However, there are certain exceptions where an agreement is valid even without consideration:

1. **Promise made on account of natural love and affection:** Section 25(1) states,

   > An agreement made without consideration is void, unless it is expressed in writing and registered under the law for the time being in force for the registration of documents, and is made on account of natural love and affection between parties standing in near relation to each other.

   This clause lays down four conditions for validity of an agreement without consideration:
   a. The agreement is in writing.
   b. It is registered.
   c. It is made in account of natural love and affection.
   d. It is between parties standing in near relation to each other.

   Example: X, out of natural love and affection, promises to give his son Y ₹9,000. X puts his promise to Y in writing and registers it. This is a valid contract. Although the act does not provide any guidance, near relatives would imply parties related by blood or marriage, and some kind of natural love and affection is also implied. But love and affection may sometimes be overruled by external circumstances.

   In the case of Rajlukhy Dabee vs. Bhootnath Mookerjee, the husband promised to pay his wife a fixed sum of money every month for her separate residence and maintenance. The agreement was contained in a registered document which mentioned certain quarrels and disagreements between the two. The court refused to hold the agreement valid, as it could not find any love and affection between the parties whose quarrels had compelled them to separate.

   But in another case, Bombay High Court declared the agreement valid. In Bhiva vs. Shivaram, X sued his brother Y for a share in certain lands. But the suit was dismissed as Y solemnly affirmed that the property was not ancestral. Y then agreed by registered deed to give X one half of the same property. In a suit to recover that property by X, the court held that in this case the brother had such natural love and affection for X that he was willing to give him his property. So in this case, Section 25(1) applied and X was held entitled for the property.

2. **Promise for compensation of voluntarily services:** Section 25(2) lays down that an agreement without consideration is enforceable: 'If it is a promise to compensate, wholly or in part, a person who has already voluntarily done something for the promisor, or something which the promisor was legally compellable to do.'

   Example: X finds Y's bag and gives it to him. Y promises to give him ₹500. This is a valid contract.

   In order that a promise to pay for past voluntary services is binding, the following conditions must be satisfied:

a. The services should have been rendered voluntarily.
b. The services must have been rendered for the promisor and not for anybody else. Thus, in the case of Durga Prasad vs. Baldeo, (already referred to in this chapter), it was held that shops were built on the order of the collector and not at the desire of the shopkeepers. So shopkeepers were not held liable.
c. The promisor must be in existence at the time when the services were rendered. Where services were rendered for a company not then in existence, a subsequent promise to pay for them could not be brought within this exception.
d. The promisor must have intended to compensate the promise. If a promise is given for any other motive, it is not covered by this exception.
e. The promisor should have been competent to contract at the time when the act was done.
f. The service rendered should not be immoral. A promise to pay for past services of the nature of past cohabitation with a woman whose husband is alive cannot fall under this exception because past cohabitation is deemed to be adulterous (Alice Mary Hill vs. William Clarke [1905]). But whether the same rule applies to promise to pay a woman for past cohabitation, which is not an infringement of the penal law, is a matter of controversy. There are different views held by courts of law on this issue.

Another situation covered by the exception is where the promisee has done something for the promisor which the promisor was legally compellable to do.

3. **Promise to pay time-barred debt:** According to Section 25(3),

> An agreement made without consideration is void, unless it is a promise, made in writing and signed by the person to be charged therewith, or by his agent generally or specially authorized in that behalf, to pay wholly or in part a debt of which the creditor might have enforced payment but for the law for the limitation of suits.

So under this exception, a promise in writing by a person liable to pay or his agent for the payment of a debt barred by law of limitation would be enforceable.

If the debtor promises to repay a loan, which had become time barred, it will be valid if the following conditions are satisfied:
a. The promise should be in writing.
b. It should be signed by the promisor or his agent.
c. The debt must be such for which the creditor would have enforced payment but for the law of limitation.
d. There must have been an express promise to pay. The intention should not be unexpressed. It may be to pay whole or part of the debt.

Example: X owes Y ₹5,000, but the debt is barred by the Limitation Act. X signs a written promise to pay Y ₹7,000 on account of the debt. This is a contract.

4. **Completed gift:** Section 25 lays down, 'Nothing in this section shall affect the validity, as between the donor and donee, of any gift actually made.' So in the case of a gift actually made, consideration is necessary. Not only this, there need not be nearness of relation and even if it is, there need not be any natural love and affection between the parties. But it should not be an agreement to give a gift.
Example: If X receives a gift on his birthday from Y, Y cannot take it back. It is valid in spite of no agreement to give a gift.
5. **For the contract of agency:** According to Section 185, 'No consideration is necessary to create an agency.' Thus, when a person is appointed as an agent, his appointment is

valid even if there is no consideration. It is the duty of the principal to support the contract of agency. Although generally an agent gets remuneration by way of commission for the services rendered, no consideration is paid for the creation of agency.

STRANGER TO CONTRACT AND STRANGER TO CONSIDERATION OR 'THE DOCTRINE OF PRIVITY OF CONTRACT'

It is a general rule of law that only parties to a contract may sue and be sued on that contract. This is the basis of the doctrine of privity of contract. In the English law, there are two propositions:

1. Consideration must move from the promisee only and no other person. If any other person furnishes it, the promisee becomes a stranger to consideration and, therefore, he cannot enforce the promise.
2. A contract cannot be enforced by a person who is not a party to it, even though it is made for his benefit. He is a stranger to the contract and cannot claim any rights under it.

These two propositions of the English law are respectively called 'privity of consideration' and 'privity of contract'. However, in India, the first principle is not applicable because Section 2(d) itself mentions 'promisee or any other person'. So in India, a person can be a stranger to consideration. An illustration is the decision of Madras High Court in Chinnaya vs. Ramayya referred to earlier.

PRIVITY OF CONTRACT

The second doctrine of privity of contract is applicable in India also. Therefore, a stranger to a contract cannot sue. A contract is a contract between the parties only and no third person can sue upon it, even if it is avowedly made for his benefit. House of Lords affirmed this rule in Dunlop Pneumatic Type Co. Ltd vs. Selfridge & Co. Ltd. In this case, Dunlop sold certain tyres to one Dew & Co. and secured an agreement from them not to sell the tyres below the list price and if they sold the tyres to another trader, Dunlop would obtain from them a similar undertaking to maintain the price list. Dew & Co. sold the motor tyres to Selfridge who in turn agreed not to sell the tyres to any private customer at less than the list price and to pay Dunlop $5 for each tyre sold in breach of agreement. Selfridge supplied tyres to their customers at below the listed price. Consequently, Dunlop sued Selfridge to recover $310 as liquidated damages and asked for an injunction to restrain further breaches of agreement. It was held that there was no privity of contract between Dunlop and Selfridge, so Dunlop could not enforce the contract and therefore could not sue upon it.

The Supreme Court in M. C. Chacko vs. State Bank of Travancore upheld the same rule. M. C. Chacko was the manager of Highland Bank, which had overdraft account with State Bank of Travancore. M. C. Chacko's father K. C. Chacko had guaranteed the payment of the overdraft. Subsequently, K. C. Chacko made a gift of his properties to his two sons, a daughter and wife. The gift deed provided that any liability under the guarantee should be met by M. C. Chacko either from the bank or from the share of the property gifted to him. The State Bank attempted to hold M. C. Chacko liable and claimed that a charge was created on the properties gifted. It was held that State Bank not being a party to the contract was not bound by the covenants of the deed, nor could it enforce the covenants against anyone. So M. C. Chacko was not held personally liable for the debt, nor were the properties allotted to M. C. Chacko liable to satisfy the debt due to the State Bank under the letter of guarantee.

Exceptions to the Rule of Privity of Contract

In the light of the above decision, it is now a settled law in India that a stranger to a contract cannot sue on the contract. This is due to the reason that there is no privity of contract. Following are important exception to this rule:

1. **Trust:** Sometimes, a charge or other interest in some property is created in the favour of some person known as beneficiary. Such beneficiary can enforce such right, though he is not a party to the contract. In the case of Rana Uma Nath Bakhsh Singh vs. Jang Bahadur, A was appointed by his father as his successor and was put in possession of the entire estate of his father. In consideration, A agreed that he would give a certain sum of money and a village to B, an illegitimate son of his father, on attaining majority. This agreement was between A and his father. In this case, B was held entitled to recover the money and village by maintaining a suit as a trust was created in his favour for the amount and the village.
2. **Marriage settlement, partition or other family arrangement:** An agreement is sometimes made in connection with marriage, partition or other family arrangements, and a provision is made for the benefit of some person. In such a case, such person for whose benefit the provision is made can enforce the agreement, even though he is not a party to the agreement. In Daropti vs. Jaspat Rai, Jaspat's wife left him because of his cruelty. He then executed an agreement with her father, promising good behaviour and proper treatment and in the alternative if he failed to do so, to pay her monthly maintenance and provide a house also. It was held that the wife was entitled to enforce this promise made by Jaspat to her father.
3. **Acknowledgement of payment or estoppels:** Sometimes, by the terms of a contract, a party is required to make payment to a third party. Such third party can sue the promisor although there is no privity of contract between the party and the third party.
   Example: When under an agreement between a tenant X and a subtenant Y, the latter was paying the rent directly to the landlord L, L was allowed to recover the unpaid rent from the subtenant Y.
4. **An agreement creating a charge on immovable property:** Where a person makes a promise to an individual for the benefit of a third party and creates a charge on certain immovable property for the purpose, the third party can enforce the promise, though he is a stranger to the contract. In Khwaja Muhammad Khan vs. Husaini Begam, the father of the bridegroom entered into an agreement with the father of Husaini Begam, in which he agreed to pay her ₹500 per month if she agreed to marry his son. He also charged certain properties with the payment. The husband and wife separated and Husaini Begam, to recover the arrears of payment, filed a suit. It was held that she was entitled to enforce her claim.
5. **Agreements relating to land:** Where the owner of a land is subject to certain rights and obligations, and buyer purchases the land with the notice that the owner is bound

by certain covenants affecting land or by agreement, such a buyer shall be bound by them although he is not a party to the agreement. Therefore, the rule of privity of contract may be modified by principles relating to immovable property.

6. **The principal can enforce contracts entered into through agents:** The contracts that are entered into by the agent on behalf of principal even though he is not aware of the contract, will be liable for the contract. But the agent must act within the scope of his authority and in the name of his principal.

Test Questions

1. What are the cases in which a contract without consideration is not void?
2. Consideration may be past, present or future. Explain with examples.
3. 'Under the Indian Contract Act, consideration may proceed from the promisee or any other person.' Critically examine this statement.
4. Can a stranger to a contract enforce it? If yes, under what circumstances?
5. Define consideration and state the exceptions to the rule that an agreement made without consideration is valid.
6. Distinguish between a stranger to consideration and a stranger to a contract. 'A stranger to a contract cannot sue.' Are there any exceptions to this rule?
7. State the exception to the rule that an agreement without consideration is void.
8. 'Consideration need not be adequate but it must have some value in the eyes of law.' Explain. Or 'Insufficiency of consideration is immaterial; but an agreement without consideration is void.' Comment.
9. 'An agreement without consideration is void, but an agreement with insufficient consideration is valid.' Comment.
10. Comment on the following statements:
    a. Gratuitous promises are not enforceable by law.
    b. A contract without consideration is void.
    c. Insufficiency of consideration is immaterial, but an agreement without consideration is void.
    d. Inadequacy of consideration is itself no ground for rescinding a contract, but it may be an evidence of undue influence or coercion.
    e. No stranger to the consideration can take advantage of a contract though made for his benefit.
    f. The offer and acceptance bring the partner together, but the law requires some further evidence of their intention to create an obligation.

Practical Problems

1. X, the only son of Y, fell into a river and Z saved him. Y, in gratitude, made an oral promise to pay Z ₹1,000, but Y died before making any payment. Z claims ₹1,000 from X. Will Z succeed? Give reasons.
   Hint. Yes. It is a promise to pay for voluntary services. The legal representative is bound to pay as no contrary intention appears from the contract.

2. X, Y and Z enter into a contract under which X promises both Y and Z that if Y will mow X's lawn, X will give ₹50 to Z. Y mows the lawn accordingly. Can Z compel X to make payment of ₹50 to Z? State reasons.
Hint. Consideration may move from the promisee or any other person.
3. X finds Y's briefcase containing some documents and gives it to him. Y promises to give X ₹300. Can X claim the money?
Hint. Under Section 25(2), Y is liable to pay the amount promised.
4. Highland Bank was indebted to the State Bank under an overdraft. One M was the manager of Highland Bank, and his father, K, had guaranteed the repayment of the overdraft. K gifted his properties to the members of his family. The gift deed provided that the liability, if any, under the guarantee should be met either by M or from the share of the property gifted to him. Can the State Bank sue M under the gift deed? Give reason.
Hint. No. Under the gift deed, the State Bank was not a party to the contract.
5. X agreed to give his house to a school for the library on the condition that the library would be named after him. The management of the school accepted his condition. Later on, X changed his mind. Could the management enforce the contract?
Hint. Yes. Consideration is present.
6. X, a father, died leaving a house for his two sons. The sons agreed to partition the house. It could not be divided into exactly equal parts and, therefore, one of the sons had agreed not to construct a door at a certain place in his portion of the house. This agreement was later on challenged by the son on the ground of absence of adequate consideration. Could he succeed?
Hint. No. Consideration need not be adequate.
7. X promised to give a reward of ₹8,000 to his nephew Y if he refrained from drinking for two years. Y does so. Is he entitled for the reward?
Hint. Yes. Abstinence of Y is a consideration for the promise of X.
8. X, the holder of a promissory note, filed a suit for the recovery of the amount due on the note against Y, the maker. Litigation being in doubt, X withdrew the suit in return for Y's promise to pay within two month. Is the compromise a valid consideration?
Hint. Yes. There is a consideration.
9. X promises to make a gift of ₹9,000 towards the repairs of a temple. The trustee of the temple incurs some liabilities on the faith of X's promise. X does not pay. Can the trustee recover the promised amount?
Hint. Yes. (Kedar Nath vs. Gorie Mohamed)
10. X took a house on rent from Y and agreed to get it repaired. He failed to pay rent or to effect repair. Y agreed that if X paid up all the arrears of rent he would get the house repaired. Is it a valid agreement?
Hint. No. There is no consideration.

4

CHAPTER

Capacity of Parties to Contract

Learning Objectives

- To understand the meaning of capacity of parties
- To understand what an agreement with a minor is
- To understand the meaning of persons of unsound mind
- To understand the meaning of disqualified persons

CAPACITY OF PARTIES

Section 10 of the Contract Act provides that a contract must have an agreement, capacity to contract, lawful object, consideration for each other and free consent. Thus, the capacity of parties to enter into a contract is very important to form a valid contract. Law has laid down certain rules as to who are competent and who are not competent to enter into a valid contract. The parties should be competent enough to understand the effects of an agreement, should be of sound mind and should not be disqualified from entering into a contract. Section 11 provides, 'Every person is competent to contract who is of the age of majority according to the law to which he is subject, and who is of sound mind and is not disqualified from contracting by any law to which he is subject.' The following persons are not competent to enter into a contract:

1. Minors
2. Persons of unsound mind
3. Persons disqualified from contracting by any law to which they are subject

In other words, a person who is of the age of majority, is of sound mind and is not disqualified by law from contracting is competent to enter into a contract. And no person is competent to enter into a contract who is not of the age of majority (is a minor), is of unsound mind and is disqualified to contract by any law to which he is subject.

MINOR

A person who has not attained the age of majority is said to be a minor. As per Section 3 of the Indian Majority Act, 1875, a person is said to have attained the age of majority when he attains the age of 18 years.

Nature of a Minor's Agreements

Sections 10 and 11 of the Indian Contract Act do not make it clear whether any agreement made by a minor is void or voidable. Section 10 only says that all agreements are contracts if they are made by parties competent to contract, and Section 11 says that every person is competent if he is of the age of majority. These provisions had, therefore, given rise to a controversy about the nature of a minor's agreement. However, in the case of Mohori Bibee vs. Dharmodas Ghose Calcutta Privy Council held that an agreement by a minor is void. It is now an accepted rule. In this case, a minor executed a mortgage deed of the house in favour of a moneylender to secure a loan of ₹20,000. The Privy Council held in this case that the minor's agreement was absolutely void. The council also rejected the point raised by appellants that the loan amount should be repaid by the minor. This claim was rejected on the ground that Section 64 applies to voidable contracts and not void contracts, as the court found that the money was advanced with full knowledge of the minority of the plaintiff. Thus, the claim for the refund of the loan under the Specific Relief Act was, therefore, disallowed by the court.

Effects of a Minor's Agreement or Position of a Minor

The Indian Contract Act, 1872, provides special protection to a minor. He is allowed to take the advantages of his minority out of an agreement without incurring any liability. No legal action can be taken against him out of an agreement with him. Even the guardians or the parents cannot be held responsible for the contract entered into by a minor, unless the minor acts as their agent. The rules relating to an agreement with a minor and their effects are as follows:

1. **An agreement with a minor is absolutely void and void ab initio:** An agreement with a minor is absolutely void and void from the very beginning. Although there was some controversy on this point, it has been finally settled after the case of Mohori Bibee vs. Dharmodas Ghose. It was observed by the Privy Council in that case that 'the question whether a contract is void or voidable presupposes the existence of a contract within the meaning of the Act and cannot arise in the case of an infant', as there is no existence of the contract in case of a minor. The contract with a minor is void ab initio.
2. **No rule of estoppel against a minor:** When a minor misrepresents at the time of entering into an agreement that he has attained the age of majority, the question which arises is: Does the law of estoppel apply against the minor, so as to prevent him from alleging that he was a minor when the contract was made? In other words, can a minor be held liable on the agreement on the ground that since earlier he had asserted that he had attained the age of majority, he should not be allowed to deny the same? In Gadigeppa vs. Balangowda, Bombay High Court held, 'Where an infant represents fraudulently or otherwise that he is of age of majority and thereby induces another to enter into a contract with him then on an action founded on the contract the infant is not stopped from setting up infancy.' The above decision of Bombay High Court was based on the decision of Madras High Court in the case of Vaikuntarama Pillai vs. Athimoolam Chettiar, where the court held that there could be no estoppel against the minor. Other courts have also followed the similar view.
3. **Doctrine of restitution does not apply against a minor:** The doctrine of restitution implies that if a person obtains property or goods by false representation, he

can be compelled to restore it to the person from whom he received it. Sections 64 and 65 of the Indian Contract Act, which deal with restitution, apply to contracts between competent parties and not to a minor's agreements. Over the years, courts have been interpreting this doctrine differently in different cases; for example, in Mohori Bibee case, the court refused to allow restitution by saying that Section 64 of the Contract Act applies to voidable and not void contracts. In Khan Gul vs. Lakha Singh, Lahore High Court ordered a minor to refund ₹17,500 taken as advance for sale of land which he failed to sell. However, the controversy has been set at rest by the new Specific Relief Act, 1963. The principle of restitution contained in Section 33 of this Act provides:

(1) On adjudging the cancellation of an instrument, the court may require the party to whom such relief is granted, to restore, so far as may be, any benefit which he may have received from the other party and to make any compensation to him which justice may require.

(2) Where a defendant successfully resists any suit on the ground ... that the agreement sought to be enforced against him in the suit is void by reason of his not having been competent to contract, under section 11 of the Indian Contract Act, 1872 (9 of 1872), the court may, if the defendant has received any benefit under the agreement from the other party, require him to restore, so far as may be, such benefit to the other party, to the extent to which he or his estate has benefited thereby.

Subsection (1) incorporates the principle that one who seeks equity must do equity. As per this, courts have the discretion to require a minor plaintiff to return the benefits obtained under a void agreement. But a court will not compel a minor to restore benefits even if he is a plaintiff in cases where the other party was aware of infancy or where false representation by minor did not influence the decision of the other party. Subsection (2) provides that where a minor is a defendant and successfully resists any suit on the ground that the contract is void by reason of his being a minor, he may be required by the court to restore the benefits obtained by him. But the court will allow restitution only to the extent to which he or his estate has been benefited.

4. **No ratification of a minor's agreement:** Ratification implies approval or confirmation afterwards. A minor cannot ratify an agreement made by him during minority on attaining majority. This is because ratification relates back to the date of making of the contract and, therefore, a contract that was void from the very beginning cannot be made valid by subsequent ratification. In Suraj Narain vs. Sukhu Aheer, a minor borrowed a sum of money by executing a simple bond for it and, after attaining majority, executed a second bond in respect of the first original loan with interest. It was held that as the second bond was without consideration, the suit upon the second bond was not maintainable.

   It should be noted that where a person, after attaining majority, not only ratifies the agreement but also pays the debt incurred during minority, he cannot recover it back afterwards. In Kundan Bibi vs. Sree Narayan, the court held that if a person has received a part of the benefits during minority and a part after attaining majority, a promise made by him to pay for the both attaining the age of majority is with valid consideration and enforceable by the law.

5. **No liability in contract or tort arising out of contract:** The term 'tort' implies civil wrong for which the affected party can file a suit. If a minor enters into an agreement by misrepresenting his age, he cannot be sued either for damages for breach or in the form of damages for tort (i.e., deceit). This is because this would be indirectly

enforcing the agreement that is void. No one can convert a contract into a tort to enable someone to sue an infant. If it were allowed, then it would defeat the provisions of the Act and the intentions of legislatures. However, if the tort is independent of the contract, the mere fact that a contract is also involved will not absolve the minor from obligations. Thus, in the case of Burnard vs. Haggis, an infant borrowed a mare only for riding and not to cause the mare to jump. He lent the mare to his friend, who got the mare jumped and killed her. He was held liable for tort. In Jennings vs. Rundall (1799), a minor hired a horse to ride for a short journey but took it on a long journey. As a result, the horse was injured. In this case, the minor was not held liable on the ground that the action was included in contract and, therefore, the minor was not held liable for tort. Thus, a minor cannot be held liable for breach of contract by changing the form of action into a tort.

6. **Beneficial contract:** The law declared in Mohori Bibee case that a minor's agreement is absolutely void. It has been generally followed by courts. But it has been confined to cases where a minor has been charged with certain obligations which the other party sought to enforce against the minor. There is nothing in the Contract Act which prevents a minor from becoming a beneficiary. Accordingly, a minor is allowed to enforce a contract which is of some benefit to him. Minority is a personal privilege and only a minor can take advantage of it and bind the other party. In the case of Raghava Chariar vs. Srinivasa, A executed a mortgage in favour of B (a minor), who advanced a certain sum of money to A. The court in this case held that the mortgage was enforceable by the minor as the transaction was for his benefit. The court held:

> The provision of law which renders minors incompetent to bind themselves by contract was enacted in their favour and for their protection and it would be a strange consequence of this legislation if they are to take nothing under transfers in consideration of which they have parted with their money.

In the following cases, a contract with a minor can be enforced:

a. **Contracts of marriage:** A contract for the marriage of a minor is also prima facie for his or her benefit. Thus, while a contract of marriage could be enforced against other parties at the instance of a minor, it cannot be enforced against the minor. In Khimji Kuverji vs. Lalji Karamsi, the question before the Bombay High Court was that whether the contract of marriage of a minor girl, entered into by her mother on her behalf, with a boy could be enforced and she could sue for the breach of the contract. The question was answered by the court in affirmation and her action was allowed by the court.

b. **Contracts of apprenticeship:** A contract of apprenticeship is also for the benefit of a minor. Such contracts are binding on minors because the purpose of the Apprentices Act is to enable the minors to learn the trade, crafts and employment. But a minor is not personally liable; only his estates are.

7. **Minor cannot be insolvent:** A minor cannot be held as insolvent because of his incapacity to a contract. Since an agreement with a minor is void and cannot have obligations, the court cannot declare him insolvent. He cannot be held personally liable even for the necessities supplied to him. The money due for necessities supplied to him can be recovered from the minor's assets only.

8. **Liability for necessities:** Section 68 of the Indian Contract Act imposes quasi-contractual obligations on every person incapable of entering into any contract. The

quasi-contractual obligations are enforceable as no person can be allowed to enrich himself at the expense of other. Section 68 states in this regard,

> If a person, incapable of entering into a contract, or any one whom he is legally bound to support, is supplied by another person with necessaries suited to his condition in life, the person who has furnished such supplies is entitled to be reimbursed from the property of such incapable person.

So if a minor or his dependents are supplied necessities by someone, minor's property is liable.

Example 1: A supplies B, a lunatic, with necessaries suitable to his life. A is entitled to be reimbursed from B's property.

Example 2: A supplies to the wife and children of B, a lunatic, with necessaries suitable to their condition in life. A is entitled to be reimbursed from B's property.

It is to be noted that a minor is not personally liable; only his property is liable. But to make his property liable, two conditions must be fulfilled: (a) the contract must be for goods necessary for minor's support in his life and (b) he should not already have sufficient supply of those necessities.

Although there is no definition of 'necessaries' in the Contract Act, some judicial decisions can be relied upon to understand its meaning. The gist of these cases appears to be that 'necessary' is a relative term and has to be determined with reference to the circumstances of the minor. Based upon these principles, the following have been held to be necessaries:

a. The funds supplied to a minor for the marriage of a female member in the family
b. The debt incurred for performing funeral obsequies of the father of a minor
c. Expenses in connection with litigation regarding his property
d. Education expenses and expenses in connection with training of minor

In the case of Roberts vs. Gray, Gray, a minor, intending to become a billiards player entered into a contract with Roberts, a famous billiards player, to pay him fees to learn the game and play matches with him during his world tour. The court held that Gray was liable as it was an agreement for necessaries as it was for teaching, instruction and employment and was therefore for the benefit of the minor.

9. **Positions of a minor's parents or guardian:** A minor's contract *does* not impose any liability on his parents or guardian, even if the contract is for necessaries. There is no obligation on a minor's parents to honour his commitments, although they may do so on moral grounds, as no one can be held liable for a void contract. However, when a minor acts as an agent of his parents or guardian, they can be held liable for his acts.
10. **Surety for a minor:** A person who stands as the surety for a minor can be sued, though the minor himself would not be liable. The liability of the surety is not necessarily simultaneous with that of the principal debtor. His liability arises out of different contracts. Therefore, even when the original contract between the principal debtor and the creditor is void (due to minority of the principal debtor), the surety is liable. Where a minor's debt is knowingly guaranteed, the surety may be held liable as the principal debtor.
11. **Minor as an agent:** A minor can be appointed as an agent. But he is not personally liable for any of his acts. The principal will be liable to the third parties for the acts of the minor agent which he does in the ordinary course of dealings. But he cannot hold the minor liable for any of his acts.

Positions of a Minor under Certain Other Laws

1. **Minor as a partner:** Partnership is based on agreement. A minor being incompetent to enter into a contract cannot enter into a partnership agreement. However, Section 30(1) of the Partnership Act provides that a minor may be admitted to benefits of partnership with the consent of all other partners. His liability is limited to his share in partnership. He cannot take part in management.
2. **Minor under Companies Act:** A minor cannot become a shareholder in a company since he is incompetent to enter into a contract. In case a minor inherits certain shares, he may become a shareholder acting through his lawful guardians. If shares are allotted to a minor through ignorance, any party can repudiate the contract. But so long as it is not repudiated, the minor continues to enjoy benefits of a shareholder. But he cannot be held liable for payment of call money. Similar views were expressed by the court in the case of Nandita Jain vs. Bennett Coleman & Co. Ltd.
3. **Minor under Negotiable Instruments Act:** A negotiable instrument is an instrument in writing containing a certain promise or order to one party to pay certain sum of money to a named party. It includes a promissory note, bill of exchange or cheque. A minor can draw or negotiate and enforce such instrument, if drawn in his favour. A minor can be a drawer or payee. He can also become an endorsee by transfer of a negotiable instrument.

Is Minority a Boon?

Infancy or minority is said to be a disability, but in practice it is really the protection granted by the law. But there is another rule which governs a minor's relations with others, namely 'minors can have no privilege to cheat others' or the law should not cause unnecessary hardship to persons who deal with minors. So in some cases, persons dealing with minors are entitled to certain benefits like restitution or claims, as are given in Section 11 of the Act:

1. A minor will be liable for necessaries (under Section 68).
2. A minor cannot be held responsible as an agent (under Section 184).
3. A minor can be a partner; however, he may be admitted to the profits of the firms (under Section 30 of the Indian Partnership Act, 1932).
4. A minor cannot bind himself (under Section 26 of the Negotiable Instruments Act, 1881).
5. A minor can be held liable for the torts but cannot be held liable if it results in the enforcement of the contract.
6. No specific relief can be given under Section 64 and 65 of the Contract Act, whereas Section 41 of the Specific Relief Act can be invoked in the protection of a minor.

PERSONS OF UNSOUND MIND

A person is said to be of unsound mind when he is not able to understand the outcome and obligations arising out of a contract. According to Section 12 of the Indian Contract Act,

> A person is said to be of sound mind for the purpose of making a contract, if, at the time when he makes it, he is capable of understanding it and of forming a rational judgment as to its effects upon

his interests. A person who is usually of unsound mind, but occasionally of sound mind, may make a contract when he is of sound mind. A person who is of usually of sound mind, but occasionally of unsound mind, may not make a contract when he is of unsound mind.

Thus, Section 12 explains the provisions regarding the soundness and unsoundness of mind. According to this section, a person of sound mind is one who fulfils two conditions:

1. He should be capable of understanding the contract.
2. He should be capable of forming a rational judgement about the effects of the contract on his interest.

If a person does not satisfy both these conditions, he is a person of unsound mind. Unsoundness of mind may arise from insanity, lunacy, idiocy and so on. In each case, it is a question of fact to be decided by the court. There are two types of unsoundness of mind:

1. Permanent unsoundness
2. Temporary unsoundness

Persons of permanent unsoundness are as follows:

1. **Idiots:** An idiot is a person who is devoid of any faculties of thinking. Idiocy is usually caused by lack of development of the brain. An agreement with an idiot is absolutely void. However, his property is liable for necessaries supplied to him or to persons dependent upon him. Also, he can be a beneficiary.
2. **Lunatics:** A lunatic is a person whose mental power has been damaged. Such a person is sometimes sane and sometimes insane. He suffers from intervals of insanity and sanity. Such a person may enter into a contract when he is of sound mind. Except the agreement made during lucid intervals, all agreements made by lunatics are void. However, agreements for necessities of life are valid. But only the property of a lunatic is liable for such contracts.

Persons of temporary unsoundness are as follows:

1. **Drunken or intoxicated person:** A person who is under the influence of intoxication or drugs or liquor stands on the same footing as a lunatic because he cannot form a rational opinion as to the effect of a contract on his interest. But in order to make his contract void, the drunkenness should be absolute so much so that he is incapable of understanding anything.

So the agreements entered into with persons of unsound mind are void. However, such persons can always enter into a valid contract during lucid intervals.

The concept of person with unsound mind is explained under Section 12 (2) of the Indian Contract Act.

Example 1: A patient in lunatic asylum, who is at intervals of sound mind, may contract during those intervals.

Example 2: A sane person who is delirious from fever or who is so drunk that he cannot understand the terms of a contract or form a rational judgement as to its effects on his interest cannot contract while such delirium or drunkenness lasts.

A contract entered into with such a delirious person or drunkard during such unsound mind conditions is void. Under Section 68 of the Contract Act, a person who has supplied necessities of life to such an incapable person or his dependant is entitled to be reimbursed from the property of such incapable person. But the incapable person is not personally liable for necessaries.

Under the English law, however, a contract by a person of unsound mind is voidable. A person who seeks to avoid the contract on this ground has to prove his incapacity as well as the fact that the other party was aware of it. But if such a person wants to ratify such a contract, he can ratify it during lucid intervals.

Other Disqualified Persons

Those persons are included under this heading who are disqualified from entering into a contract due to certain other reasons. This incompetence may arise from legal status, political status or corporate status. Such persons are partially or wholly disqualified from entering into a contract.

1. **Alien enemy:** An alien is a person who is living in a foreign country. An alien enemy is the citizen of a country at war with India. An agreement with an alien enemy is void. Such persons are also disqualified from suing in Indian courts. They can sue only after approval from the central government. Such contracts with an alien enemy are void on the ground of public policy, as these contracts may promote the economic interests of enemy or may prejudice the economic interests of the Indian economy. Contracts made before a war may be terminated or suspended during the war. If they are, in the opinion of the central government, against national interest, then these contracts may be terminated as being against public policy. Otherwise such contracts are suspended for the duration of the war and revived after the war is over, provided they have not already become time barred.
2. **Foreign sovereign and ambassador:** Foreign sovereigns and their representatives usually enjoy certain privileges and immunities. Generally, they cannot be sued in Indian courts unless and until the government gives permission or they submit themselves to these courts. This is as per the international law and protocol. Foreign sovereigns can enter into contracts through their agents residing in India. In such a case, the agent becomes personally liable for the performance of such contracts. The central government may grant permission to sue a foreigner or ambassador in the following cases:
    a. When such a person has instituted a suit against the person desiring to sue him
    b. When he has expressly or impliedly waived the privilege
    c. When he himself carries on trade in jurisdiction of the court or is in possession of some immovable property and is to be sued in connection with that property
3. **Convicts:** A convict is a person who has been held guilty and convicted of an offence. He is, therefore, undergoing sentence for an offence. A convict cannot enter into a contract while he is undergoing imprisonment. The very purpose of imprisonment is secluding the person from the society and if the convict is allowed to interact with the society, it defeats the very purpose of imprisonment. The inability comes to an end with the expiry of the period of sentence. The period of sentence is not taken into account in calculating the period of limitation under the Limitation Act.

4. **Insolvents:** An insolvent is a person who is unable to discharge his liabilities and, therefore, has applied for being adjudged insolvent or such proceedings have been initiated by any of his creditors. The property of the insolvent vests in the official receiver, and an insolvent cannot enter into contracts relating to his property and sue on his behalf. However, after the 'order of discharge', he is competent to enter into contracts.
5. **Company or statutory corporation:** Joint stock companies and corporations created under a special Act of legislature are all artificial persons created by law. They can enter into contracts through their agents such as boards of directors or chief officers. A company is usually bound by the conditions set out in its memorandum and articles of association. A company cannot enter into any contract which is inconsistent with the objects set out in its memorandum of association. Any act done outside the scope of its memorandum is ultra vires and void. Similarly, a company being an artificial person cannot enter into contracts of personal nature which can be entered into by a natural person only. In the case of a corporation, its scope is limited to such powers as are conferred by the special Act under which it is incorporated. Thus, a contract entered into by a corporation or company will be valid only if it is within the powers conferred by the special Act or memorandum of association, as the case may be. Any act done in excess of these powers is ultra vires and void. A corporation or company can hold property, sell or purchase it, and can sue or be sued in a court of law.
6. **Married woman:** According to the Indian Constitution, the right of a woman to be treated on a footing equal to man is guaranteed to her; therefore, a woman can enter into a contract irrespective of her marital status. She can even bind her husband's property for necessaries supplied to her in certain cases. But she cannot enter into contracts with respect to her husband's property. However, she enjoys absolute powers of dealing with her own property known as *streedhan*. Under Hindu Succession Act also, a daughter is placed in the same position as a son for the purpose of succession to the property of a male or female Hindu.

TEST QUESTIONS

1. Define the term 'capacity to contract'. State the law relating to contracts entered into by a minor.
2. What is the legal effect of a minor's misrepresentation of age while entering into an agreement?
3. A minor's agreements are void. Are there any agreements with a minor which can be enforced in a court of law?
4. 'A person who is usually of unsound mind but occasionally of sound mind may make a contract when he is of sound mind.' Explain.
5. Name the persons, other than minors, who are not competent to contract.
6. Discuss the contractual capacity of the following:
   a. Aliens
   b. Insolvents
   c. Convicts
   d. Companies
7. What do you understand by capacity to contract? State the rules regarding contracts made by minors.

8. What do you know about contracts entered into with a minor from the legal point of view in India? Do you know of any contracts with a minor to be valid? Explain them.
9. A contract made by an infant may be (a) valid, (b) void and (c) voidable. What contracts come under each of these heads?
10. Explain the legal position of the following:
    a. A minor promisor
    b. A minor promisee
    c. A minor agent

Practical Problems

1. A, a minor, borrowed ₹50,000 from B and executed a promissory note for the amount in favour of B. After attaining majority, A executed another promissory note in settlement of the first promissory note. Will B succeed in recovering money from A?
   Hint. No. A minor's agreement cannot be ratified on attaining majority.
2. A minor, falsely representing himself to be of age entered into an agreement to sell his house to B and received an advance of ₹80,000. Out of this sum, the minor bought a motorcycle for ₹50,000 and spent the rest of the money on a pleasure trip to a hill station. After the minor had attained majority, B sued him for conveyance of the property or refund of ₹80,000 and damages. Will he succeed?
   Hint. No. B can only get the motorcycle.
3. A shopkeeper supplies a minor of groceries. Is the grocer entitled to claim money against the estate of the minor?
   Hint. Yes. (Liability for necessaries under Section 68)
4. A minor who wanted to become a professional billiards player entered into a contract with a famous billiards player and agreed to pay him a certain sum of money to learn the game. Is he liable to pay?
   Hint. Yes. (Robert vs. Gray)
5. A supplies rice and wheat to the wife and children of B, who is a lunatic. B has assets worth ₹1 lakh. On non-payment, can A proceed against the assets of B?
   Hint. Yes. (Liability for necessaries under Section 68)
6. A, a minor, is facing a criminal prosecution for dacoity. He borrowed ₹5,000 from B to defend himself. Will B succeed in recovering the amount?
   Hint. Yes. The liberty of the minor being at state, the money is for necessaries.

5 CHAPTER

Free Consent

Learning Objectives

- To understand the meaning of consent and free consent
- To understand the meaning of coercion: Characteristics and effects on contracts
- To understand the meaning of undue influence: Meaning and contracts with pardan-ashin women
- To be able to distinguish between coercion and undue influence
- To understand the meaning of fraud
- To understand the meaning of misrepresentation
- To be able to the distinguish between fraud and misrepresentation
- To understand the meaning of a mistake: Meaning and types of mistake of law

CONSENT AND FREE CONSENT

Section 10 provides that free consent is an essential element for a valid contract. When two parties enter into a contract, the first thing required is perfect mutual understanding regarding the subject matter of the contract. Both the parties should agree upon the same thing in the same sense (consensus ad idem). This understanding is called consent. Section 13 provides, 'Two or more persons are said to consent when they agree upon the same thing in the same sense.' This means that parties should have the same subject matter in mind while they are entering into a contract. If they are not, then a contract does not come into existence.

The Contract Act further provides that the consent of both the parties entering into a contract should be free. It is an essential requirement of a valid contract. So it is not only important that there should be consent, but the consent should also be free. According to Section 14 of the Contract Act,

> Consent is said to be free when it is not caused by:
> (1) coercion, as defined in section 15, or
> (2) undue influence, as defined in section 16, or
> (3) fraud, as defined in section 17, or
> (4) misrepresentation, as defined in section 18, or
> (5) mistake, subject to the provisions of sections 20, 21 and 22. Consent is said to be so caused when it would not have been given but for the existence of such coercion, undue influence, fraud, misrepresentation or mistake.

So where consent of any party is obtained in any of the above manner, it is not free. When an agreement is caused by coercion, undue influence, misrepresentation or fraud, the contract is voidable at the option of the party whose consent was not free (aggrieved party).

COERCION

Section 15 provides, 'Coercion is committing, or threatening to commit, any act forbidden by Indian Penal Code or the unlawful detaining, or threatening to detain, any property, to the prejudice of any person whatever, with the intention of causing any person to enter into an agreement.' This means the use of force by one party or using a threat to compel a person to enter into a contract.

Characteristics of Coercion

On analysing Section 15 of the Act, the following characteristics of coercion can be pointed out:

1. **Coercion means committing any act forbidden by law:** Coercion means committing any act forbidden by the Indian Penal Code (IPC) with the intention of causing any person to enter into an agreement.
   Example: X gave severe beating to Y and caused him to sign a deed in his favour to sell his house for ₹800,000. In this case, X has used coercion.
   In the case of Ranganayakamma vs. Alwar Setti, the question before the court was regarding the validity of the adoption of a boy by a widow. On the death of her husband, the husband's dead body was not allowed to be removed for cremation by the relatives of the adopted boy until she adopted the boy. It was held that the adoption was not binding on the widow as her consent was obtained by coercion.
2. **Coercion may be threatening to commit any act forbidden by law:** Coercion may be threatening to commit any act forbidden by the IPC, with the intention of causing the other person to enter into a contract.
   Example: If X, at gunpoint, or threatening to cause hurt, compels Y to enter into a contract, he is said to have used coercion.
3. **Coercion is unlawful detaining or threatening to detain the property of another:** Coercion is unlawful detaining or threatening to detain the property of another, which is to the prejudice of another or to his property. If by such unlawful detention or threat a person is compelled to enter into a contract, coercion is said to have been employed in that case.
4. **A party to a contract need not necessarily initiate threat amounting to coercion:** Even a third party may initiate it. Also, it may be directed against either party to the contract or even a stranger.
   Example: X threatens to kill Y's son if Y does not agree to sell his bike to him for ₹25,000. Y agrees to sell. Y's consent in this case has been taken by coercion.
5. **The acts of coercion should be done with the intention of causing the other person to enter into a contract:** It must be established that there is an intention of the person making it to induce a person to enter into a contract under coercion. If there is no intention to induce the other person to enter into a contract, there is no coercion. It means that the purpose of coercion must be directed to obtain the consent of the party on whom the coercion is used.

6. **A threat to file a suit is not coercion:** A threat of criminal prosecution is not an act forbidden by IPC. But a threat to file a false charge is forbidden by IPC and, therefore, amounts to coercion.
7. **A threat to commit suicide amounts to coercion:** A threat to commit suicide is not punishable under IPC, even though an attempt to commit suicide is an offence. However, Madras High Court, faced with the same problem, gave a different opinion.

Effects of Coercion on a Contract

The effects of coercion are dealt with in Sections 19 and 72 of the Indian Contract Act. Section 19 states, 'When consent an agreement is caused by coercion ... the agreement is a contract voidable at the option of the party whose consent was so caused.' It means that an aggrieved party may set aside the contract. However, the burden of proof lies on the aggrieved party.

UNDUE INFLUENCE

In coercion, the element of physical pressure or threatening is involved, whereas in undue influence, mental pressure is used by one party to obtain the consent of another party. Undue influence is a subtle form of coercion. A contract is induced by undue influence where one party takes undue advantage of his superior position or relationship to obtain the consent of another party. Section 16(1) provides,

> A contract is said to be induced by 'undue influence' where the relations subsisting between the parties are such that one of the parties is in a position to dominate the will of the other and uses that position to obtain an unfair advantage over the other.

Following conditions are required to establish the use of undue influence:

1. The relation between two parties is such that one of them is in a position to exercise pressure on the other.
2. Such party uses his superior position to obtain willingness of the other party to enter into a contract.
3. Such party obtains an unfair advantage over the other due to his position.

Presumption of Undue Influence

Section 16(2) provides,

> In particular and without prejudice to the generality of the foregoing principle, a person is deemed to be in a position to dominate the will of another, where he holds a real or apparent authority over the other or where he stands in a fiduciary relation to the other.

A person is said to be in a position to influence the will of another in the following cases:

1. When he holds real or apparent authority over the other.
2. If that person stands in a fiduciary relationship to another. Fiduciary relationships are those which are relationships of trust and confidence. Mutual confidence is at the base

of such relationships, that is, solicitor and client, doctor and patient, creditor and debtor, trustee and beneficiary, parent and child, and so on.

3. Where the party with whom the contract is made is in mental distress. Such a person can be easily persuaded to give consent to an unfavourable contract. Such relationship exists between a doctor and a patient or a weak person and his attendants.

Burden of proof: To prove that a contract was induced by undue influence, it has to be proved that there was an unequal relationship, position to dominate the will of the other and position to obtain unfair advantage.

Cases Where Presumption of Undue Influence May Exist

The presumption of undue influence is raised in the following cases:

1. **Unconscionable bargains:** When a person who is in a position to dominate the will of another enters into a contract that on the face of it appears to be unreasonable or unfair, it is unconscionable bargain. Although unconscionable bargains have been mostly witnessed in moneylending transactions and gifts, the principle is not confined to only these cases. In Bhimbat vs. Yeshwantrao, a poor farmer was unable to pay back a loan. He, therefore, executed a sale deed of his property, which was three times the value of the sum due. The court set aside the sale and allowed the farmer to pay back to lender within a fixed period.
2. **Contracts with *pardanashin* women:** A *pardanashin* woman is one who observes complete seclusion because of the custom or the usage of a particular community and society, and any contract with such a woman is presumed to have been entered by undue influence. However, a woman who appears in a court, gives evidence, settles rents and so on cannot be called a pardanashin woman. Following facts are required to establish that the contract entered into with a pardanashin woman has not been induced by undue influence:
   a. The terms of the contract made are reasonable, fair and equitable.
   b. The transaction performed is real and bona fide.
   c. The deed when executed was fully explained to her.
   d. The woman received an independent and disinterested advice in this regard.
   e. The woman had complete knowledge of the nature and the effects of the transaction.

Further, the protection granted to a pardanashin woman is also extended to illiterate and ignorant women who are equally exposed to the danger and risk of an unfair deal. The basic purpose of this provision is to protect the interest of pardanashin and illiterate women.

Effects of Undue Influence

Section 19A states,

> When consent to an agreement is caused by undue influence, the agreement is a contract voidable at the option of the party whose consent was so caused. Any such contract may be set aside either absolutely or, if the party who was entitled to avoid it has received any benefit thereunder, upon such terms and conditions as to the Court may seem just.

The effect of undue influence is that a contract which is entered into by undue influence can be rescinded by the aggrieved party, which means whose consent is obtained by undue influence.

Distinction between Coercion and Undue Influence

1. In the case of coercion, the consent of the aggrieved party is obtained under the threat of an offence, or threat to detain property (i.e., committing or threatening to commit an offence), punishable under IPC. But in the case of undue influence, the consent is obtained by dominating the will of the weaker party by the stronger party and thereby taking advantage of one's superior position.
2. Coercion involves the use of physical or violent forces. But undue influence involves the use of moral force or mental pressure.
3. In the case of coercion, the relationship between parties will not be required to be proved for the free consent. But in the case of undue influence, some kind of relationship between the parties must exist. Due to this relationship, one party should be in a position to dominate the will of the other such as parent and child, and doctor and patient.
4. In the case of coercion, a party exercises an act that is a crime under IPC for which there may be a punishment and it will be criminal liability, whereas the use of undue influence does not involve any criminal liability.
5. Coercion need not be directly used against a party to the contract; it can be used directly against any third party who is also concerned with such aggrieved party. But undue influence must be exercised upon the other party to the contract who is the aggrieved party.
6. In coercion, party claiming to set aside the contract has to prove the act of coercion and the law will not presume coercion. But in certain types of relations, undue influence may be presumed by law and the party against whom it is alleged must prove that it has not used undue influence against the aggrieved party.
7. The law will take a note of the act of coercion; it may be committed at any time or place where IPC is in force or not in force, whereas undue influence should be exercised in India only so that the law may take notice of it in India.
8. In the case of coercion, the agreement is voidable at the option of the party whose consent was not free. Moreover, a party avoiding the contract has to restore the benefit obtained by him to the other party under Section 64. In the case of undue influence, the party avoiding the contract may or may not return the benefit under Section 19A. The courts have been given the discretionary power to set aside the contract either absolutely or upon such terms and conditions as the court may deem fit.

Fraud

The term 'fraud' includes all intentional or wilful misrepresentation of facts which are material for the formation of a contract. The most important element in fraud is the intention to deceive or mislead the other party. Section 17 provides,

> Fraud means and includes any of the following acts committed by a party to a contract, or with his connivance, or by his agent, with intent to deceive another party thereto or his agent, or to induce him to enter into the contract:

(1) the suggestion, as a fact, of that which is not true, by one who does not believe it to be true;
(2) the active concealment of a fact by one having knowledge or belief of the fact;
(3) a promise made without any intention of performing it;
(4) any other act fitted to deceive;
(5) any such act or omission as the law specially declares to be fraudulent.

Essential Elements of Fraud

The main elements of fraud are as follows:

1. **There must be a false representation of facts:** The most important element of fraud is that there must be a false statement of facts. Without a representation, there can be no fraud except in the following cases: (a) where silence may itself amount to fraud and (b) where there is an active concealment of facts. Active concealment of facts, however, amounts to fraud.
2. **It must be with the knowledge about its truth or falsehood:** If a person making a statement honestly believes it to be true, he is not guilty of fraud. But when he knows that it is false, or when he makes a reckless statement without caring for its truth, he is guilty of fraud.
3. **It must have been made by a party to the contract or by his agent:** If a statement is made by a stranger, it does not affect the contract. A fraud will make a contract voidable only if it is committed by a party to a contract or his agent.
4. **It must have been made with an intention to deceive the other party:** A false statement should have been made with an intention to deceive the other party. Section 17 states, 'Fraud means and includes any of the ... acts committed by a party to a contract ... with intent to deceive another party thereto or his agent, or to induce him to enter into the contract.'
5. **It must have induced the other party to act upon it:** Section 19 provides that fraud which did not cause the consent to a contract of the party on whom such fraud was practised does not render the contract voidable.
6. **The party who was misled must suffer some loss:** It is a common rule of law that 'There is no fraud without damage.' Therefore, the misled party must suffer a loss. The damage may be some loss in terms of money or money's worth of some other tangible detriment capable of assessment. Without damage, fraud does not give rise to any action for deceit.

Is Silence a Fraud?

Section 17 of the Act provides,

> Mere silence as to facts likely to affect the willingness of a person to enter in to a contract is not a fraud, unless the circumstances of the case are such that, regard being had to them, it is the duty of the person keeping silence to speak, or unless his silence is, in itself, equivalent to speech.

The general rule is that silence as to facts likely to affect the willingness of a person to enter into a contract is not fraud. A contracting party is under no obligation to disclose the whole truth to the other party or to give him the whole information which he may have, affecting the subject matter of a contract.

However, under certain cases, silence may be held as fraud. In the following circumstances, silence may amount to fraud:

1. **When it is duty to speak:** Silence will be a fraud if the circumstances are such that it is the duty of the person to speak. Duty arises when one party has full trust and confidence in the other. Duty to speak also arises in cases where one party is without any means to discover the truth and therefore depends on the good sense of the other party.
2. **Where silence will amount to speech:** Silence is sometimes itself equivalent to speech. So where a person knows that his silence is going to be deceptive and still keeps silent, he is guilty of fraud. When one party asks another regarding material facts, and such party keeps silence, then it will amount to fraud.
   Example: Where Y says to X, 'If you do not deny it, I shall assume that the dog is sound,' and X says nothing, X's silence will amount to speech.
3. **Change in circumstances:** Sometimes a statement may be true when it is made, but due to change in circumstances it may become false when it is actually acted upon. In such cases, the person is duty-bound to communicate the changes in circumstances.
4. **Half-truth:** Sometimes a person under no duty to disclose a fact may become guilty of fraud when he discloses only half the truth. A person may keep silence, but if he speaks he must disclose the whole truth. Half-truth will also be treated as silence if it misleads the person who is giving his consent on the basis of that half-truth.
   Example: The prospectus of a company states that the company has paid dividend over the last five years. But the fact is that during these years, the company has incurred heavy losses and utilized secret reserves to pay dividend. This non-disclosure or half-disclosure of facts is fraudulent in this case.

When Will Duty to Speak Arise?

In certain contracts, the law requires the parties to make fullest disclosure of material facts. In such contracts, one party has peculiar means of knowledge, which are not accessible to the other. Such contracts are known as contracts of utmost good faith. In contracts of insurance, there is a burden on both parties to make full disclosure of material facts. But this burden is more on the insured, since he possesses more information about the subject matter of insurance. Therefore, in contracts of insurance, the insured is bound to disclose all material facts relating to the subject matter of insurance which are likely to affect the risk. If he fails to do so, the insurer has right to rescind the contract. In the case of Derry vs. Peek, it was held that 'Fraud is proved when it is shown that a false representation has been made (1) knowingly or (2) without belief in its truth or (3) recklessly careless whether it be true or false.'

MISREPRESENTATION

Misrepresentation is any untrue statement made by a party to induce the other party to act upon the statement and enter into a contract. This false representation must relate to some fact which is material to the contract. If this false statement is made innocently and without an intention to deceive, it is called misrepresentation. But if it is made intentionally with a view to deceive the other party, it is called fraud. So an honest misstatement of facts is called misrepresentation. According to Section 18,

(1) 'Misrepresentation' means and includes—the positive assertion, in a manner not warranted by the information of the person making it, of that which is not true, though he believes it to be true;
(2) any breach of duty which, without an intent to deceive, gains an advantage of the person committing it, or any one claiming under him, by misleading another to his prejudice, or to the prejudice of any one claiming under him;
(3) causing, however innocently, a party to an agreement, to make a mistake as to the substance of the thing which is the subject of the agreement.

Characteristics of Misrepresentation

1. **It is an unwarranted statement:** When a person positively asserts that a fact is true when the information at his disposal does not warrant it to be so, though he believes it to be true, it is called misrepresentation. So in this, a person makes a statement on the basis of information from an untrustworthy source. However, he innocently believes his statement to be true.
2. **It is the breach of duty:** If a person commits a breach of duty, which brings an advantage to the person committing it by misleading the other to his prejudice, that is a case of misrepresentation. So under this clause, all such cases are covered in which there is no intention to deceive but where circumstances are such as to make the party drawing the benefit from the transaction answerable for it.
3. **Inducing mistake about subject matter:** If one of the parties leads the other party to make a mistake regarding the subject matter, it is a case of misrepresentation. If one party is, therefore, led to make a mistake as to the nature or quality of the subject matter, the agreement is voidable at his option.

Essentials of Misrepresentation

1. **False representation:** Misrepresentation is a false statement made without an intention to deceive. But the statement should be made without the knowledge of its falsehood.
2. **Must be of material facts:** Misrepresentation should be of facts which are material to the contract. Mere commendatory expressions, which are generally made by businessmen about their goods, are not sufficient to avoid the contract.
3. **Should be made before or at the time of entering into a contract:** Misrepresentation should be made before or at the time of making a contract. A subsequent statement is unimportant.
4. **By a party to the contract:** The representation must be by a party to the contract or his agent. If a stranger makes it, it does not affect the contract.
5. **Must have been addressed to the other party:** Misrepresentation must be addressed to the other party to induce him to enter into a contract. If it is not addressed to the other party, it is not misrepresentation.
6. **Must induce the other party:** It is further necessary that misrepresentation must be the cause of the consent; otherwise, the consent would not have been given. Misrepresentation must lead to the consent of the other party.

Effect of Misrepresentation

Misrepresentation makes a contract voidable at the option of the party whose consent was obtained by misrepresentation. Section19 states that when the consent to an agreement is caused by misrepresentation, the aggrieved party shall be placed in the position in which he would have been if the representation made had been true.

Remedies Available to the Aggrieved Party

Right of Rescission

As mentioned above, a contract brought about by misrepresentation is voidable at the option of the party whose consent was not free. The innocent party misled by misrepresentation may sue for rescission of the contract and restitution of the contract and restitution of anything he has transferred to the other party, but the party whose consent was so caused by misrepresentation cannot rescind the contract.

Right to Insist upon Performance

Section 19 provides,

> A party to contract, whose consent was caused by fraud or misrepresentation, may, if he thinks fit, insist that the contract should be performed, and that he shall be put in the position in which he would have been if the representations made had been true.

This means that the aggrieved party can accept the contract and compel the other party to put him in a position in which he would have been if there had been no misrepresentation.

Right to Claim Damages

In the case of misrepresentation, the aggrieved party generally cannot claim damages. At the most, he can insist on restitution. However, in the following cases, he can get damages:

1. Where promoters or directors of a company have made misrepresentation in a prospectus, they are liable for damages to persons who had applied for shares on the basis of such prospectus.
2. An agent who is guilty of breach of warranty of authority is liable to pay damages. Sometimes, an agent may induce another person to enter into a contract with him as an agent by making a misrepresentation as to his authority.
3. Where one person makes negligent representation to another person and a confidential relationship exists between them, for example, solicitor and client.

Distinction between Fraud and Misrepresentation

1. In both fraud and misrepresentation, there is a false statement. In fraud, a wrong statement is made knowingly with an intention to deceive the other party. But in the case of misrepresentation, the person making it honestly believes it to be true or does not know that it is false.

2. The remedy of rescission is available under both. But as fraud is a civil wrong, the aggrieved party can claim damages under the law of tort also. However, in the case of misrepresentation, damages cannot be claimed by the aggrieved party.
3. A person complaining of misrepresentation can be met with a defence that he had the means of discovering the truth by ordinary diligence. But accepting fraud by silence, in other cases, the person complaining of fraud cannot be met with this defence. In other words, a contract is voidable even if the aggrieved party had the means of discovering the truth with ordinary diligence.
4. In certain cases, fraud can be a criminal act and punishable under IPC. But misrepresentation does not show any criminal intent on the part of the person making the statement and it is not a criminal act and, hence, not punishable under the Act.
5. In some cases, silence can be construed as fraud, for example, in the case of contracts of utmost good faith. But silence cannot constitute an act of misrepresentation.

MISTAKE

The term 'mistake' may be defined as an erroneous belief concerning something, as a result of which there is a misunderstanding among the parties. It generally occurs when the concerned parties take the terms of the agreement in different sense. Salmond describes it as error in consensus, which prevents the existence of any consensus ad idem and, therefore, any contract. Generally, law will not help anyone to avoid a contract on the plea that he was mistaken. But law also realizes that mistakes do occur and that certain mistakes are so fundamental that there is no contract at all. Therefore, a mistake may operate upon a contract in two ways:

1. It may defeat the consent altogether that the parties are supposed to have given. As a result, there is no contract due to the absence of consensus ad idem.
2. The mistake may mislead the parties as to the purpose which they contemplated. As a result, the agreement is void.

Types of Mistakes

Mistakes can be of following types:

1. **Mistake of law:** A mistake of law may be:
   a. A mistake as to the law in India
   b. A mistake under a foreign Law
2. **Mistake of fact:** A mistake of fact may be:
   a. Bilateral
   b. Unilateral

Mistake of Law

Regarding the effect of a mistake as to law, Section 21 states, 'A contract is not voidable because it was caused by a mistake as to any law in force in India; but a mistake as to a law not in force in India has the same effect as a mistake of fact.' So if there is a mistake of law of a country, the contract is binding. This is because ignorance of law is no excuse. Everyone is supposed to know the law of the country where he lives. No relief on this basis can be allowed to a person who is ignorant of the law. It may be noted that the mistake of a foreign law has the same effect as the mistake of fact. A mistake with regard to a foreign law would be considered a question of fact. A mistake of a foreign law renders the agreement void.

Mistake of Fact

A mistake of fact may be either (a) bilateral or (b) unilateral

1. **Bilateral mistake:** A bilateral mistake occurs when both the parties to a contract are at a mistake about the facts which are essential to the agreement. Section 20 states that where both the parties to an agreement are under a mistake as to a matter of fact essential to the agreement, the agreement is void. In order that a mistake of fact may be made ground for avoiding the contract, it is necessary to show that the mistake was bilateral and was as to fact essential to the agreement. A bilateral mistake may be either a common mistake or a mutual mistake. In the case of a common mistake, the contract is void. In the case of a non-identical mistake, the contract does not come into existence at all because there is no consensus ad idem. The parties are never in agreement.

   It may be again (a) mistake about the subject matter or (b) a mistake about the possibility of performance.

   a. **Mistake about the subject matter:** Where both the parties are working under a mistake regarding the subject matter, the agreement is void. Following cases fall under this subheading:
      i. **Mistake as to the existence of the subject matter:** At the time of the contract, the subject matter may cease to exist or it may have never been in existence and the parties may have no knowledge about it. In such cases, the agreement is void. It is a common bilateral mistake.
      ii. **Mistake about the title of the subject matter:** When it is unknown to the parties, the buyer is already the owner of that which the seller purports to sell to him. Such agreement of sale is void.
      iii. **Mistake as to the identity and quality of the subject matter:** Where both the parties are mistaken as to the identity of the subject matter, the contract is void. In this case, one party thinks about one thing and the other about something else.
      iv. **Mistake as to the quantity of the subject matter:** If both the parties are under a mistake about the quantity of the subject matter, the contract is void. This is because the mistake is about an essential fact of the agreement: the quantity. This will also be treated as a mistake of facts about the subject matter.
      v. **Mistake as to the price of the subject matter:** There may sometimes be a genuine mistake as to the price of the article for sale. In this case, the contract will be void. If price is an essential fact of the agreement, the contract can be avoided.

   b. **Mistake about the possibility of performance:** Sometimes, both the parties may believe that a contract can be performed when in fact this is not the case. Both the parties in this case may not be knowing that a contract cannot be performed. In such a case, the agreement is void. Impossibility may be:
      i. **Physical:** Sometimes, unknown to the parties, a contract may be impossible to perform. In such cases, the contract is void.
      ii. **Legal:** A contract is void if it provides that something shall be done which cannot, as a matter of law, be done.

Example: In Griffith vs. Brymer, Griffith hired a room from Brymer for watching the coronation procession of King Edward VII. Unknown to both the parties, the procession had already been cancelled. This agreement was held to be void.

2. **Unilateral mistake:** It is a mistake on the part of one of the parties only as to a matter of fact. Generally, a unilateral mistake does not affect the validity of the contract. Section 22 provides, 'A contract is not voidable merely because it was caused by one of the parties to it being under a mistake as to a matter of fact.' The general common law rule is that the mistake made by one of the parties to a contract has no effect on the validity of the contract. However, a unilateral mistake will render an agreement void if (a) it is about some fact which is essential to the agreement and (b) the unilateral mistake defeats the true consent of the parties. The following types of unilateral mistake will render the agreement void:
    a. **Mistake about the identity of parties:** A mistake as to identity occurs where one of the parties represents himself to be some person other than who he really is. When anyone makes a contract in which the personality of the particular party contracted with is important, no one else is at liberty to step in and maintain that he is the party contracted with. In Sowler vs. Potter, it was held that the consideration of the person with whom the plaintiff was entering into the lease was a vital element in that agreement. So the plaintiff was at a mistake with regard to the identity of the defendant and the lease was void ab initio.
    b. **Mistake about the nature of the agreement:** When a deed of one character is executed under the mistaken impression that it is of a different character, then it is wholly void and inoperative. One of the parties fails to do so and induces the other person to sign the document under the belief that he is signing some other document of a different nature. In such cases, the agreement is nullified by mistake. In Raja Singh vs. Chaichoo Singh, the plaintiff appointed the defendant to look after his cultivation and his affairs as he had become too old to manage them. The defendant asked him to grant a lease of his land. The plaintiff agreed to it and placed his thumb impression upon a deed which was in fact a gift of the land. The court held the deed to be void ab initio.

Effects of Mistake

Where a contract is caused by mistake and is void, the following are the consequences:

1. Under Section 65, 'Any person who has received any advantage under such agreement or contract is bound to restore it, or make compensation for it to the person from whom he received it.'
2. Under Section 72, 'A person to whom money has been paid, or anything delivered, by mistake or under coercion, must repay or return it.'
3. A contract can rescind the contract.

Test Questions

1. Comment upon the following statements:
    a. 'To form a valid contract, there must be meeting of the minds of the parties.'
    b. 'To consummate a contract, there must be mutuality as well as meeting of minds of the parties.'

c. 'A contract which is regular in all other respects may still fail if there is no consensus ad idem.'
d. 'A threat to commit an act forbidden by IPC amounts to coercion.'
e. 'Mere silence may amount to fraud.'
f. 'An attempt to deceive, which does not deceive, is not fraud.'
g. 'Ignorance of law is no excuse.'
h. 'Fundamental error will not prevent a contract from coming into existence.'
2. Define consent. When is consent said to be free?
3. Define coercion. What is the effect of coercing on a contract?
4. Define the term 'undue influence'. What is the effect of undue influence on the validity of a contract? Differentiate between coercion and undue influence.
5. State the acts which constitute fraud. What is the difference between fraud and misrepresentation?
6. 'Mere silence as to facts likely to affect the willingness of a person to enter into a contract is not fraud.' Discuss.
7. What is a bilateral mistake? How does it differ from a unilateral mistake? How does a bilateral mistake affect the validity of a contract?
8. 'It is a rule of law that if a person intends to contract with A, B cannot give himself any rights under the contract.' Discuss.
9. What is a mistake? Explain different types of mistakes and their effect on the validity of a contract.
10. 'Undue influence is the subtle form of coercion.' Explain.

PRACTICAL PROBLEMS

1. A sells a horse to B knowing fully well that the horse is vicious. A does not disclose the nature of the horse to B. Can A be made liable to B for the transaction?
   Hint. No. A has no duty to disclose.
2. An illiterate woman executes a sale deed on the assumption that it was a power of attorney and that the deed after it was executed was not read over to the lady. Advise the lady.
   Hint. There is no consent and, hence, the contract is not enforceable.
3. Anil called at a jeweller's shop and chose a costly diamond. He tendered make the payment by a cheque, which he signed in the name of Ram Chandra, a man of credit. He took the ring and pledged it to Suresh, who had no notice of the fraud. Can the jeweller recover the ring from Suresh?
   Hint. No.
4. X sells a horse to Y for ₹1,200, but unknown to both the parties on the time of the transaction, the horse was dead. Discuss the rights and liabilities of X and Y. Would it make any difference to your answer if the horse was seriously ill at the time of the transaction and died within a few hours after the transaction?
   Hint. In the first case, the agreement is void on account of mutual mistake of fact. Y is entitled to the refund of any amount paid by him to X. In the second case, there was no misrepresentation on the part of X, and he is entitled to recover from Y the price of the horse.

5. A, a dealer, sold a mare to B with the knowledge that the mare had a cracked hoof, which A had filled up so as to prevent detection even after a diligent examination. Discuss the right of B when he subsequently detects it.
   Hint. As per Section 17(2) of the Act, A is liable to B for playing a fraud.
6. A man enfeebled by a disease and old age was induced by B's influence over him as his medical attendant to agree to pay B an unreasonable sum for his professional services. Discuss.
   Hint. Contract is voidable at the option of A on account of undue influence.

6

CHAPTER

Legality of Objects

Learning Objectives

- To understand when an object is unlawful
- To understand the circumstances when an object is unlawful
- To understand the agreements opposed to public policy
- To understand the unlawful and illegal agreements and their effects

Legality of Object

The object of a contract must be lawful for a valid contract. The agreement will be void if its object is unlawful. Section 10 of the Indian Contract Act says, 'all agreements are contracts if they are made for lawful consideration and with lawful object'. While consideration is an act, abstinence or promise given in return for a promise, the object is the purpose of the contract. Both consideration and object must be lawful. Section 23 says that consideration or object of an agreement is lawful, unless:

1. It is forbidden by law,
2. Is of such nature that, if permitted, it would defeat the provisions of any law,
3. Is fraudulent,
4. Involves or implies injury to the person or property of another or
5. The court regards it as immoral or opposed to public policy.

Therefore, whenever the object or consideration falls within any of the above categories, it is said to be unlawful. Every agreement of which the object or consideration is unlawful is void.

Example: X, Y and Z enter into an agreement for the division of income acquired, or to be acquired, by them through fraud. The agreement is void, as its object is unlawful.

When an Object Is Unlawful?

According to Section 23 of the Indian Contract Act, under the following conditions, an object or consideration is unlawful.

1. **Forbidden by law:** When the law forbids anything, an agreement will be void due to illegality of object. Any act which is forbidden by IPC or under any other Act for the time being in force is called unlawful. An agreement, which involves any crime or act of tort, will be said to be void because of illegal object. However, it should be noted that it is not necessary that when any penalty is imposed, law forbids the act. When the penalty is imposed to protect the revenue, the statute cannot be construed as prohibiting the act in respect of which the penalty is imposed.

   Examples:

   a. Law forbids the sale of liquor without licence. The agreement to sale without licence is void and the price is irrecoverable.
   b. An agreement for the business of prostitution is unlawful as it is prohibited under IPC.
   c. An agreement to bring the foreign exchange in India through an unauthorized route like Hawala is unlawful and void due to the fact that such an agreement is forbidden by the Foreign Exchange Management Act. So if object is unlawful, agreement will be void.
   d. When the holder of a licence for collecting toll has subleased it to another, without the permission of the collector of revenue. Fine for this is ₹200. In this case, the sublease is valid and the purpose of penalty is the protection of revenue only and not to make the contract void.

   In the case of Nutan Kumar vs. Additional Judge, Banda (AIR 1994 All 298), it was held that an agreement of lease between a landlord and a tenant without allotment or release order, as required by the law, is void and unenforceable.
2. **Defeat the provisions of any law:** If the object of an agreement is of such a nature that, if permitted, would defeat the provisions of any law, then such an agreement is void. There are certain acts which may not be expressly forbidden by law, but may result in circumventing any law, cannot be encouraged. The agreement with such an object or consideration is unlawful and void. In the case of Ram Sevak vs. Ram Charan, the parties entered into an agreement that they will not enter some transactions in books of accounts in order to avoid the tax liability. In this case, it was held that the agreement was aimed at defeating the provisions of tax laws, it is opposed to public policy and, therefore, the same is not enforceable. The court, in the case of Bebi Fatima vs. Ali Mahomed, held similar view that any agreement against public policy is void.

   Example: A entered into an agreement with B to sell the prohibited drugs in the market and agreed to share the profit in equal ratio. Here, the agreement is void because the object is against the Narcotics Laws and, therefore, is unlawful.
3. **The object of an agreement is fraudulent:** If the consideration or object of an agreement is to commit fraud, then the agreement is void. If two parties agree to practise a fraud on the third party, the agreement is unlawful and void. Any agreement to cheat another party or any third party will be an unlawful object, and such an agreement will be void. In the case Manni Ram vs. Purshottam Lal, the court held that the object of the agreement was to commit the fraud upon the Railway Company and, therefore, the agreement is void. The facts of the case were that M knew that Railway would not give tender to him, so he entered into an agreement with P that P should put forward an application for the contract and after the contract was granted to P, M should serve as the real contractor.
4. **Agreement is injuries to any person or property of some person:** An agreement to damage or to cause any damage to the property or cause any harm to any person is

void. The word injury means 'wrong', 'harm' or 'damage'. Person means one's body and property implies both movable and immovable property. So all agreements intending to harm someone or one's property are void.

Example: If an owner of a newspaper enters into an agreement with the printer to indemnify him against any claim arising from the libel printed in the newspaper, such agreement cannot be void.

In the case of Ram Sarup vs. Bansi Mandar (ILR 1915), a person borrowed certain sum and executed a bond promising to work for the plaintiff without pay for two years. In case of default, he was to pay exorbitant interest and the principal sum at once. The court held that the contract contained the terms for the bonded labour, which were indistinguishable from slavery, and thereby, involves injury to the person, and hence against the public policy. Therefore, held void.

5. **If it is an immoral agreement:** If the object of an agreement is regarded by the court to be immoral or opposed to the public policy, then it is unlawful and has been declared void by Section 23 of the Act.

   Example: A agrees to let her daughter to B for prostitution. The agreement is void because it is immoral, though the letting may not be punishable under the IPC.

   In Bai Vijli vs. Nansa Nagar, the plaintiff advanced the loan to the defendant, a married woman, to enable her to obtain divorce and then marry the plaintiff. The plaintiff was not entitled to recover the loan amount as the object of the agreement is immoral and, therefore, the agreement is void.

6. **Opposed to the public policy:** An agreement is said to be opposed to public policy when it is against public interest or harmful to public welfare. The 'public policy' cannot be defined precisely. Public policy means the policy of law at a stated time and place. An act, which is injurious to the interest of society, is regarded as against the public policy. The Supreme Court in the case of Gherulal vs. Mahadeodas explained the present position of the doctrine of public policy in India. However, in the case Ratan Chand vs. Askar, the Andhra High Court even went to the extent of suggesting that even if new head of public policy is to be created, the courts should do that because of the changing social values and concepts in the progressive modern society.

Agreements Opposed to Public Policy

Public policy means a set of rules and regulations, framed to protect the interest of public at large. Any act of person is against the public policy, if it causes any injury to any person or property. Justice Subba Rao, in the case of Gherulal Parakh vs. Mahadeodas, explains public policy that public policy is a vague and unsatisfactory term and leads to uncertainty and error when applied to the decision of the legal right; it is capable of being understood in different senses. However, it is permissible for the courts to expound and apply those principles to different situations as per case-to-case basis. There can be no fixed circumstances; it is the social circumstances, which determine the public policy. The following are the cases in which agreements are against public policy.

1. **Agreement to stifle prosecution:** An agreement to stifle the prosecution is regarded as opposed to public policy. The purpose of criminal law is to punish a guilty person and a compromise with a view to save a guilty person from liability would frustrate this

object. Some minor offences have been recognized as compoundable offences, where compromise is permitted.

Example: If A promises B to drop the prosecution which he has instituted against B for robbery, and B promises to restore the loss suffered by A, then it is held that such an agreement is void as its object is unlawful. Here, one point is noteworthy that compromise in civil suits and minor criminal offences are valid and lawful. However, in the criminal proceedings such compromise is not valid and is held as unlawful.

2. **Agreement of maintenance and champerty:** Maintenance is aiding or encouraging a party in civil proceedings by providing financial or other assistance without lawful justification. Maintenance is considered both crime and tort. Maintenance is strictly prohibited by the common law as being mala fide tendency to oppression, by encouraging and assisting persons to persist in suits, which perhaps, they would not venture to go otherwise. In Ram Sarup vs. Court of Wards, Privy Council held that any agreement to recover the money paid for the expenses of suit, and even though lender has no interest in the suit, will be a valid contract. Agreements made with the bona fide object of assisting a person in the enforcement of his legal rights are valid. However, much depends upon the fact that enforcement of his legal rights are valid. Therefore, if X agrees to supply funds to Y to enable him to file a suit for property and Y promises to give him 3/4th of the recovered property the agreement is champertous.
3. **Trading agreement with an enemy:** The object of war is to capture the territory of the enemy and to cripple the economy of the enemy country. When there is a war between two countries, it is unlawful and against public policy that a person should trade with a subject of the enemy country. In the case of Dailmer Co. Ltd vs. Continental Tyre and Rubber Co., it was held that all contracts entered into before the outbreak of war are either suspended or dissolved according to the intention of the parties. An agreement to promote hostile dealing with a friendly state is also against public policy.
4. **Marriage brokerage agreements:** Marriage brokerage contracts mean such contracts under which one person agrees to procure a marriage between two persons on some consideration. In other words, an agreement to procure the marriage of a person in consideration of a sum of money is marriage brokerage agreement. Thus, if A pays B a certain sum of money to procure a wife for him, he cannot enforce the agreement. According to the English law, such contracts are void. In this regard, the case of Hermann vs. Charlesworth is very important where the court held that advance paid for arranging a marriage can be asked back; however, if the marriage is solemnized, the money already paid cannot be recovered back. In India also, such contracts are void. Similarly, agreement to pay money to the parent of a minor to induce him to give minor in marriage is void. Likewise, an attempt to get dowry is equally void.
5. **Agreement tending to injure the public service:** An agreement to buy, sell or procure a public office or assignment or the salary of an office is unlawful. Such agreements corrupt the public life as they ensure the job for incapable persons. For example, A promises to pay ₹50,000 to B if gets him job in public service commission. The agreement is void as the object is unlawful. In N. V. P. Pandian vs. M. M. Roy, it was held that appellant could not take the money back as agreement is void.
6. **Agreements interfering with parental duties:** It is a general principle that parents cannot by an agreement transfer to another person their rights and duties with respect to their child. Agreements which contemplate an absolute transfer of rights of parents over their children are void as being opposed to public policy. However, this rule does not affect the validity of an adoption duly made under the Hindu Adoption and

Maintenance Act. In Atma Ram vs. Banku Mal, the father of a girl agreed to place his daughter at the disposal of the defendant to be married according to the wishes of the latter. Held, the agreement was void.

7. **An agreement interfering with marital duties:** Agreement interfering with martial duties is unlawful and, therefore, void. Such agreements include promises made by a married person to marry another person or interfere with the performance of marital duties of husband and wife opposed to public policy. The husband and wife owe certain duties towards each other and any agreement which restricts any one in performing their duties towards each other is void.
   Example: An agreement to lend money to a woman in consideration of her getting a divorce and marrying the lender is void, or an agreement that the husband will always stay at the mother-in law's house and that wife would never leave her parental house is void.
8. **Agreement restraining personal liberty:** The Constitution of India has provided everybody to live a free life and for this fundamental rights are provided in the Constitution. Therefore, any agreement by which a person is deprived of his liberty partially or completely is against the spirit of the Constitution of India. Hence, such an agreement is regarded against the public policy and, therefore, void.
   Example: X, a debtor, agrees to serve Y, his creditor, without any salary as long as his debt is not fully settled. This is an agreement that restricts the personal liberty of X and is therefore void.
9. **Agreements tending to create interest opposed to public and official duties:** Doctrine of public policy demands that a person must perform his official duties with honesty and due care. Therefore, any agreement that restricts any public servant to perform his duties with honesty is inconsistent with the duty of public servant and against public policy and, therefore, void.
   Example: X enters into an agreement with Y, a public servant, that he should not visit the forest on a specified date, which will help X to cut the trees without permission. This is an agreement where X stops Y from performing his duties with honesty, which conflicts with his duty, and is, therefore, void.

Unlawful and Illegal Agreements

An unlawful agreement is not enforceable by law and is void, whereas an illegal agreement is not only void but also the collateral transactions to it become infected with illegality. Every illegal agreement is unlawful but every unlawful agreement may not be necessarily illegal. Illegal acts are those acts which involve the commission of some sort of crime or may contain an element of obvious moral turpitude. Unlawful acts are those acts which involve non-criminal breach of law and are disapproved by law on some ground of public policy. Agreements opposed to public policy are unlawful. An unlawful agreement is one which is not enforceable by law. It is void ab initio, that is, from the very beginning. However, it affects only the immediate parties and not the future. On the other hand, an illegal agreement is not only void as between the immediate parties but also affects collateral transactions.

Example: X and Y enter into a partnership agreement for carrying out smuggling business and they borrow money from Z for their business, who was aware about the purpose of the loan. In this case not only the partnership is illegal, even the loan is tainted with illegality.

Effects of Illegal Agreements

An illegal contract is void ab initio and unenforceable in totality. An illegal agreement cannot give rise to any obligation or remedy to another party in spite of the ignorance of the parties about illegality. This general principle is based on public policy, which is expressed in the legal maxim as *ex turpi causa non oritur actio* meaning no action arises from a disgraceful cause. Parties to an illegal contract cannot get any protection from the court of law because no wrong person shall be allowed to touch the pure fountain of justice. The effects of illegal agreement can be studied as follows.

1. **Effects on the original agreement:** An illegal agreement is void ab initio and it does not give rise to any legal obligations between the parties. Therefore, no court can enforce it and no remedy is available to either party. Nothing can be recovered out of an illegal agreement. The courts do not interfere in the case. Due to this neutral role of the courts, the defendant may be at an advantage. The maxim used is *in pari delicto potior est conditio defendentis* which means in cases of equal guilt, more powerful is the condition of the defendant. The defendant can keep what he has received.
   Example: X promised to pay ₹150,000 to Y, if he would kill Z. If Y kills Z, he cannot recover the amount. If X has already paid the amount and Y does not kill Z, then X cannot get the amount back.
2. **Effect on collateral agreements:** Collateral agreements are incidental to the original agreement. Any transaction, which is collateral or secondary to the original agreement, also gets affected with illegality. Therefore, a collateral agreement to an illegal agreement is also void and cannot be enforced in the court of law.
   Example: R, the father of a minor girl, borrowed some money from P for marriage of the girl. P cannot recover the money, as the marriage of minor is illegal, provided that P was aware of the minority of the girl.

Exceptions

There are certain exceptions to this rule, which are given as follows.

1. **Where the contract is yet to be performed:** Where no part of the illegal agreement has been performed, then the money, which has been paid, or the goods delivered, may be recovered. However, once the illegal purpose is performed, party cannot maintain any action.
   Example: If X, a debtor, executed a transfer to deceive his creditor, but before any creditor could be deceived he repented and sought to recover back the property. He was entitled to do so.
2. **Parties not 'in pari delicto':** Where the parties are not equally guilty, the less guilty may be able to recover money paid or property transferred under the contract. This possibility can arise in three situations:
   a. The contract may be of a kind made illegal but in the interest of a particular class of persons of whom the plaintiff is one. Such persons may bring an action.
   b. The plaintiff may have been induced to enter into contract by fraud or undue pressure. In these circumstances, anything paid or delivered by aggrieved party can be recovered back as the consent is not free.
   c. A person who is under a fiduciary duty to the plaintiff will not be allowed to retain property or refuse to account for money received on the grounds of an illegal

transaction. Thus, an agent who receives money from a third party under an illegal agreement is accountable to his principal for the proceeds.

3. **Plaintiff not relying on the illegal agreement:** The plaintiff can claim back the possession or rights of ownership provided he has not relied upon the illegal agreement. So where A has let his house to a prostitute, he cannot recover rent but can sue for eviction and possession of the house. If a plaintiff is parted with possession under an illegal contract, he can recover the property provided he relies on the agreement.

AGREEMENTS PARTLY LEGAL AND PARTLY ILLEGAL

An agreement may consist of many promises, some of which are legal and some illegal or a part is legal and other part is illegal. If the illegal promise or part can be separated from the illegal one, then the legal promise or act can be enforced and the other is rejected. However, where the two parts are inseparable, the whole agreement will be void. Section 24 of the Contract Act provides, 'If any part of a single contract for one or more objects, or any one or any part of any one of several considerations for a single object, is unlawful, the agreement is void.'

Example: X promises to superintend, on behalf of Y, for legal manufacturing of indigo and for illegal trafficking in other articles, at a salary of ₹100,000 a year. The agreement is void. Where there are reciprocal promises to do certain things legal and certain things illegal, the legal part is a contract but illegal part is a void agreement.

Example: X and Y agree that X shall sell a horse to Y for ₹50,000 but if Y uses it as a gambling house, he shall pay X ₹50,000. The first set of reciprocal promises is legal but the second one is illegal. In case of alternatives promises, one branch being legal and the other illegal, the legal branch alone can be enforced.

TEST QUESTIONS

1. Comment on the following statements:
   a. Every agreement the object or consideration of which is unlawful is void.
   b. No action is allowed on an illegal agreement.
   c. The doctrine of public policy is a very unruly horse, and when once you get astride it you never know where it will carry you.
   d. The law relating to public policy cannot remain immutable. It must change with the passage of time. The wind of change blows upon it.
   e. All illegal agreements are unlawful but all unlawful agreements are not illegal.
2. Under what circumstances is the object or consideration of a contract unlawful? Illustrate with examples.
3. Explain the doctrine of public policy. What are the heads of public policy? Do you agree with the view that the heads of public policy are not closed?
4. What do you understand by an illegal agreement? What are the effects of illegal agreement on main transactions and collateral transactions?
5. Under what circumstances the object of an agreement is said to be unlawful? Explain with examples.

6. What are those cases when the object or the consideration of an agreement is deemed unlawful?
7. 'A contract shall not be enforced if the agreement is opposed to public policy.' Explain the statement and illustrate your answer.

PRACTICAL PROBLEMS

1. A borrows ₹500 from B to purchase certain smuggled goods from C. Can B recover the amount from A, if he (a) knows of A's purpose for which he borrowed money and (b) does not know of A's purpose?
Hint. (a) No (b) Yes.
2. A grants lease of certain premises at Calcutta to B for one year at a monthly rental of ₹500. Knowing that the premises will be used for the purpose of (a) prostitution or (b) installing machinery for minting base coins, B does not pay the rent. Can A recover the rent?
Hint. No.
3. X promises to drop prosecution, which he has instituted against R for robbery and R promises to restore the value of things taken. Can X enforce this promise? If so, give reasons.
Hint. No.
4. A, being already married to B, agrees with C, during B's lifetime, that he will marry C in case B dies. Can C ask for performance of the promise in the event of B's death?
Hint. No, C's contract amounts to interference with the marital status of A and B.
5. A promises to pay ₹1,000 to B who is an intended witness in a suit against A in consideration of B's absconding himself at the trial. B absconds but fails to get the money. Can he recover?
Hint. No.
6. A debtor promises his moneylender that he will not, without the consent of lender, leave his job, borrow money, dispose of his property or change his address. Is the agreement valid?
Hint. No. It is against the public policy since it restricts personal freedom.
7. A and B agree that B will murder C for which A will pay ₹50,000 to D telling him about the agreement with B. Can D subsequently recover ₹50,000 from A?
Hint. No. An illegal agreement taints collateral transactions also.
8. A promise to pay a sum of ₹5,000 to Y, who is an intended witness in a suit against X, in consideration of Y's absenting himself from the court on one pretext or the other. Y absents himself and demands payment from X who refuses to pay. Can Y recover ₹5,000 from X?
Hint. No. Since it is against public policy, the agreement is illegal.
9. A advances ₹10,000 to B, a married woman, to enable her to obtain a divorce form her husband. B agrees to marry A as soon as she obtains a divorce. B obtains the divorce but refuses to marry A. Can A recover the amount?
Hint. No.
10. A promised to pay ₹1,000 per month to B, a married woman in consideration of living in adultery with A and acting as his housekeeper. B lived with A as per agreement for three months. On A's refusal to pay any money to her, she filed a suit against him to recover her wages for three months at least for her services as a housekeeper. Would she succeed?
Hint. No.

7

CHAPTER

Performance of Contracts

Learning Objectives

- To understand the performance of contract and its types
- To understand the essentials of valid tender of performance
- To know by whom the contract must be performed
- To know who can demand performance
- To know when time is the essence of contract
- To understand appropriation of payment of debts
- To know assignment of contracts
- To know performance of joint promises
- To understand the contracts which need not to be performed

PERFORMANCE OF CONTRACTS

Every contract creates some legal obligations for the parties to the contract and they continue till the contract is performed or discharged. Performance of the contract is the natural way of extinguishing contractual obligations. Performance of a contract implies fulfilment of the terms, conditions and obligations of the contract by the parties within specified time and in the manner prescribed.

Example: X promises to sell his red car to Y for ₹150,000. Y agrees to it. When X actually gives his red car to Y and Y pay ₹150,000 to X, it will be performance of the contract.

According to Section 37, the parties to a contract must either perform or offer to perform their respective promise, unless such performance is dispensed with or excused under the provisions of this Act or under any other law. Promise binds the representatives of the promisor in case of the death of such promisor before performance, unless a contrary intention appears from the contract. The performance of contract may be of two types which are as follows:

1. **Actual performance:** Actual performance of contract refers to the fulfilment of contractual obligations either by the parties themselves or by their agents or by their legal representatives. When parties to the contract perform their obligations, the contract comes to an end. If the promisor or promisee dies before performing their obligations, it is the duty of their legal representatives to perform their obligations, if personal skills not involved.

Example: Ram and Shyam enter into an agreement that Ram will sell his house to Shyam for ₹10 lakhs. Ram transfers his house and Shyam pays ₹10 lakh to Ram. The contract is discharged by performance.

2. **Attempted performance:** It may happen that the promisor offers performance of his obligation under the contract at proper time and place but the promisee refuses to accept the performance. This is known as attempted or tender of performance. When the promisee does not accept performance, the promisor is not responsible for non-performance. It entitles the promisor to sue the promisee for breach of contract. Section 38 provides that where the promisor has made an offer of performance to the promisee, and the offer has not been accepted, the promisor is not responsible for non-performance, nor does he thereby loses his right under the contract.

   Tender or attempted performance is of two types:

   a. **Tender of goods:** A contract involving the delivery of goods is discharged when goods are tendered for acceptance according to the terms and conditions of the contract. If the promisee refuses to accept the goods, the promisor need not to offer them again and he is discharged. He can file the suit for non-acceptance or he can defend an action for non-delivery of goods, provided he has fulfilled all the requirement of a valid delivery.

      Example: X enters into a contract with Y to sell 100 bikes on 24 October. On due date, X sends a truck to Y's residence but his servant has not taken the delivery. This will be treated as tender of goods and Y cannot sue for the non-delivery of bikes.

   b. **Tender of money:** Tender of money is another way to discharge a contract, but where some money is due, tender by the debtor, if refused by the creditor, does not operate as a discharge. However, interest on debt immediately ceases to accrue from the date of the rejection of a valid tender of money. Here, it is to be noted that mere attempted performance is not enough for the debtor to discharge him from the liability but it is he who has to find out the creditor and pay the money to him. If the creditor refuses to accept the money, then he must be ready to pay the debt to the creditor whenever the creditor demands it.

Essentials of a Valid Tender of Performance

According to Section 38 of the Act, following conditions are necessary to make a valid tender of performance.

1. **The tender must be unconditional:** Section 38(1) provides that tender or offer to perform the contract must be unconditional. No person while tendering the performance for his part of promise can put forward any condition for that performance. If he does so, then it will not be valid tender of performance.

   Example: R, the debtor, offers to pay S, his creditor, the amount due to him, if M permits. This is a conditional offer and cannot be a valid tender.

2. **Tender must be an offer to perform in full:** It is not a valid tender if an offer to perform in part is made since it will be a conditional tender and is against the provisions of Section 38(1).

   Example: If X agrees to supply 100 kg of sugar to Y but on due date, he supplies only 60 kg. This is a part performance and Y can refuse to take the delivery.

3. **Tender must be made at proper time and place:** According to Section 38(2), the tender of performance must be made at the time and place fixed by the parties, with an opportunity to the promisee to ascertain that the promisor will make proper performance. If parties to the contract have not agreed regarding the place of performance, then the promisee shall be under an obligation to make tender of performance at an appropriate place and time as per the custom or practice in such business.
4. **The promisee must give a reasonable opportunity of inspecting goods:** According to Section 38(3), the promisee must have a reasonable opportunity of inspecting the goods so as to ascertain that the quality, quantity and the goods are the same, which the promisor was bound to deliver. Further, according to Section 41(2) of the Sale of Goods Act, unless otherwise agreed, when the seller tenders delivery of goods to the buyer, he is bound on request to afford the buyer a reasonable opportunity of examining the goods for ascertaining whether they are in conformity with the contract. **Example:** X contracts to deliver 250 kg sugar to Y at his shop on 31 March 2015. X must bring the sugar to Y's shop on the fixed day so that Y has a reasonable opportunity of satisfying himself that sugar is the same as contracted for and is of proper quantity as ordered.
5. **Tender of performance must be made to the proper person:** Any person or promisor, who is tendering the performance, must make it to the promisee as per the agreement between them. Any tender of performance to a stranger or to an unauthorized person is not a valid tender of performance. Any tender made to an authorized agent is a valid tender.
6. **The tender must be made in the proper form:** The tender of performance must be made in the proper form according to the terms of agreement. It means that tendered performance must fulfil all the conditions given in the agreement.
7. **An offer of performance to one of the joint promisee is a valid tender:** According to last para of Section 38, when there are several joint promisee, an offer of performance to any one of them will be as good as an offer to all of them.

Effect of Refusal of a Party to Perform the Promise Fully

According to Section 39, 'When a party to the contract has refused to perform or disabled himself from performing his promise in its entirety, the promisee may put an end to the contract unless he had signified by words or conduct, his acquiescence in its continuance.'

Example: X, a dancer, enters into a contract with Y, the manager of the hotel, to dance at his hotel for three weekends and Y promises to pay her ₹50,000 per show. On the second weekend, X absents herself wilfully. Y is at liberty to put an end to the contract.

By Whom the Contract Must Be Performed

As per Section 40 of the Act, unless it is the intention of the parties to the contract that the promisor himself should perform any promises contained therein, the promisor or his representatives may employ a competent person to perform it. The provisions of the Act provide that any of the following person may perform the contract:

1. **Promisor:** If a particular contract requires personal skill, taste or art or if it appears from the nature of the contract, then the promisor himself must perform the promise. Such contracts are usually those where the personality of promisor is a vital element such as contract to sing and paint. Such contracts end if the promisor dies.
   Example: X is a dancer who enters into an agreement with Y, manager of a hotel, that he will dance for two nights in his hotel. After performing for one night, X dies. Now contract ends as here personal skill is involved and anyone else cannot perform on behalf of X.
2. **Agent:** Contracts, which are not of a personal nature, may be performed through an agent or representative of the promisor, that is, if for the performance of a contract personal skill is not required, an agent appointed by the promisor can perform such contract. Section 40 provides that in such cases the promisor or his representative may employ a person to perform it.
   Example: X agrees to supply 100 kg of sugar to Y. In this case, X may perform this promise either himself or by causing it to be supplied by his agent.
3. **Legal representative:** In the event of the death of the promisor, the promisee can compel the legal representative or representatives, as the case may be, to perform the promise unless it involves personal skill, taste and so on of the promisor. Section 37 of the Act provides that a promise binds the representatives of the promisor in case of death of the promisor before performance, unless a contrary intention appears from the contract. However, the liability of the legal representatives is limited to the estate of the deceased, which has come in their hands.
   Example: X enters into an agreement with Y to paint a picture for him but before he could do so, he dies. In this case, Y cannot compel the legal representatives of X as this agreement involves the personal skill of X.
4. **The third person:** As per Section 41, when a promisee accepts performance of the promise from a third person, it is a valid performance and the promisee cannot afterwards enforce it against the promisor. In the case of Lala Kapurchand vs. Mir Nawab, a promisee accepted a lesser amount from the third party in the full settlement of debt. It was held that the promisee could not enforce the promise against the promisor.
5. **Joint promisors:** Sections 42 to 45 deal with rules regarding the joint promises. Section 42 deals with the voluntary discharge of liabilities of the deceased by the joint promisors but if they do not discharge their obligations on their own, Section 43 will be applied. It states three rules regarding the performance of joint promises. These provisions are explained later in this chapter.

Who Can Demand the Performance?

It is normally the promisee who is entitled to demand the performance of the promise. It is immaterial whether the promise is for the benefit of the promisee or for any other person. Even if the promise is made for the benefit of a third party, it cannot demand performance of the contract. The performance can be demanded either by the promisee or his legal representative.

Example: X promises Y to pay a sum of ₹50,000 to Z but does not pay. It is only Y who can enforce the promise against X.

However, in certain cases, a third party can enforce contract. This has already been discussed in the chapter titled 'Consideration' under the heading 'Stranger to the Contract'.

Example: X agrees to sell his laptop to Y for ₹10,000. Before the delivery of laptop, Y dies. Now, legal representative can claim the delivery of laptop.

TIME AND PLACE OF PERFORMANCE

The parties are free to decide as to when and where the performance of the contract is to be made. Sections 46 to 50 lay down the principles for the performance of the contracts containing different stipulation as to time and place. These provisions are explained as follows.

1. **Time for performance of promise, where no application is to be made and no time is specified:** Section 46 provides that where, by the contract, a promisor is to perform his promise without application by the promisee, and no time for performance is specified, then obligations must be performed within a reasonable time. The section further explains that reasonable time will depend on the terms and facts of the case.
   Example: X agrees to supply the goods to Y but they fixed no time. X has not supplied the goods for two months. Now, the circumstances will decide the time for the performance of agreement.
2. **Time and place for performance of promise, where time is specified and no application to be made:** Section 47 of the Act provides that when a promise is to be performed on a certain day, it is the promisor's duty in such a case to perform the contract during usual business hours on such day. If the goods to be delivered are supplied after usual closing time, the buyer may reject them.
   Example: A promises to deliver goods at B's warehouse on 1 January. On that day, A brings the goods to B's warehouse but after the usual hours of its closing and they are not received. A has not performed his promise.
3. **Application of performance at proper place and time:** Section 48 explains that when a promise is to be performed on a certain day and the promisor has not undertaken to perform it without application by the promisee, it is the duty of the promisee to apply for performance at a proper place and within the usual hours of business. In such cases, it is the duty of the promisee to apply for performance. What is proper time and place is a question of fact in each case and will be decided on the facts of the case.
   Example: X promises to deliver 200 kg of sugar to Y on 21 March 2016. The terms of contract required Y to specify the place later on where delivery was to be made. In this case, it is the duty of Y to apply for performance and inform X about the place of performance. Ignorance of place cannot be an excuse for non-performance of contract.
4. **Place for performance where no application is made, no place fixed:** According to Section 49, when a promise is to be performed without application by the promisee and no place is fixed for its performance, it is the duty of the promisor to apply to the promisee to appoint a reasonable place for the performance of the promise, and to perform it at such a place.
   Example: X promises to deliver 2,500 tons of sugar to Y on a particular day. X must apply to Y to fix a reasonable place for the performance of the promise and must deliver it to him at such place as specified by the Y.
5. **Manner or time by promisee to perform a promise:** Section 50 states that the performance of any promise may be made in any manner or at any time, which the promisee prescribes.

Example: B owes A ₹2,000. A desires B to pay the amount to A's account with his banker C. B also has account in the same bank. B orders C to transfer the amount from his account to A's credit and this is done by C. Afterwards, and before A knows of the transfer, the bank fails. There has been a good payment by B.

When Time Is the Essence of the Contract

The promise must be performed within the specified period as per the agreement between the parties. A breach of condition as to the time for performance entitles the innocent party to consider the breach as a repudiation of the contract. Generally, it is expected that both parties will perform their obligation at the stipulated time but if any of them fails to do so, then it will be the breach of contract. Section 55 deals with the time as the essence of the contract. It provides the rules regarding the effects of failure to perform a contract within the specified time.

In a contract, where time is the essence of the contract and if there is failure to perform the same within the fixed time, the contract becomes voidable at the option of promisee. He can rescind the contract and sue for the same. If the promisee accepts the performance after due date, he cannot claim for the compensation after such acceptance for any loss suffered by him. However, at the time of accepting delayed performance, the promisee can give the notice for the compensation or intimation to that effect. Time is generally considered to be of the essence of the contract in the following three cases:

1. Where the parties have expressly agreed to treat it as of the essence of the contract,
2. Where delay operates as an injury and
3. Where the nature of contract requires it to be so construed, for example, where a party asks for extension of time for performance.

When Time Is Not the Essence of the Contract

According to Section 55, Para 2 of the Act, where time is not the essence of the contract, failure to perform it within the fixed time does not make the contract voidable, but the promisee is entitled to get the compensation for any loss incurred by such failure.

From the above discussion, it can be said that the matter depends upon the intention of the parties. Even where a specific date is mentioned for the completion of the contract, promisor has to look at the substance of the agreement in order to know the real intention of the parties. In the contracts of sale of goods, the courts will see the facts of each case whether time was essence of contract or not. In case of contract for sale of immovable property, the Supreme Court held that the time is not the essence of the contract.

Appropriation of Payments of Debts

When the debtor owes several distinct debts to a creditor, and he makes some payment, which is not enough to cover the payment of all the debts, the question, which arises, is as to which particular debt the payment is to be appropriated. There was a very famous case in England,

Clayton's Case, which explains the rules on the above issue. As per Sections 59 to 61 of the Indian Contract Act, following are the rules, for the payment of debt and its apportionment:

1. **Appropriation of debt as desired by the debtor:** Where a debtor owes several debts to a person and makes a payment to him with express intimation or under circumstances, implying that the payment is to be applied to the discharge of some particular debt, the payment to be appropriated, if accepted, must be applied according to the instruction of the debtor. The debtor has the right to request to the creditor to apply the payment for the discharge of some particular debt. If there is no express instruction as to appropriation there may be circumstances, which imply that the debtor intended appropriation to particular debt. It is the duty of the creditor to accept the payment of debt and apply it according to the instructions of debtor as held in State of Gujarat vs. Bank of Baroda. The above rule is also as per the spirit of the Clayton's Case given under the English law. This rule was again upheld by the court in the case of Smithaben vs. ICDS (Industrial Credit and Development Syndicate).
2. **Appropriation by the creditor where indication is not made by the debtor:** Section 60 provides that where the debtor has omitted to intimate, and there are no other circumstances indicating to which debt the payment is to be applied, then creditor is free to adjust against any debt, even he may apply it to liquidate a time barred debt. The creditor may also adjust the payment against the debt, which carries simple or less interest. **Example:** X owed several debts to Y, including one debt of ₹6,000 which is time barred. X paid ₹10,000 to Y without indicating against the time barred debt and balance against any other debt, which he likes. Here, Y is free to adjust to the amount against any debt.
3. **Appropriation in order of the debts due:** According to Section 61, where neither party indicates appropriation, law provides that the debts be satisfied in order of their due dates. Even debts, which are time barred, can be adjusted against the payment. If the debts are of equal standing, the payment shall be applied in discharge of each of them proportionately. In case of current account, the first item on the credit side discharges the first item on the debit side. It is the sum first paid out.
4. **Rules regarding the payment of interest and principal when both are due:** When the principal amount and interest, both are due, the debtor can stipulate that a particular payment made by him to be considered as the repayment of the principal amount or the interest remaining due. If the creditor accepts the payment, he has to accept the debtor's appropriation. However, if a payment is made without expressly stating its appropriation, it can be applied towards interest first and then the balance to the principal. In the case of Meghraj vs. Bayabai, AIR 1970, the Supreme Court held that where debtor has not indicated anything regarding the adjustment of debt, creditor is free to adjust it against the interest and then for the principal.

Performance of Reciprocal Promises

The rules regarding the performance of reciprocal promises are provided in Sections 51 to 54 of the Contract Act. These provisions are explained as follows:

1. **Contracts requiring simultaneous performance:** According to Section 51 of the Act, when a contract consists of reciprocal promises to be simultaneously performed, no promisor needs to perform his promise unless the promisee is ready and willing to perform his reciprocal promise. When the parties agree that the performance of the

contract by each party is to be simultaneous, it is necessary that in exchange for the performance of the contract by one party, the other party should also be in a position to give simultaneous performance. In the case of Nathulal vs. Phool Chand, the Supreme Court held that it is enough that the buyer has made arrangement to make the payment of the delivery of the goods and he can do so without undue delay, whereas seller has to arrange for the goods, which he can deliver as and when money is received by him.

2. **When the order of performance is expressly fixed by the contract:** According to Section 52 of the Act, when the order in which reciprocal promises are to be performed is expressly fixed by the contract, they shall be performed in that order and where the order is not expressly fixed by the contract, they shall be performed in that order which the nature of transaction/agreement requires.
3. **One party preventing the other from performing his reciprocal promise:** According to Section 53, when a contract contains reciprocal promises, and one party to the contract prevents the other from performing his promise, the contract becomes voidable at the option of the party so prevented, and he is entitled to compensation from the other party for any loss which he may sustain in consequence of the non-performance of the contract. The above provision provides that where one party is ready to perform but prevented from doing so, in case, such party will have two remedies:
   a. He may avoid the contract.
   b. He may claim compensation for the loss suffered by him due to the non-performance of the contract.
4. **Non-performance of a reciprocal promise by the party who is to perform first:** According to Section 54, when a contract consists of reciprocal promise, such that one of them cannot be performed or that its performance cannot be claimed till the other has been performed and the promisor of the promise last mentioned fails to perform it, such promisor cannot claim the performance of the reciprocal promise and must make compensation to the party to the contract for any loss which such other party may sustain by non-performance of the contract.

Legal and Illegal Promises (Section 57)

According to Section 57 of the Act, where persons reciprocally promise to do certain things, which are legal and under specified circumstances to do certain other things, which are illegal, the first set of promise is a contract but the second part is a void agreement. It means, if there are two sets of agreements between the parties where one is legal and the other is illegal, then legal one will be enforceable but illegal part will be void and non-enforceable.

Example: X and Y agree that X shall sell to Y a house for ₹50,000, but if Y uses it for gambling purpose, he shall pay X ₹75,000 for it. The first set of reciprocal promises is a contract. The second set is a void agreement for an unlawful object (gambling).

Alternative Promises of Which One Branch Is Legal and the Other Is Illegal (Section 58)

In the case of an alternate promise, one branch of which is legal and the other is illegal, the legal branch alone can be enforced. Further, it can be said that in some cases parties may enter into promise to do certain legal things and to do certain illegal things. In such cases, only the legal part of contract is enforceable in the court of law.

Example: X and Y agree that X shall pay Y ₹50,000, for which Y shall afterwards deliver to X either rice or smuggled opium. It is a valid contract to deliver rice and it is a void agreement to deliver opium.

Performance of Joint Promises

According to Section 42, when two or more persons have made a joint promise, unless a contrary intention appears by the contract, all such persons must jointly fulfil the promise. In short, when two or more persons jointly promise to another to do or not do something, it is known as joint promise. Following rules govern the performance of joint promises.

1. **The joint promise must be fulfilled jointly:** Section 42 provides that when two or more persons have made a joint promise, unless a contrary intention appears by the contract, then all such persons must jointly fulfil the promise. In case of the death of any one of them, his legal representative jointly with survivors must fulfil the promise. On the death of all the promisors, the representatives of all of them must jointly fulfil the promise but this is subject to any private agreement between the parties.
2. **Any one of the joint promisors may be compelled to perform:** According to Section 43, when a joint promise is made, the promisee may, in the absence of any express agreement to the contrary, compel any one or more of the joint promisors to perform the whole of the promise.
3. **Each promisor may compel contribution:** According to Section 43 of the Act, each of the joint promisors may compel other joint promisors to contribute equally with him to the performance of the promise. This means that if a joint promisor has been compelled to perform the whole of the promise, he can require other joint promisors to make equal contribution to the performance of the promise.
4. **Sharing of loss by default in contribution:** Section 43 further provides that if any one of the two or more promisors makes default in contribution to the joint promise, the remaining joint promisors should bear the loss arising from such default in equal shares.
   Example: X, Y and Z are under a joint promise to pay P ₹8,000. Z is unable to pay anything and X and Y are compelled to pay the whole. However, either of them can also pay the amount and later he can recover from other person up to the amount which is due on his part. If X pays full, then he is entitled to receive ₹4,000 from Y.
5. **The contribution rule does not apply to principal debtor and surety:** Sometimes, a person gives guarantee for repayment of loan by the debtor to creditor who is called a surety. The creditor can recover the entire amount of loan from debtor or surety. If surety repays it, he can recover the whole amount from debtor. However, debtor cannot get contribution from surety in case he pays the whole sum because it is the liability of debtor to repay the loan.
   Example: X, Y and Z are under a joint promise to pay P ₹9,000. X and Y are only sureties for Z. Now, if Z fails to pay P, then X and Y are compelled to pay the whole sum and later they are entitled to recover the same from Z. However, if Z repays the loan, then he cannot recover from X and Y.
6. **The promisee may release any one joint promisor:** Section 44 of the Act provides that sometimes the promisee may release one of the joint promisors. However, this does

not discharge other joint promisors. This release does not free the joint promisor so released from responsibility to contribute to the other promisors.

Example: X, Y and Z jointly owe ₹9,000 to P. P releases X from payment, files a suit against Y and Z for the payment of ₹9,000. P releasing X does not release Y and Z, and X is not discharged from his liability to Y and Z for contribution.

DEVOLUTION OF JOINT RIGHTS

Section 44 of the Act provides that when a person makes a promise to two or more persons jointly, the persons can be called joint promisees. In such cases, unless a contrary intention appears from the contract, the right to claim rests with all of them during their lives. If one of them dies, his legal representatives must claim performance jointly with the surviving promisees. On the death of all of them, the legal representatives of all of them can jointly claim performance. But this rule will not apply if any contrary intention is clear from the contract.

CONTRACTS WHICH NEED NOT BE PERFORMED

Normally, the contracts are to be performed by the parties to the contract but in certain situations, the contract may not be performed without incurring any liability. Such cases are as follows:

1. When performance of a contract becomes impossible. (Section 56)
2. When there is an agreement between the parties to substitute or rescind or alter the original contract, then there is no need to perform the original contract. (Section 62)
3. When the promisee may dispense with or remit, wholly or in part, the performance of the promise made to him, or may extend the time for such performance, or may accept instead of it any satisfaction, which he thinks fit, such contract need not be performed. (Section 63)
4. When a person at whose option a contract is voidable rescinds the contract, the other party need not to perform his part in the contract. (Section 64)
5. If any promisee neglects or refuses to afford the promisor reasonable facilities for performance of his promise, the promisor is excused by such promisee's refusal for non-performance. (Section 67)
6. If it is an illegal agreement.
7. In case of reciprocal promises, which are to be performed simultaneously, there is no need for promisor to perform his promise unless the promisee is ready and willing to perform his reciprocal promise. (Section 54)

TEST QUESTIONS

1. When is a contract said to be discharged by performance? Discuss the rules relating to performance.
2. What do you mean by performance of a contract? State the persons by whom the contract should be performed.

3. 'Tender is attempted performance.' Comment.
4. What do you mean by time and place of performance of a contract? 'Time as the essence of the contract.' Explain.
5. What are the essentials of a valid tender of performance? What is the effect of refusal by promisee to accept correct tender of goods and money?
6. Discuss the law relating to the rights and duties of joint promisors in a contract. Also, explain the devolution of joint liabilities.
7. Explain the rules regarding performance of reciprocal promises.
8. When does the problem about appropriation of payment arise? What are the rules regarding appropriation?
9. What are the rules of law relating to time and place of performance of a contract?
10. State the rules regarding devolution of joint rights and liabilities.

PRACTICAL PROBLEMS

1. A, B and C jointly borrow ₹3,000 from D. D proceeds to recover the entire amount form C only. Will he succeed?
   Hint. Yes, (Section 43) permits.
2. A, B and C jointly promise to pay D ₹1,500. A and B are untraceable. Can D compel C to pay him in full?
   Hint. Yes (Section 43).
3. A, B and C jointly lent ₹3,000 to D. A dies. B and C file a suit against D for recovery of the money lent. Will they succeed?
   Hint. No. The suit should be filed along with the legal representative of A.
4. X lent to Y three sums of ₹100, ₹200 and ₹500. Y sent a sum of ₹100 asking X to appropriate this money towards the third debt of ₹500. X wants to appropriate this money to the first loan. Can he do so?
   Hint. No.
5. A and B enter into contract that A shall do some work for B for ₹500. A is ready and willing to do the work, but B prevents him from doing so. Advise A.
   Hint. The contract is voidable at the option of A.

8

CHAPTER

Discharge of Contract

Learning Objectives

- To understand the discharge of contract
- To know different modes for discharge of contract
- To understand discharge by impossibility of performance
- To understand cases not covered by supervening impossibility

DISCHARGE OF CONTRACT

A contract is said to be discharged when the rights and obligations created by a contract come to an end. In other words, a contract is discharged when the contractual relationship between the parties comes to an end or when the rights and obligations arising out of such a relationship are extinguished. A contract may be discharged in any of the following ways:

1. By performance
2. By agreement
3. By lapse of time
4. By operation of law
5. By impossibility of performance
6. By breach of contract
7. By assignment

DISCHARGE BY PERFORMANCE

According to the provisions of Section 37, when the parties to a contract fulfill their obligations and promises arising out of any contract within the specified time and in the manner prescribed, the contract is discharged. The performance of a contract is most usual mode of its discharge. Every person bound by an obligation must be ready to perform it at the time when he had promised to perform it. In case of death of the promisor, his legal representatives are bound to perform it, except in a few cases. Performance may be:

1. Actual performance
2. Attempted performance

A party is said to have actually performed his promise when he has fulfilled all his obligations under the contract. However, when the parties offer to perform their respective promises, it is called tender or attempted performance. (The provisions related to performance of contract are discussed in Chapter 7.)

Discharge by Agreement

An agreement is the basis for any contract and it can be discharged by an agreement between the parties or mutual consent. Such agreement can be express or implied. The rights and obligations created by an agreement can be discharged without performance by means of another agreement between the parties that provides for the extinguishment or change in earlier rights and obligations. A contract may also be rescinded by mutual agreement between the parties. In such cases, the original contract need not be performed. Again, by agreement some important changes may be made in terms of the contract. In this regard, the legal maxim used is *Eodem modo quo quid constituitur, eodem modo destruitur*, which means that a thing may be destroyed in the same manner in which it is created or constituted. There may also be cases where the parties may be changed, the contract remaining the same. In all these cases, the original contract is discharged. Section 62 of the Act provide, when the parties to a contract agree to substitute a new contract for the existing contract or to rescind or alter it, the original contract need not be performed. Further, according to Section 63, when every person who accepts a proposal may dispense with or remit, wholly or in part, the performance of the proposal made to him which he has accepted, or may extend the time for such performance or may accept instead of it any satisfaction which he thinks fit. An agreement can discharge a contract in any one of the following ways.

1. **Novation:** Novation means when an existing contract is being replaced by a new contract and whereby the obligations of the old contract between the parties end. The new contract can be entered into between the same parties or different parties. In the case of Scarf vs. Jardine, the court explained that novation might involve either change of parties, the contract remaining the same, or change of contract between the same parties. Section 62 of the Act, if the parties to a contract agree to substitute a new contract for it or to rescind or alter it, the original contract need not be performed. One of the essential requirements of novation is that there should be complete substitution of a new contract in place of old one. A substituted contract should rescind, alter or extinguish the previous contract. If the terms of two contracts are inconsistent and they cannot stand together, the subsequent contract cannot be said to be in substitution of the earlier contract (Lata Construction vs. Rameshchandra Ramniklal Shah, AIR 2000 SC 380).

   Novation can be of the following two kinds.

   a. **Change in the parties of contract:** In case there is a change in the parties of the contract or in contract, parties to the contract will be governed by the terms and conditions of the new contract. There may be a case where another person may substitute one party to the contract. The original contract remains the same. In such cases, the concurrence of all the parties is necessary. The novation of this kind takes place when a new partner is admitted into an existing firm or firm is reconstituted after retirement of a partner. The court held the similar view in the case of Citibank vs. Standard Charted Bank (2004).

   b. **Substitution by new agreement:** The parties may enter into a new contract and old contract is substituted by a new contract between the same parties. The original contract is therefore discharged and need not be performed. However, it is necessary that the original contract must be subsist. If there is a breach of original contract, then substitution is not possible. Moreover, the new agreement should be valid.

Example: A owes B certain sum of money. It is agreed between A, B and C that B shall, henceforth, accept C as his debtor, instead of A. The old debt of A to B is discharged and a new debt from C to B is contracted.

2. **Alteration:** The term alteration means change in one or more terms and conditions of the contract by the mutual consent of the parties to the contract. Alteration and novation are not one and the same thing. In alteration, there may be change in one or more condition of the contract, whereas in novation there may be change in parties also. In, alteration, original contract is not wholly rescinded, and only some terms of the original contract are varied and made inoperative. The alteration is valid when it is made with the consent of all the parties. A valid alteration discharges the original contract and parties become bound by new contract.
3. **Rescission:** Rescission means the cancellation of the contract. It takes place when all or some of the terms and conditions of the contract are cancelled. The contract may be rescinded by an agreement between the parties any time before it is discharged by performance or in some other way. If the parties agree to rescind a contract, the contract ends. Rescission of a contract may take place by parties, aggrieved party or by mutual consent of the parties to the contract.

   Example: X promises to purchase chairs from Y who agrees to supply the same on 15 November 2005. But Y does not supply the chairs as agreed upon, X may rescind the contract.
4. **Remission:** Remission refers to the acceptance of a lesser performance or the fulfilment of the promise made than what was actually agreed by the parties to the contract. Section 63 provides that every promisee may dispense with or remit, wholly or in part, the performance of promise made to him or may extend the time for such performance or may accept instead of it any satisfaction as he may think fit. According to this section any part to the contract has power to get the contract performed.

   Example: X owes Y ₹8,000. X pays to Y ₹5,000 and Y accepts it as the repayment of the whole debt. The whole debt is discharged.

   According to Section 63, a party to the contract may extend the time for performance. The Supreme Court held, in the case of Keshav Lal Lallubhai Patel vs. Lalbhai Trikumlal Mills (1959 SC R213), that the promisee cannot by a unilateral act extend the time of performance of his own accord and for his own benefit. Consent of the other party is necessary.
5. **Waiver:** Waiver means the abandonment of a right. A party to a contract may waive his rights under the contract. Thereupon, the other party is released from his obligations. Neither an agreement nor a consideration is required to constitute a waiver. A waiver is nothing unless it amounts to release. It signifies nothing more than an intention not to insist upon the right. Section 63 provides that neither consideration nor an agreement be required to constitute waiver.

   Example: X promises to paint a picture for Y. Later on, Y forbids X to paint a picture. X is no longer bound to perform the promise.
6. **Merger:** In merger, an inferior right accruing to one of the parties to a contract merges into a superior right accruing to the same party under the same or other contract.

   Example: X holds a house under a lease. Subsequently, if he buys the same, he becomes the owner of the house. His rights as a lessee merge into his rights as an owner. This is a case of merger.

Discharge by Lapse of Time

Every contract must be performed within a specified period or within a reasonable time, if no time is specified in the contract. If the contract is not performed within the time, contract ends due to lapse of time. This means that a contract cannot be enforced by the law if it is discharged due to lapse of time, since the Limitation Act provides a time to sue for the non-performance and once this period is over no suit can be filed. In case of contracts, the period of limitation is three years. If a party does not file a suit to enforce his rights within the prescribed period, the remedy becomes time-barred. The contract will be discharged due to lapse of time and aggrieved party cannot sue for such non-performance.

Example: X agrees to supply certain goods to Y for ₹8,000. If there is no agreement regarding payment, payment should be made or suit should be filed to recover it within three years from the date of delivery. If creditor does not file a suit against the buyer within this period, the debt becomes time barred and irrecoverable.

Discharge by Operation of Law

A contract is discharged by the operation of law under the following cases.

1. **Death:** In the contracts where personal skill or taste or ability is required, the death of promisor results in the discharge of contracts. However, where the personal skill or ability is not involved, the rights and liabilities of the deceased person pass to his legal representative.
2. **Insolvency:** When the court declares a person insolvent, he is released from all his liabilities to which he was liable under the provisions of any contract. After getting a certificate of discharge, all his liabilities end. Thus, an insolvent is discharged from all the liabilities incurred prior to adjudication as insolvent, and his all assets and rights will transfer to the official receiver appointed by the court.
3. **Unauthorized material alteration:** According to the provisions of this section, a contract can be discharged if there is any material alteration without the knowledge of other party. Material alteration means any alteration which changes the basic nature of the agreement and the legal position of the parties. Any material alteration in the deed without the consent of other party will make the agreement void. In cases where the alteration is made with the consent of other party, this will not result in the discharge of a contract.
4. **Complete loss of evidence:** If the evidence, which provide the existence to contract, is lost, then contract will stand as terminated. The destruction of the subject matter or the evidence related to the contract will be treated as loss of evidence and contract will be void.

Discharge by Impossibility of Performance

Section 10 provides that an agreement must be capable of being performed to make a valid contract. Section 56 provides that an agreement to do an act impossible in itself is void. Impossibility is one of the valid grounds under which a contract would be discharged. Impossibility may appear on the face of the contract, may exist unknown to the parties at the time of making the contract or may arise subsequently after the contract is made. A contract which, at the time when it is entered into, is impossible to perform is void ab initio and creates no rights and obligations. A contract which at the time it was entered into was capable of being performed may subsequently become impossible to perform or unlawful. Such impossibility is known as 'subsequent impossibility' or 'post-contractual' or 'supervening impossibility'. Therefore, impossibility may be categorized as follows.

1. **Initial impossibility:** An agreement to do an act impossible in itself is void. The object of making any contract is that parties to it must perform their part of promise. If a contract is impossible of being performed, the parties to it will never be able to fulfill their object, and hence such an agreement is void. This initial impossibility may be either known or unknown to the parties at the time of entering into the agreement. In such cases, the contract becomes void when such impossibility is discovered because parties are under mutual mistake of fact. Impossibility means not only physical impossibility but legal impossibility also.
   Example: If a person promises to find the hidden wealth by magic or does a work against law, then the contract is initially impossible.
   Example: X agreed to sell his horse to Y. But unknown to both the parties, the horse had already died. In this case, the contract is void on the ground of impossibility.
2. **Subsequent impossibility:** Subsequent impossibility is that impossibility which comes after the creation of contract where parties have no interference in it and circumstances change in such a way that the object of contract is vanished and it strikes the roots of the contract. In such cases, the parties are discharged from further performance. Section 56 provides, 'A contract to do an act which after the contract is made, becomes impossible, or, by reason of some event which the promisor could not prevent, unlawful, becomes void when the act becomes impossible or unlawful.'
   Example: X and Y entered into a contract of marriage. Before the date of marriage, B becomes mad, the contract will be discharged due to subsequent impossibility. The contract becomes void on the ground of subsequent impossibility only if the following conditions are satisfied:
   a. The act should have become impossible.
   b. The impossibility should have been caused by circumstances beyond the control of the parties.
   c. The impossibility should not be the result of the act of the parties.

Some Examples of Subsequent Impossibility

There are certain cases and situations where the principle of impossibility of performance is applicable. An exhaustive list of situations in which the doctrine is going to be applied is not possible. However, the following grounds of impossibility have become well established.

1. **If the foundation of contract is destroyed:** There are certain facts on which a contract is based and contract exists only if those facts exist, if that fact ceases to exist, the performance of the contract becomes impossible and the parties are excused from performing the contract. This point was explained in the case of 'Taylor vs. Caldwell'. In this case, defendant had given his music hall for a music concert to plaintiff for four nights at the rate of £100 per night. Before the commencement of the concert, the fire

destroyed the music hall. The court held that the foundation of the contract was dependent on the continued existence of the hall, and since the hall was no more in existence, the parties are discharged from their liabilities.

2. **Frustration due to change of object:** The doctrine of frustration has been extended to those cases where there was no physical impossibility of performance of the contract, but because of change in circumstances the purpose was frustrated, or by the literal performance of the contract the main object of the contract could not be fulfilled. This was explained in the case of 'Krell vs. Henry', the defendant hired a room in England for viewing the coronation procession of Edward VII, but due to sickness of the king, the procession was postponed. The plaintiff filed a suit to recover entire rent but the court held that the main object of contract was viewing the coronation procession march and when that object was frustrated, the parties could not be held liable. However, the contract is discharged only when the happening of the event was the basis of the contract.
3. **Frustration due to death or incapacity of a party which has to render personal service:** When the nature of contract requires the personal performance by any party to the contract, it will be subject to the health and life of that party. Thus, in case of contract based on personal skill or confidence of the parties, the death of party in such a case puts an end to the contract.
4. **Change in the law:** Sometimes, the change in law also creates the impossibility of performance and the contract is discharged by such change in the law. The change in law should be such that it fully makes impossible to perform the obligation. Merely a suspension for a particular period will not discharge the contract. It should be specific and affecting the performance of duties under the contract.

   Example: X contracts to sell trees of a forest to Y. State government by an order prohibits cutting of trees in the area.

   In the case of Noorbux vs. Kalyan, X had agreed to transport goods belonging to Y from one point to another. Subsequent to the contract, X's trucks were requisitioned by the government under a statutory power. Held, the contract discharged. However, where the change of law makes the performance unlawful, the courts would have no choice but to put an end to the contract.
5. **Outbreak of war:** A contract entered into with an alien enemy during war is unlawful, and therefore, impossible of performance. However, contracts entered into before the outbreak of the war are suspended during the war and may be revived after the war is over. A contract entered into during war with an alien enemy is void ab initio. If the intervention of the war is due to delay caused by the negligence of a party, contract is not discharged on the ground of subsequent impossibility.

   Example: X contracts to take cargo for Y at a foreign port. X's government afterwards declares war against the country in which the port is situated. The contract becomes void when war is declared.

Cases Not Covered by Supervening Impossibility (Exceptions of Supervening Impossibility)

The question arises, does the contract will discharge in every changed circumstance. The answer to this question is, no, it is not so. Apart from the cases mentioned above, impossibility does not discharge contracts. Therefore, impossibility of performance is a rule not an excuse from performance. In the following cases, the contract is not discharged on the ground of supervening impossibility.

1. **No frustration by mere likely delay in performance:** In order to establish that the doctrine of frustration is applicable, it is necessary that the performance should become unlawful or impossible. The event should be such that the object of the parties is, thereby, totally upset. Merely likely delay in performance does not amount to impossibility. This has been explained in the case of Satyabrata Ghose vs. Mugneeram. In this case, the defendant company made an offer to construct building complexes as colony in a vast land. It was stated that interested person may deposit advance money for the construction of road and drainage and soon as the road and drainage will be completed the parties will have to pay the remaining amount after which they can build their buildings. A (plaintiff) paid ₹101 as part payment and part of that land was requisitioned by the government during the Second World War due to which the roads and so on could not be built. Defendant wanted thereupon to cancel the contract on grounds that the contract stood discharged by frustration, as the performance had become impossible due to supervening events. It was held that since there was no specified period suggested in agreement for construction of above and the requisition is not of permanent nature, therefore, mere likely delay in performance could not frustrate the contract.
2. **Impossibility does not mean mere commercial difficulty:** A distinction is drawn between the happening of an event, which makes the performance of the contract impossible, beyond the control of the promisor, and an event, which makes the performance of the contract impossible. Mere commercial difficulty cannot frustrate the contract. In Ganga Saran vs. Ram Charan Ram Gopal, a contract was made for supplying certain bales of cloth manufactured by the New Victoria Mills Kanpur. The contract was for supplying goods of the Victoria Mills, as soon as they are supplied to us by the Victoria Mills. The Victoria Mills failed to supply goods to the seller and, therefore, seller pleaded impossibility of performance. The court held that they were liable.
3. **Strikes, lockouts and civil disturbances:** Strikes, lockouts and civil disturbances like riots do not discharge the contract unless the parties had specifically agreed in this regard at the time of entering into a contract. In the case of Jacob vs. Credit Lyonnais, it was held that riots and civil disturbances were no excuse for non-performance of the contract.
4. **Failure of one of the several objects:** When there are several objects or purposes for which a contract is entered into, failure of one of the objects or partial impossibility does not terminate the contract. The parties can still perform the contract to achieve other objects which have not become impossible. Therefore, failure of one of the objects of contract or partial impossibility does not relieve the parties from performing other acts, which have not become impossible. In the case of Herne Bay Steam Boat Co. vs. Hutton, X company agreed to let out a boat to Y for the purposes of:
   a. Viewing a naval review on the occasion of coronation of King Edward VII and
   b. To sail around the fleet.

   Due to King's illness, the naval review was cancelled but the fleet was assembled. The boat could be used to sail around the fleet, although the first object could not be achieved. It was held that the contract was not discharged.
5. **Impossibility due to the conduct of the third party:** The doctrine of subsequent impossibility does not apply to a case where a contract could not be performed due to the default of a third person on whose word the promisor relied upon. The parties

remain bound to perform their respective obligations if a third person has not acted in a manner agreed between the parties.

Effects of Supervening Impossibility

Section 56(2) of the Act provides that a contract to do an act, which after the contract is made, becomes impossible, or by reason of some event, which the promisor could not prevent, becomes void when the act becomes impossible or unlawful. This means when it is impossible to perform the obligations given under the contract, then contracts becomes void. According to Section 65 of the Act, when a contract becomes void any person who has received any benefit under the agreement must restore it or make compensation to the person from whom he received it. So, if any party which obtains any benefit under a contract, which becomes void subsequently, is bound to restore it to the other person.

Example: X entered into a contract with Y to give a performance at his theatre for two nights in a month for one year. Y agreed to pay him ₹50,000 in advance for two nights. X fell ill on the fifth night and could not perform. Here, X must refund the advance taken but is not liable to Y for the loss of profits, which he could have made if X had been able to perform. The effects of supervening impossibility are as follows.

1. **Contract becomes void:** Where the performance of a contact becomes impossible or unlawful subsequent to its formation, the contract becomes void.
   Example: X contracts to marry Y, being already married to Z. X is forbidden by law to practise polygamy. X must make compensation to Y for the loss caused to her by non-performance of the promise.
2. **Benefit to be restored:** Where a contract becomes void, and person who has received any advantage under it must restore it or should make compensation for it to the person from whom he received it. The English law was further explained in the case of Fibrosa vs. Fairbairn that all the sums paid to any party in pursuance of the contract before it is discharged are recoverable. Sums payable cease to be payable.

Thus, in the case of supervening impossibility, contract comes to end and the benefits received are required to be restored. However, no liability under this impossibility be imposed.

Differences between Supervening Impossibility and the Doctrine of Frustration

The following are the differences between supervening impossibility and the doctrine of frustration:

Supervening Impossibility	*Doctrine of Frustration*
1. Supervening impossibility is applicable in India.	1. Doctrine of frustration is applicable under the English law.
2. Supervening impossibility of performance is decided by the court and not for the parties to raise it as a defence.	2. Parties can raise the plea of frustration as a defence for non-performance of the contract.

3. In the Indian Law, where a contract had become impossible to be performed, any amount paid as advance or benefit already given must be refunded or returned to the party concerned under the principle of a quasi-contract.	3. In the case of frustration, money that was already advanced by the promisor to the promisee need not be refunded or returned. The status quo will be maintained.

Note: The breach of contract and its remedies and assignment will be discussed in the next chapter.

TEST QUESTIONS

1. Examine the various ways in which a contract may be discharged.
2. Discuss the different ways in which a contract may be discharged by operation of law.
3. What do you understand by the doctrine of 'supervening impossibility'? What are its consequences?
4. 'Impossibility of performance is, as a rule, not an excuse for non-performance of contract.' Discuss.
5. What is novation of a contract? How is it effected? What are its legal consequences? How does it differ from alteration?
6. What do you understand by the doctrine of frustration of contract? Differentiate with supervening impossibility.
7. 'Impossibility of performance' is, as rule, not an excuse for non-performance of a contract. Discuss.
8. Explain the doctrine of frustration and point out the limitations to it.

PRACTICAL PROBLEMS

1. X owes money to Y under a contract. It is agreed between X, Y and Z that Y shall, henceforth, accept Z as his debtor instead of X. Can Y claim payment from Z?
   Hint. Yes. Y can claim payment from Z. This is called novation of the contract. Its effect is that the original contract need not be performed but the new contract shall be performed.
2. X, Y and Z jointly promise to pay ₹50,000 to P. X and Y are not traceable. Can P compel Z to pay him in full?
   Hint. Yes. P can compel Z to pay him the full amount since the liability of joint promisors is joint and several.
3. X lent three sums to Y for ₹4,000, ₹450 and ₹5,000. Y sent a sum of ₹4,000 asking X to appropriate this money towards the third debt of ₹5,000. X wants to appropriate this money to the first loan. Can he do so?
   Hint. X cannot do so since the debtor has the primary right to specify the manner of appropriation.
4. A and B execute a promissory note in favour of X and Y for ₹4,000. Will X succeed if he sues A alone on the pronote?
   Hint. X will not succeed if he sues A alone. Y must join him because according to Section 45, the right to claim performance rests with all the joint promises jointly and a single promise cannot demand performance.

5. X obtains two loans of ₹25,000 each from a bank, one of which is guaranteed by Y. Y sends the bank a sum of ₹30,000 without any direction regarding appropriation towards the loans. The bank appropriates ₹25,000 towards the loan not guaranteed by B and ₹5,000 only towards the loan guaranteed by Y. Y objects to such appropriation. Can he succeed?
   Hint. No. Y cannot succeed since in the absence of any instruction from the debtor with regard to appropriation, the creditor is entitled to apply the payment to any of the two debts. Therefore, the appropriation done by the bank is perfectly valid and binding.
6. X was due to perform a contract on 1 June 2000, but on 20 May, he repudiated his obligation. On 30 May, the contract became illegal through a change in the law. Y, the other party to the contract, filed a suit for breach of contract on 31 May 2000. Discuss.
   Hint. Y has no remedy against X. Contracts, which become illegal because of a change in law become void as per the doctrine of supervening impossibility.
7. X agrees to sell his car to Y a month after the date of the contract. However, just after 25 days of the contract, he sells the car to Z. Hereupon, Y sues X for the breach of contract. X contends that he could still perform the contract by repurchasing the car from Z. Decide?
   Hint. Here, there is anticipatory breach of contract by conduct from X's side and, therefore, his contention will not be upheld. Y is entitled to treat the contract as rescinded and sue X for the breach of contract immediately.
8. X contracts to marry Y in three years' time. Shortly afterwards, he breaks off the engagement without Y's consent. Y writes repeatedly begging him to adhere to the contract. Just before the expiry of three years, a change in law makes it illegal for X to marry Y. On the expiry of three years, Y sues X for the breach of the contract. Will he succeed?
   Hint. No. Y will not succeed because when he filed the suit for breach, the contract had already been discharged by supervening impossibility and X is entitled to take advantage of that.
9. The unloading of a ship was delayed beyond the date agreed with the shipowners owing to a strike of dock labourers. On a suit by the shipowners for damages, the plea of impossibility of performance was raised. Advise the shipowners.
   Hint. The shipowners are bound to succeed in the suit. Strike by workers renders the performance only difficult or expensive and not impossible and as such it is not covered under the doctrine of supervening impossibility.
10. An existing mortgage was discharged by the substitution of a new agreement of mortgage. The new agreement could not be registered and, hence, it was not enforceable. Could parties fall back upon the original contract?
    Hint. Yes. In novation, if for any reason the new contract cannot be enforced, the parties can fall back upon the old contract. This principle was confirmed in the case Shankarlal Damodar vs. Ambalal Ajaipal.

9

CHAPTER

Breach of Contract and Its Remedies

Learning Objectives

- To understand a breach of contract
- To understand different types of remedies for breach of contract

Breach of Contract

When any party having obligations under a contract fails to perform them or does an act whereby the performance of the contract by him becomes impossible or he refuses to perform the obligations under the contract, there will be a breach of contract. Breach means failure or refusal of a party to perform his obligations under a contract without any lawful excuse. In some cases, a breach of contract also discharges the aggrieved or injured party from performing his obligations under the contract, which may be due from him, and he gets a right to sue the defaulting party to claim damages for the loss, which he may suffer from such breach. Breach of contract may be:

1. Actual breach, that is, non-performance of the contract on the due date.
2. Anticipatory breach, that is, due to circumstances it cannot be performed.

Actual Breach

Actual breach of contract means that breach is committed by either at the time when the performance of the contract is due or during its performance. It is also called 'present breach'. Actual breach of contract may occur:

1. During the performance of the contract, or
2. At the time the performance is due, any one party to the contract fails or refuses or neglects to perform his obligation under the contract. The refusal of performance may be express or implied. Actual breach discharges the contract.

For breach of contract, the aggrieved party will have a right to sue the defaulting party to claim for damages. In the actual breach of contract, time is the most important factor, and in case the contract is not performed on time, the legal action can be taken.

Example: X entered into an agreement with Y to dance at his hotel but on the due date X refused to dance at the hotel. This will be known as actual breach of contract. For which, Y can either claim the damages or rescind the contract.

Anticipatory Breach

Anticipatory breach of contract arises in case of executory contracts. When before the contract becomes due for performance, one of the parties to it shows his intention not to perform the contract, this is called anticipatory breach of contract. It is an announcement by one of the contracting parties of his intention not to fulfil the contract and that he will no longer be bound by it. In the case of West Bengal Financial Corporation vs. Gluco Series, X granted a loan to Y and also agreed to grant a further loan at its discretion, provided that Y makes the repayment of loan as per the agreement. Y failed to repay the loan amount. X refused to grant further loan as agreed earlier. It was held by the court that Y had already granted the loan to Y and this is not breach of contract by X on account of not granting the second loan. Anticipatory breach of contract may occur:

1. When a party repudiates his liability under the contract before the time for performance is due, or
2. When a party by his own act or conduct disables himself from performing the contract. It is a premature destruction of the contract rather than a failure to perform it. It indicates a breach before the performance is due.

Example: X agrees to marry Y, but before the agreed date of marriage, he marries Z. The marriage contract has been repudiated by X's conduct before the due date of its performance. The breach here is anticipatory breach.

Effects of Anticipatory Breach

Anticipatory breach gives the aggrieved party either of the following two remedies.

1. **Rescind the contract:** He may rescind the contract and can bring an action for damages for breach of contract immediately without waiting for the due date for performance.
2. **May not rescind the contract:** He may not put an end to the contract and treat the contract operative until the date of performance arrives and sue only after that for damages for breach.

   There are two options available to the aggrieved party: One, to sue at once for the breach or second, wait for performance from the other party. However, if he waits for the time when the contract is to be executed, certain consequences follow:
   a. The party repudiating the contract may choose to perform when the time comes and the aggrieved party will be bound to accept the performance.
   b. The contract remains open for the benefit of both the parties and the defaulter party can also take the advantage of any subsequent event, which discharges the contract otherwise than by repudiation.

Example: In the case of Avery vs. Bowden, X chartered Y's ship and agreed to load it at a port within 45 days. On arrival of the ship, X told the captain that he had no cargo and requests the captain to go away. The captain stayed there. However, before the expiry of 45 days, war broke out which rendered performance illegal. Y brought an action for breach. It was held that the contract was discharged by impossibility and not by breach.

Remedies for Breach of Contract

When the obligations are not fulfilled by the parties to the contract, it is known as breach of contract and the process of enforcing right under a contract is known as 'remedies for the breach of contract'. The remedies are of two kinds:

1. Common law remedy
2. Equitable remedy

When there is a breach of contract, the aggrieved party may have one or more of the following remedies.

1. **Rescission of the contract:** 'Rescission' means the revocation or cancellation of a contract. When one of the parties to a contract commits breach, the other party may treat the contract as cancelled or rescinded and refuse to perform his part of the contract. He may also successfully defend an action for non-performance or an action brought for specific performance. Section 75 further entitles him to compensation for any damage he may have sustained through the non-fulfilment of the contract.
   Example: A promises to deliver 10 tons of sugar to B on a certain date, and B promises to pay the price on delivery of the goods. A does not deliver the goods on the appointed day. B can treat the contract as rescinded and need not to pay the price.
   When one party breaks a contract, then the other party may sue to treat the contract as rescinded and refuse further performance. Rescission means the revocation of a contract. It is an equitable remedy under the Specific Relief Act, 1963. If the contract is void or inoperative, the court may decree rescission at the instance of either party. If the contract is voidable, rescission is not decreed at the instance of the guilty party.
   According to Section 27 of the Specific Relief Act, the court may grant rescission in any of the following cases.
   a. **Where a contract is voidable:** A voidable contract is the one which includes a condition that if a party fails to fulfil the obligation within a stipulated period, the other party may put an end to the contract.
   b. **The contract is unlawful:** Where the contract is unlawful for causes not apparent on its face and the defendant is more to blame than the plaintiff.
   c. **For specific performance:** Where, in any suit for specific performance of a contract for the sale or lease of immovable property, a decree has been made and the purchaser or lessee does not pay the purchase money or other sum within the period allowed under the decree. In such a case, the seller can sue for rescission.

   Exceptions:
   a. If plaintiff has expressly or impliedly ratified the contract
   b. If the subject matter of contract is destroyed
   c. If third parties have acquired rights in good faith and for value in the contract
   d. If the contract is not severable and a part only is sought to be rescinded

Section 30 of the Specific Relief Act provides that where one party claims rescission, then he is under obligation to restore the benefits to the other party. Section 75 of the Indian Contract act provides that a person rightfully rescinding a contract will have a right to compensation for any loss caused to him for non-fulfilment of the contract by the other party.

2. **Suit for damages:** Whenever there is a breach of contract, the injured or the aggrieved party is entitled to claim damages under the contract. Damages mean pecuniary or monetary compensation. The court in terms of money awards them. So damages can be defined as 'a monetary compensation allowed to the injured party by the court for the loss or injury suffered by him as a result of the breach of the contract'. The object of awarding damages is to put the injured party in the same financial position as he would have been had there been no breach, but performance. As such, damages are not punitive, but compensatory. Damages are not awarded as punishment for a wrong as it is in the case of torts, but only to compensate the injured party for the loss suffered by him. Its purpose is compensation and compensation alone.

The aggrieved party may claim the damages for the breach of contract and damages may be of the following types.

a. **General damages:** These are also called 'ordinary damages' or 'compensatory damages'. These damages are awarded to compensate the injured party for the actual, factual and real amount of loss. These damages are awarded for the direct and proximate consequences of the breach of contract and not for the remote and indirect consequences of the breach of contract. These are restitute and compensatory in nature. General damages are calculated as on the date of breach, taking into consideration the prevailing circumstances. Subsequent changes in circumstances are ignored in calculating general damages. General damages are granted as a matter of routine course whenever there is a breach of contract.

   In the case of Haya Raghavan vs. Leo Films, X agreed to provide money in instalments to Y for producing a feature film. After paying few instalments, X refused to pay further instalments. Y, therefore, borrowed funds at a higher rate of interest from another source and completed the production of the film. The film was not a success. Y sued X for the loss sustained by him in the production of the film. It was held that he was entitled to damages for the loss sustained by borrowing funds at a higher rate of interest and not for the loss sustained or incurred by the failure of the film.

b. **Special damages:** Special damages are also called 'particular damages'. These are the damages resulting from a breach of contract under special circumstances. Damages which arise from unusual or extraordinary circumstances known to both the parties to the contract at the time of contracting are known as special damages. They constitute the indirect loss suffered by the aggrieved party because of breach of contract. Every breach of contract of sale by businessperson may involve loss of goods, profits, reputation and so on. Loss of profits is the indirect loss arising from special circumstances and not the loss that directly arises in the usual course of things from the breach. Such losses can be recovered only when the other party had known the special circumstances giving rise to them at the time of making the contract. Subsequent knowledge of the special circumstance will not create any special liability on the guilty party. Thus, unlike ordinary damages, special damages cannot be claimed as a matter of right when there is a breach of contract. These principles are clearly brought out in the following case:

In the case of Hadley vs. Baxendale, a part of the machinery of A's flourmill was broken. As a result, the movement of the other machinery also stopped. A gave the machinery to B, a common carrier, to get it repaired. A did not let B know that delay would result in a loss of profits. B unreasonably delayed the delivery of the machine and so the mill remained idle for a number of days. The delay, thus, caused loss to A. A claimed damages covering up the loss resulted to him by the closure of the mill. It was held that since the common carrier had no knowledge about the grim situation prevailing in the factory, he was not liable for the loss of profits or special damages claimed by A. Damages due to delay, however, were awarded or allowed.

c. **Vindictive damages:** These are also called 'exemplary damages' or 'extraordinary damages' or 'punitive damages'. These damages are awarded with the intention of punishing the defaulting party. These damages are awarded by way of lesson or punishment to the wrong doer. The purpose of vindictive damages is to prevent the parties from committing a breach. These damages need not be in proportion to the loss caused to the injured party. These damages are not generally awarded for breach of contract, but there are two exceptional circumstances when they may be given:
   i. Breach of contract to marry
   ii. Wrongful dishonour of a cheque by bank

   In the case of wrongful dishonour of a cheque, damages are awarded taking into account the loss of prestige and goodwill of the customer. The rule applied in this case is 'smaller the amount of the cheque, higher the damages'. In the case of breach of contract to marry, damages will include compensation for the loss to the feelings and reputation of the aggrieved party. In the case of Prema vs. Ahmed, vindictive damages were awarded for a breach of promise to marry.

d. **Nominal damages:** Nominal damages are neither compensatory nor punitive. These are awarded for a technical violation of a legal right, although the aggrieved party might have not suffered any substantial loss because of the breach. Nominal damages are usually awarded if the contract price and the market price are the same at the time of breach of the contract and the aggrieved party has not suffered any substantial loss. Nominal damages are also known as 'contemptuous damages'.

   In the case of Ashby vs. White, a voter was prevented by a returning officer from exercising his vote. Later on, it was found that the action of the returning officer was improper. The voter claiming damages filed a suit. The court was baffled as regards to determining the quantum of damages. Although the person in whose favour the voter desired to exercise his vote got elected, the voter contended that he was deprived of his valuable right. The court awarded damages by way of a meagre sum.

Rules regarding damages

The rules regarding damages have been very well explained in the Hadley vs. Baxendale case. Section 73 of the Contract Act deals with the principles for the measurement and remoteness of damages, and is based on decision given in the Hadley vs. Baxendale case. It provides that in cases of breach of contract, the injured party is entitled to receive compensation for any loss or damages which arose naturally from the breach or which the parties knew to be likely to arise from the breach. The relevant laid down rules are as follows.

i. **Purpose of damages:** Damages are compensatory in nature and the aggrieved party is to be placed in the same financial position in which party would have been, had the contract been performed. In the case of Muralidhar Chiranjilal vs.

Harishchandra Dwarkadas, the Supreme Court observed that the primary aim or principle of the law of damages for a breach of contract is to place the injured in the same position he would be if the contract had been fulfilled or to place the injured in the position he would have occupied had the breach of contract not occurred.

ii. **Actual loss:** The aggrieved party is entitled to recover by way of compensation only the actual, factual and real loss suffered by him.

iii. **Natural and usual loss:** In calculating actual loss, the court will take into account only such loss as may fairly and reasonably be considered as arising naturally and in the usual course. Compensation is not to be given for any remote or indirect loss or damages sustained due to breach.

iv. **Special damages:** Special damages are not recoverable unless the special circumstances are brought to the notice of the other party before the contract is made. In the case of Dominion of India vs. All India Reporter Ltd, a parcel of books was sent by the consignor to himself as the consignee. In transit through the railways, three volumes were lost that rendered these whole set of reports useless. The consignor filed a suit for the recovery of the price of the set. The railways had absolutely no notice that loss of three volumes would render the whole set useless. The railways were held liable only for the loss of three volumes but not the whole set of books.

v. **Vindictive damages:** Explained earlier under 'Types of Damages'.

vi. **Nominal damages:** Explained earlier under 'Types of Damages'.

vii. **Measure of damages in case of contract for sale of goods:** Normally, the measure of damages in the case of breach of contract for sale of goods is the difference between the contract price and market price on the date of the breach.

viii. **Damages in quasi-contract:** Compensation for the breach of quasi-contract would be the same as for breach of normal contract.

ix. **Effect of a penalty clause:** If in contract, a sum of money is named as the amount to be paid in case of breach or if the contract contains any stipulation by way of penalty for failure to perform the obligation, the court will allow reasonable compensation, not exceeding the sum named.

x. **Minimization of loss:** It is the duty of the injured party to minimize the loss as much as possible. The law imposes on the injured party the duty of taking all reasonable steps to minimize or mitigate the loss. The aggrieved party is not entitled to claim any part of the damages which is due to his negligence.

xi. **Difficulty of assessment:** Difficulty of calculating damages is no ground for refusing damages. The court must make an assessment of loss and pass a decree for it.

xii. **Cost of decree:** The aggrieved party is entitled, in addition to damages, to get the cost of getting the decree for damages. The cost of the suit for damages is at the discretion of the court.

3. **Specific performance**: In certain special cases of breach of contract, damages are not an adequate remedy, since mere compensation in terms of money will not be an adequate remedy for certain losses. The defaulting party may be forced to perform the act promised under the contract. Specific performance means 'the actual carrying out of the promise by the party in breach, exactly according to the terms of the contract'.

Section 14 of the Specific Relief Act provides that the following contracts cannot be specifically enforced:

a. Where monetary compensation is an adequate remedy
b. Where the court cannot supervise the execution of the contract
c. Where the contract is for personal services
d. Where one of the parties is a minor
e. Where the contract is not certain or said to be inequitable to either party

However, in contracts for sale of land, buildings and rare articles, courts generally grant for specific performance of the contract according to the provisions of the Specific Relief Act. Section 10 of the Specific Relief Act provides that the specific performance of any contract may, at the discretion of the court, be enforced in the following cases:

a. Where compensation in money is not an adequate remedy for the breach of a contract
b. Where there is no standard for ascertaining the actual damage caused by non-performance of the act agreed to be done
c. Where the compensation in money cannot be obtained for non-performance of the act agreed to be done

When, at the instance of the aggrieved party, the court directs the other party to perform the contract made by him and in accordance with its terms, it is called specific performance. In such cases, the court may direct the defaulter party to perform his promise. 'Specific performance is equitable relief given by the court in cases of breach of contract in the form of judgment that the defendant does actually perform the contract according to its term and stipulations' (Halsbury's Laws of England).

Specific performance may also be enforced in cases where the plaintiff has done substantial acts or suffered losses in consequence of a contract capable of specific performance.

4. **Suit for injunction:** Where a party to the contract is doing something, which he promised not to do, the court may, by issuing an order, restrain him from doing what he promised not to do. Such an order of the court is known as an 'injunction'. The injunction is, thus, a mode of securing the specific performance of the negative terms of a contract. Injunction is a preventive relief and is particularly appropriate in case of anticipatory breach where damages would not be an adequate relief. The court, at its discretion, grants a temporary or a perpetual injunction for an indefinite period.

In Metropolitan Electric Supply Company vs. Ginder, G agreed to buy the whole of the electric energy required for his house from the metropolitan company. This was interpreted as a promise not to buy electricity from any other company. He was, therefore, restrained by an injunction from buying electricity from any other company.

a. **An injunction is a preventive relief:** Injunction is a negative order of the court directing the party to refrain from doing something. This is given in cases where a party is guilty of breach of a negative term of the contract. This remedy may be used as a means of enforcing an express negative stipulation in a contract or a simple promise to forbear. It is the discretion of the court to grant injunction. However, there seems to be no reason why the court should refuse to grant injunction to restrain the breach of contract:
   i. whereby a promisor undertakes not to do something or
   ii. which is negative in substance though not in form, for example, to purchase goods from one supplier.

b. **Injunction may be prohibitory or mandatory:** In prohibitory injunction, it is order of the court restraining the commission of a wrongful act, whereas in mandatory, it restrains continuance of a wrongful omission. It may also be temporary or permanent. Temporary injunction is such as is to continue till a specified time or until further orders of the court. Permanent or perpetual injunction is one whereby the defendant is perpetually enjoined from the assertion of a right or from commission of an act which would be contrary to the rights of the plaintiff. It is only granted after the full trial.

c. **Sometime a contract may comprise two agreements:** An affirmative agreement to do a certain act and a negative agreement not to do a certain act. In such a case, if the court is unable to compel specific performance of the affirmative agreement, it shall not be precluded from granting an injunction to perform the negative agreement. But before the court does that, it shall see that the plaintiff has not failed to perform the contract so far as it is binding on him. To avail this, the following requirements are essential:

   i. The contract must consist of two agreements—affirmative and negative.
   ii. The contract must be divisible and negative part should be separable from the positive one.
   iii. The applicant should not have failed to perform the contract so far as it is binding on him.

   Thus, injunction is a preventive relief and is particularly appropriate in cases of anticipatory breach where damages would not be an adequate relief.

5. **Quantum meruit:** *Quantum meruit* means 'as much as merited' or 'as much as earned'. In other words, it means 'payment in proportion to the amount of work done'. The right to claim quantum meruit is conferred outside the contract by the law. This right is quasi-contractual in nature. A right to sue on a quantum meruit arises where a contract, partly performed by one party, has become discharged by the breach of the contract by the other party. In such cases, the injured or affected party is entitled to the value of the services rendered or the goods delivered till the moment of breach. The remedy may be availed either without claiming damages or in addition to claiming of damages for breach. The object of allowing a claim on quantum meruit is to decompensate the party or person for value of work he has done. Justice Alderson explains the quantum meruit in the case of De Bernardy vs. Harding that where one party has absolutely refused to perform or has rendered himself capable of performing his part of the contract, he puts it in the power of the other party either to sue for breach of it or to rescind the contract and sue on quantum meruit.

   It covers a case where one person has rendered service to another in circumstances which indicate an understanding between them that it is to be paid for, although no remuneration has been fixed. The claim on quantum meruit arises in the following cases:

   a. When a contract is discovered to be void
   b. When something is done without an intention to do so gratuitously
   c. When the contract is divisible
   d. When one party refuses to perform the contract

   For the application of this doctrine, the condition and nature of this remedy were given in the case of Puran Lal vs. State of UP, which are given as follows:

   a. The original contract must have been so discharged by the other party that the plaintiff is entitled to treat himself free from the obligation of further performance and he must have elected to do so. If the original contract is open, the party cannot have quantum meruit, but he is to rely on his remedy in damages.

b. The claim should be brought by a party not in default. The object of allowing a claim on quantum meruit is to recompensate the party or person for value of work he has done. Damages are compensatory in nature, whereas quantum meruit is restituting. It is a reasonable compensation awarded on implication of a contract to pay remuneration.

The doctrine of quantum meruit is subject to the following limitations:

a. If a lump sum money is to be paid for complete work and the contract is not divisible into part performance, then this will not entitle the party to claim any payment.
b. A person who is himself guilty of breach cannot sue on quantum meruit. But this is only where the contract is indivisible and payment is to be made for a completed work.
c. If a lump sum is to be paid on completion of work and the work has been completed, though badly, the defaulting party can recover lump sum less deduction for bad workmanship.
d. Any claim based on quantum meruit cannot be allowed unless there is an evidence of an express or implied promise to pay for the work which has already been done.

TEST QUESTIONS

1. What do you understand by breach of contract? Distinguish between actual breach and anticipatory breach.
2. What are the remedies available to an aggrieved party in case of breach of contract?
3. Explain the rules of damages as laid down in the case of Hadley vs. Baxendale. To what extent the rule is applicable in India?
4. What are the different types of damages which can be awarded by the court?
5. 'If a contract is broken, the law will endeavour, so far as money can do it, to place the aggrieved party in the same position as if the contract had been performed.' To what extent this statement is true?
6. 'Having agreed to pay a fixed sum of money on a breach of contract, the party committing the breach may still not be bound to pay the same amount.' Do you agree with this statement?
7. What is the distinction between liquidated damages and penalty and what bearing this distinction has in India upon the question of compensation in case of breach of a contract?
8. What is meant by suing on 'quantum meruit'? Under what circumstances claim on quantum meruit arises?
9. Write short notes on:
   a. Exemplary damages
   b. Liquidated damages
   c. Specific performance

PRACTICAL PROBLEMS

1. The plaintiff hired a godown from the defendant for a period of 12 months and paid the whole rent to him in advance. After six months, the godown was destroyed by fire and the plaintiff claimed a refund of proportionate amount of the rent. Is the claim valid? State reasons for your answer.

Hint. Yes. The contract becomes void. Under Section 65 of the Act, restitution is required.

2. A, in Delhi, entrusts 100 packages of crackers with the railways to be carried to his branch at Allahabad and instructs the railway authorities to deliver the same by the first week of November 1976. Due to negligence of the railway, the packages are delivered by the third week of November after the Diwali season is over. A sues the railways for the loss of profit which he might have earned by the sale of crackers during the Diwali season. Decide giving reasons.
   Hint. A will not succeed since the special circumstances have not been made known to the defendant.
3. A agrees to pay ₹100,000 to B, a contractor, after he builds A's house as per specifications. After some time the work is abandoned. B demands part payment for the work done. Will he succeed? Give reasons for your answer.
   Hint. No. It is a lump sum contract requiring complete performance. The plaintiff himself being defaulter, his claim should be proved by a fresh contract and the defendant should have the option of refusing to accept the benefit.
4. A agrees to sell land to B for ₹30,000. B pays to A ₹1,000 as a deposit at the time of the contract, the amount to be forfeited by A if B does not complete the sale within a specified period. B fails to complete the sale within a reasonable time after the expiry of that period. A rescinds the contract and retains the deposit. B contends that deposit is a benefit received by A under the voidable contract, which is rescinded by A and so A should, under Section 64 of the Indian Contract Act, restore the benefit to B. Decide.
   Hint. A can retain the deposit. It is not a benefit but only a security that the purchaser would fulfil his contract.
5. In a bond there is a stipulation for payment of compound interest on failure to pay simple interest at the same rate as was payable on the principal. Discuss whether this stipulation is liquidated damages or penalty.
   Hint. Liquidated damages. The sum is not extravagant and unconscionable.
6. A, a tailor, expected to make good profits at a place on the occasion of a festival there. He sent a sewing machine and some cloth through a railway company to the place of festival. Due to the fault of the servants of the railway company, the machine and the cloth could not be delivered till the termination of the festival. Discuss the rights of the tailor.
   Hint. Since the railway company had no notice of the special purpose, the damages cannot be recovered.

10
CHAPTER

Void Agreements

Learning Objectives

- To understand different void agreements
- To understand agreement in restraint of marriage
- To understand agreement in restraint of trade
- To understand agreement in restraint of legal proceedings
- To understand agreement with uncertain meaning
- To understand wagering agreements
- To understand agreement to do impossible acts

VOID AGREEMENTS

Not all the agreements entered into are enforceable by law. The agreements which are not enforceable by law are said to be void. Such agreements do not give rise to any legal consequences. All agreements which are against the public policy are void. Moreover, there are some agreements which have been specifically declared as void by the Indian Contract Act. The agreements which have been declared void by the Act are as follows:

1. Agreements by incompetent parties (Section 11)
2. Agreements under mutual mistake of fact material to the agreement (Section 20)
3. Agreements with unlawful consideration or object (Section 23)
4. Agreements with unlawful consideration in part (Section 24)
5. Agreements without consideration (Section 25)
6. Agreements in restraint of marriage (Section 26)
7. Agreements in restraint of trade (Section 27)
8. Agreements in restraint of legal proceedings (Section 28)
9. Agreement having uncertain meaning (Section 29)
10. Wagering agreement (Section 30)
11. Agreements contingent on impossible events (Section 36)
12. Agreement to do impossible acts (Section 56)

Agreements 1–5 have been explained in the earlier chapters, namely 'Capacity of Parties to Contract', 'Consideration', 'Legality of Objects' and 'Free Consent'. Agreements 6–12 are explained as follows.

Agreement in Restraint of Marriage (Section 26)

According to Section 26, every agreement in restraint of marriage of any person, other than a minor, is void. An agreement which restricts a person's freedom to marry or to marry any person of his choice is against public policy and is void. Further, in some cases, employment agreement can impose some reasonable restrictions on the marriage such as in armed forces and airlines.

In the case of Lowe vs. Peers, a man promised Mrs Lowe that he would not marry any person other than her, and further promised to pay a sum of GBP 2,000, if he marries someone else. It was held as against the public policy and void. Law discourages those agreements which restrain the freedom of marriage. An agreement in restraint of marriage is the one which curbs the freedom of a person to marry; the restraint may be general or partial. In general, a person is restrained from marrying a particular person or a class of persons. In all these cases the agreement is void. However, an agreement restraining a minor's marriage is valid.

Example: X agreed to marry Y and no one else, in consideration of her father giving him the entire property. The agreement is void as it is in restraint of marriage.

However, in the case of Rao Rani vs. Gulab Rani, the Allahabad High Court held that the agreement between the two co-widows that any one of them would lose the right to the deceased husband's estate on remarriage is not a restraint on the right of marriage.

Agreements in Restraint of Trade (Section 27)

The freedom to carry on any business or trade has been guaranteed to every citizen by the Constitution of India. Public policy requires that every man shall be at liberty to work for him and shall not be at liberty to deprive himself or the state of his labour, skill or talent by any contract. Section 27 provides that every agreement by which anyone is restrained from exercising a lawful profession, trade or business of any kind is to that extent void. The restraint of trade may be partial or complete. Whether the restraint is general and unqualified or qualified, if the agreement is in the nature of a restraint of trade, then it is void. But if it is a partial restriction and is separable from the valid portion, the valid portion will be enforceable. This is made clear by Section 27 when it says 'to that extent void'.

Example: In Madhub Chander vs. Raj Coomar Dass, the court held that even a partial restriction on the trade is restraint of trade, hence any agreement of such will be void. However, in the case of Gujarat Bottling Co. Ltd vs. Coca Cola Company, the court held that any restriction on the franchisee not to deal with the competing goods is not a restraint of trade.

Exceptions of Agreements in Restraint of Trade

The general rule is that all the agreements in restraint of trade are void. Whether the restraint is general or specific, partial or complete, it is void unless the case falls within any of the statutory or judicially created exceptions given under Section 27. These exceptions may be classified into two categories:

1. Exceptions under different Acts
2. Exceptions by judicial interpretation

Exceptions under Different Acts

1. **Sale of goodwill:** When there is sale of business by a person along with its goodwill, the seller of the business may make an agreement with the buyer not to carry on the business in competition with the buyer. Any reasonable restriction on the trade will be valid. This exception is given in Section 27 of the Indian Contract Act. The restriction imposed should satisfy the following conditions:
   a. The restriction should be related to a similar business only.
   b. It should specify the geographical limits.
   c. Restriction should apply only for such period for which the buyer or any of his representatives carry on the business.
   d. The restriction must be reasonable. What is reasonable will depend on factors such as the area in which the goodwill is enjoyed, the nature of business, price paid for it and the period of restriction.

   Example: X is running a shop in Sarojini Nagar main market. He sells the business to Y and enters into an agreement with him not to carry on a similar business within specified limits as long as Y or his representative carries on the business in Sarojini Nagar market. This restriction is valid. Nevertheless, a restriction not to start a similar business anywhere in India is unreasonable and, therefore, void or any other restriction on Y to do any other business in the same locality or anywhere else is also void. (Nordenfelt vs. Maxim Nordenfelt Guns and Ammunition Co. Ltd)
2. **Under Partnership Act:** Some exceptions are given under the Indian Partnership Act, 1932 which are as follows.
   a. **An agreement between the partners of a firm:** All the partners of a partnership firm may agree not to carry on firm's business or any similar business, so long as they are partners. It is a valid restriction within the provisions of Section 11(2) of the Partnership Act and will not be a restraint of trade under Section 27 of the Indian Contract Act.
   b. **Restriction on an outgoing partner:** According to Section 36(2) of the Partnership Act, there may be an agreement between the outgoing partner and the remaining partner that he will not carry on any business which is similar to the business of partnership firm. The restriction could be with regard to the time and area within which a similar business is not to be carried out.
   c. **Agreement on or after the dissolution of firm:** According to Section 54 of the Indian Partnership Act, partners may in anticipation of dissolution or upon dissolution enter into an agreement that some or all of them will not carry on a business similar to that of the firm within a specified period or within specified local limits.
   d. **After the sale of goodwill:** According to Section 55(3), any partner may, upon sale of goodwill of a firm, make an agreement that such partner will not carry on business similar to that of the firm within a specified period or local limits, provided the restriction is reasonable.

By Judicial Interpretation

Following are the exceptions based upon the interpretation of Section 27 by the various courts in India.

1. **Restrictions imposed by the agreement between employer and employee:** An agreement between employer and employee can impose restriction on employee

that he will not serve anybody else during the period of employment with that employer.

Example: In the case of V. N. Deshpande vs. Arvind Mills Ltd, the defendant took employment as a weaving master in a mill and agreed not to serve in that capacity for three years anywhere else in any part in India. An injunction was granted to restrain him in terms of the agreement. However, the restrictions should be reasonable taking into account the facts and circumstances of the case.

The Supreme Court has laid down in the case of Superintendence Co. of India Ltd vs. Krishna Murgai that a restraint beyond the term of service would be void and the only ground on which it can be justified is by showing that it is necessary for the protection of the employer's goodwill.

2. **Restriction by trade combinations:** The trade combinations are the voluntary organizations to regulate the price and supply of goods in the market for the best interest of all. These agreements include price fixation, contributing profit to a common pool, fixing the profit margin and so on. However, a combination which tends to create monopoly and which is against public interest is void. In Bhola Nath Shankar Das vs. Lachmi Narain, the Allahabad High Court held that the agreement was valid on the ground that every trader has a privilege to regulate his own mode of carrying business according to his discretion and choice.
3. **Sole selling or solus agreement:** Sometimes, seller may agree to sell his entire product to only one buyer or buyer may enter into an agreement with supplier that he will purchase all the material required from that supplier. Such agreement is called solus agreement or exclusive dealing agreement. These kinds of agreements are valid and not treated as restraint of trade (Mackenzie vs. Striramiah).

   Example: X agreed to supply 100,000 pairs of dhotis to Y and not to sell goods of that kind to any other person for a fixed period. In this case also the court held that agreement was valid. However, in the case of Shaikh Kalu vs. Ram Saran Bhagat, the court held the agreement void as the restraint was for unreasonably long time and agreement was intended to create a monopoly.

Agreement in Restraint of Legal Proceedings (Section 28)

According to Section 28, an agreement absolutely restraining a party from enforcing his right through the court or an agreement restricting this right fully or partly will be void. Section 28 of the Indian Contract Act (as amended in 1997) provides that every agreement which restricts any party from enforcing his rights absolutely under any contract by the usual proceedings in the courts or which limits the time within which one may enforce his right is void to that extent. This section makes two kinds of agreements void which are as follows.

1. **Agreement absolutely restraining legal proceedings:** If an agreement restricts a party absolutely from enforcing his contractual rights by bringing usual legal proceedings, then it is void. An agreement to oust the jurisdiction of a court is opposed to public policy and is void. The agreement is void if restraints are absolute one. In the case of Hakam Singh vs. Gammon India Pvt. Ltd, an agreement between the parties was restricting the jurisdiction of any suit in Bombay only. The plaintiff had filed a suit in Varanasi but the court had dismissed the suit, and on appeal, the Supreme Court held that restriction on filing suit in Bombay only is not unreasonable. Hence, it is not void.

2. **Agreement limiting time for legal action:** Agreements are declared void under Section 28 if the parties have tried to restrict the time within which a suit may be filed and it is less than the period prescribed by the law of limitation, that is, in cases of breach of contract, action may be brought within a period of three years from the date of breach according to the law of limitation. If a clause in an agreement provides that no suit can be filed after two years, then it is void.
   Example: X has supplied goods to Y. X promises that he will not sue Y after a period of one year. If he fails to sue within one year, he will have no right to sue. Such an agreement is void.
   In the case of National Insurance Co. Ltd vs. S. G. Nayak, the court held that an agreement which curtails the period of limitation and provides for a shorter period than the Limitation Act is void. However, waiver of right in an agreement after the lapse of time is not void.

Provisions of Section 28(b)

Section 28(b) of the Indian Contract (Amendment) Act, 1997, provides that every agreement which extinguishes the right of any party thereto or discharges any party from any liability under or in respect of any contract on the expiry of a specified period so as to restrict any party from enforcing the rights is void to that extent. In other words, if any agreement restricts the right of suing, it is void. The Amendment Act provides following exceptions.

1. **Reference to arbitration in case of dispute:** According to Exception 1 of Section 28, any agreement between the parties by which they may refer any dispute which may arise between them in future to arbitration, and only the amount awarded in such arbitration shall be recoverable in respect of the dispute so referred, shall not be rendered illegal. In the case of New Great Insurance Co. vs. United Equipment and Stores Pvt. Ltd, court held that if an agreement to refer dispute to arbitration does not close the final door of justice, then it is not void, and if it closes the door of justice, then it is void.
2. **To refer existing questions to arbitration:** According to Exception 2 of Section 28, questions which have already arisen between the parties may be referred by them to arbitration by a contract in writing. Such an agreement is valid. In other words, it can be said that sometimes the parties may agree to refer existing dispute to arbitration. An agreement to such effect is valid, as it does not seek to oust the jurisdiction of courts.
   Example: X agreed to sell his car to Y for ₹100,000. Y agreed to pay the price on delivery. On the date of delivery, a dispute arose about the value and Y refused to pay the price. They agreed in writing to refer it to arbitration. This is a valid agreement.

Agreements with Uncertain Meaning (Section 29)

According to Section 29 of the Act, 'any agreement, the meaning of which is not certain or capable of being made certain is void'. This means that any agreement whose meaning is uncertain or incapable of being understood by the parties to contract is void.

Example: X agrees to sell to Y 1,000 tons of oil. The agreement is void for uncertainty because in this case it is not clear what kind or brand of oil the party had ordered.

In the case of Puspabala Ray vs. LIC of India, the court held that the resolution, promise or agreement contained therein is void for vagueness or uncertainty and, therefore, the suit is void. An uncertain agreement is the one whose terms are vague. Where the parties unable to express their intention clearly, the agreement is void. However, if the price is to be decided by a third party, the agreement is not void but an agreement to agree in future is void as there is no certainty whether the parties will be able to agree or not in future.

Wagering Agreements (Section 30)

According to Section 30 of the Act, agreement by the way of wager is void and no suit shall be brought for recovering anything alleged to be won on any wager or entrusted to any person to abide by the result of any game or other uncertain event on which any wager is made. However, the provisions of this section shall not be applicable in case of winnings from horse races. The Contract Act has not defined the term 'wagering agreements' but Sir William Anson (*Anson's Law of Contract*, 24th edition) has defined wager as 'a promise to give money or money's worth upon the determination or ascertainment of an uncertain event'.

Essentials of a Wagering Agreement

It is essential to a wagering agreement that each party may under it either win or lose. His win or loss depends on the happening of the event and, therefore, remains uncertain until that event is known. If any of the parties may win but cannot lose, then it is not a wagering agreement. An agreement will be known as a wagering agreement if it satisfies the following conditions.

1. **Opposite view regarding an uncertain event:** Wagering agreement depends upon an uncertain event or the determination of such event. The performance of the agreement must depend upon the happening or non-happening of an uncertain event. A wager generally contemplates a future event but it may even relate to a past event, but the parties should not be aware of its result.
2. **Chances of gain or loss for both the parties:** The second essential feature of a wagering agreement is that each party should stand a chance to win or lose. If one party may win but cannot lose or may lose but cannot win, the agreement is not wager. In the case of Baba Saheb vs. Rajaram, it has been held that if out of the money which has been recovered, the payment is to be made to winner of a certain game, then this is not a wagering contract as each party has equal chance of winning.
3. **No party should have control over the event:** No party to the contract should have control over the happening of the event. If either of the parties has the event in his hands, it is not a wager as uncertainty is the basic feature of wagering contract.
4. **No other interest in the event other than bet amount:** No party to the agreement should have any other interest in the event except winning or losing the amount of bet. If any of the parties has other interest, the agreement is not a wagering agreement. In the case of Brahm Dutt Sharma vs. LIC of India, the Court held that plaintiff can recover the money as he has financed the policy without having insurable interest in the life of deceased person. Hence, it is a wagering contract.

   Example: X promises to pay Y ₹25,000, if it rains tomorrow; but if there is no rain tomorrow, then Y will pay X ₹25,000. This is a wagering agreement.

Consequences of Wagering Agreement

According to the provisions of Section 30, the wagering agreement is void and unenforceable but law does not forbid a wagering agreement. Wagering agreement is not illegal and it does not affect collateral transaction. Therefore, the collateral transactions are not void but valid and enforceable. So money borrowed to take part in a wagering transaction is a collateral transaction and this money is repayable.

Exceptions

There are following exceptions to the provisions of Section 30 of the Act.

1. **Horse races:** Section 30 makes one exception in favour of certain prizes for horse racing. According to this section, any subscription or contribution or an agreement to subscribe or contribute towards any plate, prize or sum of money of the value of ₹500 or more to the winner of any horse race is not void.
2. **Crossword competitions:** Section 30 further states that there are certain other transactions which are not wagers. Literary competitions and other such competitions, which involve the application of skill and where an effort is made to select the best and most skilful competitor, are not wagers. But where prizes depend upon a chance, like lottery, are void. So where skill plays an important part in the result, the competition is not a lottery.

Important Transactions of Wagering Nature

1. **Lottery:** Lottery is a game of chance. The event is wholly dependent on the draw of lots. The chances of gain or loss are equal and depend upon an uncertain event. Therefore, the prize money cannot be recovered through a court of law. Some state government have given sanction for conducting lotteries. This does not change the nature of wagering transaction. The only effect of sanction is that the person conducting lottery cannot be prosecuted. However, chit fund agreements are not wagering contract.
2. **Speculative transactions:** Sometimes, it may be difficult to find out whether an agreement is by way of wager or a genuine commercial transaction. In such cases, where delivery is intended to be given and taken, it is a valid contract but where the difference in prices is intended to be paid, it is a wagering agreement. Share market transactions are not wagering contract.
3. **Option dealings:** These transactions are in the nature of pure speculation and mean a right to buy or sell certain goods at a price fixed at the time of entering into the agreement. Option dealing is not a wagering transaction unless it is proved that both parties do not intend to give and take delivery. However, option dealings in securities are prohibited by the Securities Contract (Regulation) Act, 1956.

Contracts of Insurance and Wagering Agreements

Although there are many similarities between a wagering agreement and a contract of insurance, contracts of insurance are not void. Contract of insurance is one whereby the insurer, in consideration of a sum of money, undertakes to make good the loss of the other in respect of insured parties on the happening of uncertain specified event. Wagering agreement also depends on an uncertain event. Both involve payment of money. But the following are the points of difference between the two:

1. In a wager, the parties have no interest except winning or losing. However, in contracts of insurance, the contract is to protect the insurable interest; only a person who stands to lose at the loss of an article or life is allowed to insure it.
2. Wagering agreement is a contract to pay a specified sum to the winner, whereas contract of insurance is a contract of indemnity. Only the loss is made good. However, life insurance contracts are not contracts of indemnity.
3. The amount to be paid to the winner is fixed in case of wagering agreement. But in case of insurance (except life insurance), the actual amount of loss will be paid up to the maximum of sum insured.
4. A contract of insurance is a form of social cooperation. It is very beneficial to businessmen. A wagering agreement, on the other hand, is of no use to the society.
5. In case of insurance, the premium is calculated on the basis of certain scientific principles. However, in case of wagering agreement, neither the risk is calculated scientifically nor the amount to be won or lost. It is a mere gamble and, therefore, void.

Agreements to Do Impossible Acts (Section 56)

Possibility to perform an agreement is the condition for the validity of an agreement. According to Section 56 of the Act, an agreement to do an act impossible in itself is void. Section 56 further provides.

1. **Contract to do an act which afterwards becomes impossible or unlawful:** An agreement which is unlawful at the time of making it is void ab initio. However, if impossibility arises afterwards, then it is void.
2. **Compensation for loss through non-performance of act known to be impossible or unlawful:** If the promisor receives any compensation, he is under obligation to pay it back.

Therefore, impossibility may be at the time of entering into a contract or subsequent to the formation but before performance of a contract. An agreement to do an act impossible is void ab initio. But impossibility arising later on is known as doctrine of subsequent impossibility. If the initial impossibility is known to the promisor alone, he must pay compensation to the promisee for any loss due to non-performance.

Example: A agrees with B to discover treasure by magic, the agreement is void.

Example: A contracts to marry B while being already married to C and forbidden by law to practise polygamy. A must make compensation to B for the loss caused to her by non-performance of the promise.

Doctrine of Restitution

When one party receives some benefit under a void agreement, such party is under obligation to repay the same. This restoration of benefit is called 'restitution'. This rule is based on the principle of justice and equity that no one can be allowed to enrich himself at the expense of other. The doctrine of restitution means that a person who has been unjustly enriched at the expense of another is required to make restitution to another. The doctrine of restitution is based on 'the benefits which are enjoyed by the defendant at the cost of the plaintiff, which is unjust for the defendant to retain'.

Section 64 of the Contract Act provides that when a person at whose option a contract is voidable rescinds it, the other party need not to perform any promise contained in the agreement, in which he is promisor. The party rescinding a voidable contract shall, if he has received any benefit there under from another party to such contract, restore such benefit, so far as may be, to the person from whom it was received.

Similarly, Section 65 provides that when an agreement is discovered to be void or when a contract becomes void, any person who has received any advantage under such agreement or contract be bound to restore it or make compensation for it to the person from whom he has received it. When a contract becomes void, the person receiving the benefit must restore it or make compensation for it.

Example: X agrees to sell a house for ₹100,000 to Y. Y pays an advance of ₹10,000 for it. Before the sale takes place, the house is destroyed. The contract becomes impossible and, hence, void. However, X must return ₹10,000 paid by Y to him.

However, Section 65 does not apply to:

1. Agreements which were known to be void when they were entered into. This means that no restitution is allowed in case of expressly declared void agreements.
   Example: Where X paid ₹25,000 to Y to beat Z, the money paid cannot be recovered.
2. The section does not apply to a case where the parties are wholly incompetent to contract.
   Example: Where one of the parties is a minor, he cannot be asked to restore the benefit but where he misrepresented his age, the court may, on equitable grounds, order for restoration of the benefit received or payment of compensation.
   Where the benefit cannot be restored, the party may be asked to compensate for it.

TEST QUESTIONS

1. Comment on the following statements:
   a. No action is allowed on illegal agreements.
   b. Liberty to trade is not an asset which the law will permit a person to barter except in special circumstances within well-recognized limitations.
   c. The jurisdiction of courts of law to decide dispute arising from contractual obligation cannot be ousted by agreement between parties.
   d. A person ought not to be allowed to restrain himself by contract from exercising any lawful craft or business at his own discretion and in his own way.
2. What do you understand by void agreement? What are the various agreements that have been expressly declared void?
3. 'An agreement in restraint of trade is void.' Examine this statement stating exceptions, if any.
4. What are the essentials of a wagering agreement? Discuss the effect of wagering agreements.
5. Are the following wagering agreements?
   a. Flower show
   b. Lottery

c. Crossword competitions
d. Horse races
e. Stock exchange dealings
6. Discuss the impact of uncertainty on an agreement.
7. Distinguish between wagering agreement and contract of insurance.
8. Discuss the effects of agreement of which consideration and object are unlawful.
9. Is contract of insurance a wagering agreement? Give reasons for your answer.
10. What are void agreements and void contracts? Is a party which has received some benefit under a void contract bound to restore it to the other party?

PRACTICAL PROBLEMS

1. X instructs Y to enter on his behalf into a wagering transaction. Y loses in the transaction and pays from his pocket. Is Y entitled to reimbursement from X? State reasons.
   Hint. Yes. Wagering agreements are void but not illegal except in old Bombay State. Collateral transactions are valid.
2. A had a bet of ₹1,000 with B that a certain horse would win a certain race. Under this agreement, A had to deposit ₹200 with B. Since A had no money, he approached his friend C who advanced him ₹200. Subsequently, A lost the bet and refused to repay the amount to C. Advise C.
   Hint. C can recover the sum. Wagering agreements are void but not illegal except in old Bombay State. Collateral transactions are valid.
3. Briefly discuss the legal validity or invalidity of the following:
   a. An agreement to purchase a lottery authorized by government.
   b. An agreement to pay fee to a holy man for success of a pending suit.
   c. An agreement not to plead limitation.
   d. An agreement grounded on erroneous belief that a particular debt is barred by law of limitation.
   e. An oral agreement to compensate a person who has already voluntarily done something for the promisor.
   Hint. a. Void, because it is a wagering agreement.
   b. Valid, see agreements in restraint of legal proceedings.
   c. Void, because it defeats the provisions of the Limitation Act.
   d. Valid unless inequitable and unjust.
   e. Valid, ignorance of law is no excuse.
   f. Valid, exception under Section 25(2) regarding consideration.
4. A and B each deposit ₹1,000 with C to abide by the result of a bet between them. A wins the bet, C refuses to pay the amount to A. Can A recover the amount (i.e., ₹2,000) from C?
   Hint. A cannot recover the amount from C.
5. A agrees to sell to B a horse for ₹2,000, if it wins a race, and for ₹50 if it does not. The horse wins the race. Advise A in each case.
   a. B refuses to pay ₹2,000 and buy the horse.
   b. A refuses to sell the horse to B.
   c. B agrees to buy the horse for ₹1,000.
   Hint. a. A cannot compel B to buy the horse and pay ₹2,000.
   b. B cannot compel A to sell the horse.
   c. A is not bound to sell the horse.

6. X lends ₹500 to Y in Delhi in order to enable him to bet with Z as to the result of a horse race. Can X recover money from Y?
   Hint. Yes.
7. A promises B, in consideration of ₹10,000, never to marry throughout his life. Is the agreement valid?
   Hint. No. Section 25—agreement restraint of marriage.
8. A bank appoints B as an officer subject to the condition that after leaving the service he would not join the service of any other bank in India for a period of five years. Can the bank enforce this condition in a court of law?
   Hint. No. Section 25—agreement is void.

11

CHAPTER

Quasi-contract and Contingent Contract

Learning Objectives

- To understand the meaning of a quasi-contract
- To learn the basis and types of quasi-contracts
- To understand the meaning of doctrine of restitution
- To understand the meaning of a contingent contract
- To understand the essentials of a contingent contract
- To understand the meaning of enforcement of contingent contracts
- To understand the difference between a wagering agreement and a contingent contract

QUASI-CONTRACT

A contract is the result of an agreement which is enforceable by law, and obligations arising from a contract are called 'contractual obligations'. However, under certain special circumstances, it may come into existence from the action of parties, and the law creates and enforces legal rights and obligations. Such legal rights and obligations imposed or created by law are known as 'quasi-contracts'. Dr Jenks defines a quasi-contract as 'a situation in which law imposes upon one person, on grounds of natural justice, an obligation similar to that which arises from a true contract, although no contract, express or implied, has in fact been entered into by them'.

Sections 68–72 deal with quasi-contracts. Quasi-contracts are an exceptional kind of contracts, by which one party is bound to pay money in consideration of something done or suffered by the other party. They are not founded on mutual promises, but one person has done something or paid money for another and the court comes forward on the ground of equity saying that the person receiving benefit must make compensation to the other. Quasi-contracts are not contracts because the obligation does not arise from mutual agreement of the parties.

Basis of Quasi-contracts

Quasi-contracts are based on the principles of equity and justice. It is the duty, and not a promise or agreement, which is the basis of such contracts. There is no offer and acceptance nor consensus ad idem in the case of quasi-contracts. Their main object is to prevent unjust enrichment or unjust benefit. They rest on the doctrine of 'unjust enrichment'. In the case of Mahabir Kishore & Ors vs. State of Madhya Pradesh, the Supreme Court held that in an action for unjust enrichment, the following essentials have to be proved:

1. The defendant has been enriched by the receipt of a benefit.
2. The enrichment is at the expense of the plaintiff.
3. The retention of the enrichment is unjust.

An action for a quasi-contract resembles a contractual action in so for as such an action is against a certain person or persons who have got the unjust benefits. Such an action, it may be further noted, is for a liquidated sum of money.

Example: A delivers goods to B, mistaking him to be C, and B consumes them. B is bound to pay to A the value of goods. Law imposes such a duty on B. This is a quasi-contract.

In quasi-contracts, there is no agreement at all and certain obligations are imposed by law on the parties to the contract. They do not result from the following:

1. Any express agreement
2. Any implied agreement

Types of Quasi-contracts under the Contract Act

Following are the types of quasi-contracts.

1. Claim for Necessaries Supplied to a Person Incapable of Contracting (Section 68)
2. Reimbursement to a Person Paying Money Payable by Other (Section 69)
3. Obligation of a Person Enjoying Benefit of Non-Gratuitous Act (Section 70)
4. Responsibility of the Finder of Goods (Section 71)
5. Liability of a Person Getting Benefit under Mistake or Coercion (Section 72)

Claim for Necessaries Supplied to a Person Incapable of Contracting (Section 68)

Section 68 of the Act provides that if someone supplies to a person who is incapable of entering into a contract (like a minor), or any one who he is legally bound to support, with necessaries suited to his conditions in life, the person who has furnished such supplies is entitled to be reimbursed from the property of such incapable person. Necessaries may vary according to the situations in the life of the incapable person or his peculiar circumstances at the time. The following are the relevant points which are to be considered:

1. The character of the goods supplied to an incapable person
2. The actual circumstances of the incapable person
3. The extent to which the person is already supplied with these goods

Example: A supplies B, a lunatic, with necessaries suitable to his condition in life. A is entitled to be reimbursed from B's property.

It should be noted that an incapable person's liability is not personal. It can only be recovered from his property, and if such person has no property, nothing can be recovered from him. The provision has been made to enable incapable persons to meet their primary needs if they have no ready cash at any time. Two points must be noted here:

1. The amount is recoverable only from the property of the incapable person and not from him personally.
2. The objects supplied must be necessaries. The incapable person cannot be held personally liable for the payment in India.

Reimbursement to a Person Paying Money Payable by Other (Section 69)

Section 69 provides, 'A person who is interested in the payment of money which another is bound by law to pay, and who therefore pays it, is entitled to be reimbursed by the other.'

Example: B holds land in Bengal, on a lease granted by A, the zamindar. The revenue payable by A to the government being in arrear, the government advertises his land for sale. Under the revenue law, the consequence of such sale will be the annulment of B's lease. B, to prevent the sale and the consequent annulment of his own lease, pays to the government the sum of due from A. A is bound to make good to B the amount so paid.

For the application of this section, the following two essentials are required:

1. **One should have interest in making payment:** The person who makes the payment, and then claims its reimbursement, must have an interest in making the payment. The purpose of making the payment should be bona fide protection of his interest by the plaintiff.
2. **Other person should be bound by law to pay:** The plaintiff should have an interest in the payment, and the defendant should be bound by law to pay the same. The provision is based on the principle that the plaintiff, having discharged the defendant's debt, is entitled to be reimbursed by him. If the plaintiff himself is liable to pay, then he cannot sue the defendant.

Example: In the case of Tulsa Kunwar vs. Jageshwar Prasad, A's goods were wrongfully attached to realize the arrears of government revenue due by B. A paid the dues to save his property. The court held that A was entitled to recover the amount from B.

Obligation of a Person Enjoying Benefit of Non-Gratuitous Act (Section 70)

Section 70 provides,

> Where a person lawfully does anything for another person, or delivers anything to him, not intending to do so gratuitously, and such other person enjoys the benefit thereof, the latter is bound to make compensation to the former in respect of, or to restore, the thing so done or delivered.

Section 70 provides that the following conditions must be fulfilled:

1. **A person should lawfully do something for another person, or should deliver something to him:** When a person does something for another person or

delivers something to him not intending to do so gratuitously, he is entitled to claim compensation for the same from such person. This point has been explained by Allahabad High Court in Indu Mehta vs. State of U.P. In this case, Ms Indu Mehta, an advocate, practising in a district court, was appointed as Assistant District Government Council (Criminal), in pursuance where of she rendered her services. Later, the appointment was found to be void. It was held that even though the said appointment was void, the state had enjoyed the benefit of the services rendered by Ms Mehta. The government was not entitled to recover back the fees already paid to her.

2. **The person making the payment or delivering the thing must not do so gratuitously; that is, he should expect payment for the same:** When nothing is done by the plaintiff but he merely refrains from doing something, that is not sufficient to entitle him to make a claim under Section 70. In the case of Kirori Mal vs. State of M.P., the court held that the plaintiff's claim under Section 70 could not be successful, as nothing positive was done by him to confer any benefit on the defendant.
3. **The other person should enjoy the benefit of this payment or the delivery of the thing:** For the action under Section 70, one of the essentials is that the defendant enjoyed the benefit of the work done or the thing delivered to him by the plaintiff. This has been explained in the case of Aries Advertising Bureau vs. C.T. Devaraj. The plaintiff, advertiser, made advertisements for circus at the instance of the circus owner. The advertiser was not a party to the contract between the financer and the circus owner. The advertiser brought an action against the financer to recover advertisement expenses. Since the financer did not enjoy any benefit from the advertisements, the financer cannot be made liable under Section 70 to pay advertisement charges to the advertiser.

However, it should be noted that Section 70 does not apply to persons incompetent to contract and as such, they are not under any obligation to compensate the other person for any benefit received by them. Both the parties must be competent to contract.

Responsibility of the Finder of Goods (Section 71)

Section 71 contemplates another quasi-contract situation; that is, when a person is the finder of the goods, there is no contract between him and the owner of the goods. Even then, some responsibility has been fixed by Section 71, as per which a person who finds goods belonging to another and takes them into custody is subject to the same responsibility as a bailee. A bailee here refers to a person who finds the goods and should keep it with safety and not mix it with his own goods and return it to the actual owner when found. There are two aspects of responsibility of the finder of goods:

1. **Finder's right of lien and compensation:** The finder of goods has the right to sue the owner for claiming compensation for preserving the goods in his custody. However, where the owner has offered a specific reward for the returns of goods lost, the finder may sue for such reward and may retain the goods until he receives it.
2. **Finder is a bailee against the true owner:** Finder is a bailee against the true owner only. He is not entitled to give the goods to anyone other than the true owner. If the finder of a jewel gives the jewel to a jeweller for being valued, he has the right to recover its value from the jeweller if the latter refuses to return the same.

Liability of a Person Getting Benefit under Mistake or Coercion (Section 72)

Section 72 covers a situation where money has been paid, or anything delivered, by one person to another either by mistake or under coercion. It provides that a person to whom money has been paid, or anything delivered, by mistake or under coercion, must repay or return it.

Example: A and B jointly owe ₹100 to C. A alone pays the amount to C, and B, without knowing this fact, pays ₹100 once again to C. Here, C is bound to repay the amount to B.

In Kotrabasappa vs. the Indian Bank, the Karnataka High Court held that if there is a mistaken entry in the account of a person by the bank and such person utilizes the amount, he is bound to repay or return that amount. According to Section 72, a person to whom money has been paid or anything delivered, by mistake or under coercion, must repay or return it. Money paid under a mistake is recoverable whether the mistake is of fact or of law.

Compensation for Failure to Discharge Obligations Created by Quasi-contracts

> Section 73 of the Act provides, 'When an obligation resembling those created by contract has been incurred and has not been discharged, any person injured by the failure to discharge it is entitled to receive the same compensation from the party in default, as if such person had contracted to discharge it and had broken his contract.'

So according to this section, the person failing to discharge a quasi-contractual obligation is liable to pay same compensation to the other party as is payable in the case of breach of a contract. So a person is bound to discharge obligations created by a quasi-contract.

CONTINGENT CONTRACTS

According to Section 31, 'A "contingent contract" is a contract to do or not to do something, if some event, collateral to such contract, does or does not happen.' When a contract is dependent or conditional upon the happening or non-happening of a certain future event, it is contingent. In other words, the performance of a contract becomes due only after the happening or non-happening of some uncertain event. Such a contract is known as a contingent contract.

Example: X contracts to pay Y ₹50,000 if Y's house is burnt. This is a contingent contract.

In the case of Bashir Ahmad vs. Government of Andhra Pradesh, the court held that if consideration is to be paid in instalments, and the agreement is not dependent on the happening of an event, then the contract is not contingent and the plaintiff has the right to recover the amount.

The condition which is collateral to the performance of a contract can be a condition precedent or a condition subsequent. Condition precedent is one which has to be satisfied first and then performance can be demanded. Condition subsequent is one which has to be satisfied after the formation of the contract. In the case of Velammal vs. Daivasigamani, the court held that if the contingency of a contract was neither pleaded by the defendant in the written statement nor argued before the trial court, the plea for the same could not be raised in appeal.

Essentials of a Contingent Contract

Section 31 of the Act and various decisions of courts provide for following essentials of a contingent contract:

1. **It is a valid contract:** The basic requirement is that there must be a valid contract between the parties which fulfils all the essential requirements of a valid contract as explained under Section 10 of the Act.
2. **It depends on happening or non-happening of a future event:** The contract should be dependent on the happening or non-happening of an event in the future. The parties to the contract should not be in the control of the outcome of the contract.
3. **The event should be uncertain:** The first condition regarding a contingent contract is that the event upon which the performance of the contract depends must be an uncertain event. If it is a certain event, the contract is not a contingent contract.
4. **The event is collateral to the main contract:** The event upon which the performance depends should not form part of reciprocal promises that constitute a contract. The event should be independent or ancillary to the contract.
5. **The event should not be the discretion of the promisor:** If the performance of a contract depends upon the sweet will or discretion of the promisor, the contract is not a contingent one. Discretion of one party is not an event for the purpose of a contingent contract.

Enforcement of Contingent Contracts (Sections 32–36)

1. **Happening of a future uncertain event:** According to Section 32, 'Contingent contracts to do or not to do something if an uncertain future event happens cannot be enforced unless and until that event has happened. If the event becomes impossible, such contract becomes void.'
   Example: X makes a contract with Y to buy Y's horse if X survives Z. This contract cannot be enforced unless Z dies in X's lifetime.
2. **Non-happening of a future event:** According to Section 33, if a contract is dependent upon the non-happening of a future event, it can be enforced only when that event becomes impossible. Contingent contracts to do or not to do anything if uncertain future event does not happen can be enforced when the happening of that event becomes impossible and in no case earlier to that. However, if the event happens or does not become impossible, law cannot enforce the contract.
   Example: X agrees to pay Y a sum of money if a certain ship does not return. The ship is sunk. The contract can be enforced as the return of ship becomes impossible.
3. **Event depends on the conduct of a human being:** Section 34 provides,

   > If the future event on which a contract is contingent is the way in which a person will act at an unspecified time, the event shall be considered to become impossible when such person does anything which renders it impossible that he should so act within any definite time, or otherwise than under further contingencies.

   When the event is linked with the future conduct of a person, the event shall be considered to have become impossible if that person does anything which makes it impossible that he could act in that way in any definite time or without further contingencies being fulfilled.

Example: X agrees to pay Y a sum of money if Y marries Z. Z marries P. The marriage of Z and Y must be considered impossible, although Z can marry Y after P's death.

4. **Happening of a specified event within a fixed time:** According to Section 35 of the Act, 'Contingent contracts to do or not to do anything, if a specified uncertain event happens within a fixed time, become void if, at the expiration of the time fixed, such event has not happened, or if, before the time fixed, such event becomes impossible.'
5. **Non-happening of a specified event within a fixed time:** According to Section 35 of the Act,

   > Contingent contracts to do or not to do anything, if a specified uncertain event does not happen within a fixed time, may be enforced by law when the time fixed has expired, and such event has not happened, or before the time fixed has expired, if it becomes certain that such event will not happen.

   In the case of a contingent contract dependent upon non-happening of an event within a fixed time, the contract cannot be enforced within the fixed time. It can be enforced only if the event does not happen within a fixed time or if it becomes certain that such event will not happen.
6. **Agreements contingent upon an impossible event:** Section 36 of the Act provides that a contingent agreement to do or not to do anything if the impossibility of an event is known or not known to the parties at the time of agreement is void. A contract dependent on an impossible event is void. It can never be enforced, as the impossible event is void because it can never be enforced, as the impossible event will never happen.

Differences between a Wagering Agreement and a Contingent Contract

Contingent contracts and wagering agreements are dependent on an uncertain event. Even then a wagering agreement is void but a contingent contract is enforceable by law. The following are the main points of difference between the two:

Reasons	*Wagering Agreement*	*Contingent Contract*
Meaning	It is an agreement where one party promises to pay something on happening of some uncertain event in consideration of other party's promise to pay if that event does not happen. (Section 30)	It is a contract to do or not to do something if some event collateral to such contract does or does not happen. (Section 31)
Nature	Every agreement is of a contingent nature.	Not every contract may be of a wagering nature.
Enforceability	A wagering agreement is void and illegal.	A contingent contract is valid.
Reciprocal promises	A wagering agreement always consists of reciprocal promises.	It may not contain reciprocal promises.

Reasons	*Wagering Agreement*	*Contingent Contract*
Effect of future event	A future event is the sole determining factor in a wagering agreement.	In a contingent contract, a future event is collateral.
Interest in the subject matter	Except for winning or losing of money or money's worth, the parties to a wagering agreement have no other interest in the subject matter.	Parties have interest in the subject matter. In the absence of such interest in the subject matter, a contingent contract may turn to be wagering in nature.
Performance of contract	No party intends to perform an agreement itself. They are only interested to pay or receive money or money's worth, and therefore a wagering agreement is considered as a game of chance.	In a contingent contract, parties intend to perform the contract themselves.

Meaning of Restitution

Restitution means to restore the benefit which a person has obtained and its main purposes are, first, to restore the position of victim, that is, 'plaintiff' in case of a contract, to original position which he enjoyed before entering into the contract and, second, to prevent the unjust enrichment of the defendant, that is, to stop him from making wrongful gains which he is not entitled as per the law to make.

Example: Mr Mohan entered into a contract with M/S Ram and Sons for a purchase of 200 ton of wheat. Mr Mohan paid an advance of ₹500,000 which was 10 per cent of the total value of the contract. Later at a future date, M/S Ram and Sons rescinded the contract due to some financial loss after which they were declared as insolvent and decided to wind up their business. Now, in this case, the contract becomes void and M/S Ram and Sons must return ₹500,000 to Mr Mohan.

The Doctrine of Restitution in the Indian Contract Act

Section 65 deals with doctrine of restitution and it relates to the obligation of the person who has received some advantage under a void agreement or contract. This doctrine is based on a very common rule of consideration which means that a person pays consideration only when he gets something in return. It applies only when an agreement at a subsequent stage is discovered to be void or when a contract becomes void later on by one person or the other. However, Section 65 will never come into play if the contract was void ab initio. The Supreme Court in the case of Kuju Collieries Ltd vs. Jharkhand Mines Ltd held that an agreement which was discovered to be void at a later stage will invite Section 65 into the picture and in such a case an advantageous person is bound to restore the disadvantaged party. In another case of The Bank of Rajasthan Ltd vs. Sh. Pala Ram Gupta, it was held that an agreement or contract which was void and illegal from the very beginning can never apply the provisions of this doctrine.

The doctrine of restitution includes the following key points:

1. One party has entered into a contract with another for consideration.
2. There was some consideration involved in the said contract.
3. Both parties were competent to enter into a contract.
4. Thereafter, one party failed to perform his part of the contract or the contract became void due to any unforeseen condition.
5. Now the party which has paid any consideration as the advance is entitled to recover the same from the other party, and the other party is not entitled to receive an unfair advantage over it.

Exceptions

- **Where an agreement is known to be void:** This doctrine will not be applied for an agreement known to be void, for example, where an agreement is for some illegal act or an impossible act like an agreement that A will pay B ₹10,000 if B picks stars from the sky. A pays ₹500 as security to B; this being an impossible act to perform, A cannot recover even his ₹500.
- **Where an agreement has been entered into between incompetent persons:** Contract entered into between incompetent persons like a person suffering from insanity, intoxication or a minor will not invite this doctrine to play.
- **Where the party is required to give some earnest money as security and later on defaults:** This provision deals with a situation like paying application money for a residential scheme. Now if a person fails to pay future allotment money, then his application money will also be forfeited and he cannot claim his earlier earnest money by revoking the doctrine of restitution.

Difference between Restitution and Compensation

Most of the times, these two terms are treated as synonyms, but the difference between them lies in the manner in which the monetary award is calculated; for instance, in compensation the award is calculated based on how much loss the plaintiff suffered, whereas in restitution the award is calculated based on how much gains the defendant has earned. However, on certain occasions on the discretion of the judge based on the facts of a particular case, the judge can very much give a choice to the plaintiff to choose from restitution and compensation. Restitution involves restoring the position of the affected party to his original position before entering into the contract, and one party is not entitled to have an unfair advantage over the other. By enforcing the provisions of Section 65, he can very much claim compensation or restitution as the case may be.

Test Questions

1. 'A quasi-contract is not a contract at all. It is an obligation which the law creates.' Discuss.
2. What do you understand by a quasi-contractual obligation? Amplify and state the quasi-contracts under the Contract Act.

3. What are quasi-contracts? Enumerate the quasi-contracts provided for by the Indian Contract Act.
4. What are the rights and duties of a finder of goods?
5. Define a contingent contract. Discuss the rules relating to the enforcement of contingent contracts.
6. Discuss the points of distinction between a contingent contract and a wagering agreement.
7. To what extent the impossibility of the contingency affects the performance of the contract?

PRACTICAL PROBLEMS

1. K was levied a sales tax on his forward transactions in bullion which he paid. The levy of this tax was declared ultra vires. K demanded refund of the amount of the sales tax on the ground that payment was made under a mistake of law. Will he succeed?
   Hint. Yes. K will succeed. Section 72 of the Indian Contract Act provides, 'A person to whom money has been paid, or anything delivered, by mistake or under coercion, must repay or return it.' Money paid under a mistake is recoverable whether the mistake is of fact or of law. A similar decision was given in the case of Kanhaiya Lal vs. Sales Tax Officer.
2. A, a tradesman, leaves his goods at B's house by mistake. B treats the goods as his own and appropriates them. Can A file a suit against B for the price of such goods?
   Hint. Yes. Section 72 of the Indian Contract Act imposes a quasi-contractual obligation on the person to whom money has been paid or anything delivered by mistake to repay or return it. Hence, in the given case, B should return the goods to A or pay for it.
3. A finds a man B lying unconscious on the road and fetches C, a doctor, to attend him. Does C has any right to be paid for his services against A or B?
   Hint. C should press his claim for payment of his services against B under provisions of Section 70 of the Indian Contract Act.
4. G wrongfully attached the goods belonging to A in order to realize arrears of the government revenue due. A paid the amount to save the goods from sale. Can A recover the amount?
   Hint. Yes. A is entitled to recover the amount from G. The case illustrating the rule is Abid Husain vs. Ganga Sahai.
5. A agrees to sell land to B at a price to be fixed by C. C refuses to fix the price. Is the contract enforceable?
   Hint. No. (Section 34)
6. During his wife's lifetime, A promised to marry B when his wife dies. The wife died, but A refused to marry B. Does B has any remedy?
   Hint. No. A's promise is not valid.
7. A enters into a contract with B to construct a building for a fixed price. B has to supply the necessary timber. B fails to supply the timber and the work cannot be executed by A. Can A sue for compensation for the loss caused to him?
   Hint. B is bound to compensate A for the loss caused to A. Here, the promise is mutual and dependent.

UNIT II

The Indian Contract Act, 1872: Special Contract

12

CHAPTER

Contract of Indemnity and Guarantee

Learning Objectives

- To understand the meaning of a contract of indemnity and rights of an indemnity holder
- To understand the rights and liabilities of an indemnifier
- To understand the meaning of a contract of guarantee, and types of guarantee
- To understand the meaning of continuing guarantee and its revocation
- To understand the difference between indemnity and guarantee contracts
- To understand the meaning of a surety, and his rights and liabilities
- To understand the meaning of discharge of surety
- To understand the meaning of a surety as a favoured debtor

CONTRACT OF INDEMNITY

Indemnity means protection against loss by way of a promise to pay for loss of money and goods. To indemnify means to compensate or make good the loss. The object of a contract of indemnity is essentially to protect the promisee against the anticipated loss. Section 124 defines a contract of indemnity as 'a contract by which one party promises to save the other from loss caused to him by the conduct of the promisor himself, or by the conduct of any other person'. The person who promises or undertakes to indemnify or make good the loss is called 'indemnifier' or 'promisor'. The person whose loss is to be made good is called 'indemnified'. He is also called 'indemnity holder' or 'promisee'. A contract of indemnity is really a class of contingent contracts.

Example: X contracts to indemnify Y against the consequences of any proceedings which Z may take against Y in respect of a certain sum of ₹65,000. This is a contract of indemnity. X is the indemnifier or promisor. Y is the indemnified or promisee. The contract between X and Y is a contract of indemnity.

In the case of United India Insurance Co. Ltd vs. M/S Aman Singh Munshi Lal, the court held that the goods insured will be liable for the loss incurred to the indemnifier as it was covered within the insurance contract.

Position under English Law

The English law defines *indemnity* as 'a promise to save another from loss caused as a result of a transaction entered into at the instance of the promisor'. In other words, indemnity includes the loss caused by events or accidents such as death, disability, destruction by fire, cyclone and so on, the occurrences of which do not depend upon the conduct of human beings. However, the Indian Contract Act does not provide that there can be an implied contract of indemnity. Section 124 should be extended to include cases of loss caused by events which may or may not depend on the conduct of any person. It should also provide clearly that the promise might also be implied.

Essentials of a Contract of Indemnity

A valid contract of indemnity should fulfil the following conditions:

1. There must be two parties, namely the indemnifier and the indemnified.
2. There must be a promise to save the other party from some loss.
3. The loss may be due to the promisee himself or any other person.
4. A contract of indemnity has to be express.
5. A contract of indemnity, being a species of a general contract, must fulfil all the essentials of a valid contract such as free consent, competence of parties, lawful object and lawful consideration.

Rights of an Indemnity Holder

Section 125 deals with the rights of an indemnity holder. He can bring an action against the indemnifier (the promisor) to recover the damages, compensation and so on. As per Section 125, an indemnity holder acting within the scope of his authority is entitled to the following rights:

1. **Right to recover damages:** An indemnity holder is entitled to recover from the indemnifier all damages which he is compelled to pay in any suit in respect of any matter covered by the contract of indemnity.
2. **Right to recover costs:** The indemnified is entitled to recover from the indemnifier all costs which he is compelled to pay in filing a suit or defending a suit. The indemnified in these cases should have acted prudently and with some reason.
3. **Right to recover sums paid under compromise:** An indemnity holder is entitled to recover from the indemnifier all sums which he has paid under the terms of a compromise suit. The said compromise suit should not be adverse to the interest and benefit to the indemnifier.
4. **Right to sue for specific performance:** An indemnity holder is entitled to sue the indemnifier for the specific performance of a contract if he has incurred absolute liability and the contract covers such liability.

It has been held that the rights of an indemnity holder, under Section 125, are not exhaustive. An indemnity holder may be entitled to other equitable reliefs as well.

Rights of an Indemnifier

There is no provision in the Contract Act about an indemnifier's rights. The rights of an indemnifier refer to terms and conditions of the contract under which he has agreed to indemnify. However, by reading Section 141, which deals with the rights of a surety and as per the provisions of the English law, the rights of an indemnifier are virtually the same as those of a surety in a contract of guarantee.

Indemnifier's Liability

There has been a controversy regarding the question that whether an indemnifier can be held liable for anything or not. The Indian Contract Act does not have any provision regarding the time of the commencement of an indemnifier's liability and the quantum of liability under the contract of indemnity. Further, in the case of Gajanan Moreshwar vs. Moreshwar Madan, the Bombay High Court had concluded that the rights of an indemnity holder should be more defined and the remedies to him should be indicated even in the cases of where he has not been sued. Therefore, the court of equity held that the indemnity holder was entitled to get the indemnifier to pay off as soon as his liability became absolute. Therefore, if the indemnified had incurred a liability and that liability was absolute, he was entitled to call upon the indemnifier to save him from that liability and pay it off. Justice Chagla further held that the provisions of Section 124 and 125 are not exhaustive and the courts would apply the equitable principle. Therefore, if an indemnified has incurred a liability and that liability is absolute, he is entitled to call upon the indemnifier to save him from that liability and to pay it off.

CONTRACT OF GUARANTEE

A contract of guarantee is also called a 'contract of surety ship'. It is entered into for enabling a person to get a loan or goods on credit or an employment. Section 126 defines a contract of guarantee as 'a contract to perform the promise, or discharge the liability, of a third person in case of his default'. There is a contract to perform the promise of another person or discharge his liability in case of his default. A guarantee may be either oral or written.

Parties in a Contract of Guarantee

In a contract of guarantee, there are three parties. They are as follows:

1. **Surety:** The person who gives the guarantee is called the 'surety'.
2. **Principal debtor:** The person in respect of whose default the guarantee is given is called the 'principal debtor'.
3. **Creditor:** The person to whom the guarantee is given is called the 'creditor'.

Nature of a Contract of Guarantee

A contract of guarantee is a tripartite agreement among a principal debtor, creditor and surety. In it, there are three collateral contracts: (a) between a creditor and a principal debtor,

(b) between a surety and a creditor and (c) between a surety and a principal debtor. Guarantee may be specific or continuing.

Requisites of a Valid Guarantee

The following are the essentials of a valid contract of guarantee:

1. **Requirements of a valid contract:** The essentials of a valid contract such as competence of parties, free consent and lawful object must be present to make the contract of guarantee enforceable by law.
2. **The contract must be supported by consideration:** Like every other contract, a contract of guarantee must be supported by consideration. However, law presumes that considerations received by the principal debtor are sufficient consideration for surety. There need not be direct consideration between the surety and the creditor.
3. **There must be someone primarily liable:** There must be a primary liability on someone other than a surety. There must be someone liable as a principal debtor, and the surety undertakes to be liable on his default. If that liability does not exist, there cannot be a contract of guarantee.
4. **There must be utmost good faith:** A contract of guarantee is a contract of absolute good faith. So the guarantee obtained by means of misrepresentation or concealment of material facts by a creditor is invalid. A surety ought to be acquainted with the whole contract entered into with his principal.
5. **The contract may be oral or in writing:** Section 126 explains that a contract of guarantee may be either written or oral. It will not make any difference to its validity.
6. **Concurrence:** A contract of guarantee requires concurrence of all the three parties to it, namely the principal debtor, the creditor and the surety. The surety appears at the request of the principal debtor.

Types of Guarantee

The function of a contract of guarantee is to enable a person to get a loan or goods on credit or an employment. It may cover one transaction or a number of transactions. Therefore, a contract of guarantee may be of any of the following types:

1. **Existing guarantee:** A guarantee which is given for an existing or past debt or obligations is known as existing guarantee or 'retrospective guarantee'.
2. **Future guarantee:** A guarantee which is given for a future debt or obligation is called future or 'prospective guarantee'.
3. **Fidelity guarantee:** A guarantee which is given for the good conduct or honesty of a person employed in a particular office is called 'fidelity guarantee'.
4. **Specific guarantee:** A guarantee which extends to a single transaction is called a specific or simple guarantee. It ends when the debt is duly discharged or the promise is duly performed.
5. **Continuing guarantee:** A continuing guarantee is one which extends to a series of transactions.

Continuing Guarantee

Section 129 defines a continuing guarantee as 'a guarantee which extends to a series of transactions' and is not exhausted or confined to a single credit transaction. It is, thus, prospective in its operation. It is just a standing offer. Under a continuing guarantee, the surety is prima facie liable in respect of any of the successive transactions which come within its scope. Whether a guarantee is continuing or not depends upon the language of guarantee and the surrounding circumstances.

Examples: X guarantees payment to a tea dealer to the amount of ₹10,000 for any tea transaction he may, from time to time, supply to Z. Y supplies Z with tea to the value of ₹10,000 and Z pays Y for it. Afterwards, Y supplies Z with tea to the value of ₹20,000. Z fails to pay. The guarantee given by X was a continuing guarantee, and he is accordingly liable to Y to the extent of ₹10,000 only.

Revocation of a Continuing Guarantee

The revocation of a continuing guarantee means the cancellation of the guarantee. On revocation, the liability of the surety ends. A continuing guarantee may be revoked in any of the following ways:

1. **By notice of revocation:** A surety may revoke a continuing guarantee by giving a notice of revocation to the creditor. Section 130 provides, 'A continuing guarantee may at any time be revoked by the surety, as to future transactions, by notice to the creditor.'
2. **By death of surety:** Section 131 explains, 'The death of the surety operates, in the absence of any contract to the contrary, as a revocation of a continuing guarantee, so far as regards future transactions.' Guarantee is automatically revoked or cancelled on the surety's death. But the estate of the surety is liable for all transactions entered into prior to the death of the surety unless there was a contract to the contrary. No notice of death is required to be given to the creditor.
3. **By variance in the terms of contract:** Section 133 provides, 'Any variance, made without the surety's consent, in the terms of the contract between the principal debtor and the creditor, discharges the surety as to the transactions subsequent to the variance.' In the case of Amrit Lal vs. State Bank of Travancore, the court held that the surety will be discharged only when the variance in the contract is within the meaning of Section 133. If it is not so, then the surety will not be discharged.
4. **By release or discharge of the principal debtor:** The surety is discharged by any contract between the creditor and principal debtor, by which the principal debtor is released or by any act or omission of the creditor, the legal consequence of which is the discharge of the principal debtor. In this case, the surety will automatically be discharged.
5. **By creditor's act or omission impairing surety's eventual remedy:** According to Section 139 of the Act,

> Discharge of surety by creditor's act or omission impairing surety's eventual remedy. If the creditor does any act which is inconsistent with the rights of the surety, or omits to do an act which his duty to the surety requires him to do, and the eventual remedy of the surety himself against the principal debtor is thereby impaired, the surety is discharged.

6. **By loss of security:** Section 141 provides,

> A surety is entitled to the benefit of every security which the creditor has against the principal debtor at the time when the contract of suretyship is entered into.... If the creditor loses, or without the consent of the surety, parts with such security, the surety is discharged to the extent of the value of the security.

In the case of R. Lilavati vs. Bank of Baroda & Ors, the court held that if the securities are lost without the fault of a creditor, then it will not discharge the surety from his liability.

DIFFERENCES BETWEEN INDEMNITY AND GUARANTEE CONTRACTS

A contract of indemnity differs from a contract of guarantee in following respects:

1. **Parties:** In a contract of indemnity, there are two parties only. They are the indemnity holder and the indemnifier. In a contract of guarantee, there are three parties, that is, the creditor, the principal debtor and the surety.
2. **Number of contracts:** There is only one contract in the case of a contract of indemnity, and that is between the indemnifier and the indemnified. But in the case of a contract of guarantee, there are three contracts: one between the creditor and the principal debtor, another between the creditor and the surety, and the third, an implied contract between the principal debtor and the surety. Thus, an indemnity contract is a simple or single contract, while a guarantee contract is a compound contract.
3. **Purpose of contract:** A contract of indemnity is for making good the loss suffered by a party to it. It provides security against loss. A contract of guarantee, on the other hand, is for the security of the creditor. It provides security to the creditor against default by the principal debtor.
4. **Nature of liability:** The liability of an indemnifier is primary in the case of a contract of indemnity. The indemnifier undertakes to discharge the liability in any event. In the case of a contract of guarantee, however, the liability of the surety is only collateral or secondary. It is only the principal debtor who is primarily liable for the contract.
5. **Acting upon request:** In a contract of indemnity, the indemnifier voluntarily accepts to indemnify the indemnified. In the case of a contract of guarantee, the surety gives guarantee to the creditor at the request of the principal debtor.
6. **Existing liability:** In the case of indemnity, there is no existing liability. It is only a contingency. The indemnifier becomes liable on the happening of the contingency. But in the case of guarantee, the liability already exists. There is an existing debt or duty, the performance of which is guaranteed by the surety. Thus, in the case of indemnity, the liability is contingent, while in the case of guarantee, the liability is subsisting.
7. **Interest in the transaction:** In the case of indemnity, the promisor has some interest in the transaction apart from indemnity. But in the case of guarantee, the surety has no other interest in the transaction. He is not connected with the contract except by means of the promise to pay the debt.
8. **Right to sue third parties:** In indemnity, the indemnifier cannot sue a third party for loss in his own name. He can sue only in the name of the indemnity holder. But in

the case of guarantee, the surety can sue the principal debtor in his own name after discharging the debtor's liabilities. He steps into the shoes of the debtor and creditor after discharging the debtor's liabilities.

RIGHTS OF A SURETY

A surety has certain rights against the creditor, the principal debtor and his co-sureties.

Rights against the Creditor

The following are the various rights of a surety against the creditor:

1. **Right to insist on creditor suing:** At any time after the guaranteed debt has become due, and before being called upon to pay, the surety may insist upon the creditor suing the principal debtor to recover the guaranteed debt.
2. **Right of exoneration:** In the case of fidelity guarantee, the surety can call upon the creditor or the employer to dismiss the employee in the event of his proved dishonesty. In that case, the surety is exonerated.
3. **Right to claim securities:** The surety is entitled to the benefit of every security held by the creditor at the time of making the contract, whether the existence of the security is or is not known to him. If such security is lost or parted with or without the consent of the surety, the surety is discharged to the extent of the value of the security. However, if the security is lost for reasons beyond the control of the creditor, such as an act of god and accident, the surety is not discharged.
4. **Right of subrogation:** 'Subrogation' implies the substitution of one person for another. After the surety pays the guaranteed debt or performs the guaranteed duty, he becomes entitled to every remedy which the creditor had against the principal debtor.
5. **Right to set-off:** Set-off implies a counter-claim or deduction from the loan. The surety can demand the creditor to give credit in respect of all amounts paid by the principal debtor. This is known as the surety's right to set off, and this right to set off is also extended in respect to counter-claims made by the debtor as against the creditor.

Rights against the Principal Debtor

The following are the various rights of the surety against the principal debtor:

1. **Right to indemnity:** In case of a contract of guarantee, there is an implied promise by the principal debtor to indemnify the surety. The surety has a right to recover from the principal debtor whatever he has legitimately paid under the contract to the creditor. But if the surety pays an amount which the principal debtor is not liable to pay, he cannot recover from the principal debtor. The surety, thus, cannot recover sums which he has paid wrongfully.
2. **Right to seek relief from liability:** Before the guaranteed debt is paid, the surety has a right to compel the principal debtor to relieve him from the liability by paying off the debt.

Right against Co-sureties

The following are the various rights of a surety against co-sureties:

1. **Right to equal contribution:** The co-sureties are liable to contribute equally, whether they are co-sureties jointly or severally. But this rule is subject to any contract to the contrary. Section 146 of the Contract Act provides that when a surety has paid more than his share of the debt to the creditor, he is entitled to contribution from the co-sureties who are equally bound to pay with him.
Example: A, B and C are sureties to D for the sum of ₹3,000 lent to E. E makes default in payment. A, B and C are liable, as between themselves, to pay ₹1,000 each.
2. **Right of contribution if different sums:** Where the co-sureties have agreed to guarantee different sums, they are bound under Section 147 to contribute equally up to the maximum limit fixed by them.
Example: A, B and C as sureties for D enter into three several bonds, each in a different penalty, namely A in the penalty of ₹10,000, B of ₹20,000 and C of ₹40,000 conditioned for D's duly accounting to E. D makes default to the extent of ₹30,000. A, B and C are each liable to pay ₹10,000.
3. **Right to share benefits of security:** Sometimes, at the time of guarantee, one of the co-sureties receives a security from the principal debtor, or on payment of the debt, he receives security from the creditor. In such cases, the co-sureties are entitled to share the benefits of security.

Discharge of Surety

A surety is said to be discharged from liability when his liability comes to an end. He is discharged from liability by the acts of parties either to the guarantee contract or by operation of law. A surety may be discharged by the following.

Discharge of a Surety by Revocation of a Contract of Guarantee

Revocation means withdrawal or taking back. The revocation of a guarantee contract takes place in any of the following circumstances:

1. **Revocation by giving a notice:** A specific guarantee cannot be revoked by the surety if the liability has already accrued. The surety as to future transactions may at any time revoke a continuing guarantee by giving notice to the creditor.
2. **Revocation on death:** A continuing guarantee is revoked by the death of the surety so far as future transactions are concerned. The termination is effective for future transactions only. The surety's heirs remain liable for liability already incurred.
3. **Revocation by novation:** A contract of guarantee may be discharged by novation, that is, substitution of an old contract of guarantee by a new contract. The new contract may be entered into either between the same parties or between one of the old parties and a new party.

Discharge of Surety by the Conduct of the Creditor

A surety is discharged by the improper conduct of the creditor in the following cases:

1. **Variation (alteration) in terms without the consent of the surety:** The letter of guarantee given by the surety to the creditor binds him. Any alteration made without the surety's consent in the terms of the contract between the principal debtor and the creditor will discharge the surety as to transactions subsequent to the variation. In the case of Pratapsingh vs. Keshavlal, X agreed to give a loan to Y on the security of Z for ₹50,000; later, X extended the time for loan repayment. It was held that Z was discharged as the surety.
2. **Release or discharge of the principal debtor:** A surety will be discharged if the creditor makes a fresh contract with the principal debtor by which the principal debtor is released. The release of the principal debtor amounts to the release of the surety also. This is because the surety's liability is collateral with that of the principal debtor. But if the principal debtor is discharged due to insolvency, this will not operate as discharge of the surety.
3. **Compounding by the creditor with the principal debtor:** According to Section 135 of the Contract Act, 'A contract between the creditor and the principal debtor, by which the creditor makes a composition with, or promises to give time to, or not to sue, the principal debtor, discharges the surety, unless the surety assents to such contract.'
4. **Impairing surety's right:** The term 'impairing' implies damaging or diminishing the rights of the surety. It is the duty of the creditor not to do anything which is inconsistent with the right of the surety. If the creditor does anything which is inconsistent with the rights of the surety, the surety is discharged. In simple words, if the creditor fails to protect the surety's rights, the surety is discharged of his liability.
5. **Loss of security:** If the creditor has any security against the principal debtor, the surety is entitled to its benefit; if the creditor loses or parts with such security without the consent of the surety, the surety is discharged to the extent of the value of security.

Discharge of Surety by Invalidation of a Contract

A contract of guarantee, like any other contract, may be avoided if it is either void or voidable. A contract of guarantee is invalid in the following cases:

1. **Guarantee obtained by misrepresentation:** Any guarantee which the creditor has obtained by means of misrepresentation is invalid. Surety, in such a case, will be discharged from liability.
2. **Guarantee obtained by concealment of facts:** Any guarantee which the creditor has obtained by concealment of material facts is invalid. The surety in such a case will be discharged.
3. **Not supported by consideration:** If a contract between the creditor and the principal debtor fails for want of consideration, the surety is discharged.
4. **Co-surety not joining:** If a co-surety fails to join according to the terms of the contract, the surety is discharged.

When Surety Will Not Be Discharged

A surety will, however, not be discharged from his liability in the following cases:

1. **Release of a co-surety:** When there are co-sureties, release of one co-surety by the creditor does no discharge the other sureties.
2. **Forbearance to sue:** Mere forbearance on the part of the creditor to sue the principal debtor or enforce any other remedy against him does not, in the absence of any provision in the contract of guarantee to the contrary, discharge the surety.
3. **Negligence of the creditor:** Negligence or delay on the part of the creditor to sue the principal debtor does not discharge the surety.
4. **Agreement by the creditor with a third person to give time:** When there is a contract to give time to the principal debtor, the surety is not discharged because his liability will continue for such extended period also.

Liability of a Surety

A surety is a person who has guaranteed the performance of the promise or discharge of the liability of a third person in the case of his default. Section 128 of the Contract Act defines the nature and extent of a surety's liability. The liability of the surety may be discussed under the following heads:

1. **Secondary liability:** The liability of the surety is only secondary, collateral, accessory or contingent. He becomes liable to the creditor only on default by the principal debtor. On becoming liable to the creditor by the default of the principal debtor, he would be in the same position as that of the principal debtor.
2. **Surety is a favoured debtor:** According to Lord Seaborne, 'A surety is undoubtedly and not unjustly an object of some favors at law and at equity.' It only means that the surety being a favoured debtor can insist on a rigid adherence to the terms of the contract and his obligation to the creditor. The surety can be made liable only to the extent specified in the contract, and he cannot be asked to perform any promise which he has not expressly undertaken. No liability can be thrust on the surety which is not covered by the contract.
3. **No privities of contract:** The law does not treat the principal debtor and surety on one platform. Therefore, any admission by the principal debtor or a judgment obtained against the principal debtor will not be enforceable against the surety without a special agreement to that effect.
4. **Liability is co-extensive:** Section 128 explains that the liability of the surety is co-extensive with that of the principal debtor, unless it is otherwise provided by the contract. The expression 'co-extensive' refers to the maximum extent of surety's liability. The amount of the liability of the surety is the same as that of the principal debtor. The liability of the surety will neither be more nor less than that of the principal debtor. The surety is liable for what the principal debtor is liable.
5. **Surety's right to limit the liability:** Although the liability of the surety is co-extensive with that of the principal debtor, he may limit his liability at the time of

entering into the contract. If the surety limits his liability to a fixed amount, he cannot be held liable for more than that, regardless of the amount due by the principal debtor.

6. **Liability for a minor's debt:** Where the guarantee contract is between the creditor and the principal debtor, who is a minor, the surety will be liable as if he is the principle debtor.
7. **Surety's liability in the case of a voidable contract:** Where the contract between the creditor and the principal debtor is voidable, the surety may not be discharged from liability.

Surety as a Favoured Debtor

A surety is a person who has guaranteed the due discharge of a liability or the performance of a promise of a third person in the case of his default. The Contract Act recognizes certain rights of the surety, besides imposing liability on him. The surety and the principal debtor do not constitute a single person in the eyes of law. A judgment against the principal debtor is not a judgment against the surety. As such, the surety is not bound by any admission made by the principal debtor. It is not open to the creditor to call upon the surety to pay under the contract unless the creditor has performed his part of the contract. It is also necessary to fulfil the conditions precedent to the surety's liability before making him liable.

Example: If the surety agrees to be only one of several co-sureties, he will not be liable unless the others also join him. The special position of the surety is recognized by giving him favoured treatment. He is considered with favour at both law and equity. His position is superior to that of the principal debtor. He is a privileged debtor.

The following provisions contained in the law of indemnity and guarantee bring out the fact that a surety is a favoured debtor:

1. **Surety's liability for payment:** A surety's liability arises only on the default of the principal debtor. Hence, it is rightly said, 'A surety's liability is secondary, collateral, accessory or contingent.' The surety cannot be called upon to pay unless the principal debtor has made a default.
2. **Extent of liability:** A surety's liability is co-extensive with that of the principal debtor. He is liable for those sums that the principal debtor is liable for. His liability cannot be more than that of the principal debtor. The maximum extent of the liability of the surety is limited to that of the principal debtor.
3. **Not responsible for fruitless litigation:** A surety is not liable for fruitless litigation the creditor may bring against the principal debtor unless the creditor has given a sufficient notice to this effect to the surety.
4. **Variation of terms without the consent of the surety:** A surety is liable only for what he has positively undertaken in the guarantee contract; any alteration made without the surety's consent in the terms of the contract between the principle debtor and the creditor will discharge the surety as to transactions subsequent to the variation.
5. **All remedies of the creditor:** A surety is entitled to every remedy which the creditor has against the principal debtor. The rights of surety stand not merely upon the contract but also upon natural justice.
6. **Right of exoneration:** In the case of fidelity guarantee, the surety can call upon the employer to dismiss the employee in the event of his proved dishonesty. In that case, the surety is exonerated from his liability.

7. **Not responsible for admissions of the principal debtor:** The judgment against the principal debtor is not a judgment against the surety. As such, the surety is not bound by any admission made by the principal debtor.
8. **Right to claim set-off:** The surety is also entitled to the benefit of any set-off or counter-claim which the principal debtor might possess against the creditor in respect of the same transaction.
9. **Right to indemnity:** In every contract of guarantee, there is an implied promise by the principal debtor to indemnify the surety. So the surety is entitled to demand from the principal debtor whatever he has paid under the guarantee.
10. **Contribution from co-sureties:** If there are two or more sureties, and one of them has paid the debt, he can recover from other the excess of what he has paid above his share.
11. **Right of marshalling:** In some cases, the creditor, in addition to the guarantee given by the surety, might have collected or obtained some securities from the principal debtor. In such cases, the surety can ask the creditor to first proceed against the securities obtained by him from the principal debtor before proceeding against the surety. In such cases, the surety will be liable only for deficiency, if any.

TEST QUESTIONS

1. Define a contract of indemnity. What are the essentials and legal rules for a valid contract of indemnity?
2. State the rights of an indemnity holder, when sued. Does the law confer any right on the indemnifier? If yes, state and explain.
3. When does the liability of an indemnifier commence? Explain, in detail, the different views in this regard.
4. Define a contract of guarantee. What are the essentials of a valid contract of guarantee? Explain the difference between a contract of indemnity and a contract of guarantee.
5. 'The liability of a surety is secondary. It is co-extensive with that of the principal debtor.' Discuss.
6. 'A surety is a favoured debtor.' Discuss.
7. 'There can be no contract of guarantee unless there is someone primarily liable.' Discuss.
8. What are the various kinds of guarantee?
9. State the nature and extent of a surety's liability. How and in what circumstances a surety is discharged forms his liability?
10. What are a surety's rights against the principal debtor and the creditor? Does he have any rights against co-sureties? If yes, enumerate them.

PRACTICAL PROBLEMS

1. A is employed as a cashier on a salary of ₹2,000 a month by a bank for a period of three years, C, standing the surety for A's good conduct. Nine months afterwards, when the financial position of the bank deteriorates, A agrees to accept a lower salary of ₹1,500 a month. Two months later, it is discovered that A has been misappropriating cash all through. What is the liability of C?

Hint. C is liable as a surety for the loss suffered by the bank due to misappropriations by A during the first nine months but not for misappropriation committed after the reduction in salary.

2. A advances ₹500 to a minor B on the guarantee of X. On demand for repayment, the borrower pleads minority. Can A recover the amount from X?
   Hint. Yes. The surety in such a case will be taken as the principal debtor. In this case, X is liable to A as B is a minor.
3. B is the principal debtor of A. C is the surety of the debt. A, the creditor, makes a promise to a neighbour of B to give time to B. Discuss the effect, if any, of this promise on the contract of guarantee.
   Hint. The surety is not discharged because the contract is with a third party and not with the debtor.
4. A guaranteed the honesty of a servant in the employment of B. The servant was guilty of dishonesty in the course of his service, but B continued to employ him and did not inform A of what had occurred. Subsequently, the servant committed further acts of dishonesty. B required A to make good the loss. Discuss the liability of A.
   Hint. In the given case, A cannot be held liable because of change of circumstances not brought to the notice of A having knowledge of the same. Under such circumstances, Section 139 of the Indian Contract Act becomes operative. It provides that if the creditor does any act which is inconsistent with the right of the surety, or omits to do any act which his duty to the surety requires him to do, and the eventual remedy of the surety himself against the principal debtor is thereby imparted, the surety is discharged. Thus, in the present case, the omission of the creditor to inform A of the servant's dishonesty and his conduit of continuing to employ him shall discharge the surety A.
5. A stood as the guarantor for B to the extent of ₹10,000 for discounting bills which are to be presented by B to C within a period of one year. A informs C not to discount the bills further after three months. C without taking this into account continues to discount the bills even after the instructions given by A. There was a default on the part of B to clear off the amounts received by him by discounting the bills after the revocation by A. Is A liable?
   Hint. The guarantee was a continuing guarantee for one year. A continuing guarantee may be revoked at any time by the surety as to further transactions by giving a notice to the creditor. Hence, A is not liable for the payment of bills discounted after the instructions given by him.

13 CHAPTER

Contract of Bailment

Learning Objectives

- To understand the meaning, features and classification of bailment
- To understand the duties and rights of a bailor and a bailee
- To understand the meaning of a lien and its kinds: particular and general lien
- To understand the differences between general and particular lien
- To understand termination of a lien
- To understand the meaning of a finder of goods and his rights and duties
- To understand termination of bailment
- To understand the meaning of a pledge
- To understand the rights and duties of a pledgor and a pledgee

BAILMENT

The term 'bailment' is derived from the French word *baillier*, which means to deliver or handover. Bailment is a delivery of goods by one person to another for a specific purpose. The goods are delivered with a condition that they shall be returned to the owner after the fulfilment of the purpose. Bailment involves change of possession and not transfer of ownership. Section 148 defines bailment as

> the delivery of goods by one person to another for some purpose, upon a contract that they shall, when the purpose is accomplished, be returned or otherwise disposed of according to the directions of the person delivering them. The person delivering the goods is called the 'bailor'. The person to whom they are delivered is called the 'bailee'.

The examples of a contract of bailment are delivering a watch or radio for repair, leaving a car or scooter at a parking stand, leaving luggage in a cloak room, delivering gold to a goldsmith for making ornaments, leaving garments with a dry cleaner and so on.

The essence of bailment is the transfer of possession. The ownership remains with the owner. There cannot be a bailment of immovable property.

Examples: X lends a book to Y to be returned after the examination. It is a contract of bailment between X and Y.

Essential Features of Bailment

The definition of bailment reveals certain essential features of bailment. They are as follows:

1. **Contract:** Bailment is created by a contract between two parties. The contract may be express or implied. But sometimes bailment may arise without a contract. Courts in many cases decided that there can be bailment without a contract. The Supreme Court in State of Bombay (Now Gujarat) vs. Memon Mahomed observed that it is not correct to say that there cannot be a bailment without a contract. 'A finder of goods of another has been held to be a bailee in certain circumstances.' Thus, the finder of goods is treated in law as a bailee of the lost article.
2. **Delivery of goods:** There must be delivery of goods by the bailor to the bailee. Delivery involves change of possession in legal sense. Mere custody of goods does not involve change of possession. Delivery of goods, which involves change of possession, may be either actual or constructive. In the case of actual delivery, the bailor hands over the physical possession of goods to the bailee. Delivery of gold to a goldsmith for making jewels is an instance of actual delivery. Constructive delivery, on the other hand, does not involve change of physical possession. Goods remain where they are. However, something is done which has the effect of putting the goods in the possession of the bailee.

   In the case of Ultzen vs. Nichols, an old customer went to a restaurant to have dinner. When he entered the room, a waiter took his coat without being asked and hung it on a hook behind him. When the customer was about to leave, he found the coat missing. In this case, the restaurant keeper was held liable. The waiter by taking coat in his possession assumed the responsibility as a bailee.
3. **Delivery of goods must be for some purpose:** The bailor should deliver the goods to the bailee for some purpose. The purpose may be lending, giving or depositing the goods for safe custody, security for a debt, repair or conversion of form. Moreover, where goods are delivered by mistake to a person, there is no bailment.
4. **Return of goods:** When the purpose for which the goods were delivered has been accomplished, the goods may be returned to the bailor either in the original form or in an altered form. If there is no contract to deliver back or otherwise to dispose of the goods according to the directions of the bailor, there is no bailment at all.
5. **Bailment relates only to moveable property:** Bailment is concerned with goods only. Goods mean every kind of movable property other than money. Thus, bailment does not relate to money. A deposit of money in a bank is not a bailment, as the bank is not bound to return the same notes and coins. Moreover, bailment does not relate to immovable property.
6. **Consideration:** Consideration for transactions of bailment may be in the form of money payment by the bailor to the bailee or in the form of the benefit derived by each other for valuable consideration. Detriment suffered by the bailor in parting with possession of goods is sufficient consideration to support the contract of bailment.

Classification of Bailment

A contract of bailment may be classified as follows:

1. **On the basis of benefits:** On this basis, bailment may be of two types:
   a. **Bailment for the benefit of bailor only:** In this case, the bailor for his exclusive benefit delivers goods. Delivery of some valuables to a neighbour for safe custody without charge is an example of bailment.
   b. **Bailment for the mutual benefit of both bailor and bailee:** In this case, the bailor for mutual benefit of both bailor and bailee gives goods. Giving a watch for repair is a good example of this type.
2. **On the basis of reward:** Bailment may be classified on the basis of charge or reward as follows:
   a. **Gratuitous bailment:** A gratuitous bailment is one in which neither the bailor nor the bailee is entitled to any remuneration. For example, lending of a book to a friend is a bailment without any charge or reward to anybody.
   b. **Non-gratuitous bailment:** It is also called 'bailment for reward'. It is a bailment in which either the bailor or the bailee is entitled to some remuneration. Furniture let out for hire, cloth given to a tailor for stitching and articles given to a person for repairs are examples of non-gratuitous bailment.

Duties of a Bailor

The provisions regarding the duties of a bailor are provided in Sections 150, 158 and 184 of the Indian Contract Act, which are as follows:

1. **Duty to disclose faults in goods bailed:** The bailor's duty to disclose faults in the goods bailed is different for gratuitous and non-gratuitous bailment. If the bailment is gratuitous, it is the duty of the bailor to disclose to bailee known faults in goods bailed. Failure to make such disclosure will make the bailor liable for damages arising to the bailee directly from such faults.
   Example: X lends a horse to Y, which X knows to be vicious. He does not disclose the fact to Y. Y is thrown and injured and the horse runs away. X is responsible to Y for the damage sustained.
   However, if the bailment is non-gratuitous, the bailor is responsible or liable for known as well as unknown faults in goods bailed. Section 150 clearly lays that if the goods are bailed for hire, the bailor is responsible for damage, whether he was or was not aware of the existence of such faults in the goods bailed.
   Example: A hires a carriage of B. The carriage is unsafe, though B is not aware of it, and A is injured. B is responsible to A for the injury.
2. **Duty to bear extraordinary expenses:** In the case of gratuitous bailment, it is the duty of the bailor to bear the necessary expenses incurred by the bailee for the purpose of bailment. However, in the case of non-gratuitous bailment, it is the duty of the bailor to bear extraordinary expenses only. The ordinary and reasonable expenses are to be borne by the bailee.
   Example: X delivers some gold ornaments to Y for converting them into new gold ornaments. Y is to receive no remuneration. Y incurs an expenditure of ₹1,000 in making jewellery. X must repay these expenses to Y.
3. **Duty to indemnify the bailee for loss:** If the bailee is compelled to return goods, in the case of gratuitous bailment, before the specified time and suffers a loss which

exceeds the benefit derived by him, it is the duty of the bailor to indemnify the bailee for such loss.

4. **Duty to make good the loss due to defect in title:** The bailor is bound to make good the loss suffered by the bailee due to defective title of bailor. The bailor's title to goods may be defective at the time of bailment, or at the time of receiving back goods, or at the time of giving directions regarding goods bailed. The bailor is liable to compensate the bailee for loss due to defective title.
5. **Duty to receive back the goods:** It is the duty of the bailor to receive back the goods bailed when the bailee returns them. If he refuses, the bailee has the right to receive compensation from him for the expenses incidental to safe custody of goods.

Rights of a Bailor

There are certain rights, which a bailor enjoys under a contract of bailment. These rights are as follows:

1. **Right of termination:** A bailor has a right to terminate the contract and claim damages, if any, if the bailee does not follow the conditions of the bailment. The bailor can terminate or put an end to the bailment only when the bailee does any act inconsistent with the conditions of the bailment.
2. **Right to demand restoration of goods lent gratuitously:** In the case of gratuitous bailment, the bailor has a right to demand goods back any time he chooses in spite of the fact that he had lent them for a fixed period or for a specific purpose. The bailee can, however, claim compensation from the bailor in the case of return of goods before the expiry of the agreed time.
   Example: A delivered his car to his friend B for one week. B got the petrol tank filled. The next day, A demanded the car back. A must compensate B for the price of petrol.
3. **Compensation from a wrongdoer:** If a wrongdoer does some harm to goods or deprives the bailee of the use of goods, the bailor may file a suit against him and recover compensation. However, the compensation shall be divided between the bailor and the bailee according to their rights.
4. **Right to get profit or any addition to goods bailed:** A bailor is entitled to any profit and any addition accruing from the goods bailed.
5. **Enforcement of duties imposed upon a bailee:** The duties of a bailee are the rights of a bailor. A bailor has a right to sue the bailee for the enforcement of bailee's duties and responsibilities in case he neglects his duties.

Duties of a Bailee

A bailee is a person to whom goods or articles are delivered for some temporary purpose under a contract of bailment. The following are his main duties:

1. **Duty to take reasonable care of the goods bailed:** The first and foremost duty of a bailee is to take care of the goods entrusted to him. Section 151 defines the scope and extent of care to be taken by a bailee. It prescribes a uniform standard of care in all cases

of bailment. The standard and the degree of care required from a bailee are the same whether the bailment is for reward or gratuitous. If a bailee takes reasonable care of the goods, as a man of ordinary prudence, he will be no more liable for any loss, destruction or deterioration of the goods bailed. He will be, however, liable for all losses arising out of his negligence. However, he cannot be held answerable for any act of nature, fire or tremors, or by public enemies. In the case of Shanti Lal vs. Tara Chand, X deposited his goods in Y's godown. On account of unprecedented floods, a part of the goods were damaged. It was held that Y was not liable for the loss.

2. **Duty not to make unauthorized use of the goods bailed:** A bailee is under a duty to use the goods according to the conditions of the contract of bailment or directions of the bailor. He should not use the goods in a manner inconsistent with the terms of the contract. Section 153 explains, 'A contract of bailment is voidable at the option of the bailor, if the bailee does any act with regard to the goods bailed, inconsistent with the conditions of bailment.'

   Example: A lends a horse to B only for riding. B drives the horse in a carriage. It is voidable at the option of A, and he can terminate the bailment contract.
3. **Duty not to mix the goods bailed with his own goods:** As a general rule, a bailee should not mix the goods of the bailor with his own goods. He should keep the bailor's goods separate from his own goods. If the bailee mixes his own goods with those of the bailor, the following rules apply:
   a. **Mixing goods with the consent of the bailor:** A bailee may mix the goods with the consent of the bailor. If the goods are mixed with the consent of the bailor, both shall have a proportionate interest in the mixture.
   b. **Mixing goods without the consent of the bailor:** If the goods are mixed without the consent of the bailor and the goods can be separated, the expenses of separation and any damage arising thereby are to be borne by the bailee.
   c. **Mixing goods without the consent of the bailor and not separable:** If the bailee, without the consent of the bailor, mixes the bailor's goods and such goods are not separable, the bailee is bound to compensate the bailor for the loss of goods.
4. **Duty not to set up adverse title:** A bailee cannot deny the title of the bailor and his right to bail. As per the Indian Evidence Act, a bailee is stopped from denying the title of the bailor. A bailee must hold goods on behalf of and for the bailor. He should not set up his own title or that of a third party. Even if the bailor has no title, the bailee cannot deny the title of the bailor unless he gets orders from the court.
5. **Duty to return the goods:** It is the duty of a bailee to return or deliver the goods, without demand, on the expiry of the time fixed or when the purpose is accomplished. If he does not return or deliver as directed by the bailor or tender the goods at the proper time, he becomes liable for any loss, destruction or deterioration of the goods even without negligence during the period it is detained.
6. **Duty to return profit or the addition to the goods bailed:** It is the duty of the bailee to return to the bailor any profit from or addition to the goods bailed. However, it is subject to a contract to the contrary.

Rights of a Bailee

The duties of a bailor are the rights of a bailee. As such, a bailee can, by suit, enforce the duties of a bailor. Some other rights of a bailee are as follows:

1. **Right to apply to court to stop delivery:** If a person other than the bailor claims the goods bailed, the bailee may apply to the court to stop the delivery of goods to the bailor, and to decide the title to the goods. This right is known as the 'right to interplead'.
2. **Right of action against trespassers:** If a third party or person wrongfully deprives the bailee of the use or possession of the goods bailed to him, he has a right to bring an action against that party.
3. **Right to indemnity:** A bailee is entitled to be indemnified by the bailor for any loss arising to him because of the bailor not being entitled to make bailment or to receive the goods back or to give directions regarding them. If the bailor has no title to the goods and the bailee delivers them back to the bailor in good faith, the bailee is not responsible to the owner in respect of such delivery.
4. **Right to claim compensation in case of faulty goods:** If a bailor does not disclose faults of the goods bailed, of which the bailor was aware, the bailee is entitled to damages arising directly from such faults.
5. **Right to claim necessary expenses:** A bailee can also claim all necessary expenses incurred by him for the purpose of gratuitous bailment.
6. **Right of delivery of goods to any one of several joint owners:** In the case of joint ownership of the goods bailed, the bailee has a right to return the goods to any one of the joint owners unless there is an agreement to the contrary.
7. **Right of a particular lien for payment of services:** Where a bailee has rendered any services in accordance with the purpose of bailment, involving the exercise of labour or skill in respect of goods bailed, he has, in the absence of a contract to the contrary, a right to retain such goods until he receives due remuneration for the service rendered by him. This right is restricted to the right of retaining the goods and not to their sale.
8. **Right of a general lien:** Bankers, factors, attorneys of high courts and policy brokers are entitled to retain as security for a general balance of account any goods bailed to them in the absence of a contract to the contrary. Even other types of bailees may also be given this right by a specific contract in this regard.

Meaning of a Lien

A 'lien' means the right to retain goods or property until some debt or claim is paid. The right of lien may arise by statute or by contract. In the case of bailment for some purpose, the bailee can detain the goods until the bailor pays his charges in respect of labour and skill used. Possession of goods is essential for exercising the right of lien. A bailee's lien is known as a 'possessory lien'.

Kinds of Lien

Lien are of two kinds which are as follows.

Particular Lien

A 'particular lien' means the right to retain particular goods until claims on account of those goods are paid. As a rule, the bailee is entitled to a particular lien.

Example: Where a bailor sends his car to the bailee for repair, the bailee has a lien on the car for the cost of repairs. Section 170 explains that where a bailee has rendered any service involving the exercise of labour or skill, he has a right to retain such goods until he receives his due remuneration. But this right is available only when there is no contract to the contrary.

Conditions for Exercising Particular Lien

The right of a particular lien is subject to the following conditions:

1. The bailee must have rendered some services involving the exercise of labour or skill in respect of goods bailed. There is no lien for custody charges or other charges for work not involving labour or skill.
2. The labour or skill must have led to improvement of the goods.
3. The services must have been performed in full and must be duly performed. Where the services are not rendered in accordance with the terms of the contract, the bailee cannot exercise his right of lien.
4. The bailee keeping the goods to enforce his lien cannot charge for keeping them. The right of lien is lost when possession is lost.
5. The lien cannot be claimed if there is an agreement to pay the money on a future date.

In the case of Andu vs. Maruti, it was laid down that there was no lien for safe custody charges because there was no exercise of labour or skill.

General Lien

A 'general lien' means the right to retain all the goods of the other party until all the claims of the holder are paid. Section 171 confers the right of general lien to bankers, factors, wharfingers, attorneys of high courts and policy brokers. These parties can exercise general lien against any goods under their possession and for any sum legally due on a general balance of account. Bankers can have a general lien over bank accounts balances subject to the approval and consent of the customer. In Kunhan Mayan & Ors vs. the Bank of Madras, Kunhan deposited certain jewels with the Bank of Madras to secure certain debt. After payment of this debt, he demanded the return of these jewels from the bank. He was still indebted to the bank for certain other debts. On bank's refusal to return the jewels, it was held that Kunhan was not entitled to recover unless he proved that the bank had agreed to give up its general lien.

According to the provisions of Section 171, a general lien is available only to the specified categories of bailees. These provisions are as follows:

1. **Lien of bankers:** The general lien of bankers attaches to all goods and securities deposited with them as bankers by a customer or third person on a customer's account, provided there is no contract, express or implied, inconsistent with such lien.
2. **Lien of factors:** A factor is an agent entrusted with the possession of goods for the purpose of sale on behalf of the principal. He usually sells the goods in his own name. He has a general lien on goods of his principal.

3. **Wharfingers:** He is a person who keeps the goods belonging to another in his godown or wharf place adjoining water used for purposes of loading and unloading of goods for safe custody.
4. **Attorneys of high courts:** There are solicitors who act legally for others. An attorney or a solicitor is entitled to a general lien until his professional fee and other costs incurred by him are paid. But such a lien is available only for professional fees and not for ordinary loans and advances.
5. **Policy brokers:** An insurance agent has a general lien on the policies in his possession not only for any premium due on the policies but also for other charges due for the purpose. His lien extends to any balance on any insurance account due to him from the person who employed him to affect the policy.

Differences between Particular Lien and General Lien

Both general lien and particular lien are possessory liens. However, there are certain differences between the two. They are as follows:

	Particular Lien	*General Lien*
1.	A particular lien is a contractual lien. It arises out of a contract between a bailor and a bailee.	A general lien is a statutory lien. It arises under the operation of law.
2.	A particular lien signifies that the right to retain could be exercised only against that particular property which has been given to the bailee for a specific purpose.	A general lien, as the name itself suggests, gives an authority to retain or detain not only goods but also balance of money in an account by mercantile agents over debts due to them.
3.	In a particular lien, the bailee should have used some labour or skill to improve upon the goods bailed to him.	In the case of a general lien, there is no need either to improve the goods or to improve the funds entrusted to the bailee.
4.	A particular lien could be exercised only by such a bailee who has exercised his labour and skill on the goods bailed to him.	A general lien could be exercised only by bankers, factors, policy brokers, attorneys, insurances agents, wharfingers and so on, and not by others.

Termination of a Lien

The right of lien of a bailee is terminated in the following circumstances:

1. **Surrender of possession:** The right of lien is a personal right which continues so long as the bailee is in possession of goods. It is lost as soon as the bailee surrenders the possession of goods.
2. **Payment or tender of the amount due:** The right of lien is terminated as soon as the amount due to the bailee is tendered or paid to him.
3. **Abandonment:** The bailee may give up his right of lien by entering into an agreement to abandon his right.

Rights of Bailors and Bailees against Third Parties

Following are the rights of bailors and bailees against third parties:

1. **Suit against wrongdoer:** Section 180 provides,

   If a third person wrongfully deprives the bailee of the use or possession of the goods bailed, or does them any injury, the bailee is entitled to use such remedies as the owner might have used in the like case if no bailment had been made.

2. **Apportionment of relief or compensation obtained by such suits:** Section 181 provides, 'Whatever is obtained by way of relief or compensation in any such suit shall, as between the bailor and bailee, be dealt with according to their respective interests.' The bailee has to account for anything that he recovers over and above his interest to the bailor.
3. **Right of a third person claiming goods bailed:** Section 167 provides that the bailee has a right to sue, if a person, other than the bailor, claims goods bailed. He may apply to the court to stop the delivery of goods to the bailor and to decide the title to the goods.

Finder of Goods

A 'finder of goods' is a person who finds goods belonging to another person and takes them into his custody. He may or may not pick up the goods. However, once he takes the goods into his possession, he becomes a gratuitous bailee of such goods. Section 71 explains that a person who finds the goods belonging to another and takes them into his custody is subject to the same responsibility as a bailee. A finder has to trace or chase the true owner in order to hand over the goods. Until such time, his position would be that of a bailee. He is bound to exercise reasonable care in preserving the goods found.

Rights of a Finder of Goods

Sections 168 and 169 of the Contract Act define the rights of a finder of goods. They are as follows:

1. **Right of possession:** The finder of goods is entitled to retain possession of goods against everyone except the true owner. This is a special privilege enjoyed by the finder of goods under law.
2. **Right of lien:** The finder of goods has a right of particular lien over the goods or property. He is entitled to retain the possession of goods against the true owner until he receives compensation for expenses incurred in connection with preservation of goods and finding out of the owner. But he cannot sue the owner for such compensation.
3. **Right to sue for reward:** Where the owner has offered a specific reward for the return of goods lost, the finder may sue for such reward, and also retain the goods until he receives the reward.

4. **Right of sale of goods:** The finder of goods may sell the goods if:
   a. The owner of the goods cannot be found with reasonable diligence.
   b. The owner refuses to take delivery of the goods.
   c. The goods are in danger of perishing or losing their greater part of the value.
   d. The lawful charges of the finder exceed two-thirds of their value and the owner refuses to pay such lawful charges.

Obligations or Duties of a Finder of Goods

The following are the important obligations or duties of a finder of goods:

1. **To take reasonable care of the goods:** The finder of goods has to take reasonable care of the goods. If, in spite of reasonable care, the goods are destroyed, he is not liable. The measure or degree of care depends upon the nature, quality and quantity of the goods found.
2. **To find the true owner:** It is the duty of the finder of goods to use reasonable diligence to find the true owner.
3. **Not to use the goods for his own purpose:** The finder of goods should not use the goods for his own purpose. If he appropriates the goods for his own use, he becomes trespasser and would be criminally liable.
4. **Not to mix the goods with his own goods:** The finder of goods should not mix the goods with his own goods.
5. **To return the goods:** The finder of goods must return the goods to the real owner who has paid the expenses incurred by the finder.
6. **To return any addition to the goods:** The finder of goods also has the duty to return any addition to the goods to the real owner.

Termination of Bailment

A contract of bailment is terminated under the following circumstances:

1. **Expiry of the period:** When the bailment is for a specific period, it terminates after the expiry of the period.
2. **Accomplishment of the purpose:** A bailment for a specific purpose terminates as soon as the purpose is achieved.
3. **Inconsistent use of goods:** The bailor may terminate a contract of bailment if the bailee does any act with regard to the goods bailed, inconsistent with the conditions of bailment.
4. **Death of bailor or bailee:** A gratuitous bailment is terminated by the death of either the bailor or the bailee.
5. **Destruction of subject matter:** A bailment is terminated when the subject matter of bailment (a) is destroyed or (b) by reason of a change in its nature becomes incapable of use for the purpose of bailment.
6. **Termination by bailor:** In the case of a gratuitous bailment, the bailor may terminate it any time even if it was lent for a specified time or purpose. However, if any loss is caused to the bailee because of such premature termination, it must be made good by the bailor.

PLEDGE

A pledge is a special kind of bailment. It is a form of bailment in which goods are delivered as security for the repayment of a debt. The object of delivery of goods is to provide security for a loan or fulfilment of an obligation. Section 172 defines a 'pledge' as 'the bailment of goods as security for payment of a debt or performance of a promise'. The bailor in the case of a pledge is called the 'pawnor' or 'pledger', and the bailee is called the 'pawnee' or 'pledgee'. Since a pledge is a bailment of goods, delivery of the goods, whether actual or constructive, is necessary to constitute a pledge.

Example: X borrows ₹1,000 from Y and keeps his ring as security for the payment of the debt. The bailment of ring is pledge. X is the bailor or pledger. Y is the bailee or pledgee.

Essential Characteristics of a Pledge

The following are the essential requirements or characteristics of a pledge:

1. **Delivery of possession:** The property pledged should be delivered to the pawnee. Only the possession is transferred and not ownership. The delivery of possession to the pawnee may be actual or constructive. In the case of Bank of Chittoor Ltd vs. Narasimhulu Naidu & Ors, a cinema projector and accessories were pledged with a bank. The bank allowed the property to remain with pledgers since they formed the equipment of running a cinema. Subsequently, the pledgers sold the machinery. The court held that the sale was subject to the pledge as there was a constructive delivery.
2. **Delivery should be in pursuance of contract:** It is essential for a valid pledge that the delivery of the goods or property should be made in pursuance of the contract of the pledge. Both delivery and loan need not be contemporaneous. A pledge may be perfected by delivery after the advance is made.
3. **Delivery should be for the purpose of security:** The pawnor should deliver goods to the pawnee as a security for the payment of loan, or fulfilment of an obligation. If the delivery of goods is not as security but for some other purpose, it is mere bailment but not pledge.
4. **Delivery should be upon a condition to return:** The delivery of possession should be upon a condition that when the loan is repaid or promise is fulfilled, the goods should be returned to the pawnor.
5. **Movable property:** A pledge can be made of movable property only. Movable property includes goods, valuables and document. Money cannot be pledged. Immovable property also cannot be a subject matter of pledge.

Rights of a Pledgor

The rights of a pledgor are almost similar to those of a bailor. The following are the important special rights of a pawnor or pledgor:

1. **Right to redeem the goods pledged:** It means the right to recover back the goods by paying the debt and other charges, if any. The pawnor can get the pledged goods redeemed any time before the actual sale of goods by the pawnee.

2. **Right to have his goods duly preserved by the pledgee:** The pledgor has every right to insist upon the pledgee to preserve the goods pledged and to ensure that they are properly maintained.
3. **Right of an ordinary debtor:** The pledgor can also exercise his right as an ordinary debtor, which are conferred under various statutes, for protecting the interest of the debtor.
4. **Right to receive back the addition to the goods:** The pawnor has a right to take back with the goods any increase that the goods have undergone during the period of pledge.

Duties of a Pledgor

The following are the duties of a pledgor:

1. **To disclose faults:** The pledgor should disclose to the pledgee the faults in the goods pledged about which he is aware. If he does not disclose the faults, he will be liable for the loss resulting therefrom.
2. **To indemnify the pledgee:** If the title of the pledgor to the goods pledged is defective and the pledgee suffers any loss due to this fact, the pledgor should indemnify or compensate the pledgee.
3. **To meet extraordinary expenses:** The pledgor should bear the extraordinary expenses incurred by the pledgee in respect of the goods pledged.
4. **To repay the loan:** The pawnor is under the duty to repay the loan to the pawnee as per the terms of the contract. If he fails to do so, the pawnee can file a suit to recover the loan.
5. **To bear expenses in case of late payment:** If, after making default, the pawnor subsequently repays the loan, he is liable to pay the expenses incurred by the pawnee due to default in repaying the loan at the stipulated time.

Rights of a Pledgee or Pawnee

The following are the various special rights of a pawnee:

1. **Right of retainer:** Section 173 confers a pawnee only the right of particular lien to retain possession of the goods pledged till he recovers the debt, interest and other expenses incidental to the possession or preservation of goods. However, he can retain the goods only for the payment of the particular debt for which the goods were pledged and not for any other debt or promise unless there is a contract to the contrary.
2. **Right to recover extraordinary expenses:** The pawnee is entitled to receive any extraordinary expenses incurred for the preservation of goods pledged. He can sue to recover these expenses and is entitled to sue even if the pawnor has violated some provisions of law in respect of goods pledged.
3. **Right to bring civil suit for amount due:** Where the pawnor makes default in the payment of the debt or performance of the promise at the stipulated time, the pawnee has the right to bring a civil suit against the pawnor for the payment of debt or performance of the promise. He can retain the goods pledged as collateral security.
4. **Right to sell the goods:** In the case of default by the pawnor, the pawnee can sell the goods pledged after giving a notice to the pawnor. If the proceeds of such sale are

insufficient to meet the claims of the pledgee, the pledgor is still liable to pay the balance. If the sale of the pledged goods results in surplus, such excess amount has to be returned to the pawnor.

5. **Right to be compensated for damage suffered:** If the pledgee suffers any damage due to non-disclosure of faults in the goods pledged known to the pledgor, he has a right to be compensated for any damages suffered.
6. **Right against wrongdoers:** In the case of injury to the goods or deprivation by a third party, the pledgee would have all such remedies as the owner of the goods against them.
7. **Right to payment in priority:** The pledgee has a right to be paid in priority before the unsecured creditors' claims are satisfied.

Duties of a Pledgee

The following are the main duties of a pledgee:

1. **To take reasonable care:** The pawnee must take reasonable care of the property pledged to the extent to which an ordinary prudent man would take of his own goods under similar circumstances.
2. **Not to make unauthorized use of goods:** Normally, a pledgee is not entitled to use the goods as they are pledged to him as security and not for use. He can use the goods only if authorized. Otherwise, he is liable to pay damages for the loss caused due to such use.
3. **To return goods on repayment:** The pledgee must return the goods on payment of the debt. If he does not return the goods at proper time, he is responsible to the pledgor for any loss or deterioration of the goods pledged.
4. **To return any increase:** The pledgee must return to the pledgor any increase in or profit accrued from the goods pledged.
5. **Not to set up adverse title:** The pledgee should not deny the pledgor's title. He should not set up his own title or that of a third party.

Differences between Bailment and Pledge

1. Bailment is a wider term and includes a large variety of transactions, but pledge is a specific category of bailment.
2. A pledge is distinguished from other types of bailments by the nature of the lien possessed by the pledgee. The pledge lien gives the pledgee the right to sell the goods in the event of non-payment of the debt or non-performance of the obligation secured.
3. Goods are pledged to ensure repayment of a debt or for performance of a promise. But goods may be bailed for any purpose.
4. Goods are pledged as a security, but these are bailed for carrying out a specific purpose or for a particular period of time.
5. The purpose of bailment may be to enable the bailee to make use of bailed goods. Such a personal use of goods is decided to a pledgee.

Both bailment and pledge can be effected only of movable property and in both, there is only transfer of possession and not that of ownership.

PLEDGE BY NON-OWNERS

The general rule is that only the owner of goods or anyone who is duly authorized by the owner can make a valid pledge. This rule is based on the maxim that no one can pass a better title than he himself has. This rule applies to both contracts of sale and contracts of pledge. This principle is necessary to protect the individual interest in the ownership of property. However, in the following cases, even persons other than the owner can make a valid pledge:

1. **Pledge by a mercantile agent:** Section 178 of the Contract Act provides that a pledge by a mercantile agent, who is not authorized by the owner of goods, will be valid if the following conditions are satisfied:
   a. The mercantile agent is in possession of goods or documents of title to goods.
   b. The possession of goods is with the consent of the owner.
   c. The mercantile agent makes the pledge in the ordinary course of his business as an agent.
   d. The pawnee acts in good faith.
   e. The pawnee has no notice of the pawnor's defective title.

   Example: A salesman of a company pledged the goods of the company. The pawnee acting in good faith gets a perfect title.
2. **Pledge by a person in possession under a voidable contract:** A pledge made by a person who has obtained goods by fraud, misrepresentation, undue influence and coercion will be valid, provided the following conditions are satisfied:
   a. The contract under which the pawnor obtained possession of goods has not been rescinded at the time of the pledge.
   b. The pawnee acts in good faith.
   c. The pawnee has no notice of the pawnor's defective title.
3. **Pledge where a pawnor has only limited interest:** Section 179 states, 'Where a person pledges goods in which he has only a limited interest, the pledge is valid to the extent of that interest.'
4. **Pledge by a co-owner:** Where there are several joint owners of goods, and one of them is in possession of goods with the consent of other co-owners, he can make a valid pledge of the goods.
5. **Pledge by a seller in possession after sale:** A seller who has got possession of goods even after sale can make a valid pledge, provided the pledgee acts in good faith and has no notice of sale.
6. **Pledge by a buyer in possession of goods:** A buyer who has got possession of goods, with the consent of the seller before ownership is obtained, can create a valid pledge, provided the pledgee acts in good faith and has no notice of the pledger's defect in the title to the goods pledged.

TEST QUESTIONS

1. Define bailment and state its characteristic features. Discuss various types of bailment.
2. Discuss the rights and duties of a bailor and a bailee.
3. What are the circumstances when a contract of bailment stands terminated?

4. What are the rights and obligations of a finder of goods? What is the nature of lien he has over the goods?
5. Distinguish between 'general lien' and 'particular lien'. In what categories you would place a bailee's lien? Who are entitled to general lien?
6. Define a pledge. Discuss rights and duties of a pledger and a pledgee.
7. When do non-owners create a valid pledge?
8. Distinguish between bailment and pledge.

PRACTICAL PROBLEMS

1. A lends his motorcar to B for a drive only by him. B allows his daughter C, who is an expert car driver, to drive the vehicle. C drives carefully but the axle suddenly breaks and the car is damaged. Is B liable for the damage?
   Hint. Yes. B is liable for the damage to A's car since the use of the car by C is unauthorized. (Section 153)
2. Jewellery was pledged with a moneylender as security for a loan. The moneylender gave this jewellery to his wife for putting it on at a social gathering. While returning from this function, his wife was attacked by a gang of dacoits, who relieved her of all her jewellery. Is the moneylender liable for the loss?
   Hint. Yes. The moneylender is liable to make good the loss as he used the jewellery for an unauthorized purpose.
3. A hires a carriage of B. The carriage is unsafe, although B is not aware of it and A is injured. Is B responsible to A for the injury?
   Hint. Yes. B is responsible to A for the injury caused to him. Where bailment is for hire, the bailor is responsible for the damage arising out of the faults of the goods whether he was aware of the faults or not.
4. X entrusted a white tiger to the railway for carriage. The cage broke by the jolts received during the journey, and the tiger escaped. It killed a bullock belonging to Y and was almost immediately crushed by the engine. Is the railway administration liable to pay loss to X and Y?
   Hint. The railway administration is liable neither to X nor to Y. The cage broke by jolts and the owner gave the cage.
5. A lends a sum of ₹500 to B on the security of 20 shares of a limited company on 1 January 1985. On 15 January 1985, the company issued five bonus shares. B repays the amount of ₹500 with interest. A returns 20 shares but refuses to return the 5 bonus shares. Advise B.
   Hint. Section 163 provides that B is entitled to any increase in shares. Hence, A must return not only 20 shares but also 5 bonus shares.

14
CHAPTER
Contract of Agency

Learning Objectives

- To understand the meaning of a contract of agency
- To understand the relationship between an agent and a principal
- To understand the authority of an agent
- To understand the creation of an agency
- To understand the meaning of an agency by ratification
- To understand delegation of authority by an agent
- To understand the differences between a sub-agent and a substituted agent
- To understand the termination of an agency

Contract of Agency

There are many transactions which a trader cannot do himself, so he appoints some other person to perform those on his behalf known as an agent. The contract which creates the relationship between an agent and a principal is known as an 'agency'. It is based on the consent of the two parties, that is, a principal and his agent. The term agency may be defined as the relationship between an agent and his principal created by an express or implied agreement. The provisions relating to an agency are contained in Sections 182–238 of the Indian Contract Act, 1872.

Example: It may be making of a contract, the institution of an action, the conveyance of land or, in the case of power of attorney, the exercise of any proprietary right available to the principal himself.

Meaning of an Agent and a Principal

Section 182 defines an agent as a person employed to do any act for another or to represent another in dealings with a third person. The person for whom such an act is done, or who is so represented, is called the principal. The function of the agent is to bring his principal into contractual relations with the third person. This means that an agent is merely a connecting link between the principal and the third party. It may even imply a servant, an employee and the like as an agent.

Example: X appoints Y to purchase 5,000 books on his behalf. X is a principal and Y is the agent of X, and the relationship between X and Y is called as an agency.

Who Can Employ an Agent?

Section 184 provides that any person who is more than 18 years of age and is of sound mind may employ an agent. As such, a minor, a lunatic or a drunken person cannot employ an agent. An agent acts for and on behalf of his principal with a third party and, as such, an agent does not incur any personal liability. When he acts within his authority, the principal is held liable to the third party on the contracts entered into by his agent. This is based on legal maxim *qui facit per alium facit per se*, which means he who does through another does by himself.

Section 226 explains,

> Contracts entered into through an agent, and obligations arising from acts done by an agent, may be enforced in the same manner, and will have the same legal consequences as if the contract had been entered into and the acts done by the principal in person.

Who May Be an Agent?

Any person who is authorized to act as such may be an agent. An agent does not make contracts on his own behalf. It is not necessary that he should have contractual capacity. Even a minor may be an agent. If a person who is not competent to contract is appointed as an agent, the principal is liable to the third party for the acts of the agent. In other words, if a minor, lunatic or idiot is appointed as an agent, then the principal will be liable and not the agent. However, if an agent has the contractual capacity, then he will be *held liable for those acts which he has not performed in the capacity of an agent.*

ESSENTIALS OF AN AGENCY

The relationship of an agency is based upon a contract, and the essentials of an agency are as follows:

1. **Agreement:** The agreement between a principal and an agent is the basis for a contract of agency. The agreement may be express or implied. There is no need for consideration in a contract of agency; however, if any consideration is present, the relationship becomes contractual.
2. **Competency of principal:** Section 183 provides that any person who is of the age of majority, and is of sound mind, may employ an agent. So a minor or a person of unsound mind cannot employ an agent. However, a minor or a person of unsound mind can be an agent. In other words, whatever a person can do himself personally, he can do the same through another person.
3. **Consideration not necessary:** Section 185 provides that no consideration is required to create an agency. Law specially provides that consideration is not necessary to create an agency.

4. **Authority:** The principal should confer authority on the agent to act for him. The authority of an agent to bind the principal may be of two types:
   a. Actual or real authority
   b. Ostensible or apparent authority

Authority of an Agent

An agent is a connecting link between the principal and the third party and thereby establishes a privity of contract between them. All acts of an agent done in the discharge of his duties and within the scope of his authority are binding upon the principal. The principal is responsible for the acts of the agent in the same manner as if he has himself done those acts. However, the authority of an agent is not unlimited. Section 186 provides that the authority of an agent may be express or implied. The authority of an agent to bind the principal may be actual or real authority, or it may be ostensible or apparent authority.

1. **Actual authority:** Actual authority is the authority conferred by the principal on the agent. It may be express or implied. Express authority is that which is given by words spoken or written. Implied authority is that which is to be inferred from the circumstances of the case. The extent of authority of an agent, whether express or implied, depends upon the following:
   a. The nature of the act or business he is appointed to do
   b. Things which are incidental to the business or are usually done in carrying it out
   c. The usual customs and usages of the trade
2. **Ostensible authority:** Ostensible authority is the authority of an agent as it appears. When a person is appointed as an agent for a particular purpose or business, persons dealing with him are entitled to presume that he has the authority to do all such lawful acts as are necessary or incidental to such a business. The ostensible authority may coincide with the actual authority or may sometimes exceed it.
   Example: A constitutes B, his agent, to carry on his business of shipbuilding. B may purchase timber and other materials, and hire workers, for the purpose of carrying on the business.

Agent's Authority in Emergency

An agent has the authority, in an emergency, to do all such acts for the purpose of protecting his principal from loss as would be done by a person of ordinary prudence, in his own case, under similar circumstances.

Examples: A consigns provisions to B in Calcutta, with directions to send them immediately to C in Vijayawada. B may sell the provisions at Calcutta, if they will not bear the journey to Vijayawada without spoiling.

RULES OF AGENCY

The law of agency is based on the following general rules:

1. Whatever a person can do personally, he can do through an agent.

2. He who does an act through another does it by himself. This means that the principal is bound by the acts of his agent and can get the benefit of such acts as if he had done them himself. The acts of the agent shall, for all legal purposes, be considered the acts of the principal.

The Test of Agency

An agent is a person employed by his principal to do certain acts on behalf of his principal or to represent him in dealing with third parties. However, a person who merely gives an advice to another person in matters of business or in some other respects does not become an agent. The true test of an agent's authority is his power or authority of making his principal answerable to third parties. However, if an agent does some unauthorized act, he can be held personally liable for the same but it should also be kept in mind that if his principal thinks it proper, he may accept the unauthorized act of his agent by way of ratification. In short, it can be said that an agency between the persons exists if one has the capacity of binding the other from his acts.

Creation of an Agency or Modes of Creation of an Agency

1. **Agency by express agreement:** Sections 186 and 187 explain that an agency may be created by an express agreement which may be oral or in writing. An agency may be created by a letter or document or by a deed in writing or oral. The written contract of an agency is called as 'power of attorney'. The power of attorney gives the agent the power to act as an agent on behalf of the principal in accordance with the terms and conditions mentioned therein. The power of attorney is executed where an agent has to carry out several transactions.
   Example: To present a document before the registrar for registration.
2. **Agency by implied agreement:** An agency may be created by an implied agreement from the conduct of the parties or the relationship between them. An implied agency arises from the conduct, situation or relationship of the parties. Partners, servants and wives are usually regarded as agents by implications because of their relationship. An implied agency includes an agency by estoppels, by holding out and by necessity.
   a. **Agency by estoppels:** An agency by estoppels is based on the 'doctrine of estoppels'. Where the principal by his conduct or statement wilfully induces another person to believe that a certain person is his agent, he is subsequently stopped or prevented from denying the fact of agency. An agency by estoppels may also arise in cases where an agent is terminated and no public notice is given to that effect.
   Example: A tells B in the presence of C that he is C's agent. C does not object to this statement. Later on, B supplies certain goods to A, taking him as an agent of C. C is liable to pay the price to B. Here, the agency is said to be created by estoppels.
   b. **Agency by holding out:** An agency by holding out resembles with estoppels. In this case, a prior positive or affirmative act on the part of the principal is necessary to establish an agency subsequently. The principal will be bound by the acts of the

agent if, on an earlier occasion, he has induced the other person to believe that such acts are done with his authority.

Example: A allowed his servant B to purchase some goods on credit from C. B usually purchased goods from C on credit and A used to pay. On one occasion, A gave cash to B to purchase goods. B misappropriated the money and purchased goods on credit in A's name. A is bound to pay C. Here, B is an agent by holding out.

In both agency by estoppels and by holding out, there is no express appointment of an agent by the principal, but the agent acquires the authority through principal. However, in the case of estoppels, the principal is passive and allows another person to give the impression of himself to act as an agent. In the case of holding out, the principal himself holds to the world that somebody is his agent. Here, there is some active assertion or representation by the principal.

c. **Agency of necessity:** An agency may also arise from the necessities which may arise in a number of circumstances. In certain circumstances, a person who has been entrusted with another's property may have to insure against unauthorized expenses to preserve it. However, to constitute a valid agency of necessity, the following conditions must be satisfied:
   i. There must be a real emergency and necessity to act on behalf of the principal.
   ii. It must be impossible for the agent to communicate with the principal or to obtain his instructions.
   iii. The agent must act honestly in the interest of the principal.
   iv. The agent must adopt a reasonable and practical course under the circumstances of the case.

   Example: A horse sent by a train arrived at a station with nobody to receive it. The railway company fed the horse. It was held that the railway company is an agent of necessity and was entitled to recover the expenses from the owner of the horse.

3. **Agency by operation of law:** Sometimes, an agency arises by operation of law. In this case, law treats any person as the agent of another person.

   Example: When a company is first established, the promoters are its agents. A partner is the agent of the firm for the purpose of the business of the firm. The acts of a partner are binding on the firm. In all these cases, the agency is implied by the operation of law.

4. **Agency by ratification:** An agent may act on behalf of the principal either with or without his authority. All acts of an agent done in the discharge of his duties and within the scope of his authority are binding upon the principal. However, acts performed by an agent beyond the scope of his authority are not binding upon the principal. In case the principal adopts the act of the agent without his authority, he is said to have ratified the act. The subsequent adoption by a person of an unauthorized act done by another is called 'ratification'. On ratification, the act of the agent becomes the act of the principal, and he becomes bound by the same. The agency in this case is called *exposit facto agency* because it is created subsequent to the contract. This agency is also called the 'agency arising after the event'. Ratification is an approval of a previous unauthorized act or contract. It implies the adoption or recognition by the principal of an act made by an agent on his behalf, but without his authority. Section 196 of the Contract Act provides,

   > Where acts are done by one person on behalf of another, but without his knowledge or authority, he may elect to ratify or to disown such acts. If he ratifies them, the same effects will follow as if they had been performed by his authority.

Effect of Ratification

Ratification relates back to the date on which the agent was first contracted; it is tantamount or equivalent to prior authority. It authorizes an unauthorized act. It is a cure of the lack of authorization or a substitute for authorization.

Example: A buys five bags of wheat on behalf of B. B did not appoint A as his agent. B may, upon hearing of the transaction, accept or reject it; if B accepts it, the act is ratified and A becomes his agent with retrospective effect. In the case of Williams vs. North China Insurance Company, an agent insured the goods of the principal without authority. Later, the principal ratified his agent's act of insurance. The parties were bound by the contract.

Essentials of Valid Ratification

Sections 196–200 explain the rules relating to ratification to make it legal and valid. These are as follows:

1. **Agent must act on behalf of the principal and not on his own behalf:** An agent must have contracted as an agent for a principal. The principal must be named or identified. An undisclosed principal cannot ratify his agent's contract or act. An act done by a person on his own account cannot be ratified. If the agent acts in his own name, ratification does not become valid. In the case of Keighley vs. Durant, an agent was authorized to buy wheat at a certain price. The agent purchased the wheat at a higher price in his own name but not in the name of his principal. Subsequently, the principal ratified the contract. The ratification was held to be invalid.
2. **Principal must be in existence:** The principal must be in existence at the time the agent had made the contract. A contract cannot be ratified by a principal who was not in existence at the time of contract. In the case of Kelner vs. Baxter, A entered into a contract with B on behalf of a company yet to be formed. The company on being formed ratified the contract. The ratification was held void on the ground that the company was not in existence at the time of the contract.
3. **Contractual capacity of the principal:** The principal must have contractual capacity at the time of making the contract and at the time of ratification. If the principal is not competent to enter into a contract, he cannot ratify it subsequently when he attains competence to contract. Thus, he cannot ratify an act done on behalf of a minor, on attaining majority.
4. **Void acts:** An act which is void from the very beginning cannot be ratified.
   Example: Payment of dividend out of capital is void and cannot be ratified. Similarly, a forgery of signatures, being a crime, cannot be ratified.
5. **Legal acts:** An act to be ratified must be legal or lawful. It must not be criminal or unlawful.
   Example: Forgery cannot be ratified because it is a crime.
6. **Full knowledge of material facts:** Ratification must be made with full knowledge of all the material facts. Ratification without such knowledge is invalid. Section 198 declares, 'No valid ratification can be made by a person whose knowledge of the facts of the case is materially defective.'

7. **No partial ratification:** Ratification must relate to the whole act or transaction and not to a part of it. There cannot be partial ratification or partial rejection. The principal cannot accept the profitable part and reject the unprofitable one.
8. **Reasonable time:** Ratification must be made within the time fixed for this purpose or within a reasonable time after the original contract is made. If it is done after a long delay, it may not be valid.
9. **Communication:** Ratification must be communicated within a reasonable time to the agent and the third parties; otherwise, it will not be a valid ratification.
10. **Power of the principal to ratify:** Ratification can be made of those acts alone which the principal had the power to do. In other words, the act to be ratified must be within the principal's authority.
11. **Third parties rights:** Ratification must not cause loss to a third party. An act which puts a third party to loss or damage cannot be ratified.
12. **Nature of ratification:** Ratification may be express or implied.

Limitations of Ratification

1. **Where an agent purports to act as an agent for a principal not in existence:** If someone acts for a principal who is not in existence, then the agency cannot be ratified, as it is the first requirement for an agency that one can act only for that person who is in existence.
2. **Where the principal is incapable of contracting:** If any person who acts for the principal and the principal is incapable of entering into contract, that is, a minor, lunatic, idiot and the like, such acts cannot be ratified.
3. **Where the principal does not have full knowledge of facts:** Without the knowledge of the entire facts, the principal cannot ratify the agency.
4. **Where the act to be ratified is void or illegal:** The principal cannot ratify any act which is illegal or void.
5. **Only the whole of the transaction can be ratified:** Only a transaction as a whole can be ratified, not any part of it, which means that a transaction cannot be ratified in part.
6. **Where the ratification puts a third party to damages:** If any ratification puts a third party in the state of damages, then it cannot be ratified.
7. **Where the knowledge of the facts of the case is materially defective:** If the facts of the contract are materially defective, then also an agency cannot be ratified.

Delegation of Authority by an Agent

Section 182 defines an agent as 'a person employed to do any act for another, or to represent another in dealings with third persons'. An agent is a connecting link between the principal and third parties. An agent has to act within the scope of his authority. The reason is that the authority given to an agent is personal and cannot be exercised through another. The maxim *delegates non protest delegate* means a delegate cannot further delegate. In other words, a person to whom authority has been given cannot delegate that authority to another. A contract of agency is based on good faith. Therefore, the agent should perform his responsibilities himself. Section 190 provides that an agent cannot lawfully appoint a sub-agent to perform acts which he has expressly or impliedly undertaken to perform personally. So ordinarily, an agent cannot delegate or pass on his duties to another.

Exceptions: These circumstances are as follows:

1. Where the ordinary custom of trade permits employment of a sub-agent
2. Where the nature of work demands that a sub-agent should be appointed
3. Where the principal has expressly allowed his agent to appoint a sub-agent. His consent may also be implied from the circumstances
4. Where, in the course of agent's appointment, unforeseen emergencies arise which render it necessary to delegate his authority
5. Where the principal knows that the agent intends to appoint a sub-agent
6. Where the power of the agent to delegate can be inferred from the conduct of the parties
7. Where acts to be done are purely ministerial in nature. Ministerial acts are those which are of routine nature and can be done by the agent or delegated by him

Effects of Delegation

Sections 192 and 193 deal with the legal consequences of appointment of a sub-agent. The appointment of a sub-agent may be either proper or improper. The legal relations between a principal and a sub-agent depend upon whether the appointment of the sub-agent is proper or improper.

Where a Sub-agent Is Properly Appointed

Delegation is proper if it is within any of the recognized exceptions. Where a sub-agent is properly appointed, the following consequences emerge:

1. The principal is liable to third parties for the act of the sub-agent.
2. The agent is responsible to the principal for the acts of the sub-agent.
3. The sub-agent is not responsible to the principal except in cases of fraud and wilful wrong.

Where a Sub-agent Is Improperly Appointed

Delegation is improper if it is not within any of the recognized exceptions. Where a sub-agent is improperly appointed, the following consequences emerge:

1. Such a sub-agent does not represent the principal, and so he is not liable for any of the acts of the sub-agent.
2. The agent is responsible to his principal as well as to third parties for the acts of his sub-agent.
3. The sub-agent is not responsible to the principal at all. He is answerable only to the agent.

Types of Agents

There are different types of agents, which are as follows.

Based on Their Authority

1. **Special agent:** A special agent is one who has the authority to do some particular act or represent his principal in some particular transaction. Such an agent has a limited authority and as soon as the act is performed, the authority ends. He has no authority to bind the principal in any matter other than that for which he is appointed.
2. **General agent:** A general agent is one who is employed to transact generally all the business of the principal about which he is employed. Such an agent has the authority to do all acts connected with a trade or business. His authority is continuous, and it continues until the principal withdraws it. In the absence of a notice of restriction, third parties have a right to assume certain acts to be within the apparent authority of the agent, whether they are within the scope of actual authority or not.
3. **Universal agent:** A universal agent is one who is authorized to transact all the business of his principal of every kind and to do all the acts which the principal can lawfully do and can delegate. He has the authority to bind his principal by any act which he does, provided it is legal and conforms to the law.

Based on Their Nature of Work

1. **Mercantile agent:** A mercantile agent is an agent who has the authority to sell the goods or to consign goods for sale, or to buy goods or to raise money on the security of the goods on behalf of his principal. Some of the important mercantile agents are as follows:
   a. **Factor:** He is one to whom the possession of goods is given to sell them. He usually sells the goods in his own name. He gets remuneration by way of factorage. He is an agent who is in possession of the goods with the consent of his principal, and if he sells or pledges the goods in the ordinary course of business, such a transaction is binding on the principal, whether he had authorized it or not.
   b. **Broker:** A broker is also an agent appointed by a person to buy or sell goods on his behalf. However, a broker is not given the possession of the goods. He is employed to bring a contractual relationship between his principal and third parties. He makes contracts in the name of the principal and has no right of lien. He is a mere negotiator whose business is to find purchasers for those who wish to sell, and sellers for those who wish to buy. He gets his remuneration by way of brokerage.
   c. **Auctioneer:** He is an agent appointed by a seller to sell his goods by public auction for a reward generally in the form of a commission. Primarily, he is the agent of the seller. When the property has been knocked down, he becomes the agent of the buyer. He has the authority to receive the price of the goods sold and sue for it in his own name. An auctioneer cannot give warranties as to the goods sold in an ordinary case.
   d. **Commission agent:** A commission agent is similar to a broker. He is paid commission on finding out a seller or buyer of goods. He may or may not be

entrusted with goods. He is engaged to buy or sell goods at the best available terms. The duties and responsibilities of a commission agent depend upon his agreement with the principal.

e. **Del credere agent:** He is an agent who assumes for a special commission the responsibility of ensuring that the parties with whom his principal is brought into contractual relations will pay the money on due date. He occupies the position of a guarantor as well as an agent. However, his liability is secondary and arises only in cases of insolvency or failure of the other party. A del credere agent is generally appointed when the principal deals with a person about whom he knows nothing.
f. **Banker:** Generally, the relationship between a banker and a customer is that of a debtor and a creditor. However, when the banker buys or sells securities and collects cheques, dividends and the like on behalf of his customer, he also acts as an agent.

2. **Non-mercantile agent:** These agents do not deal in mercantile transactions. Such agents usually perform certain acts which are not done by mercantile agents. Some of the important non-mercantile agents are insurance agents, solicitors, guardians, promoters, wives, estate agents and so on.

SUB-AGENT

A person who is appointed by an agent in the business of agency is called a sub-agent and acts under the control and direction of the original agent. A sub-agent is a person employed by, and acting under the control of, the original agent. So an agent appointed or employed by an agent is called a sub-agent. Such a sub-agent acts under the control of the original or main agent. The relationship between a sub-agent and an agent is fully that of an agent and a principal. Section 191 defines a sub-agent as 'a person employed by, and acting under the control of, the original agent in the business of the agency'. There is no privacy of contract between the principal and sub-agent. Hence, the principal cannot sue the sub-agent except for fraud or wilful wrong. The original agent is responsible to the principal for the acts of the sub-agent, and the sub-agent is generally not responsible to the principal. A sub-agent is, however, bound by all the duties of the original or ordinary agent.

SUBSTITUTED AGENT

A substituted agent is a person who is named by the agent, on an express or implied authority for the principal, to act for the principal. He is not a sub-agent but an agent of the principal for such part of the business of the agency as is entrusted to him. He is an agent of the principal, though the agent names him at the request of the principal. There is a privity of contract between the principal and the substituted agent. Therefore, the principal can sue the substituted agent for damages on an account. The ordinary agent is not concerned about the work of the substituted agent.

Example: A authorizes B, a merchant in Markapur, to recover the money due to A from Murali. B instructs Mr Venu, a solicitor, to take legal proceedings against Murali for the recovery of money. Venu is not a sub-agent; he is a full-fledged agent of A.

Differences between a Sub-agent and a Substituted Agent

A substituted agent is superior to a sub-agent in status and position. The following are the main differences between a sub-agent and a substituted agent:

1. **Appointment:** An agent appoints a sub-agent. However, an agent or a principal may appoint a substituted agent.
2. **Responsibility:** A sub-agent is not responsible to the principal for his acts except those that are fraudulent or wrong. However, a substituted agent is responsible to the principal for all his acts.
3. **Direction and control:** A sub-agent does his work under the control of the agent. However, a substituted agent works under the control and directions of the principal.
4. **Privity of contract:** After the appointment of a substituted agent, a privity of contract is established between the principal and the substituted agent. However, there are no privities of contract between the principal and the sub-agent. Therefore, he cannot sue or be sued by the principal.
5. **Responsibility of the agent:** An agent is responsible to the principal for the acts of the sub-agent. However, the agent is not responsible and liable for the acts of the substituted agent, provided he has taken due care in selecting him.
6. **Discharge of duty of the agent:** In the case of a sub-agent, the agent remains liable and answerable for the acts of the sub-agent as long as the sub-agent continues. However, in the case of a substituted agent, the duty of the agent ends once he has named a substituted agent.
7. **Right of action:** A sub-agent has no right of action against the principal for remuneration due to him. A substituted agent, on the other hand, can sue the principal for remuneration due.
8. **Delegation of work:** An agent delegates a part of his own duties to the sub-agent. However, the agent does not delegate any part of his duty to the substituted agent.

Duties of an Agent

The duties of an agent mainly depend upon the terms and conditions of the contract of agency. The following are the main duties of an agent:

1. **Duty to act according to the principal's directions:** The primary duty of an agent is to act within the scope of his authority and to conduct the business of his principal according to the directions given by him. If the agent fails to act according to the directions, the ordinary rules of contract will apply and he will become liable for breach.
   Example: A, an agent, engaged in carrying on a business for B, in which it was the custom to invest from time to time, on interest, the moneys which he may have in hand, but he omits to make such investments. A must make good to B the interest usually obtained by such investments. (Lilley vs. Doubleday)
2. **Duty to act with reasonable skill and diligence:** An agent is bound to conduct the business of an agency with as much skill as is generally possessed by persons

engaged in similar business. This rule will not apply in cases in which the principal has notice of want of skill of the agent. Further, the agent is bound to observe reasonable diligence and skill in the discharge of his duties.

Example: A, an insurance broker, employed by B to effect insurance on a ship, omits the usual clauses that are inserted in the policy. The ship is afterwards lost. In consequence of the omission of the clauses, nothing could be recovered from the underwriters. A is bound to make good loss to B.

3. **Duty to render proper accounts:** An agent is bound to render proper accounts to the principal on demand. Rendering accounts means not only producing accounts with relevant vouchers but also explaining them.
4. **Duty to communicate with the principal:** It is the duty of the agent, in case of difficulty, to use all reasonable diligence in communicating with his principal, and in seeking to obtain his instructions. However, if there is urgency and the principal cannot be communicated without losing time, the agent can act on his own in good faith and in the best interests of the principal.
5. **Duty to remit sums:** An agent is bound to pay to his principal all moneys received in the course of agency. He is, however, entitled to deduct his lawful charges. When an agent receives money on behalf of the principal under an illegal or void contract, the agent must account to the principal for this money so received and cannot set up the illegality of the contracts as a justification for withholding payment.

   Example: X, an agent of P, entered into a number of wagering contracts with third parties. X made good profits in these contracts and refused to pay to P on the plea of illegality. It was held that P could recover the money.
6. **Duty not to set up an adverse title:** It is a duty of an agent not to set up an adverse title against his principal. If he acts otherwise, the principal can stop him from doing so. However, he can set up a superior title of his principal against third parties.
7. **Duty not to use information obtained in the course of agency against the principal:** It is a duty of an agent not to use information obtained in the course of agency against the interest of the principal. If he does so, the principal can restrain him from doing so by an injunction from the court.
8. **Not to deal on his own account:** It is a duty of an agent not to deal on his own account. In fact, the agent should not do anything which would bring his personal interest and his duty to the principal in conflict with each other. This conflict is more likely to arise in cases where the agent is personally interested in the transaction of the principal. An agent must not become a principal party to the transaction as against the principal. However, if he was to do so, he must fully disclose all the facts in respect of the transaction and obtain his consent, before acting on his own account.
9. **Duty not to make secret profits:** As the relationship of an agent and a principal is of fiduciary nature, it is, therefore, a duty of the agent not to make any secret profit.
10. **Duty to protect the interest of the principal on his death or insanity:** Where an agency is terminated by death or insanity of the principal, the agent is bound to take, on behalf of the principal's representatives, all reasonable steps for the protection and preservation of the interest entrusted to him.
11. **Duty not to delegate authority:** A principal appoints an agent because he has full faith and confidence in his integrity and confidence. Therefore, the agent should not further delegate the work delegated to him by his principal. But there are certain cases in which an agent may delegate his duties or a part of his work to another person.

Rights of an Agent

The following are some of the important rights of an agent:

1. **Right to receive remuneration:** Where the services rendered by an agent are not voluntary or gratuitous, the agent is entitled to receive the agreed remuneration. If the remuneration is not fixed, the agent is entitled to receive reasonable remuneration. In the absence of any special contract, payment for the performance of an act is not due to the agent until the completion of such act.
2. **Right to retain money due to himself:** An agent may retain, out of any sums received on account of the principal in the business of agency, all moneys due to himself in respect of his remuneration and advances made or expenses properly incurred by him in conducting such business.
3. **Right of lien:** In the absence of any contract to the contrary, an agent is entitled to retain goods, papers and other property of the principal received by him, until the amount due to himself for commission, disbursements and services in respect of the same has been paid or accounted for to him. However, the lien of the agent is a particular lien. But by a special contract, an agent may have a general lien extending to all claims arising out of the agency.
4. **Right of indemnification:** An agent has a right to be indemnified against the consequences of all lawful acts done by him in exercise of the authority conferred upon him. This right of indemnity, however, does not extend to criminal acts of the agent, even though the principal authorizes them.
   Example: A employs B to beat C and agrees to indemnify him against consequences of the act. B, thereupon, beats C and has to pay damages to C for doing so. A is not liable to indemnify B for those damages.
5. **Right of compensation:** An agent has the right to be compensated for injuries sustained by him by neglect or want of skill on the part of the principal. Section 225 explains, 'The principal must make compensation to his agent in respect of injury caused to such agent by the principal's neglect or want of skill.'

Duties of a Principal

A principal owes a number of duties to an agent. The following duties of a principal are provided in Sections 222–225:

1. To indemnify the agent against the consequences of all lawful acts
2. To indemnify the agent against the consequences of acts done in good faith
3. To indemnify the agent for injury caused by principal's neglect
4. To pay the agent his commission or other remuneration agreed for his services

Rights of a Principal

A principal has the following rights against an agent:

1. To see that the agency business is conducted according to his instructions and to be compensated for loss or any profit accruing owing to departure from instructions

2. To be entitled to compensation in respect of the direct consequences of the agent's negligence, want of skill or misconduct
3. To get proper accounts when demanded by him
4. To repudiate the transaction, if a material fact is concealed by the agent while dealing on his own account
5. To receive all moneys due to him on his account subject to deductions in respect of expenses incurred by the agent and his remuneration.
6. To refuse to pay the remuneration if the agent is guilty of misconduct

Personal Liability of an Agent

An agent works for a principal and acts on behalf of the principal. Hence, he cannot personally enforce contracts entered into by him on behalf of the principal. Similarly, an agent is not personally liable for the contracts entered into by him on behalf of the principal.

Section 230 explains, 'In the absence of any contract to that effect, an agent cannot personally enforce contracts entered into by him on behalf of his principal, nor is he personally bound by them.' However, if there is such a contract, the agent may sue or be sued on the contract. This rule applies even where the agent has contracted beyond his authority and the principal would not be liable. Thus, the rule is that an agent cannot personally sue or be sued.

Example: A principal sent goods through the railway to his agent. The railway did not deliver the goods to the agent. The agent cannot sue the railway, as the railway receipt confers no ownership on him. The principal alone can sue the railway as the consignor.

Exceptions or When an Agent Will Be Personally Liable

The rule that an agent cannot personally sue or be sued has certain exceptions. An agent is personally liable in the following cases:

1. **When the agent acts for a foreign principal:** When an agent for sale makes a contract or purchases goods for a merchant residing abroad, the agent is personally liable. However, he can exclude his personal liability by express provision to this effect in the contract. If he does so, he cannot be sued on the contract.
2. **When the agent acts for an undisclosed principal:** Where an agent does not disclose the name of the principal, he is personally liable for such a contract. The third party may, however, on discovering the identity of the principal sue the principal also, if he so chooses.
3. **When the agent acts for a disclosed principal who cannot be sued:** An agent incurs personal liability when he contracts on behalf of a principal who though disclosed cannot be sued.
   Example: Where an agent acts for a minor or an ambassador, he is personally liable.
4. **Where the agent's authority is coupled with interest:** Where an agent has an interest in the subject matter of the contract entered into by him with a third party, his authority is coupled with interest. He has, in such a case, the right to sue or be sued, but only to the extent of his interest in the subject matter.

5. **Where the agent receives or pays money by mistake or fraud:** When an agent pays some money by mistake or fraud, he has a right to recover it back from the receiver. Similarly, when a third party pays to an agent some money by mistake or fraud, the agent can be sued for refund of the amount.
6. **Where an agent is liable for breach of warranty of authority:** When an agent exceeds his authority, or represents to have a kind of authority, which he in fact does not have, he commits breach of warranty of authority. In such a case, he is personally liable to the third party for any loss caused to him by reasons of acting under the false representation.
7. **Where the trade usage or custom makes him personally liable:** Where there is a trade usage or a custom making the agent personally liable, he is liable unless there is a contract to the contrary.
8. **Where the agent signs a contract or a negotiable instrument in his own name:** Where an agent signs a negotiable instrument or a contract without making it clear that he is signing on behalf of the principal, the agent is personally liable.
9. **Where the agent acts for a non-existing principal:** When an agent enters into a contract on behalf of a fictitious or non-existing principal, such a person in presumed to have contracted personally. No agent can bind a non-existent principal.

Rights of a Person Dealing with a Personally Liable Agent

In cases where the agent is personally liable, a person dealing with him may hold either him or his principal, or both of them, liable. Thus, the liability of the principal and the agent is not alternative but joint. However, under the English law, the third party can sue either the agent or the principal, but not both. Thus, the liability of the principal under the English law is only alternative and not joint.

Undisclosed Principal

If the name of the principal is not disclosed to the contracting parties, such a principal is called 'undisclosed principal' or 'unnamed principal'. According to Section 231, the positions of the undisclosed principal, the agent and the third party are as follows.

Position of a Principal

1. If the third party comes to know of the existence of the principal before obtaining judgment against the agent, he may sue either the principal or the agent or both.
2. The principal, if he likes, may intervene and sue the third party for non-performance of the contract.
3. The third party can claim any set-off for payment made to the agent, against the principal, when sued by the principal.
4. The third party may refuse to fulfil the contract if he can show that if he had known him as the principal, he would not have entered into the contract.

Position of an Agent

1. An agent has all the rights of an agent as against the principal.
2. As regards the third party, the agent is personally liable on the contract.
3. He may be sued on the contract, and he has the right to sue the third party.

Position of a Third Party

1. The third party may elect to sue either the principal or the agent or both.
2. The third party can also claim a right to set-off against the agent.

   In the case of Rabone vs. Williams, A sold to T goods of P, an undisclosed principal. When P sued T, T claimed set-off of debt by A to T. The set-off was allowed by the court.
3. The third party has, as against the principal, the same rights as he would have had as against the agent if the agent himself had been the principal.

TERMINATION OF AN AGENCY

An agency may be defined as the relationship between an agent and his principal created by an express or implied agreement. Termination of an agency occurs when the relationship between the principal and the agent ends. The contract of agency may be terminated by the following modes:

Termination of an Agency by the Act of the Parties

An agency may be terminated by the act of the parties in the following ways:

1. **By agreement between the principal and the agent:** An agency can be terminated at any time and at any stage by the mutual agreement between the principal and the agent. The parties are free to terminate the contract of agency by mutual agreement.
2. **By revocation of the agent's authority by the principal:** The principal can revoke the authority of the agent at any time. When the agent is appointed to do a single act, the authority can be revoked any time before the act is begun. In the case of a continuous agency, a notice of revocation should be given to the agent. If a reasonable notice is not given, the principal will be liable to compensate the agent and be bound by the acts of the agent with respect to third parties. The principal, however, cannot revoke the agency when it is said to be coupled with interest.
3. **By renunciation of the agency business by the agent:** Section 201 empowers the agent to renounce his authority. Renunciation may be express or implied. An agent can after giving a reasonable notice of his intention to the principal renounce the contract of agency. Where an agency is for a fixed period and the agent renounces it without a sufficient cause before the time fixed, he shall have to compensate the principal. An agent may renounce the agency by:
   a. tendering resignation
   b. ceasing to discharge his duties

c. mere abandonment of his service
d. setting up an adverse title to the principal

Termination by Operation of Law

An agency may be terminated by operation of law in any of the following ways:

1. **By completion of agency business:** The agency is automatically terminated when the business is completed for which it was made. Where the agency is for a single transaction, the agency terminates when the transaction is completed.
   Example: An agency for the sale of property ends when the sale is completed and does not continue until the payment of the price.
2. **By the expiry of time:** If the authority is given for a fixed period, the agency ends on the expiry of the period even if the business is not completed.
3. **By the death or insanity of the principal or the agent:** When the agent or the principal dies or becomes of unsound mind, the agency is terminated. When the principal has expired or has become insane, the agent has a duty to protect and preserve the interest entrusted to him by taking all reasonable steps. Till such time, the agency is not terminated.
4. **By insolvency of the principal:** Section 201 of the Contract Act states that the insolvency of the principal puts an end to the agency. Insolvency is a disqualification in entering into a contract, and so insolvency of the principal terminates the agency. But in regard to the insolvency of the agent, the law is silent.
5. **By destruction of the subject matter:** Where the subject matter in respect of which the agency was created has been destroyed, the agency comes to an end. There is no scope, in such a case, for continuation of the agency.
6. **By principal becoming an alien enemy:** Sometimes, an agency becomes unlawful by the happening of an event after the agency is created. If the principal and the agent belong to two different companies and war breaks out between the two countries, the performance of the contract of agency would become impossible and, therefore, the agency would be terminated.
7. **By the dissolution of a company:** When a company, whether principal or agent, is dissolved by winding up, the contract of agency with or by the company automatically ends.
8. **Termination of the sub-agent's authority:** The termination of the authority of the chief agent appointed by him will also terminate the authority of the sub-agent working under his control.

When Does Termination of an Agent's Authority Take Effect?

The termination of an agency is complete or takes effect, as regards the agent, when it comes to the knowledge of the agent. As regards the third parties, it becomes effective when they know it. It implies that the principal must also give a public notice of termination of the agency, so that it is effective with regard to the third parties as well. Even in the case of death or insanity of the principal, the agency terminates when the agent gets to know of the death or insanity of the principal. If a notice is not given to the public, the principal would become liable for the act of the agent.

IRREVOCABLE AGENCY

An irrevocable agency is one which cannot be revoked by the principal. In other words, when an agency cannot be terminated or put to an end, it is known as an irrevocable agency. The principal cannot revoke the authority of the agent at his pleasure in the following cases:

1. **Where the agency is coupled with interest:** An agency is said to be coupled with interest when it is created for the purpose of securing some benefit to the agent over and above his remuneration. Such an agency cannot, in the absence of a contract to the contrary, be terminated to the prejudice of such interest. Section 202 provides that where the agent has himself an interest in the property which forms the subject matter of agency, the agency cannot, in the absence of an express contract, be terminated to the prejudices of such interest. The agency coupled with interest cannot be terminated even on the death or insanity of the principal.
   Example: A gives an authority to B to sell A's land and to pay himself out of the proceeds the debts due to him from A. A cannot revoke his authority, nor can it be terminated by his insanity or death.
2. **Where the agent has incurred personal liability:** When the agent contracts in his own name and incurs a personal liability, the agency becomes irrevocable. The principal in such a case cannot be permitted to withdraw authority, leaving the agent exposed to the risk or liability, which he has incurred.
3. **Where the agent has partly exercised the authority:** Where the authority has been partly exercised by the agent, it becomes irrevocable, in particular with regard to obligations which arise from acts already done. The principal is bound by the acts already done on his behalf.
   Example: A asks B, his agent, to pay out of A's funds, remaining in B's hands, a sum of ₹100 to C in two instalments. By a subsequent letter, A revokes B's authority. Before this revocation, B had already paid ₹50 to C. A is bound by this payment.

Agency Coupled with Interest

An agency is said to be coupled with interest when an agent himself has an interest over the subject matter of the contract belonging to the principal over and above his remuneration. The authority to collect rent due to the principal is called 'authority coupled with interest'.

Example: A consigns certain wheat to B for sale. B subsequently advances some money to A, the principal. The subsequent advances could not convert the agency into an agency coupled with interest.

Termination or Revocation

An agency coupled with interest cannot, in the absence of a contract to the contrary, be terminated to the prejudice of such interest. Section 202 of the Act provides, 'Where the agent has himself an interest in the property which forms the subject-matter of the agency, the agency cannot, in the absence of an express contract, be terminated to the prejudice of such interest.'

Thus, an agency coupled with interest cannot be terminated even on the death or insanity of the principal. The principle laid down in Section 202 of the Contract Act applies only if the following conditions are fulfilled:

1. The interest of the agent should exist at the time of the creation of the agency and should not have arisen after the creation of the agency.
2. The authority given to the agent must be intended for the protection of the interest of the agent.
3. The interest of the agent in the subject matter must be substantial and not ordinary.
4. The interest of the agent should be over and above his remuneration. Mere prospect of remunerations is not sufficient interest.

Test Questions

1. Define the term 'agency'. What are the essentials and legal rules for a valid agency?
2. 'No one can become an agent of another except by the will of the person.' Comment. Briefly explain the various modes by which an agency may be created.
3. What is meant by agency by ratification? State the conditions that must be fulfilled before the doctrine can apply to an act of the agent.
4. What is the difference between the agent's actual authority and ostensible authority? State the scope and extent of an agent's authority.
5. State the rights and duties of an agent. What is the degree of skill required of him?
6. Discuss the rights and duties of a principal.
7. Define the term 'sub-agent'. When can he be appointed? State the position of a sub-agent in relation to an agent, a principal and third parties. What is the difference between a sub-agent and a substituted agent?
8. State the rule relating to the personal liability of an agent for a contract entered into by him on behalf of the principal.
9. Discuss briefly the modes in which an agency can be terminated. When does the termination take affect?
10. When is an agency irrevocable? When is an agency coupled with interest? When can it be revoked?

Practical Problems

1. A, who owes B ₹2,000, appoints B as his agent to sell his landed property in Kanpur and after paying himself (B) what is due to him, to hand over the balance to A. Can A revoke his authority delegated to B?
   Hint. No. A cannot revoke the authority delegated to B. The doctrine of agency coupled with interest applies in the instant case.
2. X, being Y's agent for the sale of goods, induces K to buy them by a misrepresentation, which X was not authorized by Y to make. Can this contract be set aside at the option of K. State reasons for your answer?

Hint. The principal is bound by the misrepresentation made by the agent acting in the course of agency business. K can, therefore, set aside the contract.

3. A consigns 300 cases of tea to B, who has advanced the amount to him and desired to sell the tea and to repay himself out of the price the amount of his own advance. A wants to revoke his authority. Decide.
   Hint. A cannot revoke the authority since the 'agency is coupled with interest'. According to Section 202 of the Indian Contract Act, 'Where the agent has himself an interest in the property which forms the subject-matter of the agency, the agency cannot, in the absence of an express contract, be terminated to the prejudice of such interest.'
4. A, who owes ₹500 to B, sells 1,000 rupees worth of rice to B. A is acting as the agent for C in the transaction, but B has no knowledge or reasonable ground of suspicion that such is the case. Can C compel B to pay ₹1,000 for the rice?
   Hint. C cannot compel B to pay ₹1,000 for the rice. B did not know nor did he have sufficient reasons to believe that A is the agent. Hence, C can compel the performance of the contract only subject to the set-off of the debt between A and B.
5. A holds a lease from B terminable on three months' notice. C, without B's authority, gives notice of termination to A. B ratifies the notice and files a suit for ejectment. Is B entitled to get a decree?
   Hint. No. B is not entitled to get a decree in the suit of ejectment, since ratification in this case would amount to the termination of A's right to hold a lease.
6. A asks his agent B to get a ship for him. B asks C, a competent surveyor, to get a good ship for A. C makes a bad selection and suffers a loss. Discuss the liability of B and C to A.
   Hint. C is liable to A but not B to A—substituted agent.
7. A, who owes ₹50,000 to B, appoints him as his agent to sell A's land and after paying himself what is due to him, B is to hand over the balance to A. A becomes insane. Is B's agency revoked thereby?
   Hint. No. The agency is coupled with interest. (Section 202)

UNIT III

The Sale of Goods Act, 1930

15

CHAPTER

Contract of Sale

Learning Objectives

- To know the meaning of a contract of sale and its essentials
- To understand the difference between a sale and an agreement to sell, and difference between a sale and a hire-purchase agreement
- To understand the term goods, classification of goods and effects of perishable goods
- To understand the meaning of price and modes of fixing price

The law relating to sale of movable goods is contained in the Sale of Goods Act, 1930. The Act came into force on 1 July 1930. It extends to whole of India except the State of Jammu and Kashmir. It contains provisions relating to sale of movable property and the special features of a contract of sale. It may be noted that the Sale of Goods Act does not limit or restrict the discretion of the parties to agree to any terms and conditions in their contract.

Contract of Sale of Goods

A contract of sale of goods is the most important legislation in business laws. It is a contract whereby a seller transfers the ownership in goods to a buyer or agrees to transfer it for a price. Section 4(1) defines a contract of sale as 'a contract whereby the seller transfers or agrees to transfer the property in goods to the buyer for a price'. A contract of sale includes both a sale and an agreement to sell. It is made by an offer to buy or sell goods for a price and the acceptance of such an offer. It creates rights and obligations. According to Section 4(2), 'a contract of sale may be absolute or conditional'. An absolute contract of sale is a contract without any conditions.

According to Section 2 of the Act, '"property" means the general property in goods, and not merely a special property'. When the goods are sold, the property in goods is passed from the seller to the buyer and as a result, the seller ceases to be the owner of goods, while the buyer becomes its owner. It must be kept in mind that this Act deals with sale of only movable goods and not immovable goods.

Example: X has sold 500 bags of sugar to Y @ ₹1,000 per bag. It is a contract of sale since the ownership of 500 bags of sugar has been transferred from X to Y for ₹500,000.

ESSENTIALS OF A CONTRACT OF SALE

Based on the definition given under Section 4 and explanations given thereto, the following essentials of a contract of sale are revealed:

1. **Two parties:** Like any other contract, a contract of sale is a contract between two parties. Thus, there must be two distinct parties, a seller and a buyer. The parties must be competent to contract. According to Section 2(13), a '"seller" means a person who sells or agrees to sell goods'. Section 2(1) explains that a '"buyer" means a person who buys or agrees to buy goods'. A contract of sale is a bilateral contract where the property in goods has to pass from one party to another. A person cannot buy the goods himself. However, according to the provisions of Section 64(3), a person may buy his own goods under certain cases such as auction sale and execution of a decree.
2. **Goods:** The subject matter of a contract of sale must be some goods. Goods mean every kind of movable property including stock and shares. Immovable property cannot be the subject matter of a contract of sale of goods. The seller must be the owner of goods. Section 2(7) explains that '"goods" means every kind of movable property other than actionable claims and money; and includes stock and shares, growing crops, grass, and things attached to or forming part of the land which are agreed to be severed before sale or under contract of sale'. Actionable claims means claims which a legal action or a suit can enforce.
3. **Transfer of property:** Transfer of property or the agreement to transfer the property is yet another important essential of a contract of sale; however, mere transfer of goods from one place to another cannot amount to sale. The object of a contract of sale must be the transfer of ownership in goods from one party to another. 'Property' here means 'ownership'. A mere transfer of possession is not sale. Thus, the essence of a contract of sale is transfer of property in goods.
   Example: X owns a car and if he pledges the goods with Y, this is a transfer of goods but not a sale.
4. **Price or money consideration:** The goods must be sold for some price. 'Price' means the money consideration for sale of goods. Where there is no money consideration, the transaction is not a contract of sale. Where goods are exchanged for goods, it is not a sale but barter. However, there is nothing to prevent the consideration from being partly in money and partly in goods. For example, when an old car is returned to the dealer and the difference is paid in cash, it would also be a sale.
5. **Essential elements of a valid contract:** All the essential elements of a valid contract must be present in a contract of sale, such as agreement, free consent, competence of parties and consideration.
6. **Mode of formation:** No particular form is necessary to constitute a contract of sale. It may be made in writing or by words of mouth or may be implied from the conduct of the parties. Therefore, it may be express or implied. It may be absolute or conditional.

DIFFERENCES BETWEEN SALE AND AGREEMENT TO SELL

Contract of Sale

A contract of sale is 'a contract whereby the seller transfers or agrees to transfer the property in goods to the buyer for a price'. A 'contract of sale' is a generic term and includes both a sale and an agreement to sale.

Sale: According to Section 4(3) of the Sale of Goods Act, 'Where under a contract of sale the property in the goods is transferred from the seller to the buyer, the contract is called a sale.' In other words, where the property in the goods is immediately transferred to the buyer, the contract of sale is called a 'sale'. Thus, the sale has the immediate effect of transferring the legal ownership of the goods.

Example: A agrees to sell certain goods to B on 1 July for ₹2,500. B agrees to pay the price after one week. It is a sale, since the ownership of goods has been transferred from A to B.

Agreement to sell: Section 4(3) explains, 'where the transfer of property in the goods is to take place at a future time or subject to some condition, thereafter to be fulfilled, the contract is called an agreement to sell'. Thus, in an agreement to sell, ownership in the goods is not immediately transferred from a seller to a buyer; where the goods are to be weighed or measured by a seller for ascertaining price; the transaction is an agreement to sell.

Example: A, on 1 July, agrees to sell certain goods to B for ₹2,500 after one week. B agrees to pay the price for the goods on delivery. It is an agreement to sell, since A agrees to transfer the ownership of the goods to B in future.

An agreement to sell becomes a sale when the time lapses or the conditions in the agreement are fulfilled. The conditions may have to be fulfilled by the buyer or the seller.

The distinction between a sale and an agreement to sell can be done based on the following points:

Basis of Difference	*Sale*	*Agreement to Sell*
Transfer of ownership	Ownership or property in the goods passes to the buyer at the time of the contract. The seller is no more the owner of the goods.	Ownership or property in goods does not pass to the buyer at the time of the contract. The ownership passes to the buyer at a future time or is subject to the fulfilment of a condition.
Nature of contract	It is an excepted contract. The transfer of property and delivery of goods are done immediately.	It is an executor contract. It is to be performed in future.
Incidence or risk of loss	After sale, the buyer is responsible for any loss or destruction of goods in the possession of the seller. This is because the seller ceases to be the owner immediately on completion of the contract.	Loss of goods shall be borne by the seller. This is because the seller remains the owner until the agreement to sell becomes a sale.
Nature of goods	A sale can only be made with regard to the goods which are specific and ascertained at the time of the contract.	An agreement to sell can only be with regard to unascertained and existing goods at the time of the contract.
Conveyance	A sale is a contract plus conveyance of ownership in the goods.	An agreement to sell is merely a contract, pure and simple.
Suit for price	If the buyer fails to pay for the goods, the seller can sue for the price even though the goods are still in his possession.	The seller can only sue for damages if the buyer fails to accept and pay for the goods. He cannot sue for payment of the price.

Basis of Difference	*Sale*	*Agreement to Sell*
Right to resell	The seller cannot resell the goods. If, after the sale, the seller disposes the goods, the buyer has double remedy suit for damages against the seller and recovery of goods from the third party.	If, after the agreement to sell, the seller disposes the goods, the buyer can sue only for damages. The goods are still the property of the seller, and he can dispose them of as he likes.
Nature of rights	A sale creates rights in rem. It gives a right to the buyer to enjoy the goods as against the world at large including the seller.	An agreement to sell creates rights in personal. It gives a right to the buyer against the seller only to sue for damages.
Insolvency of buyer	If the buyer becomes insolvent, the seller, in the absence of the right of lien over the goods, must deliver the goods to the official receiver. The seller can claim only a proportionate dividend for the price due.	If the buyer becomes indolent before paying the price of the goods, the seller may refuse to deliver goods to the official receiver.
Insolvency of seller	If the seller becomes insolvent, the buyer will be entitled to recover the goods from the official receiver. This is because the buyer is the owner of the goods.	If the seller becomes insolvent and the buyer has paid the price, he can claim only a proportionate dividend from the official receiver. This is because the buyer is not the owner of goods.
Liability for sales tax	A sale is liable for sales tax.	An agreement to sell is not liable for sales tax until it is actually converted into a sale.

Differences between a Sale and a Hire-Purchase Agreement

Hire-Purchase Agreement

An agreement of hire-purchase is not a sale. A hire-purchase agreement is an agreement under which the owner delivers his goods on hire basis to a 'hirer' for his use. The hirer has the option to purchase the goods by paying the agreed amount in specified instalments. A hire-purchase agreement gives the hirer the possession of only goods. The hirer may return the goods at any time without any obligation to pay the balance rent. A hire-purchase agreement is a bailment plus an agreement to sell.

Whether an agreement is a hire-purchase agreement or a contract of sale? The test is whether any option is given to the hirer to terminate the contract. If the answer is yes or in affirmation, it would be a hire-purchase agreement. If the answer is in negative, it would be a contract of sale. Where the buyer has no right to terminate the agreement and is bound to pay the price, the agreement is a contract of sale.

Basis of Difference	*Sale*	*Hire-Purchase Agreement*
Transfer of ownership	In the case of a contract of sale, the ownership in goods is transferred from the seller to the buyer as soon as the contract is made.	In the case of a hire-purchase agreement, the ownership in goods is transferred to the hire-purchaser only when all the agreed instalments are paid.

Basis of Difference	*Sale*	*Hire-Purchase Agreement*
Return of goods	In the case of a sale, the buyer has no option to return the goods. He cannot terminate the contract.	In the case of a hire-purchase agreement, the hirer may terminate the agreement at any stage. He need not pay the remaining instalments on termination of the agreement.
Positions of the buyer	The position of the buyer is that of the owner, and he gets all rights of the owner in the case of a sale.	In a hire-purchase, the hire-purchaser does not become the owner. He becomes owner only when he has paid all the instalments. Before paying all the instalments, his position is only that of a bailee.
Treatment of instalments paid	In a sale, if the purchaser opts to pay in instalments, then each instalment is regarded as part payment.	But in the case of a hire-purchase, each instalment paid is regarded as hire charges.
Governing law	A contract of sale is governed by the Sale of Goods Act, 1930.	However, a hire-purchase agreement is governed by the Hire-Purchase Act, 1972.
Implied conditions and warranties	A sale is subject to implied conditions and warranties.	A hire-purchase agreement is not subject to such implied conditions and warranties.

Definition of Goods

Goods form the subject matter of a contract of sale. Section 2(7) defines goods as 'every kind of movable property other than actionable claims and money, and includes stock and shares, growing crops, grass, and things attached to or forming part of land which are agreed to be severed before sale or under the contract of sale'. Thus, goods include the following:

1. Every kind of movable property, including stock and shares, growing crops and grass.
2. Things attached to earth such as growing grass and trees can be the subject matter of sale, provided they are agreed to be separated from the earth under the contract of sale.
3. The term 'goods' does not include money and actionable claims. Money means currency money and it is not goods. Currency means the legal tender. But foreign coins or antique coins or old coins may be treated as goods. An actionable claim means 'a claim which can be enforced through the court of law. Debts due from one person to another are actionable claims. They cannot be the subject matter of sale'.

Classification of Goods

Goods forming the subject matter of a contract of sale may be as follows:

1. **Existing goods:** Goods owned or possessed by the seller at the time of making the contract of sale are called 'existing goods'. Only existing goods can be the subject matter of a sale. Generally, the seller is the owner of such goods. However, in the case of a sale by an agent or pawnee, the goods are possessed but not owned by the seller.

Existing goods may be specific goods, ascertained goods or unascertained goods. These are as follows:

a. **Specific goods:** Goods identified and agreed upon at the time a contract of sale is made are called 'specific goods'. For example, if A agrees to sell his horse or car to B, it is a sale of specific goods.
b. **Ascertained goods:** Goods which are ascertained or identified only after the formation of a contract of sale are known as 'ascertained goods'. The terms ascertained and specific are commonly used for the same kind of goods.
c. **Unascertained goods:** Goods which are not identified and ascertained at the time of sale are called 'unascertained goods'. They are also called 'generic goods'. They are not definite and specific. They are goods defined by description only and may form part of a lot.

2. **Future goods:** Future goods are goods which are manufactured or produced or acquired by the seller after the making of a contract of sale. There cannot be a sale of future goods. A contract for the sale of future goods is an agreement to sell goods. This is because ownership cannot be transferred before the goods are manufactured or produced.
   Example: P agrees to sell to Q all the mangoes which will be grown in his garden next year. This is an agreement for the sale of future goods.
3. **Contingent goods:** Goods, the acquisition of which by the seller depends upon an uncertain contingency, which may or may not happen, are called 'contingent goods'. A contract for sale of contingent goods is enforceable only when the event on the happening of which the performance of the contract depends has happened. If the event does not happen, the contract becomes void. Contingent goods come within the class of future goods.
   Example: X agrees to sell to Y a 'ring', provided he is able to purchase it from its present owner. This is an agreement for the sale of contingent goods.

Effects of Perishable Goods

There are some goods which are perishable. In a contract of sale of specific goods, the goods may perish before the sale is complete. The Sale of Goods Act provides the following provisions regarding the perishable goods:

1. **Goods perishing before contract:** Section 7 of the Act provides,

> Where there is a contract for the sale of specific goods, the contract is void if the goods without the knowledge of the seller have, at the time when the contract was made, perished or become so damaged so damaged as no longer to answer to their description in the contract.

However, this rule applies subject to the following conditions:

a. The goods must be specific goods, and the contract of sale should be for specific goods.
b. Goods must have perished before the contract is made, and the seller should have no knowledge about it.

If the seller was aware of the destruction and still entered into the contract, he is stopped from disputing the contract. In that case, he must either make his contract good or pay compensation for breach, except where the buyer also knows that the goods have perished.

2. **Goods perishing after agreement to sell but before sale:** Section 8 provides,

> Where there is an agreement to sell specific goods, and subsequently the goods without any fault on the part of the seller or buyer perish or become so damaged as no longer to answer to their description in the agreement before the risk passes to the buyer, the agreement is thereby avoided.

However, the contract can be avoided on this basis only when the following conditions are satisfied:

a. The contract must be an agreement to sell.
b. The loss should relate to specific goods.
c. The goods must have perished or damaged before the property or risk passes to the buyer.
d. The perishing or damage to goods must not be due to fault on the part of the buyer or the seller.

The section applies only to sale of specific goods. If the sale is of unascertained goods, the perishing of the whole quantity of such goods in the possession of the seller will not relieve him of his obligation to deliver.

In the case of Howell vs. Coupland, Coupland agreed to sell to Howell 200 tons of regent potatoes to be grown on the land belonging to Coupland. Coupland sowed sufficient land to grow more than 200 tons, but without his fault, a disease attacked the crop, and he was able to deliver only 8 tons. The agreement was held to have become void.

CONTRACT OF SALE AND CONTRACT FOR WORK AND LABOUR

A contract of sale involves the transfer of ownership and possession to the buyer for a price. However, a contract of work and materials involves exercise of skill and labour by one party in respect of materials supplied by another. Delivery of goods is a subsidiary condition or incidental to the contract.

The test generally applied to distinguish between the two is that if as a result of the contract, the property in goods is transferred to the other for a price, it is a sale. Where the substance of the contract is the exercise of skill and labour, it is a contract for work and labour. The court would have to find out in each case the principal object of the transaction and the intention of the parties to determine whether a contract is one of a sale or that of work and labour.

Example: In Lee vs. Griffin, a dentist agreed to supply a set of artificial teeth to fit the mouth of a patient. The material was wholly supplied by the dentist. It was held to be a contract of sale of goods.

The Supreme Court clarified in State of Gujarat vs. Variety Body Builders that whether the contracts for construction of coaches on under-frames supplied by Western Railway administration were contracts of sale of goods or work and labour. The court concluded that the predominant element in the contract was that the parties intended that the contractor should transfer the property in railway coaches to the Railway administration after their completion. However, much depends upon circumstances. The court held that it was a contract of work or labour.

Sale and Bailment

In a contract of bailment, the goods are delivered by one person to another for certain purpose and ownership does not pass to the bailee, but in the case of a sale, the seller makes delivery of goods to the buyer for a price and the buyer becomes the owner of the goods. Following are the main differences between a sale and bailment:

1. **Transfer of property and possession:** In a sale, the property in goods is transferred from the seller to the buyer and therefore the buyer can deal with the goods in any way he likes. However, in bailment, there is only transfer of possession from the bailor to the bailee for some specific purposes such as safety, use and carriage.
2. **Return of goods:** In bailment, the bailee is under an obligation to return the goods, after achieving the purpose for which they were bailed. But in the case of a sale, there is transfer of ownership for money consideration and there is no question of return of goods.
3. **Consideration:** In a sale, there is money consideration. However, in bailment, the possession may be transferred with or without any money consideration. Bailment can be gratuitous (without charge) or non-gratuitous (with charge).
4. **Right to goods:** In the case of a sale of goods, the buyer may deal with the goods in any way he likes, as he is the absolute owner. But in the case of bailment, the bailee has to use the goods according to the terms of bailment.

Modes and Forms of Contract of Sale

Section 5(1) provides,

> A contract of sale is made by an offer to buy or sell goods for a price and the acceptance of such offer. The contract may provide for immediate delivery of the goods or immediate payment of the price or both, or for the delivery or payment by instalments, or that the delivery or payment or both shall be postponed.

The above provision states the following:

A contract of sale is made by an offer to sell or buy goods by one person and acceptance of such offer by another person. It may provide for the following:

1. Delivery of goods immediately, simultaneously with payment of price
2. Immediate delivery of goods but price to be paid in future
3. Payment of price immediately, with delivery of goods in future
4. Postponement of delivery of goods and payment of price
5. Payment of price and delivery of goods in instalments

How Is a Contract of Sale Made?

A contract of sale can be made in any of the following ways:

1. In writing
2. By word of mouth

3. Partly in writing and partly oral
4. May be implied from the conduct of the parties or by the course of their business

However, if any law prescribes any particular mode, then the contract of sale must be made in that particular mode (Section 5(2)).

PRICE

Section 2(10) provides, '"price" means the money consideration for a sale of goods'. No sale of goods can take place without a price. The price must be expressed in money terms. If any consideration other than money is to be given, it is not a price.

MODES OF FIXING PRICE

Sections 9 and 10 provide the following modes of fixing the price:

1. **Price fixed by the contract:** The price in a contract of sale may be fixed by the contract itself. The parties are free to fix any price and the court will not interfere in this matter to determine its adequacy.
2. **Price fixation in the manner provided in the contract of sale:** The contract itself might provide for some manner in which the price is to be fixed. In such cases, the price may be fixed in a manner provided in the contract. However, (a) where the price is agreed to be whatever sum the seller is offered by any third party or (b) where the price is left to be fixed only by one of the contracting parties, the agreement would be uncertain as to price and hence void. However, where no price is fixed, the contract is not void for uncertainty, as in such a case, the buyer is bound to pay to the seller a 'reasonable price'.
3. **Price to be determined by the course of dealings between the parties:** Where the price is not expressly stated in the contract or no provision is made for its determination. It may be determined by the course of dealings between the parties.
4. **Reasonable price:** Where the price is not determined by any of the foregoing provisions, the buyer shall pay the seller a reasonable price. The term 'reasonable' price is a question of fact depending upon the circumstances of each particular case.
5. **Price fixation by third parties:** Section 10 provides that the parties may agree to sell and buy goods on terms that the price is to be fixed by the valuation of a third party. If such third party fails to make valuation, the contract becomes void. However, if the buyer has received the goods or any part thereof and has appropriated them, he is bound to pay a reasonable price to the seller.

ADDITION TO OR DEDUCTION FROM PRICE ON ACCOUNT OF TAX

Section 64 provides that unless a different intention appears from the contract, if after making of the contract any duty of customs or excise on goods or any tax on sale or purchase of goods is imposed or increased, in respect of any goods, the seller may add it to the contract price.

How Is the Payment to Be Made?

A seller is not bound to accept the payment for goods otherwise than in the form of currency unless there is an agreement to the contrary or unless the seller is stopped from disputing the mode of payment. A seller is not bound to accept the payment by cheque.

Earnest Money or Deposit

Sometimes the buyer pays a part of price in advance to the seller for due performance of the contract. This is known as earnest money. If the contract is duly performed, it is adjusted against the purchase price and only balance of the price is payable. However, if the contract is not performed or cannot be performed due to the fault of the buyer, the seller forfeits the earnest money. If the seller does not perform the contract, he must return the earnest money.

Stipulations as to Time

Section 11 provides,

> Unless a different intention appears from the terms of the contract, stipulations as to time of payment are not deemed to be of the essence of a contract of sale. Whether any other stipulation as to time is of the essence of the contract or not depends on the terms of the contract.

However, regarding the time of delivery of goods, the section provides that it depends on the terms of the contract whether it is of the essence of the contract or not.

Therefore, failure by the buyer to pay the price in time would not as a rule entitle the seller to treat the contract as repudiated. As regards the time for performing any other part of the contract, whether time is of the essence or not depends on the terms of the contract. Such intention is to be gathered from the nature of goods, language used, conduct of the parties and surrounding circumstances at the time of making of the contract.

Test Questions

1. Define a contract of sale of goods. What are the essential features of a contract of sale of goods? Distinguish between a contract of sale and an agreement to sell.
2. Define goods and mention how goods are classified.
3. What are the characteristics and formalities of a contract of sale? What is price? How and when price can be determined?
4. Distinguish between bailment and sale, and sale and hire-purchase?
5. How is price fixed in a contract of sale? If the price is not determined by the parties, what price, if any, is the buyer liable to pay?

Practical Problems

1. X agrees to sell to Y his two bikes on the terms that the price will be fixed by Z. Y takes the delivery of one bike immediately. Z refuses to fix the price. X ask for the return of bike already delivered, whereas Y insists on the delivery of the second bike and requests to pay a reasonable price for both the bikes. Decide.
   Hint. Y can keep the first bike after paying a reasonable amount; however, he cannot insist for the delivery of the second bike as the contract is void. (Section 10)
2. X agrees to sell a horse to Y, who tells X that Y needs the horse for riding to Kolkata. The horse was ill at the time of agreement. What are the rights of X and Y?
   Hint. The agreement is void. (Section 8)
3. X agrees to exchange with Y 500 tins of baby food at ₹20 per tin, for 10 cows at ₹500 per cow and pay the difference in cash. State with reasons whether this is a contract for sale of goods.
   Hint. It is a contract for sale of goods since money values have been taken into consideration.
4. There was a sale of 800 bags of nuts. Unknown to the seller, before the sale, 84 bags had been stolen. Is the sale valid? Can the buyer be compelled to take the remainder?
   Hint. The sale is void. The buyer cannot be compelled to take the remainder as the subject matter is not complete.
5. X sold 500 quintals of groundnut oil to Y. Before it would be delivered to Y, the government of India requisitioned the whole quantity lying with X in public interest. Y wants to sue X for breach of contract.
   Hint. The contract becomes void.

16 CHAPTER

Conditions and Warranties

Learning Objectives

- To understand condition and warranties
- To understand when condition is to be treated as warranty
- To understand express and implied conditions as to the contract of sale
- To understand when implied condition can be removed
- To understand the doctrine of caveat emptor and its exceptions

Every contract of sale usually contains a number of stipulations or terms or statements regarding the nature, time of delivery and quality of goods. However, not all stipulations are of equal importance. Some stipulations form the very basis of the contract of sale or may be essential to the main purpose of the contract. Some other stipulations may be less essential, collateral or subsidiary to the main purpose of the contract. Major stipulations are called 'conditions' and minor stipulations are called 'warranties'. In Wallis vs. Pratt, it was observed that a condition is a term which goes so directly to the substance of the contract or in other words is so entitled to its very nature that non-performance may fairly be considered by the party as a substantial failure to perform the contract at all. A warranty is a term which, though must be performed, is not so vital that a failure to perform goes to the substance of the contract.

Condition: A condition in a contract of sale is a stipulation of fundamental nature. It is essential to the main purpose of the contract. If there is a breach of condition, the aggrieve party has a right to treat the contract as repudiated and refuse to accept the goods. He can also claim damages. Section 12(2) defines a condition as 'a stipulation essential to the main purpose of the contract, the breach of which gives rise to a right to treat the contract as repudiated'.

Warranty: A warranty is subsidiary to the main purpose of the contract. It is not as vital to the existence of the contract as a condition. The breach of warranty does not give right to treat the contract as repudiated. The aggrieved party can only claim damages for any loss, which may arise. Section 12(3) defines a warranty as 'a stipulation collateral to the main purposes of the contract, the breach of which gives the aggrieved party a right to sue for damages only and not to avoid the contract itself'.

In the case of Baldry vs. Marshall, M bought two small ships from K relying upon the particulars furnished by K that the capacity of each ship was 460 tons. While the actual capacity was 360 tons only. M wanted to reject the ships. It was held that the representation of capacity was a warranty for which M could only sue for damages. Therefore, the court generally looks at the intention of the parties and the construction of the contract to know whether a stipulation is a condition or warranty.

In the case of Gomathy Nayagam vs. Palaniswami, it was held that the intention to make time as essence of the contract may be evidenced by either express stipulations or by circumstances which are sufficiently strong to displace the ordinary presumption that in a contract of sale of land, the stipulation as to time is not the essence.

Whether a stipulation in a contract of sale is a condition or warranty depends in each case on the intention of the parties and the structure or construction of the contract. Conditions and warranties may be either express or implied. Thus, a condition in a contract of sale is stipulation of fundamental nature, the breach of which gives the opposite party a right to treat the contract repudiated. However, warranty is subsidiary to main purpose of the contract. The breach of warranty only gives rise to a right to claim damages for any loss, which may arise.

Differences between Condition and Warranty

The following are the main differences between condition and warranty:

Basis of Difference	*Conditions*	*Warranties*
Importance	A condition is very essential to the main purpose of the contract of sale. It is of a fundamental nature.	A warranty is collateral or secondary to the main purpose of the contract. It is of a subsidiary or inferior character.
Right in case of breach	On breach of condition, contract may be repudiated or avoided. Damages also can be claimed.	On breach of warranty, contract cannot be repudiated. Only damages can be claimed.
Rejection of goods	On breach of condition, buyer may reject the goods.	On breach of warranty, buyer cannot reject the goods.
Performance of contract	In breach of condition, aggrieved party is not bound to perform the contract.	In breach of warranty, aggrieved party is bound to perform the contract.
Treatment	The buyer may treat a breach of condition as breach of warranty only.	The buyer cannot treat a breach of warranty as breach of condition.

When to Treat Condition as Warranty (Sections 13(1) to 13(3))

Section 13(1) provides that a buyer can treat the breach of condition as a breach of warranty. Further, a breach of condition would be treated as a breach of warranty in the following circumstances.

1. **Voluntary waiver:** Where a contract of sale is subject to any condition to be fulfilled by the seller, the buyer may waive the condition. If he does so, he cannot afterwards insist on fulfilment of the condition. A buyer may accept either defective goods or beyond the stipulated time. The conditions are for the benefit of the buyer. He may decide not to take benefit of any condition. Waiver may be express or implied.

2. **Election by the buyer to treat a breach of condition as a breach of warranty:** Where a contract of sale is subject to any condition to be fulfilled by the seller and the seller commits a breach of the condition, the buyer can treat the contract as repudiated and refuse to accept the goods. However, he is not bound to do so. He may accept the goods treating the breach of condition as a breach of warranty and may sue the seller for damages for breach of warranty.
3. **Acceptance of goods by the buyer:** Where the contract is indivisible and the buyer has accepted the goods or part thereof, the breach of condition can only be treated as breach of warranty. The buyer can only claim damages and cannot reject the goods or treat the contract as repudiated. Section 42 provides that the buyer is deemed to have accepted the goods:
   a. When he intimates to the seller that he has accepted them
   b. When he does any act in relation to the goods which is inconsistent with the ownership of the seller
   c. When, after the lapse of a reasonable time, he retains the goods without intimating to the seller that he has rejected them

   Thus, where the buyer after receiving the goods resells them or pledges them, it will be regarded that the buyer has accepted the goods.

   Example: X purchased 500 bags of sugar from Y according to the sample. When the goods were delivered, X resold the sugar to Z. Z rejected the goods on the ground that it was not according to sample. Now X also wants to avoid the contract. Here, X will not succeed because by reselling the goods to Z, X has accepted the goods. Now, he is to treat this breach of condition as a breach of warranty.
4. **Impossibility of performances:** Where the performance of the contract becomes impossible subsequent to the formation of the contract, performance will be excused. However, this rule will not be applicable in the following circumstances:
   a. Where the performance was made impossible owing to the negligence or default of any of the parties to contract.
   b. The parties expressly provide in contract with reference to occurrence of supervening event.
   c. Where the promise is capable of being performed in itself, the promisor cannot be excused from his obligation to perform by stating that the inability to perform was due to circumstances beyond his control.
   d. A party will also be excused from performance, if subsequent to the promise, an act is passed by the state or an event occurs, thus rendering the performance illegal.
   e. In case of two alternative promises, where one of the promises becomes impossible, the promisor will have to perform the other promise.
   f. Where after making two promises the promisor elects to perform one of them, the impossibility of performance of that promise will not excuse the promisor from performing the other.

Express Conditions as to the Contract of Sale

Section 62 provides that parties to the contract are free to include any number of express conditions and warranties in contract, but there will be some conditions and warranties by law or by the usage and custom of trade. Express conditions are those which are expressly provided in the contract. It is open for the parties to include in their contract any number of express conditions. Implied conditions and warranties are those which the law implies in a contract of sale. The provisions of law are based on the following maxims:

1. *Expressum facit cessare tacitum*, that is, what is expressed makes what is tacit or implied to cease.
2. *Modus et conventio vincunt legem*, that is, custom and agreement overrule law (implied conditions and warrants).

Thus, express conditions are provided by the terms of the contract.

Implied Conditions as to the Contract of Sale

In addition to express conditions, law implies into every contract of sale of goods a number of conditions. Such conditions are called 'implied conditions'. Both the parties to a contract of sale are bound by implied conditions unless they are excluded by an express agreement between themselves. Sections 14 to 17 lay down the following implied conditions.

1. **Conditions as to title:** In every contract of sale, there is an implied condition that seller has the right to sell goods. In case of agreement to sell, there is an implied condition, that seller will have the right to sell the goods at the time when the property is to pass and this condition is called 'condition as to title'. If a person sells goods, he can recover the purchase price from the seller. In the case of Rowland vs. Divall, R purchased a second-hand motorcar from D and used it for four months. Subsequently, the police seized the car, as the car was a stolen one. R sued D to recover the price, which he had already paid. It was held that D had broken the condition as to title and R was, therefore, entitled to recover the purchase money from D.
2. **Condition in sale by description:** In the case of sale of goods by description, goods shall correspond with the description. It is a condition which goes to the essence of the contract. The breach of this condition entitles the buyer to reject the goods. The description may be in terms of the qualities or characteristics of the goods. This rule applies to all the cases where the purchaser has not seen the goods but is relying on the description alone. The conditions as to description must be strictly fulfilled. The seller must provide the goods ordered and described and not something different, however excellent and merchantable they may be.

   In the case of Varley vs. Whipp, A agreed to buy a second-hand reaping machine which he had never seen. The seller stated that the machine was almost new and had been used to cut only about 50 acres. A found that it was old and had been mended. Therefore, he returned it to the seller. The court held that as the machine did not correspond with the description, A has the right to return the machine to the seller and recover the money paid.

   In Beale vs. Taylor, a car that was described 'Herald Convertible' 1961 model was put to sale. Having seen the car, the buyer went ahead and purchased it. Later, he discovered that the rear part of the car was part of a 1961 model, but the front half was a part of an earlier model. He could reject the car and recover the amount paid.

3. **Condition as to sample:** A contract of sale is a contract of sale by sample where there is a term in the contract, express or implied to that effect. Where goods are sold by sample, there are the following implied conditions:
   a. The bulk shall correspond with the sample in quality.
   b. The buyer shall have a reasonable opportunity of comparing the bulk with the sample.
   c. The goods shall be free from latent defect, rendering them un-merchantable. Latent defect means a defect which is discoverable by reasonable examination.

   Thus, the goods sold should match the sample in quality. If the bulk does not correspond with the sample, there is a breach of condition and the buyer is entitled to reject the goods. In the case of Lorymer vs. Smith, A agreed to sell by sample two parcels of wheat to B, one containing 7,000 bushels and the other 1,400. The buyer was allowed to inspect the smaller parcel but was refused inspection of the larger parcel. It was held that the buyer was entitled to refuse to take any of these wheat parcels.
4. **Sale by description as well as sample:** Where a contract is made for the sale of goods by sample as well as description, there is an implied condition that goods must correspond with the sample as well as with the description. If the goods supplied correspond only with the sample and not with the description or vice versa, the condition is broken and the buyer is entitled to reject the goods. In Wallis vs. Pratt, there was a contract for sale of seeds. However, the seeds supplied to the buyer were of a different quality. The defect also existed in the sample. The discrepancy in quality was discovered only after the seeds were sown. The buyer could recover damages as there was a breach of condition.
5. **Condition as to quality or fitness:** According to Section 16(1), in a contract of sale there is no implied warrantee or condition as to the quality or fitness for any particular purpose of goods supplied. The general principle is caveat emptor, that is, let the buyer beware, and the buyer should buy the goods after satisfying himself that they will serve his purpose. The implied condition as to quality or fitness shall apply, if the following conditions are satisfied:
   a. The buyer, expressly or impliedly, informs the seller about the particular purpose for which the goods are required.
   b. The buyer should rely on seller's skill or judgement.
   c. The goods must be of a type which is normally dealt with by the seller.
   d. Where the goods are capable of more than one use, the buyer must inform the seller the particular purpose and then only this condition shall apply.
   e. Where the goods are fit for one particular use alone or if the nature of goods itself tells the purpose by implication, then the buyer need not inform the seller the particular purpose for which they are being bought.
   f. If a person buying goods for a particular purpose is suffering from some abnormality and it is not made known to the seller at the time of sale, the implied condition as to fitness shall not apply.
6. **Sale under patent or trade name:** Sometimes a buyer may rely more on the trade name of an article than the judgement of the seller. Section 16(1) provides that in the case of contract of the sale of a specified article under its patent or other trade name, there is no implied condition as to its fitness for any particular purpose.

   Example: A person buys 'Disprin tablets' to get relief from severe headache, if he does not get any relief, he cannot avoid the contract and the seller of 'Disprin tablets' cannot be held liable.

7. **Condition as to merchantability:** Section 16(2) provides that where goods are brought by description from a seller who deals in goods of that description (whether he is the manufacturer or producer or not), there is an implied condition that the goods shall be of merchantable quality. Even goods sold under a patent or trademark must be of a merchantable quality. Goods must be of such a quality as to be capable of being resold in the market by that description. However, for applying this condition, the following requirements must be satisfied:
   a. The goods should have been bought by description.
   b. The goods should have been bought from a seller who deals in goods of that description (whether he is the manufacturer or producer or not).

   Merchantable quality: The term 'merchantable' or 'merchantable quality' has not been defined in the Act. It means that goods must correspond with the description and must be in such condition that a reasonable man would accept them. If the goods are purchased for self-use, they must be reasonably fit for the purpose for which they are generally used. In Jones vs. Just, a firm of Liverpool merchants contracted to buy from a London based merchant, a number of bales of Manila hemp which will arrive from Singapore. The hemp was so much damaged by the seawater that it could not be sold as Manila hemp. The goods had to be sold at a reduced rate. It was held that the goods were not merchantable and the seller was liable to make good the loss caused by selling at the reduced price.
8. **Condition as to wholesomeness:** This condition applies in the case of eatables and other provisions. The provision supplied must not only answer to description and be merchantable but also wholesome, pure, unadulterated and suitable for consumption at the time of sale. In the case of Chaproniere vs. Mason, a person bought a bun from a baker's shop. The bun contained a stone because of which the buyer broke one of his teeth. The subject matter of this contract did not satisfy the condition as to wholesomeness, and hence the buyer was entitled to recover damages from the baker.

When Can Implied Conditions Be Removed

The implied condition as to the contract of sale may be removed by any of the following means.

1. **By express agreement:** The implied conditions and warranties may be negated or varied by express agreement. The seller can exclude his liability by expressly providing that he will not be liable for breach of any condition or warranty. However, when the seller is guilty of fundamental breach, he cannot exclude liability by express agreement.
2. **By course of dealings:** The parties may vary rights, duties and obligations implied by law by the 'course of dealings' between them. Course of dealings implies repeated occurrence of similar transactions between the parties. A single transaction is not sufficient to establish course of dealings between parties.
3. **Usage of trade:** Implied conditions may be excluded by trade usage also. The agreement between the parties is always subject to established customs and trade usages. If such usages provide for exclusion of the liability, the parties are not liable for breach of implied terms in a contract of sale.

Implied Warranties

Subject to the contract to the contrary, following are the implied warranties in a contract of sale of goods.

1. **Warranty of quiet possession:** According to the provisions of Section 14(b), unless the circumstances are such as to show a different intention there is an implied warranty that the buyer shall have and enjoy quiet possession of the goods.
   Example: A purchased a second-hand typewriter from B. A spent some money on its repairs but was dispossessed of it after six months by B. It was held that A was entitled to recover from B not only the price paid but also the cost of repair.
   The breach of implied condition as to title may also result in breach of warranty as to quiet possession. The buyer, therefore, will be entitled to recover compensation for breach of both, a condition as well as a warranty.
2. **Warranty of freedom from encumbrance:** Section 14(c) provides that the goods shall be free from any charge or encumbrance in favour of a third party not declared or known to the buyer before or at the time when the contract is made. Buyer shall have no right of action if the seller had disclosed the charge or encumbrance at the time of contract.
3. **Warranty as to quality or fitness by usage of trade:** Section 16(3) provides that an implied warranty or condition as to quality or fitness for a particular purpose may be annexed by the usage of trade. In the case of Jones vs. Bowden, where drugs were sold by auction and where it is a usage of trade to disclose beforehand any sea damage, such disclosure must be made. In case no such disclosure has been made and the goods are found to be defective, it will be taken as a breach of warranty.

Warranty to Disclose Dangerous Nature of Goods

Where the goods are dangerous and the seller knows that the buyer is ignorant about the dangerous nature of the goods, the seller should warn the buyer about the probable danger, otherwise he would be liable for damages for the injury caused to the buyer because of the dangerous quality of the goods. In the case of Clarke vs. Army & Navy Cooperative Society Ltd, A sold a tin of disinfectant powder to C, A knew that the tin was to be opened with special care otherwise it might prove dangerous. He also knew that C was ignorant about it. He did not warn C. C opened the tin and the powder injured his eyes. It was held that A was liable, as he should have warned C of the probable danger.

Effect of Breach of Warranty

In case of breach of warranty, the buyer cannot repudiate the contract. In terms of the provisions of Section 59, he may, of course, set up the breach of warranty in diminution or extinction of the price and may bring an action against the seller and claim damages for the breach.

Doctrine of Caveat Emptor

The 'caveat emptor' means 'let the buyer beware'. The doctrine of caveat emptor means that seller is not bound to disclose the defects in the goods which he is selling. A buyer purchases at his own risk. It is the duty of buyer to satisfy himself before buying the goods that the goods will serve the purpose for which they are being bought. If the goods turn out to be defective or do not serve his purpose or if he depends on his skill or judgement, the buyer cannot hold the seller responsible. Section 16 has enunciated the rule of caveat emptor that there is no implied warranty or condition as to the quality or fitness for any particular purpose of goods supplied under a contract of sale.

Example: X purchased rice from Y. X erroneously thought that the rice was old. The rice was, however, new. Here, X cannot avoid the contract because he has depended on his own skill and judgement. Therefore, the rule of caveat emptor will be applicable.

In the case of Ward vs. Hobbes, a vendor was bound to emptor no artifice or disguise for the purpose of concealing defects in the article sold, since that would amount to a possible fraud on the buyer, yet under the general doctrine of caveat emptor, he is not undoubtedly bound to disclose every defect of which he may be cognizant; although his silence may operate virtually to deceive the buyer. The reason was that the buyer bought the things on his own assessment. Therefore, the rule of caveat emptor applied to the case.

Exceptions to the Rule

The doctrine of caveat emptor is, however, subject to the following exceptions.

1. **Fitness for buyer's purpose:** Section 16(1) provides that where the buyer makes known to the seller the particular purpose for which the goods are required, so as to show that he relies on the seller's skill or judgement and the goods are of a description which it is in the course of seller's business to supply, it is the duty of the seller to supply such goods as are reasonably fit for that purpose. In this case, the buyer must prove the following:
   a. The buyer required the things for the particular purpose.
   b. The buyer expressly or by implication makes known to the seller that particular purpose.
   c. The buyer relied on the seller's skill and judgement.
   d. The seller's usual course of business is to sell goods whether he is the actual manufacturer or producer or not.

   In the case of Shivallingappa Shankarappa vs. Balakrishna & Son, the buyer ordered for the best quality of dal. However, on arrival at the destination, the dal had been damaged by moisture and was no longer of merchantable quality. It was held that the buyer could reject the goods and claim damages from the seller.
2. **Goods purchased under patent or brand name:** Section 16(1) provides that in case where the goods are purchased under its patent name or brand name, there is no implied condition that the goods shall be fit for any particular purpose. In Baldry vs. Marshall, B who wanted to purchase a car to be used as a touring car approached M, a motor car dealer, for his advice. M recommended a Bugatti car, and subsequently, B

purchased it. It was later discovered that car was not reasonably fit for use. The buyer could reject the car.

3. **Goods sold by description:** Section 15 provides that where the goods are sold by description, there is an implied condition that the goods shall correspond with the description. In the case of Shepherd vs. Kain, a ship was advertised for sale as copper fastened without allowance for any defects whatsoever. The ship was not fully copper fastened as is understood in the trade. It was held that it was a sale by description and the buyer could reject the goods.
4. **Merchantable quality:** Section 16(2) states that where the goods are bought by description from a seller who deals in goods of that description, there is an implied condition that the goods shall be of merchantable quality. The rule of caveat emptor is not applicable. But where the buyer has examined the goods, this rule shall apply if the defects were such which ought to have been revealed by ordinary examination. In case of Jones vs. Just, a firm of Liverpool merchants contract to buy from a London merchant a number of bales of Manila hemp to arrive from Singapore. The hemp was so much damaged by the seawater that it could not be sold as Manila hemp. The goods were not merchantable and the seller was liable to make good the loss caused by selling at the reduced price.
5. **Goods purchased by sample:** According to Section 17 of the Act, where the goods are bought by sample, this rule of caveat emptor does not apply if the lot does not correspond with the sample. In Woods vs. Michaud, there was a contract for sale of cane corn. The buyer was shown a sample of corn, which was supposed to have been grown in the previous year. This was not a sale by sample, as it was likely that there would be a difference in quality.
6. **Goods purchased by sample as well as description:** Section 15 provides that where the goods are bought by sample as well as description, the rule of caveat emptor is not applicable in case the goods do not correspond with both the sample and description. In the case of Wallis vs. Pratt, there was a contract for sale of seeds. However, the seeds supplied to the buyer were of a different quality. The defect also existed in the sample. The discrepancy in quality was discovered only after the seeds were sworn. The buyer could recover damages, as there was breach of condition.
7. **Condition implied by trade usages:** An implied warranty or condition as to quality or fitness, for a particular purpose, may be annexed by the usage of trade and if the seller deviates from that, this rule of caveat emptor is not applicable. In Jones vs. Bowden, where drugs were sold by auction and where it is a usage of trade to disclose beforehand any sea damage, such disclosure must be made. In case no such disclosure has been made and the goods are found to be defective, it will be taken as a breach of warranty.
8. **Goods sold by misrepresentation:** Where the seller sells the goods by making some misrepresentation and the buyer relies on it or when the seller actively conceals some defect in the goods so that the same could not be discovered by the buyer on a reasonable examination, then the rule of caveat emptor will not apply. In such a case, the buyer has a right to avoid the contract and claim damages. In Beale vs. Taylor, a car that was described as 'Herald Convertible' 1961 model was put to sale. Having seen the car, buyer went ahead and purchased it. Later, he discovered that the rear part of the car was part of a 1961 model, but the front half was a part of an earlier model. He could reject the car and recover the amount paid.

Test Questions

1. Explain the terms 'condition' and 'warranty'. Distinguish between a 'condition' and 'warranty'. What conditions and warranties are implied in a contract of sale?
2. What is meant by sample? What are the conditions implied in such a sale?
3. Explain the doctrine of caveat emptor and state the conditions to it. What are the exceptions of it?
4. Distinguish between a 'condition' and 'warranty' in a contract of sale. What are implied conditions in a contract of sale?
5. In a contract for the sale of goods, there is no implied condition or warranty regarding the quality of the goods or their fitness for any purpose.

Practical Problems

1. A hirer, who obtains possession of a car from its owner under a hire purchase agreement, sells the car to a buyer who buys in good faith and without notice of the right of the owner. Does the buyer get a good title to the car?
   Hint. No, the hirer has obtained possession under a contract of hire purchase and not a contract of sale.
2. Pioneer Timber Store entered into a contract with A for the sale of timber 0.5 inch. The timber supplied varied in thickness from 0.5 inch to 0.67 inch. A's purpose of buying timber was to make cement barrels and timber as supplied was not fit for that purpose. A rejected the goods. Can A succeed?
   Hint. Yes, it is a sale by description. Goods should correspond with the description. (Section 15)
3. X finds a costly ring and after making reasonable efforts to find out the owner, sells it to Y, who buys without knowledge that X was a mere finder. Can the owner recover the ring from Y?
   Hint. The true owner can recover the ring from Y. The sale by X is an invalid sale and no valid title is transferred to the buyer. Section 169 of the Contract Act regarding rights of finder of goods does not apply here.
4. A bought a car from B, who had no title to it. A used the car for several months. After that the true owner came forward and demanded the car. State the right of A and the true owner of the car.
   Hint. A is bound to hand over the car to the true owner. He can sue B for breach of condition as to title.
5. N agreed to buy rice from S on inspection. He accepted part delivery of the goods and later refused to accept the remaining quantity on the ground that the rice was of inferior quality. Was N entitled to do that?
   Hint. No. Part delivery has the effect of passing property in the whole. (Section 34)

17

CHAPTER

Transfer of Ownership in Goods

Learning Objectives

- To explain the transfer of property
- To learn the rules regarding transfer of property
- To learn transfer of title by non-owners and exception to this

TRANSFER OF PROPERTY

'Property' means 'the right of ownership'. Transfer of property implies 'transfer of ownership'. It is different from transfer of possession. A person may be the owner of goods but goods may not be in his possession. Similarly, a person may have possession of goods but he may not have ownership, like agent or bailee. So in case of sale of goods, ownership in goods may be transferred with or without possession. The main object of a contract of sale is the transfer of property from seller to the buyer. Transfer of property is important to determine the time at which the property in goods passes to the buyer. It is important to note that the terms 'property' and 'possession' have different meanings. Even though the property in the goods has passed to the buyer, the seller might still have possession of the same. 'Property in goods' means the ownership of the goods. The term 'property in goods' must be distinguished from 'possession of goods' which refers to the custody or control of goods.

RULES REGARDING TRANSFER OF PROPERTY

In case of sale of ascertained or specific goods, the property in them passes to the buyer when parties to the contract intend it to pass. The parties may fix a time or stage of the transaction where the property may pass from the seller to the buyer. For the purpose of ascertaining or determining the intention of the parties, following factors shall be considered:

1. Terms of the parties
2. Conduct of the parties
3. Circumstances of the case

If intention is clear from the contract itself, there is no difficulty. But, if the intention of the parties cannot be ascertained from the contract, the aforementioned factors come into the play. In order to understand the rules in regard to passing of property, goods can be divided into the following three categories.

Passing of Property in Case of Ascertained Goods

Specific goods mean goods identified and agreed at the time of sale. This means that their identity must have been established at the time of sale. Section 18 provides that where there is a contract for the sale of unascertained goods, no property in the goods is transferred to the buyer unless and until the goods are ascertained. Thus, for transferring the ownership it is essential that goods must be ascertained. No property in goods can pass, if the goods are unascertained. In the case of Commissioner of Sales Tax vs. Husenali Adamji and Company, it was held that where the contract is for sale of unascertained goods, the property in the goods cannot pass until the goods are ascertained.

In case of specific or ascertained goods, following rules are applicable regarding the transfer of property.

1. **Time as intended by parties:** In the case of sale of ascertained goods, the property in the goods is transferred to buyer when the parties to contract intend it to be transferred. The parties to contract of sale of goods may fix a time or stage of the transaction when the property may pass form the seller to the buyer.
   Example: A agrees to sell his horse to B for ₹15,000, the horse to be delivered on Monday and price to be paid on the next day. B accepts the offer. The horse becomes B's property as soon as the offer is accepted. It is immaterial whether the time of payment of the price or the time of delivery of the goods or both is postponed.
2. **When no time has been prescribed in the contract:** If in a contract of sale, no time has been prescribed for transfer of property, following rules shall be applicable.
   a. **Unconditional contract for sale of specific goods in deliverable state:** When contract of sale is unconditional and specific goods are in deliverable state and price is fixed, the property in the goods passes to the buyer at the time of making the contract. It is not necessary that price of the goods has been paid or goods have been delivered.
   b. **Specified goods not in deliverable state:** Where there is a contract for the sale of specific goods and seller is bound to do something to the goods for putting them into a deliverable state, the property does not pass until such a thing is done and the buyer has notice of it. Two conditions are to be fulfilled if the goods are not in a deliverable state. They are as follows:
      i. The seller has done his act of putting the goods in a deliverable state, and the buyer has knowledge thereof.
      ii. The seller might be required to do certain acts to put the goods into a deliverable state such as packing and filling in containers. No property in goods passes unless such act is done and buyer knows about it.

   Section 21 provides that where there is a contract for sale of specific goods and seller is bound to do something to the goods for the purpose of putting them into a deliverable state, the property does not pass until such thing is done and the buyer has notice thereof. The conditions in Section 21 are as follows:

i. The goods should be specific goods whether existing or future goods.
ii. The seller should be required to do something so as to put goods in a deliverable state.
iii. The seller should have fulfilled the above specified obligation.
iv. The buyer should have notice of the fact that seller has done that thing which has the effect of putting the goods in a deliverable state.

In the case of Rugg vs. Minett, turpentine oil lying in a cistern was sold. The oil had to be filled by the seller in casks. Some of the casks were filled in the presence of the buyer, but before the buyer could remove them, the entire stock was destroyed by fire. The buyer had to bear the loss for the casks, which had been filled up in his presence because the goods were put in the deliverable state in the presence of the buyer.

c. **Conditional sale of specific goods in a deliverable state:** If the contract is for sale of specific goods in a deliverable state, but the seller is bound to weigh, measure, test or do some other act or thing with reference to goods for the purpose of ascertaining the price, the property in goods does not pass to buyer until that act or thing is done and buyer has notice thereof. In the case of Turley vs. Bates, T sold to B a heap of fireclay at a certain price per ton. B was to load the clay on his carts and take it away at his own expense. The clay was to be weighed on a certain weighing machine, while the carts were to pass from T's ground to B's ground to B's place. It was held that ownership of clay passed to B on completion of the bargain and nothing remained to be done by T.

Passing of Property in Case of Sale of Unascertained Goods

Unascertained goods are those goods which are not specifically identified and agreed upon at the time of sale. In case of sale of unascertained goods, no property in the goods is transferred to the buyer unless and until the goods are ascertained. A contract to sell unascertained goods is not a complete sale but a promise to sell. Following rules will be applicable in case of unascertained goods.

1. **Goods must be ascertained:** Ascertainment is the process by which goods to be delivered are identified and set apart. So if the goods are to be taken out from the larger stock and when such stock is taken out, then sale will be complete and property in the goods will be transferred to the buyer.
   Example: A agrees to sell 250 quintals of wheat out of 2,000 quintals stored in his godown. Property in the goods will be transferred to the buyer when 250 quintals of wheat are taken out of total quantity stored in the godown.
2. **Goods must be appropriated:** Mere ascertainment of goods is not enough, appropriation is also required. Appropriation involves selection of the goods with the exclusive intention of using them in performance of the contract and with the mutual consent of the parties. Once appropriation with mutual consent is done, the goods become the property of buyer. The seller will act as bailee, if goods are with him.
3. **Delivery to carrier:** When the seller delivers the goods to a carrier for being taken to the buyer, there is unconditional appropriation on his part and the property passes to the buyer.

Passing of Property in Case of Sale of Goods on Approval

A sale on approval is one in which the buyer may return the goods within a reasonable time, if they do not serve his purpose. This sale is a conditional sale. The property in goods will pass to the buyer:

1. When the buyer signifies his approval or acceptance to seller.
2. When the buyer does any other act adopting the transaction.
3. When the buyer retains the goods, without giving notice of rejection, beyond the time fixed for the return of goods, or if no time is fixed, beyond a reasonable time.

Example: A has sent some books to B on approval. B does not return them or ask the seller to take them back for six months. B is deemed to have the sale and must pay the price.

Section 24 provides that when goods are sent on approval or on sale or return basis. In this case, if buyer use these goods or sell it to someone else than it shall be treated as sale. The property passes to the buyer:

1. When he signifies his approval or on sale or return basis.
2. If he does not signify his approval or acceptance to the seller but retains the goods without giving notice of rejection, then, if a time has been fixed for the return of the goods, on the expiration of a reasonable time. If no time is fixed for return of goods, the property in goods will pass if the goods are not returned on the expiration of reasonable time.

Exceptions to Section 24

A buyer shall be held responsible in the following cases:

1. Where an express agreement provides for some condition, then fulfilment of such condition is required. In the case of Weiner vs. Smith, jewellery was delivered on sale or return basis. The contract expressly provided 'on sale for cash only or return'. The buyer pledged the jewellery without making payment. It was held that the jeweller could recover the jewellery since the property had not passed to the buyer because payment of the price was a condition precedent for passing the property to buyer.
2. Where buyer fails to return goods within reasonable time or if time is fixed, then on the expiry of that time. Thus, until the expiry of such time, the goods remain the property of the seller.
3. Where contract stipulates 'sale for cash only or return', the ownership of the goods will pass to the buyer only when the price is paid.

RISK FOLLOWS OWNERSHIP

Risk means the liability to bear the loss or destruction or deterioration that may be caused to goods. In a contract of sale, the risk follows the property which means the owner has to bear the loss. Section 26 provides that unless otherwise agreed, the goods remain at seller's risk until the property therein is transferred to the buyer. The general rule is that in absence of special terms, the risk prima facie follows ownership.

Example: A buys goods from B. A agrees to take delivery of the goods after 12 days. So the goods remain in B's godown. Before delivery of goods to A, there is fire in B's godown and all the goods are destroyed. A must bear the loss and pay the price of goods as the ownership in the goods has already passed to A.

The rule 'risk follows ownership' is subject to following exceptions.

1. **Agreement between the parties regarding the time of passing of risk:** The parties may agree by an agreement that risk will pass at a time different from the time of passing of the ownership. The parties may fix the point of time when the risk is to pass. In the case of M. Champak vs. C. P. Shah, the agreement specially provided that during transport, the goods shall be the property of the seller but they shall be at the buyer's risk. The goods were destroyed during transport. It was held that the buyer was bound to bear the loss because he had agreed to bear the loss.
2. **Delay in delivery:** Where delivery of goods has been delayed by the fault of either buyer or seller, the party at fault has to bear the risk of loss. Thus, the goods are at the risk of the party who is responsible for delay in delivery.
3. **Custom in a particular trade:** If there is a custom in a particular trade that risk does not pass with property, the risk will pass as per the custom. In the case of Bevington vs. Dale, certain 'furs' were delivered to a buyer 'on approval'. It was a custom in the trade that the goods were at the risk of the person ordering them on approval. It was held that buyer will bear the loss.
4. **Bailee of goods of the other party:** The rule that 'risk prima facie passes with ownership' does not affect the duties and liabilities of either seller or buyer as a bailee of goods of the other party even when the risk is passed.

Transfer of Title by Non-owners or No One Can Pass a Better Title than He Himself Has

The general rule is that owner of goods can sell the goods and convey or transfer goods' title or ownership. However, no one can convey to a transferee a better title than he himself has. If a person transfers articles not belonging to him, the transferee gets no title. The Latin maxim expresses this principle *nemo dat quod non habet*, which means none can transfer a better title that he himself has. So a buyer purchasing goods from a non-owner does not get any title to them. Section 27 explains that where goods are sold by a person, who is not owner and who does not sell them under the authority of or with the consent of the owner, the buyer acquires no better title to the goods than the seller had. Hence, a person who is not the owner of the goods cannot make a third person or buyer owner of the goods. Real owner can recover the goods from any innocent purchaser, if the seller had no authority to sell. This rule applies to both movable and immovable property.

Example: A found a ring in a garden and after making reasonable efforts to discover the owner, he sold it to B. B bought it without the knowledge that A was merely a finder. Held, the true owner could recover the ring from B.

Exceptions to the Rule

In the interest of trade and commerce, following are the exceptions of 'nemo dat quod non habet' recognized by law.

1. **Sale by a mercantile agent:** Mercantile agents are regular dealers or businessmen transacting on goods who buy and sell goods as their business and who are not owners. Section 27(2) provides that when the mercantile agent, who is in possession of goods with the consent of the owner, sells goods in the ordinary course of business to a buyer who buys them in good faith, the buyer gets a better title, even though the seller had no authority to sell. Sale by a mercantile agent gives a good title to the purchaser, provided the following conditions are satisfied:
   a. The agent is in possession of the goods or of a document of title to the goods.
   b. Such possession is with the consent of the owner.
   c. The agent sells the goods in the ordinary course of business.
   d. The purchaser acts in good faith and has no notice that the agent has no authority to sell at the time he enters into the contract.
2. **Sale by one of several joint owners:** Joint owners are persons who own the goods jointly. For example, partners are said to be joint owners. Section 28 provides that where one of several joint owners of goods has the sole possession of them by permission of the co-owners, the property in the goods is transferred to any person who buys them from such joint owner in good faith and without notice that the seller had no authority to sell. Sale by one of the several joint owners is valid, if:
   a. He is in sole possession of the goods with the permission of his co-owners.
   b. The buyer should purchase the good for value and in good faith.
   c. The buyer has no notice at the time of the contract of sale that the seller has no authority to sell.
3. **Sale by a person in possession of goods under a voidable contract:** A contract is voidable if consent of one party to it is caused by coercion, undue influence, misrepresentation or fraud. Section 29 provides that when the seller of goods has obtained possession of the goods under a voidable contract and he sells those goods before the contract is rescinded, the buyer of such goods acquires a better title provided the buyer acts in good faith and without notice of the seller's defect of title. A sale by a person in possession of goods under a voidable contract is valid, if:
   a. He sells them before the contract is rescinded.
   b. The buyer acts in good faith.
   c. He has no notice of the seller's defective title.

   In the case of Phillips vs. Brooks, A obtained possession of a costly ring from B, a jeweller, by fraud. Before the fraud could be detected, A pledged the ring with P who received it in good faith. It was held that P got a better title.
4. **Sale by seller in possession of goods after sale:** Section 30(1) provides that where a person, having sold the goods, continues to be in possession of the goods or of the documents of title and sells them over again to a buyer, the buyer gets a better title provided he has acted in good faith and without notice of the previous sale. For the application of this exception, it is necessary that the goods must be in the possession of the seller after sale in the capacity of a seller and not as hirer or bailee.

   Example: A sells certain goods to B and promises to deliver the goods the next day. Before delivery, A again sells and delivers the goods to C, who buys them in good faith and without notice of the previous sale to B; C, therefore, gets a good title to the goods. B cannot hold C liable.

5. **Sale by buyer in possession of goods over which the seller has some rights:** Section 30(2) provides that when goods are sold subject to some lien or right of seller, buyer may sell, pledge or otherwise dispose of the goods to a third party and give a good title, provided the following conditions are satisfied:
   a. The first buyer is in possession of the goods or of the documents of title to the goods with the consent of the seller.
   b. The transfer is by the buyer or by a mercantile agent acting for him.
   c. The person receiving the same acts in good faith and without notice of any lien or other right of the original seller.

   In the case of Marten vs. Whale, A agreed to buy a car if his solicitor approved. The possession of the car was given to A. A sold the car to B, who buys it in good faith. It was held that B got a better title.
6. **Sale by an unpaid seller:** Section 54(3) provides that where an unpaid seller who is in possession of goods after having exercised the right of lien or stoppage of goods in transit resells the goods, the buyer gets a good title thereto as against the original buyer. The title of the subsequent buyer will not be affected by the fact that notice of such resale was not given to the original buyer.
7. **Sale under implied authority of owner or title by estoppel:** When owner of goods by his conduct or out of omission makes the buyer to believe that the seller has a right to sell goods, and thereby induces the buyer to buy such goods, later on the owner of the goods cannot deny the title of the seller. The owner is also prevented or estopped from saying that the seller has no right or authority to sell. In such cases, buyer gets a better title than that of the seller. In certain cases, the true owner is prevented by his conduct from denying the seller's authority to sell.
   Example: A sells the goods of B in his presence. B does not raise any objection. B cannot subsequently deny A's authority to sell and the sale is binding on B.
8. **Exceptions under other Acts:** The following are some of such cases.
   a. **Sale by a finder of goods:** Section 169 of the Contract Act provides that a finder of goods can sell the goods and the purchaser will get a good title.
   b. **Sale by pawnee:** The pawnee or pledgee may sell the goods pledged to him on giving the pawnor reasonable notice of the sale. The purchaser under such a sale gets a good title.
   c. **Sale by official receiver or assignee:** In case of insolvency of an individual, his official receiver or any liquidator of a company can confer a good title on the buyer under authority of law.
   d. **Execution sales:** Under Order 21 of Civil Procedure Code, officers of court can sell goods and convey title to the buyer even though they are not owners.
9. **Sale in market overt (open market):** These markets sell sometimes even stolen goods and old goods in broad daylight. In India these markets are dealing in second-hand goods. Any goods bought from these markets are considered to convey title to the buyer, irrespective of the facts that such goods might have been stolen goods.

TEST QUESTIONS

1. Define 'goods'. State the rules that govern the passing of property from the seller to the buyer.

2. Why is it important to know the exact time when the property in the goods passes from a seller to buyer? Explain with examples the rules governing the transfer of ownership of goods from seller to buyer.
3. Discuss the provision of the Sale of Goods Act, 1930, in regard to the passing of property in (a) specific goods and (b) unascertained goods.
4. 'No seller of goods can give the buyer of goods a better title to those goods than what he himself possesses.' Examine the statement and mention whether there are any exceptions to this rule.
5. Explain 'nemo dat quod non habet' along with exceptions to the above rule.

PRACTICAL PROBLEMS

1. A sold 100 quintals of groundnut oil to B. Before it would be delivered to B, the government of India requisitioned the whole quantity lying with A in public interest. B wants to sue A for breach of contract.
   Hint. The contract becomes void.
2. A, a hirer, obtains possession of a refrigerator from its owner under a hire-purchase agreement, and sells the refrigerator to a buyer who buys in good faith and without notice of the right of the owner. Does the buyer get a good title to the refrigerator? State reasons for your answer.
   Hint. Yes, refer case Lee vs. Butter.
3. A agreed to purchase 200 tons of wheat from B out of a larger stock. A sent his men with sacks and 150 tons of wheat were put into the sacks. Then there was a sudden fire and entire stock was gutted. Who will bear the loss and why?
   Hint. Buyer has to bear the loss of 150 tons. The seller had done an act necessary to put the goods in a deliverable state. Hence, property had passed.
4. There is a contract for the sale of timber standing at B's land. It is the duty of the buyer A to cut the timber and take it away on his own. But due to sudden fire the timber got destroyed. Who will suffer the loss and why?
   Hint. Property in the goods had not passed as the goods were not identified; hence, loss is borne by the seller.
5. A delivered his horse to B on trial for a week with a condition that if found suitable he will buy the horse for ₹1,000. The horse died on the third day. Is B liable to pay the price?
   Hint. No, ownership was not transferred.

18
CHAPTER

Performance of Contract of Sale and Unpaid Seller

Learning Objectives

- To understand performance of contract of sale
- To understand delivery of goods and rules regarding delivery
- To understand unpaid seller and his rights
- To understand the difference between right of lien and right of stoppage in transit
- To understand rights and duties of buyer of goods
- To understand auction sale and rules regarding auction sale

In the case of a contract of sale 'performance' means the delivery of goods by the seller and acceptance and payment for the same by the buyer. Section 31 provides that it is the duty of the seller to deliver the goods and of the buyer to accept and pay for them in accordance with the terms of the contract of sale. The delivery of goods and payment are concurrent conditions. Section 32 provides that unless otherwise agreed, delivery of the goods and payment of the price are concurrent conditions, that is to say, the seller shall be ready and willing to give possession of the goods to the buyer in exchange for price of the goods. Therefore, a contract of sale consists of two reciprocal promises:

1. The seller has to deliver the goods.
2. The buyer has to make payment of the price.

Delivery of Goods

Section 2(2) defines delivery as 'voluntary transfer of possession from one person to another'. Section 33 states that delivery be made by doing anything which the parties agree shall be treated as delivery. Thus, there are three characteristics of delivery:

1. A person has possession.
2. He transfer that possession to another person.
3. He does so voluntarily.

Kinds of Delivery

Delivery is a bilateral act. Delivery can be of the following kinds.

1. **Actual delivery:** When seller physically hands over the goods to buyer or his agent, it is called 'actual delivery' or 'physical delivery'.
   Example: A purchases a scooter from B and takes possession from B's showroom and goes on the scooter. It will be actual delivery of goods.
2. **Symbolic delivery:** Where the goods are bulky, heavy and incapable of actual delivery, 'the means of obtaining possession' of the goods are delivered by the seller to the buyer; like handing over the key of a warehouse or godown to the buyer is symbolic delivery of the goods to the buyer. Similarly, transfer of documents of title to the goods is also a symbolic delivery.
3. **Constructive delivery:** Section 35(3) provides that where the goods at the time of sale are in the possession of a third person, there is no delivery by seller to buyer unless and until such third person acknowledges to the buyer that he holds the goods on his behalf. In the case of Hammond vs. Anderson, there was a sale of specific goods lying at a wharf. The buyer paid the price and the seller directed the wharfinger to deliver goods to the buyer. After weighing them, the buyer took away a part of the goods and left the remainder with the wharfinger, who misappropriated it. It was held that it amounted to delivery of the whole of goods.

Rules Regarding Delivery of Goods

Sections 31 to 44 provide following rules for delivery of goods.

1. **Mode of delivery:** Delivery should have effect of putting goods in possession of buyer or his agent. A seller must put the goods not only out of his own possession but also into the possession of the buyer. Delivery of goods may be actual, symbolic or constructive.
2. **Delivery and payment are concurrent conditions:** Delivery of goods and payment of the price must be according to the terms of contract unless otherwise provided. The delivery of goods and payment of price must take place simultaneously.
3. **Effect of part delivery:** Section 34 provides that a delivery of part of goods has same effect as a delivery of whole, when the parties have intended and agreed.
   Example: A ship arrives in a harbour laden with cargo consigned to A, the buyer. The captain begins to discharge it and delivers over part of the goods to A in progress of the delivery of the whole. The part delivery of the cargo is equivalent to the delivery of the cargo as a whole and the ownership in whole of the goods shall pass on to the buyer.
4. **Buyer to apply for delivery:** In the absence of an express agreement, the seller is under no obligation to deliver the goods unless the buyer applies for delivery. Section 34(6) provides that it is the duty of the buyer to demand delivery of goods, otherwise he cannot hold seller liable in damages for his failure to deliver. The demand for delivery should be made at a reasonable hour. Whereas it is the duty of the seller to deliver the goods.
5. **Place of delivery:** Section 36(1) provides that place at which delivery is to be made will be generally governed by agreement between parties. Where place or places for

delivery is not mentioned, then it should be the place where goods are to be manufactured or produced. Where the place at which delivery of the goods is to take place is specified in the contract, the goods must be delivered at that place during business hours on a working day.

6. **Time of delivery:** Delivery of goods must be made within a reasonable time, if no time is fixed by the contract. Demand or tender of delivery should be made at a reasonable hour. In the case of Startup vs. McDonald's, a quantity of oil sold was to be delivered in the last fortnight of March. The seller tendered delivery at 8.30 PM on 31 March. This was held to be delivery within time and the buyer's refusal to accept it as wrongful.
7. **Expenses of delivery:** Section 36(5) provides that unless otherwise agreed, all expenses of and incidental to making of delivery are borne by the seller, but all expenses of and incidental to taking of delivery are borne by the buyer.
8. **Delivery of wrong quantity:** Section 37 provides that seller is under a duty to comply with the order of the buyer in kind, quality and quantity and must deliver goods of the exact quantity ordered. A defective delivery entitles the buyer to reject the goods. Thus, three different contingencies which may arise in case of a defective delivery are as follows.
   a. **Less delivery:** Section 37 provides that where the seller delivers to the buyer a quantity of goods less than he contracted to sell, the buyer may reject them.
   Example: A agrees to sell and deliver to B 100 quintals of sugar. However, he could supply only 75 quintals. B has a right to reject the goods. When the buyer is refusing to accept the goods, it is sufficient if he informs the seller that he is not accepting the goods, that is, the buyer is not bound to return them to the seller. If, however, the goods have been rejected for short delivery, the seller can make, within the limited period, another delivery according to the terms of the contract.
   b. **Excess delivery:** Section 37(2) provides that where the seller delivers a quantity larger than that ordered or contracted to sell, the buyer has the option:
   i. To accept the whole of the goods, in that case he shall be liable to pay for them at the contract rate
   ii. To accept the goods included in the contract and reject the excess
   iii. To reject the whole of the goods
   However, if the excess is so small as to be negligible and the seller is not asking any payment for the excess, then the buyer may not reject. In the case of Vilas Udyog Ltd vs. Prag Vanaspati Products, court held that the contention of the buyer was right and the seller could supply only contracted cases.
   c. **Mixed delivery:** Section 37(3) provides that where the seller delivers to the buyer the goods mixed with the goods of a different description, not included in the contract, the buyer has the option:
   i. To accept goods which are in accordance with the contract and reject the rest
   ii. To reject the whole of the goods
9. **Instalment delivery:** Section 38 provides that unless otherwise agreed, the buyer of goods is not bound to accept delivery thereof by instalments. In case of contract of sale of goods need to be delivered in instalments than payment may also be in instalment or as provided in the contract. When seller makes no delivery or defective delivery of goods in instalments to buyer then buyer can pay in instalments. Then it will depend on the terms of the contract and circumstances of the case whether the breach of contract is a repudiation of the whole contract or it is a severable. The breach gives rise to a claim for compensation but not to a right to treat the whole contract as repudiated.

10. **Delivery to carrier:** Section 39(2) provides that where in pursuance of a contract of sale, goods are delivered to a carrier for purpose of transmission to buyer or to a wharfinger for safe custody, delivery of goods to them is prima facie deemed to be a delivery of the goods to the buyer. In the case of Siddayya Mudaliar vs. M. N. Muthayanna Chettiar, the seller failed to inform the railways that the goods fall under the list of expected category of articles. The buyer could not be held responsible for the consequences.
11. **Liability of buyer for refusing delivery:** Section 44 provides that if the buyer neglects or refuses to take delivery within a reasonable time, he is liable to seller for loss and charges for the care and custody of the goods. If the buyer neglects to take the delivery of the goods, it does not give any right to the seller to terminate the contract. It shall apply only in those cases where the property in goods has passed to the buyer.
12. **Delivery at a distant place:** According to Section 40 of the Act, where the seller agrees to deliver the goods at his own risk at a different place than the one at which they were at the time of sale, the buyer himself is responsible for deterioration in the goods incidental to transit. This rule is, however, subject to an agreement to the contrary.
13. **Buyer has right to examine the goods:** Sections 41(1) and (2) provide that on delivery of the goods, which the buyer has not previously examined, he is considered not to have accepted them until he has had a reasonable opportunity to examine them for the purpose of determining whether they are in conformity with the contract.
14. **Deemed acceptance by the buyer:** As per Section 42, the buyer is deemed to have accepted the goods:
    a. When he intimates to the seller that he has accepted them.
    b. When he receives delivery of the goods or he does any act in relations to them which is inconsistent with the ownership of the seller.
    c. When after the lapse of a reasonable time, he retains the goods without intimating to the seller that he has rejected them (Section 42).
15. **Buyer is not bound to return rejected goods:** According to Section 43, the buyer, who has rejected the goods delivered to him, having a right to do so, is not bound to return them to the seller. It is sufficient if he intimates to the seller that he refuses to accept them. This rule is subject to an agreement to the contrary. However, it is the responsibility of the buyer to keep the goods at the disposal of the seller.

Unpaid Seller

Section 45 provides that seller of goods is deemed to be an unpaid seller when whole of the price has not been paid or tendered, or when a bill of exchange or other negotiable instrument has been received as conditional payment and the same has been dishonoured. A seller will be considered as an unpaid seller when he satisfies following conditions:

1. He must have sold goods on cash terms and he has not yet received the price money. In case the goods are sold on credit, he cannot be called as an unpaid seller during the period of credit because the payment has not become due. It is only on the expiry of the period of credit, if he remains unpaid, he will become an unpaid seller.
2. As long as some portion of the price remains unpaid, the seller will be considered as an unpaid seller.

3. He must not have received the whole of the price. The seller is treated as an unpaid seller so long as any portion of the price, however small, remains unpaid. Where the whole of the price was tendered, and the seller refused to accept such a tender, the seller cannot be called an unpaid seller.
4. However, if the price tendered is in all respects a valid tender, the seller loses his status of an unpaid seller. As a result he will be deprived of his right of lien or of stoppage in transit.
5. A bill of exchange or other negotiable instrument has been received in payment for the price but the same has been dishonoured.
6. Where the buyer becomes insolvent before the maturity of the negotiable instrument, he is regarded as not having fulfilled the condition upon which the seller received the instrument.

Rights of an Unpaid Seller

Section 46(1) provides that an unpaid seller will have expressly two kinds of rights: rights against the goods and rights against the buyer.

Rights against the Goods

These can be further divided under two heads:

1. Rights when ownership is transferred/passed
2. Rights when ownership is not transferred

Rights When Ownership Is Transferred or Passed

An unpaid seller has the following rights even if the property in goods has not been transferred to the buyer.

1. **Right of lien:** The unpaid seller has the right of lien until he receives their price. The term 'lien' means a right to retain possession of goods until the payment of the price is paid. An unpaid seller can exercise lien only in the following cases:
   a. Where the goods have been sold without any stipulation as to credit.
   b. Where goods have been sold on credit, but period or time of credit has expired.
   c. Where the buyer becomes insolvent.

   The following are the conditions for exercise of lien:
   a. The ownership in goods must have passed to the buyer.
   b. The goods must be in the possession of the seller.
   c. The entire part of the price must remain unpaid.

   The lien of unpaid seller is a possessory lien. It is a personal lien and can be exercised either by him or by his agent. The buyer is not entitled to claim delivery of a portion of goods on payment of a proportionate price. The right of lien is available only for the price of goods and not other charges like warehouse or dock charges.

In the following cases, an unpaid seller of goods loses his right of lien on the goods (this is called the termination of lien).

a. **By delivery to the carrier:** When the seller delivers goods to a carrier or other bailee for the purpose of transmission to the buyer without reserving the right of disposal of the goods. If the seller takes back the goods from the carrier for any other purpose, the right of lien does not revive.
b. **By delivery to the buyer:** If the buyer or his agent lawfully obtains possession of the goods, the lien is lost. If the goods are delivered back to the seller for specific purpose like repair, the right of lien does not revive.
c. **By waiver:** Where the seller expressly or impliedly waives his right of lien. An implied waiver takes place when the seller grants a fresh term of credit or takes a bill of exchange for the price payable at a future date or when the seller assents to a sub-sale by the buyer.
d. **Tender of price:** When the buyer tenders price for the goods, the seller ceases to be an unpaid seller. Even if the seller refuses to receive money, he cannot exercise the right of lien on the goods.

2. **Right of stoppage in transit:** The right of stopping the goods while they are in the possession of a carrier and resuming possession is known as the right of stoppage in transit. Right of stoppage in transit is just an extension of the unpaid seller's right of lien, that is, the goods are no more under his physical possession. This right of stoppage in transit can be exercised when:
   a. The seller must be unpaid.
   b. The buyer must be insolvent.
   c. The seller must have parted with the possession of goods.
   d. The goods must be in transit.
   e. The buyer must have not acquired the goods. Goods should be in transit.

   Accordingly, in protecting the interests of the unpaid seller, this section prevents the goods of the seller from falling into the hands of an insolvent buyer. The unpaid seller or vendor may exercise the right of stoppage in transit either:
   a. By taking actual possession of the goods
   b. By giving notice of his claim to the carrier or other bailee in whose possession the goods are

   The carrier on receipt of notice must redeliver the goods to the seller. The expenses of such redelivery are to be borne by the seller.

   Section 51(1), which deals with the duration of transit, provides that goods are deemed to be in course of transit from the time when they are delivered to a carrier or other bailee for the purpose of transmission to the buyer until the buyer or his agent takes delivery of them.

   The transit comes to an end and seller loses the right to stop the goods in transit:
   a. When goods are delivered to the buyer or his agent
   b. When the carrier holds the goods as the agent of the buyer
   c. When the carrier wrongfully refuses to deliver the goods to the buyer or his agent
   d. When goods are delivered in part to the buyer or his agent and part delivery shows an agreement to give up possession of the whole of the goods

3. **Right of resale:** Section 54 provides that a contract of sale is not rescinded by the mere exercise of his right of lien or stoppage in transit by an unpaid seller. The unpaid seller can resell the goods:
   a. Where the goods are of a perishable nature.
   b. Where the seller expressly reserves the right of resale in case the buyer makes a default in the payment of price.

c. Where the unpaid seller has exercised his right of lien or stoppage in transit and serves notice to the buyer of his intention to sell the goods.

The seller is bound to give reasonable notice to the buyer stating that he is going to resell the goods, if the buyer fails to pay the price of goods within reasonable time after receiving the notice. If, on resale, there is profit, the seller is not bound to pay it to the buyer. Resale of perishable goods, however, does not require any such notice. They may be sold at once without notice.

Rights When Ownership Is Not Passed

Where the property in the goods has not passed to the buyer, the unpaid seller has, in addition to his other remedies, a right of withholding property. The seller has a right to withhold delivery of the goods until the price is paid even though the sale was on credit. This right is similar to and co-extensive with his right of lien and stoppage in transit where the property has passed to the buyer.

Rights against the Buyer

An unpaid seller, in addition to the rights against the goods, has the following rights against the buyer. These rights are called 'rights in personam' as these are available against the buyer personally.

1. **Suit for price:** Section 55(1) provides that where the property in the goods has passed to the buyer and the buyer wrongfully neglects or refuses to pay for the goods, the seller can sue the buyer for the price of the goods.
2. **Suit for damages for non-acceptance of the goods:** Section 56 provides that where the buyer wrongfully neglects or refuses to accept and pay for goods, the seller may sue him for damages for non-acceptance. This section deals with general damages.
3. **Suit for damages for repudiation of contract before the due date:** Where the buyer repudiates the contract, the seller may file the suit for the damages, and the seller may also file suit for the amount of the price from the date of the tender of the goods or from the date on which the price was payable.
4. **Suit for interest and special damages:** Section 61 provides that the seller is entitled to recover interest or special damages in any case where, under the law, interest or special damages may be recoverable, or to recover the money paid where the consideration for the payment of it has failed.

Distinction between Right of Lien and Right of Stoppage of Goods in Transit

The following are the main points of distinction between the right of lien and the right of stoppage of goods in transit.

1. **Solvency of the buyer:** Right of stoppage in transit arises only when the buyer becomes insolvent. However, the right of lien can be exercised even when the buyer is able to pay but does not pay. Solvency of the buyer is immaterial in this regard.

2. **Possession of goods:** The right of lien can be exercised when the goods are in actual possession of the seller. However, the right of stoppage in transit can be enforced so long as the goods are in the possession of a middleman (carrier) between the seller and the buyer.
3. **Retention of goods:** Right of lien is exercised to retain possession of goods. But the right of stoppage in transit is exercised to regain or resume the possession of goods by the seller from the carrier or other bailee.
4. **Termination of the right:** Right of lien ends as soon as the goods go out of the possession of the seller. However, the right of stoppage in transit comes to an end as soon as the goods are delivered to the buyer.
5. **Test:** Possession is the test of the right of lien. But the test for stoppage in transit is the non-delivery of goods to the buyer.
6. **Right of force:** Right of lien remains in force till the right of stoppage in transit begins, whereas the right of stoppage starts when the right of lien ends and remains in force till the delivery of goods to the buyer.

Buyer's Remedies against the Seller

'Buyer' means a person who buys or agrees to buy goods. If the seller is guilty of default, the buyer has the following remedies against the seller.

1. **Suit for damages for non-delivery of goods:** Where the seller wrongfully neglects or refuses to deliver the goods to the buyer or where the seller has unreasonably delayed the delivery of goods, the buyer may sue the seller for damages for non-delivery.
2. **Suit for specific performance:** Where there is a contract for sale of specific or ascertained goods and seller refuses to deliver them, the buyer may file a suit for the specific performance of the contract. However, the court subject to certain conditions allows this remedy. Specific performance may be ordered by the court where damages would not be an adequate remedy.
3. **Remedy for breach of warranty:** Where there is a breach of warranty, the buyer cannot reject the goods. He has two remedies:
   a. He may deduct from the price payable the loss suffered by him.
   b. He may file a suit for damages where the loss is more than the price.

   If he has already paid the price, his only remedy is to bring an action for damages suffered by him due to the breach of warranty.
4. **Repudiation of the contract before the due date:** Where the seller repudiates the contract before the date of delivery, the buyer can:
   a. Treat the contract as rescinded and bring an action for damages.
   b. Wait till the actual date of delivery.

   If the buyer chooses the first remedy, damages shall be assessed based on price prevailing on that date and contract price. In the case of second alternative, the contract remains open for the benefit of both the parties.
5. **Interest by way of damages:** Where the consideration for the payment has failed, the buyer can recover the money paid for the goods along with the interest.

AUCTION SALES

A sale by auction is a public sale, where the goods are offered to be taken by the highest bidder. The auctioneer who sells the goods by auction is an agent of the seller. The intending buyer can inspect the goods during the fixed timings before sale. Thus, auction sales are very much different in their method of selling goods from the ordinary cash sales. In an auction sale, the auctioneer invites bids from the prospective buyers and the goods are sold to the highest bidder. The auctioneer accepts the highest bid in a customary manner by 'knock down', that is, by the fall of the hammer or by using the words 'one, two and three'. The property in goods passes to the buyer on the fall of the hammer and by paying the margin money.

Kinds of Auction Sales

1. Sale without reserve price.
2. Sale with condition that the highest bidder shall be the purchaser, nothing being said about reserve price.
3. Sale with a right expressly reserved to bid by or on behalf of the seller.

Legal Rules Regarding Auction Sales

The various legal rules regarding auction sales are contained in Section 64. They are as follows.

1. **Goods put up for sale in lots:** Section 64(1) provides that where goods are put up for sale in lots, each lot is prima facie deemed to be the subject of a separate contract of sale. The auctioneer is deemed to offer each lot separately for sale when he calls the bids and offers it to the highest bidder.
2. **Completion of sale:** The sale in an auction is complete when the auctioneer declares the acceptance of the bid by the fall of the hammer or in any other customary manner. The goods then become the property of the buyer. Until such announcement is made, any bidder may withdraw his bid. The condition in the auction sale that 'a bid once made shall not be withdrawn' is against the provisions of law and, therefore, is not enforceable.
3. **Right of the seller to bid:** A right to bid may be reserved expressly by or on behalf of the seller. Where the right is expressly so reserved, the seller or any one person on his behalf may bid at the auction.
4. **Fraudulent sale:** Unless the right to bid is expressly reserved by or on behalf of the seller, the seller cannot bid at the auction or employ any person to bid on his behalf. It shall not be lawful for the auctioneer to knowingly take any bid from the seller or any such person.
5. **Auction sale with preset or reserve price:** The sale may be notified to be subject to a reserve price or upset price. Reserve price is the minimum price below which the auctioneer will not sell the goods put up for auction sale. However, even when there is no reserve price, the auctioneer is not bound to accept the highest bid.
6. **Dumping:** Dumping is an illicit act discouraging the would-be purchaser from buying. Dumping is illegal and the auctioneer can withdraw goods from auction.

Implied Warranties in an Auction Sale

In an auction sale, the following warranties are implied:

1. The auctioneer warrants his authority to sell.
2. He warrants that he has no knowledge of any defect in his principal's title.
3. He warrants giving possession of the goods to the buyer against payment of the price.
4. He undertakes that his principal or he himself will not disturb such possession.

Some Important Terms

1. **Knockout agreement:** A bona fide agreement between persons not to bid against each other at an auction sale is called a 'knockout agreement'. Such an agreement is not unlawful. It is perfectly valid. The seller can protect his interest against knockout agreement by reserving his right to bid at an auction or by fixing a reserve price on the goods.
2. **Dumping:** Dumping is an illicit act to dissuade the intending purchasers from bidding:
   a. By pointing out defects in the goods.
   b. By doing some other act so that the intending purchaser is not in a position to have proper estimate of the price of the goods.
   c. By scaring the intending purchaser away by some other service. Dumping is illegal. The auctioneer is, therefore, entitled to withdraw the goods from the auction.
3. **Puffers:** 'Puffer' is a person employed by the seller to raise the price by fictitious bids. Such a person has no intention to purchase the goods. Such persons are also known as 'by bidders' or 'decoy ducks'.
4. **CIF contract:** 'CIF' stands for cost, insurance and freight. Under such a contract, the seller himself has to pay the cost of the goods, insurance during transit to the buyer and the freight. The price agreed to be paid between the parties to a contract of sale includes all these three. Traders residing at distant places separated by sea, who want to protect their rights to the utmost, resort to this type of contract.

Test Questions

1. What do you mean by delivery of goods? Explain.
2. Explain the term 'delivery' as used in a contract of sale and state the rules regarding valid delivery of goods.
3. What are the rights and duties of the seller in respect of delivery of goods?
4. What ate the effects of part delivery, instalment delivery and delivery of wrong quantity?
5. When is a seller of goods deemed to be an 'unpaid seller'? What are his rights?
6. Distinguish between right of lien and stoppage in transit.
7. Define sale by auction. Also, state the rules regarding sale by auction.
8. Write short notes on:
   a. Modes of delivery
   b. Part delivery
   c. Instalment delivery
   d. Rules regarding resale of goods

PRACTICAL PROBLEMS

1. Sale of 1,000 pieces of blue gum wood to be delivered in two instalments, the first instalment of 750 pieces was of very inferior quality and the buyer refused to accept it. The seller tendered the second instalment. Is the buyer under an obligation to accept it?
Hint. No. The buyer is not under any obligation to accept it.
2. X agrees to sell Y 2,000 bags of fine sugar lying in his godown for ₹12,000. Before the delivery of sugar, there is a fire in the godown which completely destroys the stock. Can Y compel X to supply sugar as per agreement?
Hint. No. The contract is for sale of specific goods and they have been destroyed without any fault on the part of any party. The contract becomes void.
3. A buys certain bags of wheat from B. Without making proper inspection to the quality of wheat, B sells these bags to different buyers. After a few days, A comes to know that the wheat is not of the quality as agreed. Can he repudiate the contract?
Hint. No. Sale of wheat amounts to his acceptance of goods.
4. A sells to B a certain quantity of rice. It is agreed that three months' credit shall be given. B allows the rice to remain in A's warehouse till the expiry of the three months and then does not pay for them. Can A retain the goods for price?
Hint. Yes. A may retain the goods for price, seller's right of lien.
5. In the month of May, certain articles of furniture were delivered by a dealer to X 'on sale or return' within a week. Three days after, two of X's creditors in execution of a decree seized the articles. The dealer claims his goods. Decide.
Hint. The dealer can claim his goods and creditors must return because X was not the owner of goods. There was no transfer of ownership because fixed time of one week had not passed and the goods remained the property of the dealer.
6. X of Delhi orders Y of Madras to deliver certain goods to him at Delhi. While the goods are lying at the Delhi Railway Station, the station master informs X that the goods are held at X's risk. But X has become insolvent. Has Y any right over the goods as an unpaid seller?
Hint. The transit is at an end and hence Y cannot exercise the right stoppage of goods in transit.
7. A bought from B a shipment of nuts and B sent to A the bill of lading. A handed over the bill of lading to C in return for a loan, and then became insolvent. B attempted to stop the goods in transit, but C claimed them. Is C's claim justified?
Hint. Yes. (Section 53)
8. X sells and consigns goods to Y, X being still unpaid. Y becomes insolvent and while the goods are still transit, Y assigns the bill of lading for cash to Z who know that Y is insolvent. Can X stop the goods in transit?
Hint. X can still stop the goods in transit since the assignee has not acted in good faith.
9. Goods were sold and sent by the sellers at the request of the buyer to shipping agents of the buyer and were put on a ship by those agents. Subsequently, they were re-landed and sent back to sellers for the buyer became insolvent. The sellers refused to deliver them to the buyer's trustee in bankruptcy except upon payment of price. Are the sellers entitled to refuse the delivery of the goods? Give reasons.

Hint. The sellers had lost their lien by delivering goods to the shipping agents. Their refusal to deliver goods to the trustee in bankruptcy was wrong.

10. X sold a quantity of wheat to Y, who paid by cheque which was dishonoured upon presentation. X gave a delivery order to Y for the wheat and Y resold it to Z, a purchaser in good faith, for consideration endorsing the delivery order to him. X refuses to deliver the goods to Z on the plea of non-receipt of price. Advise Z.
    Hint. Z is entitled to the goods.

UNIT IV

The Limited Liability Partnership Act, 2008

19
CHAPTER

Introduction to Limited Liability Partnership and Its Incorporation

Learning Objectives

- To understand the meaning of limited liability partnership (LLP) and its incorporation
- To learn important concepts of LLP
- To understand the difference between LLP and partnership and LLP and company
- To understand the process of incorporation of LLP

Limited liability partnership (LLP) is a new form of business entity that enables professional expertise and entrepreneurial initiative to combine, organize and operate in an innovative and efficient manner. Several expert committees have recommended for legislation on LLPs. Consequently, the concept of LLP was initiated as an alternative to the traditional partnership. The law of LLP is contained in the Limited Liability Partnership Act, 2008. The LLP Act came into force, for most of the provisions, on 31 March 2009, and for the remaining provisions on 31 May 2009. LLPs can be formed to carry on a lawful 'business'. Section 2(1)(e) defines the term 'business' to include every trade, profession, service and occupation.

DEFINITION OF LLP

Section 2(1)(n) of the LLP Act defines LLP as 'a partnership formed or registered under this Act'. The definition does not explain the substance of what constitutes an LLP. In the light of the nature of the LLP, Section 3 provides that, 'Limited Liability of Partnership is a body corporate, which is an artificial person, having a separate legal entity, with a perpetual succession, a common seal and carrying limited liability.'

CHARACTERISTICS OF LLP

There are following essential characteristics of an LLP.

1. **Body corporate:** LLP is a body corporate and has a legal entity distinct and separate from its constituents and having perpetual existence and a common seal with capacity to hold property, sue and be sued in its own name. It is a body corporate formed and incorporated under the LLP Act.
2. **Artificial legal person:** LLP is an artificial legal person as it is created by a legal process other than natural birth. It is created by law and will come to an end by law only. It is formed by registration of an incorporation document with the registrar of companies (RoC) of the state in which the registered office of the LLP is to be situated.
3. **Separate legal entity:** LLP is legal person having a juristic personality entirely distinct as an independent individual person from its members who are for the time being its partners. It has the right to own and transfer the title to property in any way it likes. No partner can either individually or jointly claim any ownership rights in the assets of the LLP during its existence or in its winding up. Creditors of the LLP are creditors of the LLP alone, and they cannot directly proceed against the partners personally.
4. **Perpetual existence:** LLP is an incorporated entity and has a stable form of a business organization and its life does not depend upon the death, insolvency or retirement of any or all partners. It also has provisions for transferability of economic right of a partner as also for cessation of partnership interest. Partners can come and go but the LLP goes on forever. LLP has perpetual existence, irrespective of changes of its partners.
5. **Common seal:** LLP acts through its partners and designated partners. It has legal personality and may have a common seal in accordance with Section14 of the Act. The name of LLP shall be engraved on the common seal. It shall be used as a substitute for its signature in the presence of at least two of the designated partners of the LLP.
6. **Limited liability:** Every partner of an LLP would be for the purpose of the business of LLP but not of the other partners. Liability of partners of an LLP shall be limited only to the extent to their investment extent in case of unauthorized acts, LLP fraud and negligence. A partner shall not be personally liable for the wrongful acts or omission of any other partner. An obligation of LLP, whether arising in contract or otherwise, shall solely be the obligation of the LLP only.
7. **Mutual rights and duties of partners:** The mutual rights and duties of partners of the LLP inter se and those of the LLP and its partners shall be governed by an agreement between the partners inter se or between the LLP and the partners subject to the provisions of the Act. The Act provides flexibility to devise the agreement as per their choice. In the absence of any such agreement, the mutual rights and duties shall be governed by the provisions of the Act.
8. **Minimum partners:** Every LLP shall have at least two partners and at least two individuals as designated partners, of whom at least one shall be resident of India.
9. **Accounts:** LLP shall be under an obligation to maintain annual accounts reflecting true and fair view of its state of affairs. A statement of accounts and solvency shall be filed by every LLP with the registrar every year. The accounts of LLPs shall also be audited subject to any class of LLPs being exempted from this requirement by the central government.

DISTINCTION BETWEEN LLP AND PARTNERSHIP

The main points of distinction between an LLP and erstwhile partnership firm are as follows:

1. An LLP is required by the LLP Act, 2008, whereas a partnership firm is governed by the provisions of the Indian Partnership Act, 1932.
2. The maximum number of partners in the case of a partnership firm is fixed at 10 for banking business and at 20 for any other business, but no such maximum limit of partners is fixed in case of LLP.
3. An LLP is a legal entity separate from its partners. The death or lunacy of its partners would not dissolve it. LLP may hold property in its own name and be sued in its own name. On the other hand, partnership does not have a distinct legal entity separate from its partners and its existence comes to an end upon the death or lunacy of its partners. Moreover, the firm cannot hold property in its own name and cannot sue or be sued in its own name.
4. In the case of a partnership firm, each partner has unlimited liability and is personally liable for all the debts of the firm. In an LLP, on the other hand, a partner has limited liability to the extent of his agreed contribution in the LLP except in the case of unauthorized acts, fraud and negligence of partner, when the delinquent partner will be personally liable.
5. Every partner of a partnership is an agent of other partners, whereas every partner of an LLP is not an agent of other partners. As such in a partnership each partner has an implied authority to bind his co-partners by acts done within the ordinary course of business, but in an LLP a partner has no such authority, there being no mutual agency between various partners.
6. The responsibility for carrying out the legal obligations as laid down by the LLP Act shall be solely of the 'designated partners' and other partners would not be liable for any omission in fulfilling the legal obligations. On the other hand, in the case of a partnership, every partner would be responsible for carrying out the legal obligations.
7. A partnership firm may or may not be registered, whereas in the case of LLP, registration is mandatory.
8. Every LLP shall file within the prescribed time the 'statement of accounts and solvency' and an 'annual return' with RoC each year. A partnership firm is not required to file 'statement of accounts and solvency' or 'annual return' with the registrar of the firms.
9. A partnership can be wound up at any time by any of the partners, if it is 'partnership at will', without legal formalities. In the case of an LLP, one member cannot wound up the partnership at will as it involves legal formalities.

DISTINCTION BETWEEN LLP AND COMPANY

The main points of distinction between limited liability company and LLP are as follows:

1. An LLP is required by the LLP Act, 2008, whereas a company is governed by the Companies Act, 2013.
2. No maximum limit of partners has been laid down by the LLP Act. Similarly, no maximum limit of members is fixed in the case of public company. The maximum number of members of a private company, however, must not exceed fifty excluding members who are or were in the employment of the company. The maximum number

of members in a public company is seven and in the case of private company is two. In the case of LLP, the minimum number of partners is two.

3. In the case of LLP, management rests with those partners including designated partners who are authorized by LLP agreement. But in the case of a company, the right to control and manage the business is vested in the board of directors elected by the shareholder. Thus, the management ownership divide inherent in a company is not there in LLP.
4. The internal governance structure of a company is protected by the Companies Act, 2013, whereas for an LLP it would be by a contractual agreement between the partners. LLP will have more flexibility as compared to the company. In the case of LLP, change either in the business to be conducted or in the manner of functioning could be mutually agreed upon between the partners, documented and filed with the registrar of the companies.
5. In the case of an LLP, a partner's economic rights (i.e., right to a share of the profits and losses and to receive contribution at the time of winding up) shall be transferable (Section 42). However, such transfer shall not by itself cause the disassociation of the partner and a dissolution and winding up of the LLP. Further, such transfer would not make the transferee a 'partner' of the LLP entitled to participate in this management (Section 42). For becoming a partner of LLP, unless otherwise provided in the LLP agreement, consent of all the existing partners is required (Schedule 1 appended to the LLP Act). In the case of a private company also, transfer of shares requires the prior permission of the board of directors. But in the case of a public company, a shareholder can transfer his share freely without restriction and the transferee succeeds to all the rights of membership.
6. The audit of the accounts of a company is a legal necessity, but it is not so in the case of an LLP, if the capital contribution does not exceed ₹25 lakh or if the annual turnover does not exceed ₹40 lakh. However, the turnover limit has been raised from ₹40 lakh to ₹60 lakh by the Finance Act, 2010.

DEFINITIONS

Financial year, in relation to LLP, means the period from 1 April of a year to 31 March of the following year. However, in case of LLP incorporated after 30 September, financial year may end on 31 March of the year next following that year. (Section 2(1)(l))

Foreign LLP means an LLP formed, incorporated or registered outside India which establishes a place of business within India. (Section 2(1)(m))

LLP means a partnership formed and registered under the LLP Act. (Section 2(1)(n))

LLP agreement means any written agreement between the partners of LLP or between the LLP and its partners which determines the mutual rights and duties of the partners and their rights and duties in relation to that LLP. (Section 2(1)(o))

Partner in relation to LLP means a person who becomes a partner in an LLP in accordance with the LLP agreement. (Section 2(1)(q))

NATURE OF LLP

Section 3 deals with the nature and legal character of LLP and provides that an LLP is a body corporate formed and incorporated under the LLP Act and as such it is a legal entity separate from that its partners. LLP shall have perpetual succession. Any change in the partners of an LLP shall not affect the existence, rights or liabilities of the LLP.

INCORPORATION OF LLP

For incorporation of LLP, following steps need to be taken.

1. **Name of the LLP:** For incorporation of LLP, the persons who want to form LLP should find out availability of the purposed name from RoC. Any suitable name can be chosen by an LLP, subject, however, to the following restrictions:
   a. It shall have either 'limited liability partnership' or the abbreviation 'LLP' as suffix.
   b. The name chosen must not be undesirable in the opinion of the central government or it should not be identical or resemble any other partnership firm, or LLP or body corporate or a registered trade mark or a trade mark the application of which is pending. The reason for this rule is that the reputation of a company, LLP or partnership firm may be injured, if a new LLP adopts an allied name.

   Section 16 provides that application for reservation of name for purposed LLP is to be made to RoC in whose jurisdiction, registered office of the LLP is to be situated. It is advisable that six names in order of priority should be submitted to afford flexibility to the registrar. Where the registrar informed the applicant about the reservation of name with which the LLP is to be registered, such name shall be available for reservation for a period of three months from the date of intimation by the registrar. Further, Section 19 provides that if an LLP is registered by a name which is identical with the name of another existing LLP or body corporate or is undesirable, the central government may direct such LLP to change the name. The LLP must comply with direction within three months from the date of direction.

   Section 21 requires that every LLP shall ensure that its name, address of its registered office, registration number and the statement that it registered with limited liability are mentioned on all its invoices, official correspondence and publications.
2. **Incorporation document (Section 11):** Section 11 provides that two or more persons who want to carry on a lawful business with a view to earn profit will be required to subscribe their name to an 'incorporation document' for getting an LLP incorporated. The 'incorporation document' shall be filled and with prescribed fees with RoC of the state in which the registered office of the LLP is to be situated. The LLP cannot be formed for charitable or non-profit making activities.

   A 'statement' in prescribed form shall be filled along with 'incorporation document' stating that all the requirements of the LLP Act and the rules made there under precedent to incorporation are completed with. The 'statement' must be signed by either an advocate or a company secretary or a chartered accountant or a cost accountant, who is engaged in the formation of LLP and by anyone who has subscribed his name to the 'incorporation document' and it is open to public inspection in the office of registrar on payment of the prescribed fee.

   Contents of incorporation documents: The 'incorporation document' shall contain the following information:
   - The name of the LLP.
   - The proposed business of the LLP.

- The address of the office of registrar of the LLP.
- The name and address of each of the person who is to be partner of LLP on incorporation.
- The name and address of the person who is to be designated partner of LLP on incorporation.
- Other information concerning the purposed LLP as may be prescribed.

Penalty: Section 11 provides that the punishment for a person making the statement about compliance either knowing it to be false or not believing in it being true is a fine of not less than ₹10,000, which may extend to ₹5 lakh, and also imprisonment for a term which may extend to two years.

Incorporation or registration: Section 12 provides that ROC will scrutinize whether the 'incorporation document' and other papers presented to him satisfy the requirements of the Act, and if they are in order, he will register the LLP within a period of 14 days from the date of submission of documents. On registration, ROC shall issue a 'certificate of incorporation' signed by him and authenticated by his official seal stating therein that the LLP is incorporated by the name specified in the incorporation document. The certificate is LLP's 'birth' certificate. The registrar shall enter LLP's name in the 'Register of LLPs' statutorily maintained by him and shall assign an LLP identification number to LLP.

Conclusiveness of Certificate of Incorporation

Section 12 provides that certificate of incorporation issued in respect of any LLP shall be conclusive evidence of the fact that LLP is duly registered by the name specified in the incorporation document. Once the certificate of incorporation is issued, nothing is to be enquired into as to the regularity of the prior proceedings. Even though the signatories come out to be forged, once the certificate of incorporation is issued, the registrar has no power to revoke or cancel it. The logic of the provision is that once the LLP is held out to the world as LLP ready to contract engagements, then it would be most disastrous if, years after, any person is allowed to show that it was not properly registered.

It may, however, be noted that if LLP with an illegal object has been registered, the illegal object does not become legal by issue of the certificate. But the certificate would be all the same conclusive and the legal personality of the LLP cannot be extinguished by cancellation of the certificate of incorporation. The remedy in such a case would be 'to wind up' the LLP.

Effect of Incorporation or Registration

Section 14 provides that after 'certificate of incorporation' is issued, an LLP becomes a body corporate, having separate legal entity and perpetual succession. The effect of registration is that from the date of incorporation or giving the certificate, the LLP shall be capable of suing and being sued, acquiring, owning, holding and developing or disposing of property, whether movable or immovable, tangible or intangible, can have a common seal and can do other acts as bodies corporate may lawfully do.

Registered Office of LLP (Section 13)

According to Section 13, every LLP shall have a registered office to which all communications and notices shall be received. LLP may, in addition to registered office, have other address for service of documents as per the LLP agreement. Where LLP agreement does not provide for such place, then consent of all the partners will be required for declaring any other address as the address for service for documents.

Change of Registered Office

The LLP may change its registered office from one place to another by the following procedure:

1. The procedure provided in the LLP agreement should be followed. Where the LLP agreement does not provide it, then consent of all partners shall be required. However, in case of change of registered office from one state to another state, consent of secured creditors, if any, shall also be required.
2. In the case of change of registered office from one state to another state, the LLP shall publish a public notice at least 21 days before filing any notice of change in Form 15 with the registrar and in daily newspapers published in English and local language.
3. Where the change in the place of registered office is from the jurisdiction of one registrar to another registrar or from one state to another state, the LLP shall file the notice in Form 15 with the registrar from where the LLP proposes to shift, it requires that a copy of Form 15 shall be sent for the information of registrar in whose jurisdiction registered office is proposed.
4. Change of registered office shall be notified to the RoC through Form 15 within 30 days of complying with the requirements along with the requisite filling fee in the case of change of place of registered office from one state to another state or from the jurisdiction of one registrar to that of another registrar in the same state. The notice in Form 15 should also be filled with the other registrar under whose jurisdiction the registered office is proposed to be shifted for information. The changes shall take effect only after such filling.

   Form 15 should be signed by a designated and certified company secretary/chartered accountant in practice.

Procedure for Incorporation of LLP

The procedure for the incorporation of LLP requires that applicants first file application for the reservation of name with RoC. Once the name applied is approved by RoC, the documents for incorporation of LLP need to be filed. Name of every LLP shall end with the words 'limited liability partnership' or 'LLP'. Name which is undesirable or nearly resembles that of any other partnership firm or LLP or any body corporate or trade mark is not allowed. Any entity with a similar name to an LLP that has been incorporated subsequently may seek change of name through RoC within 24 months from date of registration. No person shall carry on business under any name/title which contains the words 'limited liability partnership' or 'LLP' without duly incorporating it as an LLP under the LLP Act. LLP is required to file with RoC the LLP agreement ratified by all the partners within 30 days of incorporation of LLP.

Penalty for Improper Use of Words

Section 20 provides that if any person or persons carry a business under any name or title of which the words 'limited liability partnership' or 'LLP' is or are last word or words, that person or each of those persons shall, unless duly incorporated as LLP, be punishable with fine which shall not be less than ₹50,000 and which may extend to ₹5 lakh.

Conversion from Firm into LLP

Section 55 of the Act provides that a partnership firm, whether registered or not, is allowed to convert itself into LLP. The conversion of the firm into LLP means a transfer of the property, assets, interest, rights, privileges, liabilities, obligations and the undertaking of the firm into LLP as a going concern. After conversion, all the partners of the firm, now partners of LLP, shall be bound by the provisions of the LLP Act.

Eligibility for Conversion

A firm may apply to RoC for converting itself into an LLP, provided all the partners of the existing firm become partners of the proposed LLP. No one else is allowed to become the partner during the process of conversion.

Procedure of Conversion

The conversion of firm is effected by registration with the RoC. Before getting the firm converted into LLP, one has to take the following preparatory steps:

1. Decide about the designated partner.
2. Obtain designated partner identification number (DPIN).
3. Obtain the digital signature of the designated partners as all the applications and documents are to be filed electronically.
4. Ascertain from RoC whether the name of LLP into which the firm is to be converted is available or not.
5. Get LLP agreement and incorporation document drafted and printed. Application is to be submitted online in Form 17 to RoC of the state where the registered office of proposed LLP is to be situated for conversion of firm into LLP. The application is to be accompanied by the following documents:
    a. A statement by all of its partners in the prescribed form containing the name and registration number of firm, the date on which firm was registered under the Indian Partnership Act, 1932, or under any other law, if applicable.

b. Incorporation document.
c. Statement made by either an advocate or a company secretary or a charted accountant or a cost accountant, who is engaged in the formation of LLP and by anyone who subscribed his name to the incorporation document that all the requirements of this Act and the rules made there under have been complied with in respect of incorporation and matters precedent and incidental thereto.
d. Statement of assets and liability of the firm duly certified as true and correct by chartered accountant in practice. The statement should be made up to a date not preceding 30 days from the date of application.
e. The clearance, approval or permission from the concerned body/authority, if needed.
f. Other attachments such as details of income tax returns filed, particulars of pending proceedings, if any, and rejection letter by registrar for conversion applied earlier, if any.

Along with the other documents, necessary filing fee and registration fee at the prescribed rates are also to be paid.

Registration of Conversion

Section 58(1) provides that on receiving the documents, RoC will scrutinize the documents and if he is satisfied with the particulars and other information furnished therein, he will register the documents and issue a 'certificate of registration' stating that LLP is registered on and from the date specified in the certificate. The registrar has the power to refuse the conversion to LLP, if he is not satisfied with the particulars or the information furnished under the provisions of this Act. The firm, however, can file an appeal to the Company Law Board (CLB) in case of refusal by the registrar for conversion of the form.

After conversion, the firm needs to inform to registrar of the firm with which it was registered within 15 days from the date of registration of the LLP about the conversion and particulars of LLP. A delay in information to the registrar of firms will require LLP to pay a fee of rupees 100 per day.

Effects of Registration or Consequences of Conversion of Firm into LLP

Section 58 provides that after the conversion, the effects of conversion as LLP shall be as follows:

1. LLP comes into existence by the name specified in the certificate of registration.
2. All tangible and intangible property, all assets, interests, rights, privileges, liabilities, obligations relating to firm stand transferred to LLP without further act or deed.
3. The firm is deemed to be dissolved. If the firm is registered, then its name is also deemed to be removed from the registrar of firm maintained by the registrar of firm.
4. If any property transferred to the LLP is registered with any authority, then the LLP is required to notify that authority about the conversion with details of LLP.
5. All the proceedings by or against the firm which are pending in any court or tribunal or before any authority on the date of registration may be continued, completed and enforced by or against the LLP.
6. Any conviction, ruling, order or judgment of any court, tribunal or other authority in favour of or against the firm may be enforced by or against the LLP.

7. Every agreement to which the firm was a party on or before registration shall have same effect as if LLP were party to such agreement instead of firm and for any reference to firm will be substituted a reference to LLP.
8. All deeds, contracts, schemes, bonds, agreements, applications, instruments and arrangements subsisting on or before the date of registration relating to firm or to which firm is a party shall continue in force as if they are related to LLP and shall be enforceable by or against the LLP instead of the firm.
9. Every existing contract of employment shall continue to be in force on or after the date of registration as if the LLP were the original employer instead of the firm.
10. Every appointment of the firm in any role or capacity or any authority or power conferred on the firm which is in force immediately before the date of registration shall effect and operate from the date as if it were appointed, or conferred the authority or power by LLP.
11. If any approval, permit or licence has been issued to a firm under any other Act which is in force on or before the date of registration of the LLP, then the LLP is subject to the provisions of the Act under which such approval, permit or licence has been issued.
12. Personal liability of partners shall continue jointly and severally along with the LLP for the liabilities and obligations of the firm which were incurred prior to the conversion or which arise from any contract entered into prior to the conversion. If any partner discharges any liability or obligation of existing firm as referred above, then he shall be entitled, unless otherwise agreed, to be fully indemnified by the LLP.
13. The LLP is required to ensure that for a period of 12 months, commencing not later than 14 days after the date of registration, every official correspondence of LLP bears a statement that it was converted from a firm into an LLP along with the date of registration and name and registration number, if applicable, of the firm from which it was converted.

    Any LLP which does not mention the above facts in its official correspondence shall be punished with a fine which shall not be less than ₹10,000 and may extend to ₹100,000. If the default continues, then LLP shall pay a further fine which shall not be less than ₹50 but which may extend to ₹500 for every day during which such default continues.

Conversion from Private Company into LLP

Section 56 provides that a private company may convert itself into LLP. The conversion of the private company into LLP means a transfer of the property, assets, rights, interests, privileges, obligations and whole of the undertaking of the private company to LLP as a going concern.

Eligibility for Conversion

A private company may apply to RoC for converting itself into an LLP, if there is no security interest in its assets in force at the time of application and the partner of LLP to which is converts comprises all the shareholders of a private company and no one else. After conversion, the company, its shareholders, the LLP and all the partners of the LLP shall be bound by the provisions of the Third Schedule that are applicable to them.

Procedure of Conversion

The conversion of a private company into an LLP is effected by registration with RoC. Before getting the company converted into LLP, one has to take the following preparatory steps:

1. Decide about the designated partner.
2. Obtain DPIN.
3. Obtain the digital signatures of designated partners as all applications and documents are to be filed electronically.
4. Ascertain from RoC whether name of LLP into which the private company is to be converted is available or not.
5. Get 'LLP agreement' and 'incorporation document' drafted and printed.

   After this, an application is to be submitted online in Form 18 to RoC of the state in which the registrar office of the proposed LLP is situated along with the following documents:

   a. Statement by all of the shareholders in the prescribed form containing name and registration number of the company.
   b. The date on which the company was incorporated.
   c. Incorporation document of the company.
   d. Statement made by either an advocate, company secretary, chartered accountant or a cost accountant, who is engaged in the formation of the LLP or by anyone who subscribed his name to the incorporation document that all the requirements of this Act and rules made there under have been complied with regard to incorporation and matters precedent and incidental thereto.
   e. Statement of assets and liabilities of the private company should be made up to a date not preceding 30 days from the date of application.
   f. List of all creditors along with their consent to the conversion.
   g. The clearance, approval or permission from the concerned body/authority, if needed.
   h. Other attachments such as details of income tax returns filed, particulars of pending proceedings, if any and rejection letter by registrar for conversion applied earlier, if any.

   Along with the above documents, necessary filing fees and registration fees at the prescribed rates are also to be paid.

Registration of Conversion

On receiving documents, the RoC will scrutinize all documents and if he is satisfied with the particulars or other information furnished, he will register the LLP. On registration, he will issue a 'certificate of registration' stating the date of registration of the LLP.

RoC has the power to refuse the conversion of LLP, if he is not satisfied with the documents and other information furnished. The private company, however, can file an appeal to the CLB in case of refusal by ROC for conversion within 60 days from the date of notice of refusal.

Intimation of Registrar

The private company so converted is under an obligation to inform the concerned RoC with which it was registered within 15 days from the date of registration of LLP about the conversion and particulars of LLP. Section 69 provides that a delay in information to RoC will require an LLP to pay a fee of ₹100 for every day of such delay.

Effects of Registration

Section 68 provides that effects of registration on conversion are:

1. An LLP comes into existence by the name specified in the certificate of registration.
2. All tangible (movable and immovable) property as well as intangible property vested in the private company, all assets, interests, rights, privileges, liabilities, obligations relating to the private company and the whole of the undertaking of the private company stand transferred to and shall vest in the LLP without further assurance, act or deed.
3. The private company is deemed to be dissolved and its name is also to be removed from the registrar of the companies maintained by RoC.
4. If any property transferred to an LLP is registered with any authority, then the LLP is required to notify that authority about the conversion of private company into an LLP with details of the LLP.
5. All the proceedings by or against the private company which are pending in any court or tribunal or before any authority on the date of registration may be continued, completed and enforced by or against the LLP.
6. Any convention, ruling, order or judgment of any court, tribunal or other authority in favour of or against the private company may be enforced by or against the LLP.
7. Every agreement to which the private company was a party on or before the date of registration, the LLP would become a party, whether or not the rights and liabilities arising out of the agreement could be assigned, on and from the date of registration. Further, any reference to the private company shall be taken as reference to LLP.
8. All deeds, contract, schemes, bonds, agreements, applications, instruments and agreements subsisting immediately before the date of registration relating to the private company or to which the private company is a party shall continue in force on and after that date as if they relate to the LLP and shall be enforceable by or against the LLP instead of the private company.
9. Every existing contract of employment shall continue to be in force on or after the date of registration as if the LLP were the original employer instead of the private company.
10. Every appointment of the private company in any role or capacity or any authority or power conferred on the private company on or before the date of registration shall take effect and operate from that date as if it were appointed or inferred the authority or power by the LLP.
11. If any approval, permit or licence has been issued to private company under any Act on or before the date of registration of the LLP, then the LLP is subject to the provisions of the Act under which such approval, permit or licence has been issued.
12. The LLP is required to ensure that for a period of 12 months commencing not later than 14 days after the date of registration, every official correspondence of the LLP bears a statement that it was converted from a private company into an LLP as from the date of registration along with the name and registration number of the private company from which it was converted. Any LLP which does not mention the above facts in its official correspondence shall be punished with fine which shall not be less than ₹10,000

but which may extend to ₹100,000. If the default continues, then the LLP shall pay a further fine which shall not be less than ₹50 but which may extend to ₹500 for every day during which such default continues.

TEST QUESTIONS

1. Define LLP and bring up clearly its characteristics. How does it differ from a traditional partnership?
2. Write a comment on 'incorporation document'.
3. 'The validity of a certificate of incorporation cannot be disputed on any ground whatsoever.' Critically examine the statement.
4. What is the procedure for incorporation of an LLP? Discuss the legal effect of incorporation of an LLP.
5. State the procedure to be followed for effecting the change of registered office from one place to another, as laid down in Rule 17 of the LLP Rules, 2009.
6. Discuss the procedure of conversion from partnership firm into an LLP. Also discuss the effect of registration of conversion.
7. Discuss the procedure of conversion from private company into an LLP. What are the consequences of conversion?

20

CHAPTER

Functioning of LLP: Partners, Their Relations, Accounts, Audit and Taxation

Learning Objectives

- To understand the functioning of LLP
- To understand the partners and their relationship
- To understand the designated partners and their role
- To understand the accounting system of LLP
- To understand the audit and taxation of LLP

Who Can Be a Partner in LLP?

Section 5 provides that any individual or body corporate may be a partner in LLP. The following can be the partners in LLP:

- Any individual
- An Indian company or body corporate
- Any other LLP
- A foreign LLP
- A foreign company

Designated Partners

Section 7 of the Act provides that LLP shall have at least two 'designated partners' who are individuals and at least one of them shall be 'resident in India'. In case one or more of the partners of LLP are bodies corporate, at least two individuals who are partners of such LLP or nominees of such bodies corporate shall act as 'designated partners'.

'Resident in India' means a person who has stayed in India for minimum 182 days during the immediately preceding one year. Designated partner is responsible for compliance with the provisions of the LLP Act. Designated partner is required to obtain DPIN from the central government. Application for allotment of DPIN needs to be submitted online on the LLP website along with the necessary proof duly attested and certified as prescribed.

Disqualifications of Becoming a Partner (Section 5)

An individual shall not be capable of becoming a partner of LLP, if he is of an unsound mind, or an undischarged insolvent or has applied to be adjudged insolvent.

Minimum and Maximum Number of Partners (Section 6)

Section 6 of the Act provides that every LLP shall have at least two partners and there is no upper limit on number of partners. It further provides that if the number falls below 2, then within six months it needs to be again 2. If not, then such sole partner, who has knowledge of such station, shall be liable personally for the payments of whole debts of LLP contracted during that period.

Every LLP is required to have at least two 'designated partners' who are individuals and at least one of them shall be a resident of India, provided in case of LLP in which all the partners are bodies corporate or in which one or more partners are individuals and bodies corporate, at least two individuals who are partners of such LLP or nominees of such bodies corporate shall act as designated partners.

Appointment

The name of designated partners shall be given in incorporation document and if it states that each of the partners is designated partner, then every partner of LLP shall be a designated partner on incorporation. The LLP agreement will provide how any partner may become or cease to be designated partner. The designated partner is required to give his prior consent to act as designated partner. Every LLP shall file with RoC the particulars of every designated partner who agrees to act as may be prescribed within 30 days of the appointment. However, if no partner of LLP has been intimated to the registrar as designated partner or at any time there is only one designated partner, then every partner of LLP would be deemed to be a designated partner.

Designated Partner Identification Number (DPIN)

Every designated partner would be required to obtain a DPIN. Rule 10 of the LLP (Amendment) Rules, 2010, prescribes the conditions and the procedure which would have to be fulfilled by an individual for obtaining DPIN. Application for allotment of DPIN needs to be submitted online on the LLP website along with the necessary proof duly attested and certified. DPIN so allotted is valid for the lifetime of applicants. It will help the government to keep track of people who run LLPs and shall help prevent a defaulting designated partner from hiding his past deeds and joining another LLP. This would also facilitate effective legal action against the designated partner, keeping in view the possibility of fraud by LLPs.

Eligibility Condition for the Appointment of Designated Partner

Rule 9 of the LLP Rules, 2009, provides that a person shall not be capable of being appointed as a designated partner of an LLP, if:

1. He has any time within preceding five years been adjudged insolvent.
2. He suspends, or has any time within the preceding five years suspended payments to his creditors or has not any time within the preceding five years made a composition with them.
3. He has been convicted by a court for any offence involving moral turpitude and sentenced in respect thereof to imprisonment for not less than six months.
4. He has been convicted by a court for an offence involving Section 30 of the Act. Section 30 deals with punishment for carrying out acts by LLP or its partner with intent to defraud its creditors or for a fraudulent purpose.

Liabilities of Designated Partners

Unless expressly provided otherwise in the Act, a designated partner shall be:

1. Responsible for doing all acts, matter and things as are required to be done by LLP in respect of compliance including filing of any document, return, statement, report and so on.
2. Liable to all penalties imposed on LLP for any contravention of any provisions of the Act and the LLP agreement.

It can be said that he is a compliance officer accountable for regulatory and legal compliances. Section 9 provides that LLP may appoint a designated partner within 30 days of a vacancy arising for any reason.

LLP AGREEMENT

Section 23 provides that LLP agreement is the most important document which explains rights and duties of partners and also their rights and duties in relation of LLP. However, an LLP agreement is not mandatory but it should be as it avoids unnecessary disputes in future. Where no LLP agreement has been executed between the partners of LLP or the agreement of LLP is silent on certain issue, the provision of the First Schedule to the LLP Act, 2008, shall apply. The promoters of the new LLP may execute the LLP agreement either before incorporation or after incorporation of LLP. If there is a pre-incorporation LLP agreement, it should be ratified by all the partners immediately after the incorporation of LLP. The LLP agreement and any changes made therein must be filed with the registrar of the company in Form 3 within 30 days of incorporation of LLP or the date of change made in the agreement, as the case may be, along with the filing fee. It may be noted that the LLP agreement is not open to public inspection.

Rights of Partners

Following are rights of partners:

1. The mutual rights and duties of partners and rights and duties of LLP and its partners shall be determined by the LLP agreement or by the provision of schedule.
2. All partners of LLP are entitled to equal share in capital, profits and losses of LLP.
3. LLP shall indemnify each partner in respect of payments made and personal liabilities incurred by him.
4. The proper conduct of the business of LLP or anything necessarily done for preservation of business or property of the LLP.
5. Every partner shall indemnify LLP for any loss caused to it by his fraud in the conduct of the business of LLP. Every partner may take part in the management of LLP.
6. No partner shall be entitled to remuneration for acting in the business or management of LLP.
7. No person may be introduced as a partner without the consent of all the existing partners.
8. Any matter relating to LLP shall be decided by a resolution passed by majority of the partners and each partner shall have one vote for this purpose. However, no change can be made in the nature of business of LLP without consent of all the partners.
9. Every LLP shall insure that decisions taken by it are recorded in the minutes within 30 days of taking such decisions and are kept and maintained in the registered office of LLP.
10. Each partner shall render true accounts and full information of all things affecting LLP to any partner of his legal representatives.
11. If a partner without consenting LLP carries on any business of the same nature and/or competes with the LLP, he must be accountable to pay the LLP all profits made by him in that business.
12. Every partner shall account to LLP for any benefit derived by him without the consent of LLP from any transaction concerning LLP, or from any use by him of the property, name or any business connection of LLP.
13. No majority of the partner can expel any partner unless a power to do so has been conferred by express agreement between the partners.
14. All disputes between the partners arising out of the LLP agreement which cannot be resolved in terms of such agreement shall be referred for arbitration as per the provision of the Arbitration and Conciliation Act, 1996.

How Can a Partner Cease to Be a Partner?

According to Section 24(1), a person may cease to be a partner of LLP either by an agreement with other partners or in absence of agreement with other partners as to cessation of being a partner, by giving a notice of not less than 30 days to the other partners of his intention to resign as partner. A person may also cease to be a partner of LLP on his death, unsound mind, adjudged insolvent, applied for adjudged insolvent or dissolution of LLP.

Effect of Cessation of Partnership Interest

Section 24 provides that where a person has ceased to be a partner of LLP, he continues to be liable for the act of LLP unless person dealing with LLP has given notice that he has ceased to be a partner of LLP or a notice has been delivered to the registrar. The fact of cessation of a partner from LLP by itself does not discharge him from any obligation to LLP or to other partners or to any other person. Section 25 provides that unless the LLP agreement provides otherwise, he or his legal heir is entitled to receive his share in consequence of his death or insolvency from LLP, an amount equal to his capital contribution along with his share in accumulated profit of LLP after the deduction of its losses, if any. However, he shall not have any right to interfere in the management of LLP after ceasing to be partner in LLP.

Registration of Changes of a Partner (Section 25)

Section 25 provides that every partner shall inform LLP of any change in his name or address within a period of 15 days of such changes. LLP, in turn, would be under obligation to file such details with the registrar within 30 days of such change. LLP will also be required to file a notice with the registrar within 30 days from the date of which any person becomes or ceases to be a partner. The documents delivered to the registrar will be available for public inspection at the registrar's office on payment of prescribed fee.

Partner as Agent of LLP vis-à-vis Third Parties or Position of Partner

Every partner of LLP will be an agent of LLP for the purpose of the business of LLP but not of other partners. Only such partners who are authorized by the LLP agreement to conduct its business are the agents of LLP and can make LLP liable towards the third party only if they act within the scope of their express or implied authority.

Authority of Partner

The authority of partner can be classified as express, implied and in emergency. These are given as follows.

1. **Express authority of a partner:** When a partner is expressly authorized by an agreement of all the partners to do a certain act on behalf of LLP, it is called express authority of a partner. LLP is bound to third party by all acts of a partner done within the scope of his express authority.
2. **Implied authority of a partner:** An agent can also bind LLP to third parties by acts done within the scope inferred from the circumstances of case. Such acts of a partner are incidental to or usually done in the course of proper conduct of business come within the scope of his implied or apparent authority. For example, in the case of

trading of commercial firm, a partner, in the exercise of his implied authority, can bind LLP by following acts:

a. Buying and selling goods in which LLP deals
b. Receiving payments and debts on behalf of LLP
c. Contracting debt and paying debt on behalf of LLP
d. Settling accounts with persons dealing with LLP
e. Drawing cheques, accepting or endorsing bills of exchange and promissory notes in the name of LLP
f. Employing servants for LLP
g. Pledging movable property of LLP
h. Suing on behalf of LLP and defending suits in the name of LLP

3. **Authority in emergency:** In any emergency, an agent's authority extends to do all such acts which are required for protecting the principal as would be done by a person of ordinary prudence, in his own case, acting under similar circumstances and such act binds the principal. In regard to the act done by the agent without the principal's authority, the principal may elect to ratify or disown such acts; and if he ratifies them, which may be express or implied, same effects follow as if those acts were done by his authority.

Extent of LLP's Liability

LLP is not bound by an act of a partner in dealing with a person, if the partner has no authority to act for LLP and the person knows that he has no authority or does not believe that he is a partner of LLP. Where by the wrongful act or omission of a partner acting in the ordinary course of business of LLP, or with its authority, loss or injury is caused to any third party, or any penalty is incurred, LLP is liable, therefore, to the same extent as the partner. The wrongful act may be tort or negligence.

Section 27(3) provides that an obligation of LLP, whether arising out of contract or otherwise will solely be the obligation of LLP. Section 27(4) further provides that the liabilities of LLP shall be met out of the property of LLP. This is the greatest advantage of LLP conferring limited liability upon its partners as compared to the traditional partnership where partners are exposed to unlimited personal liability.

Section 28 provides that a partner is not personally liable, directly or indirectly, for an obligation of LLP, whether arising out of a contract or otherwise, solely by reason of his being a partner of LLP. It further provides that a partner of LLP would be personally liable for his wrongful act or omission done without its authority, but would not be liable for any other partner's wrongful act or omission.

Liability of Partner by Holding Out (Section 29)

Section 29 provides that if a person (not being a partner in LLP) represents to the outside world by words spoken or written or by his conduct, or knowingly permits himself to be represented that he is a partner in a certain LLP, he is then estoppel from denying his being a partner, and is liable as a partner in that LLP.

Actually such a person is not a partner in that LLP. No agreement, no sharing in profits and losses, no say in the management, may not be knowing exact place of business, but as he holds himself out to be a partner, he becomes responsible to outsiders as a partner on the principal of estoppel or holding out. It is for this reason that such a person is called as 'partner by holding out' or 'partner by estoppel'.

Example: Where P represent to R that he is a partner in LLP, while actually he is not a partner, and on the faith of this representation, R gives credit to LLP, and LLP becomes insolvent, R can make P liable on the basis of 'holding out' and P is estoppel from denying that he is a partner in LLP.

It is to be emphasized that in order to entitle a person to bring an action under the doctrine of holding out, it must be shown that he acted on the faith of the representation while giving credit to LLP.

DECEASED PARTNER'S LIABILITY

Where after a partner's death the business is continued in the same LLP's name, the continued use of that name or of the deceased partner's name as part thereof shall not of itself make his legal representative or his estate liable for any act of LLP done after his death. The deceased is liable only for liabilities undertaken during his lifetime. It is worth mentioning here that the liabilities of a partner of LLP shall be limited only to the extent of their investment in LLP.

UNLIMITED LIABILITY IN THE CASE OF FRAUD (SECTION 30)

Section 30 provides that where an act by LLP or a partner thereof is done with the intent of defrauding the creditor of LLP or any other person, or for any fraudulent purpose, the liability of LLP and partners who acted with the intent to defraud creditors or for any fraudulent purpose shall be unlimited for all or any of the debts or other liabilities of LLP. However, in case any such act is carried out by a partner, LLP will be liable to the same extent as the partner unless it is provided by LLP that such act was without the knowledge or the authority of LLP.

Where any business carried on with the intent to defraud creditors of LLP or any other person or for any fraudulent purpose, every person who was knowingly a party of the fraudulent act shall be punishable with imprisonment for a term which may extend to two years and with fine which shall not be less than ₹50,000 but which may extend to ₹5 lakh. Further, such partner, designated partner or employee shall be liable to pay compensation to any person who has suffered any loss or damage by reason of fraudulent conduct.

WHISTLE-BLOWER (SECTION 31)

Section 31 provides that 'whistle-blower' means a person who informs people in authority or the public that the company or firm they work for is doing something wrong or illegal. In the present context, it means the partners or employees of LLP shall be enabled to report to the management about actual or suspected dishonesty, fraud or unethical practice. Consequently, the LLP Act has given adequate protection to the whistle-blower. Section 31 provides that the court or tribunal may reduce or waive penalty leviable against any partner or employee, if he has provided useful information during investigation of such LLP for finding out the offence. No such partner or employee shall be discharged, demoted, suspended, threatened, harassed or in any manner discriminated against the terms and conditions of his LLP or employment merely because of his providing information to the court or tribunal. A whistle-blower who helps in the convention of the guilty will thus be protected.

CONTRIBUTIONS

Partner's contributions in the form of money or property towards the capital of LLP correspond to contribution of share capital in a company formed under the Companies Act, 2013. The sum total of partner's contributions towards the capital forms the security for the creditors of LLP, just as the company's share capital is the cushion of safety to its creditors. The LLP Act provides for the preservation and maintenance of LLP's capital (partners' contribution). It may be recalled that the provision of Section 24(4) provides that withdrawal of partner's contribution on his cessation as a partner shall be subject to continued liability towards the obligation incurred while being a partner until discharged. Section 33(2) also provides that a creditor of LLP may enforce the original obligation described in partnership agreement against any partner of LLP without notice of any subsequent compromise between partners.

Form of Contribution

Section 32 provides that contribution of a partner towards LLP may be in form of money, tangible or intangible property or by contracts for services performed or to be performed. The monetary value of contribution of each partner, if made in any form other than money, shall be accounted for and disclosed in the accounts of LLP. Rule 23 of the LLP Rules, 2009, provides that where the contribution of a partner consists of tangible, movable, immovable or intangible property or other benefits brought in or otherwise contributed by way of contract of services, it shall be valued by a practising chartered accountant or cost accountant or by an approved valuer drawn from the panel maintained by the central government.

Obligation to Contribute (Section 33)

The obligation of a partner to contribute money or property or perform services for LLP shall be as per the LLP agreement. In the absence of any provision to contrary in the LLP agreement, all partners are entitled to equal share in the capital, profits and losses of LLP.

ACCOUNTS, AUDITS AND TAXATION OF LLP

Accounts

According to Sections 34 and 35, every LLP shall maintain the prescribed books of accounts relating to its affairs on cash or accrual basis and according to the double entry system of accounting. LLP needs to ensure transparency and make disclosures of its solvency and financial position through filing of various returns and statements with RoC.

Book of Accounts

Section 34 provides that annual accounts of LLP shall reflect true and fair view of its business; however, the LLP Act does not expressly mention as to what particular books of account must be maintained. The LLP Rules provide that every LLP must keep proper books of account to show and explain the transactions of LLP. The accounts shall be kept in a manner to disclose the financial position of LLP as on that date with reasonable accuracy. The accounts should also enable the designated partner to ensure that the statement of account and solvency is being prepared as per the rules of LLP.

According to the LLP Act, a financial year is a period of 12 months starting from 1 April of the year to 31 March of the following year. It is important to note that for LLP which is incorporated after 30 September, the first financial year ends on 31 March of the year next following that year. Therefore, such LLP may have the first financial year having more than 12 months. For example, LLP incorporated on 1 October 2010 may end its financial year on 31 March 2012.

Form and Content

The LLP Rules have provided that LLP must keep books of accounts with respect to the particulars of all sums of money received and expanded by LLP and the matters in respect of which the receipt an expenditure takes place, the assets and liabilities of LLP, the statement of cost of goods purchased, inventories, work in progress, finished goods and cost of goods sold. The partners may mutually decide among themselves for keeping books of account for any other matter which they feel necessary. The books of account of every LLP relating to a period of not less than eight years immediately preceding the current year must be preserved in good condition at its registered office. Every LLP is required to prepare a 'statement of account and insolvency' each year and file the same with the registrar of company. This annual statement is one of the most important disclosures made by LLP annually which is open for public inspection. The statement of account and insolvency is to be prepared within a period of six months from the end of its financial year for each year of its existence. Therefore, for the financial year ending on 31 March 2017, every LLP must prepare its annual statement by 30 September 2017.

Time Period for Filing

Once the statement is prepared, a copy of it has to be filed with the registrar within a period of 30 days from the end of six months of the financial year ending on 31 March; therefore, every LLP must file its annual statement by 30 October.

From the Content

The annual statement of accounting and solvency has to be submitted in the format prescribed in Form 8. The statement has two parts—statement of solvency and statement of account. The statement of solvency consists of solemn affirmation and sincere declaration by the designated partner that they have made a full enquiry into the affairs of LLP and have formed the opinion about its solvency. In other words, it is to ensure if the LLP would be able to pay its debts in full in the normal course of its business or not. Statement of account essentially presents a detailed summary of financial position of LLP. It consists of a statement of assets and liability and a statement of income and expenditure. The two sub statements have to report the figures of the two financial years—for the current financial year and for the immediately preceding financial year to the current financial year.

Signing and Inspection

The statement of account and solvency shall be signed on behalf of LLP by its designated partners, further each designated partner shall be taken to be a party to its approval unless he shows that he took all reasonable steps to prevent their being approved and signed. Section 36 provides that statement of account and solvency field by each LLP with the registrar shall be open for public inspection at the office of the registrar and shall be available for obtaining a certified copy thereof on payment of a nominal fee.

Any LLP which fails to prepare and file the annual statement of account and solvency on or before the due date shall be punishable with fine which shall not be less than ₹25,000 but which may extend to ₹500,000. The LLP Act has also provided that every designated partner of such LLP shall be punishable with fine which shall not be less than ₹10,000 but which may extend to ₹100,000.

Annual Return of LLP

Section 35 of the Act provides that annual return shall be filed every year by LLP duly authenticated with RoC within 60 days of closure of its financial year in such form and manner and accompanied by such fee as may be prescribed. The annual return has to state the particulars as they stood on that day on Form 11 annexed to the LLP Rules, 2009. The annual return shall contain:

1. The name and address of registered office of LLP.
2. The main business activities of LLP.
3. The summary of partners and designated partners including DPIN of designated partners.
4. Number of individual(s) as partners and number of bodies corporate as partners.
5. Obligation of each partner to contribute and the contribution received.
6. The particulars of the penalties imposed, if any, on LLP or designated partner or non-designated partners.
7. Particulars of compounding of offences.

Verification and Signing

The copy of the return to be filed with the registrar must be verified and digitally signed by designated partner. The annual return filed by LLP with the registrar shall be open for public inspection at the office of the registrar and available for obtaining a copy of certification on payment of a nominal fee.

Section 34(5) provides that any LLP which fails to file the annual return in the prescribed form on or before the due date shall be punishable with fine which shall not be less than ₹25,000 but which may extend to ₹500,000. The LLP Act has provided that every designated partner of such LLP shall be punishable with fine which shall not be less than ₹10,000 but which may extend to ₹100,000.

Audit

Section 34(4) provides that the accounts of LLP shall be audited in accordance of such rules as may be prescribed. However, the central government may exempt any class or classes of LLPs from the afore-stated requirement. Rule 24(8) provides that LLP whose turnover does not exceed, in any financial year, ₹60 lakh or capital contribution does not exceed ₹25 lakh is exempted from getting its accounts audited. But if partners of such LLP decide to get the account of such LLP audited, the accounts shall be audited in accordance with the LLP Rules, 2009.

LLP Rules Regarding Auditors

Qualification of auditors: A person is qualified for appointment as an auditor of LLP, if he is a charted accountant in practice. It may be noted that LLPs may be appointed as auditors and they will not be treated as body corporate. The remuneration of an auditor may be fixed by the designated partner or by following the procedure written in the LLP agreement.

Appointment of auditors: An auditor or auditors shall be appointed for each financial year of LLP for auditing its account by designated partners. The casual vacancy and the vacancy by removal of the auditors may also be filled by the designated partners. The first auditor(s) shall be appointed at any time for the first financial year but before the end of the first financial year. The subsequent auditor(s) may be appointed at least 30 days prior to the end of the each financial year. The auditor(s) so appointed shall hold office according to the terms of his appointment. He shall continue to hold such office until new auditor is appointed or re-appointed. Where no auditor has been appointed by the designated partner or the partners, then on failure to appoint auditors, the retiring auditors shall be deemed to be re-appointed, unless:

1. The LLP agreement requires actual re-appointment.
2. The majority of partners have determined that he should not be appointed and have given a notice to his effect of LLP. The notice may be given either in hard copy or in electronic form.

Where an auditor is unwilling to be re-appointed, he is required to give a notice, in writing, expressing his unwillingness to continue as an auditor accompanied by the statement of the circumstances connected with his ceasing to hold office. The notice is to be deposited at the registered office of LLP not less than 14 days before the end of the time allowed for appointing the new auditor. The auditor's term comes to an end as on the date on which the notice is deposited or such later date as may be specified in the notice.

Removal and resignation of auditors: The auditors of LLP can be removed from their office at any time by the partners of LLP. The removal shall be according to the LLP agreement. However, if the agreement is silent about the removal of an auditor, consent of all the partners shall be required for removal of the auditors from their office.

An auditor of LLP may resign his office by giving a notice in writing and the notice becomes effective only when it is accompanied by the statement of the circumstances connected with his ceasing to hold office. The auditor's term comes to an end as on the date on which the notice is deposited at the registered office of LLP or such later dated as may be mentioned in the notice of resignation.

Penalty for non-compliance: Any LLP which fails to comply with the provisions relating to audit of accounts shall be punishable with fine which shall not be less than ₹25,000 but which may extend to ₹500,000. In addition, the LLP shall also be punishable with fine which shall not be less than ₹10,000 but which may extend to ₹100,000.

Powers and duties of an auditor: The powers and duties of auditors are given as follows:

1. The auditor has a right of access during business hours to the books of account of LLP.
2. The auditor is entitled to require such information and explanations as he may think necessary for the performance of the duties.
3. The auditor must act honestly and with reasonable skill, care and caution in the discharge of his duties. He must not be negligent.
4. The auditor is not bound to be suspicious unless there is something to arouse suspicion. 'He is a watch dog but not the bloodhound.'
5. The auditor is required to bring to the notice of the partner any irregularities affecting their interests.
6. The auditor must personally verify the matters capable of direct verification.
7. The auditor is required to make auditor's report to the partners of LLP on the accounts examined by him. He must expressly state in his report whether in his opinion the accounts examined by him give a 'true and fair view' of LLP's state of affairs.

Taxation of LLPs

The LLP Act, 2008, does not contain any provisions regarding tax regime of LLP. Hence, the taxation scheme of LLP is governed by the provision of the Income Tax Act, 1961. The tax provisions treat LLP similar to a partnership firm for tax purpose. It is provided that the provisions applicable to a partnership firm will apply to LLP automatically unless otherwise provided. The specific provisions are as follows:

1. Firms shall have the meaning assigned to it in the Indian Partnership Act, 1932, and shall include LLP as defined in the LLP Act, 2008.
2. Partner shall have the meaning assigned to it in the Indian Partnership Act, 1932, and shall include a partner of LLP as defined in the LLP Act, 2008.
3. Partnership shall have the meaning assigned it in the Indian Partnership Act, 1932, and shall include a partner of LLP as defined in the LLP Act, 2008.

Conditions for Being Taxed Partnership Firm

In order to be taxed LLP, it has to fulfil the same conditions as are applicable to a partnership firm under Section 184 of the Income Tax Act. LLP will be taxed as a firm, if it satisfies the following conditions:

1. LLP must be evidenced by an LLP agreement.
2. The individual shares of the partners must be specified in the agreement.

3. A certificate copy of the LLP agreement must accompany the return of income of LLP.
4. If during a financial year, a change takes place in membership of LLP or in profit-sharing ratio of partners, a certified copy of the revised LLP agreement must be submitted along with the return of income of the financial year.
5. There should not be any failure on the part of LLP while attending to notice given by the income tax officer for completion of the assessment of LLP.
6. LLP shall file the income tax return on due date. The annexures are not required to be filed now a days, but LLP must keep these documents ready which have to be produced to the assessing officer on demand during assessment proceeding.

Taxation Scheme

Under the Income Tax Act, a partnership firm pays tax on its profit after deducting its expenditure, salaries and interest to partners. The share of profit is exempted in the hand of partners and they are taxed for salary, interest which was allowed as a deduction in the hands of the firm. The deductions of salary of partners shall be taxed as income from business and profession in the hands of partners. If a partnership firm is converted into an LLP, the same scheme is applicable. The current schemes thus provide taxation of income in the hands of partnership firm and LLP, an exemption from tax in the hand of partners. As per Explanation 2 of Section 139(1) of the Income Tax Act, LLP has to file an income tax return on or before 31 July, if the accounts are not to be audited. The due date for filing the income tax return is on or before 30 September, if the accounts are to be audited under the Act. A designated partner shall sign and verify the income tax return of LLP. However, the income tax return shall be signed and verified by any one of the partners in the following cases:

1. Where the designated partner is not able to sign and verify the income tax return for any unavoidable reason
2. Where there is no designated partner as such

Liability of a Partner towards Tax of LLP in Liquidity

The Income Tax Act makes every partner of LLP jointly and severally liable for the taxes to be paid by LLP in liquidation for the period during which he was a partner. However, he can escape this liability if he proves that the non-recovery of taxes cannot be attributed to any gross neglect, misfeasance or breach of duty on his part.

TEST QUESTIONS

1. Who can be a partner in LLP? What are the disqualifications for becoming a partner in LLP? How can a person become a partner of LLP? Discuss.
2. What is meant by 'designated partner'? Discuss the provisions of the LLP Act, 2008, regarding appointment and eligibility conditions for the appointment of designated partner.
3. Discuss the mutual rights and duties as between the partners of LLP in the absence of an express agreement between them.

4. What is the nature and extent of a partner's authority to bind LLP by his act? Discuss.
5. Explain (a) liability of a 'partner by holding out', (b) liability of a deceased partner and (c) DPIN under the LLP Act, 2008.
6. Discuss the main statutory requirements as regard maintenance of accounts under the LLP Act, 2008. Write a note on annual return of LLP.
7. 'The statement of account and solvency is one of the most important disclosures made by LLP annually.' Comment on the statement.
8. 'The audit of the books of account of LLP has not been made compulsory by the LLP Act, 2008, relating to qualification, appointment, remuneration and removal of an auditor.' Explain. Discuss briefly powers and duties of auditors of LLP.

APPENDIX

Obligations under the LLP Act, 2008, with respect to e-filing of forms, returns and documents with registrar.

Description e-Form:

1. Application for reservation or change of name—Form 1
2. Incorporation document and statement—Form 2
3. Information with regard to limited liability—Form 3
4. Partnership agreement and changes, if any, made therein, notice of appointment of partners/designated partner and changes among them, intimation of DPIN by LLP to registrar and consent of partner to become a partner/designated partner—Form 4
5. Intimation of particulars of name or address of a partner/change in such particulars by a partner to LLP—Form 6
6. Application for allotment of DPIN—Form 7
7. Statement of account and solvency—Form 8
8. Consent to act as designated partner—Form 9
9. Intimation of changes in particulars by designated partners—Form 10
10. Annual return of LLP—Form 11
11. Specimen of notice of cessation by a ceasing partner to other partners—Form 13
12. Form for intimating the registrar of Firms/RoC of conversion of firm/company into LLP—Form 14
13. Notice of change of place of registered office—Form 15
14. Application and statement for the conversion of a firm into LLP—Form 17
15. Application and statement for conversion of a private company/unlisted public company into LLP—Form 18
16. Application for direction to LLP to change its name—Form 23
17. Application for reservation/renewal of name by a foreign LLP/foreign company—Form 25
18. Form for registration of particulars by foreign LLP—Form 27

21 CHAPTER

Winding Up and Dissolution of Limited Liability Partnership

Learning Objectives

- To understand the meaning of winding up of an LLP
- To understand the difference between dissolution and winding up of an LLP
- To understand the meaning of winding up by court
- To understand the meaning of voluntary winding up
- To understand the appointment, role, powers and duties of a liquidator

Meaning of Winding Up

An LLP is an artificial person created by law and it comes to an end by law, which is called dissolution. The process of winding up involves the realization of the assets, payment of the liabilities and distribution of surplus, if any, among the partners of an LLP by the LLP liquidator.

Winding Up vs. Dissolution

Winding up should not be taken to mean the same thing as dissolution of an LLP. Winding up of an LLP proceeds its dissolution. Prior to dissolution and after winding up, the legal entity of an LLP remains, and it can be sued in a court of law. On dissolution, an LLP ceases to exist, its name is actually struck off the 'registrar of LLP' by the RoC and the fact is published in the official gazette.

Modes of Winding Up

Section 63 provides that an LLP may be wound up by the court (Tribunal) or voluntary winding up.

Winding Up an LLP by Court (Tribunal)

Section 64 provides that winding up of an LLP by court (Tribunal) can take place on following grounds:

1. **Petition by LLP:** If the LLP has resolved that the LLP will be wound up by the court. Then it need to make a petition to the court. Before making a petition to the court, a resolution may be passed by a majority vote unless by LLP agreement provide for specified majority or unanimous. The court may refuse if it finds that winding up would be opposed to public interest or LLP's interest.
2. **Number of partners below minimum:** If the number of partners is reduced below the minimum limit, that is, below two, the court is bound to make a winding up order on this ground.
3. **Inability to pay debts**: An LLP may be ordered to be wound up if it is unable to pay its debts. The court in its discretion may make or refuse to make a winding up order if majority creditors oppose the petition for a good reason and prove to the satisfaction of the court that in which of the total assets and liabilities of the LLP it must continue to trade.
4. **LLP acting against the national interest:** An LLP may be wound up by the court if it has acted against the interests of the sovereignty and integrity of India, the security of the State or public order.
5. **Default in filing the statement of account and solvency or annual return:** If an LLP has made a default in filing with the registrar statement of account and solvency or annual return for five consecutive financial years, the court will make a winding up order on this ground.
6. **Just and equitable:** An LLP may also be ordered to be wound up if the court is of the opinion that it is just and equitable. The meaning of 'just and equitable' will depend upon facts of each case. The court may order winding up on 'just and equitable' on the basis of judicial decision.
   a. Where the main object of the LLP has failed or its whole or substantially the whole of the capital has been lost and there is no reasonable hope of trading at profit.
   b. When there is a complete deadlock in the management of the LLP owing to the partners not being on speaking term. This is applicable to a closely held LLP in which there are only two partners.
   c. When the LLP was conceived to carry out illegal business or when the business of the LLP becomes illegal.
   d. When it is a mere 'bubble' LLP and it does not carry on any business or does not have any property.

Commencement of the Winding Up

Winding up of an LLP commences at the time of the petition, not from the date of winding up order. Where before the presentation of the petition a resolution has been passed by the LLP for voluntary winding up, the winding up shall commence from the date of passing resolution. The date of commencement is important for various matters to avoid objectionable voluntary transfers and fraudulent preferences.

Power of the Court on Presentation of the Court

An application for winding up of an LLP shall be filed by a petition to the court by the LLP, or by any creditor(s) or by registrar. An LLP shall file a petition with the court for winding up along with a statement of affairs. After receiving the petition, the court fixes a date for hearing by giving a 14-day notice to the LLP to appear and present its case for the winding up and shall also cause the issue of public notice of the same in order to notify all creditors and partners of the LLP about the winding up petition.

On the hearing date, upon hearing all concerned parties and keeping in mind all the circumstances of the case, the court may within 90 days from the date of presentation of petition may:

- Dismiss the petition, with or without costs
- Make any interim order that it thinks fit
- Direct the action for revival or rehabilitation of the LLP
- Appoint a 'liquidator' as the provisional liquidator of the LLP till the making of a winding up order
- Make an order for the winding up of the LLP with or without costs

Consequences of the Winding Up Order by the Court

The consequences of the winding up order by the court are as follows:

1. The petitioner and the LLP are required to file a certified copy of court's order with the RoC within 15 days from the date of order.
2. The order for winding up shall be the notice of discharge of the officers and employees of the LLP, except when it is required for beneficial realization of assets.
3. For computing the period of limitation in respect of the suits and applications on behalf of or in the name of LLP, which is being wound up by the court, the period between the date of making the application of winding up and the date of the order of winding up order should be excluded.
4. No suit or legal proceeding can be commenced against the LLP without the leave of the court. Similarly, if a suit is pending against the LLP at the date of winding up order, it shall not be proceeded with, except with the permission of the court.
5. The court which is winding up the LLP shall have full power to entertain or dispose of any new or pending suit or proceeding by or against the LLP. Companies Act, 2013 provide that any suit or proceeding pending in any other court shall also be transferred to the court in which the winding up of the LLP is proceeding (Section 446).

Voluntary Winding Up

Voluntary winding up may be either by members or by creditors. The procedure for voluntary winding up by members is as follows:

1. **Passing of resolution:** An LLP can be wound up voluntarily by passing of a resolution for such winding up by at least three-fourths of the total number of its partners. A copy

of the resolution shall be filed with the registrar within 30 days of passing of the resolution in Form 1.

2. **Declaration of solvency:** The majority of the designated partners shall make a declaration in the format provided under Form 2 verified by an affidavit to the effect that the LLP has no debt or that it will be able to pay its debt in full within such period not exceeding one year from the commencement of the winding up. Such declaration is to be registered with the registrar in Form 3 within 15 days of passing of the resolution for voluntary winding up along with the statement of assets and liabilities in Form 4 for the period commencing from the date declaring that the LLP is not being wound up to defraud any person up to which the last account was prepared and ending with the latest practicable date immediately before the making of the declaration duly attested by at least two designated partners.
3. **Creditors' consent for winding up:** In case the creditors are subsisting, whether secured or unsecured, the approval of the creditors would also be required for such winding up. A copy of the aforesaid declaration, the estimated amount of the claims due to each of the creditors and an offer for creditors to accept such claims shall be sent to the creditors by registered or speed post or any of the modes specified in Rule 15. The creditors shall, within 30 days of receipt of the declaration, give to the LLP their opinion in respect of voluntary winding up proposed by the LLP or acceptance of offer for satisfaction of their claims. At least two-thirds of the creditors of the LLP shall give their consent for such voluntary winding up. In case the debts of the creditors would not be payable from the proceeds of the assets of the LLP, the LLP may be wound up voluntarily by creditors. In case the debts of the creditors would not be payable and it is proposed by the Tribunal to wind up the LLP, the LLP shall file an application within 14 days thereafter. Notice of any decision of creditors shall be given by the LLP to the registrar in Form 5 within 15 days of the receipt of the consent of creditors.
4. **Publication of resolution:** Within 14 days of the receipt of the creditors' consent, the LLP shall give notice of the resolution by advertisement in a newspaper circulating in the district where the registered office or the principal office of the LLP is situated.
5. **Appointment of liquidator:** Within 30 days of the passing of the resolution where no creditors are subsisting or within 30 days of intimating the decision of the creditors to the registrar in the case of creditors, the liquidator of the LLP has to be appointed with the consent of the partners. The LLP liquidator shall file a declaration in Form 6 with the registrar disclosing conflict of interest or lack of independence in respect of his appointment if any with the LLP or the creditors and the LLP shall give notice to the registrar in Form 10 within 10 days of the appointment of the liquidator. On the appointment of the LLP liquidator, all the powers of the designated partners and other partners, if any, shall cease.
6. **Audit of LLP liquidator's account:** The accounts of the LLP liquidator shall be audited in accordance with the manner specified in Rule 56.
7. **Liquidator's report:** After the winding up of the affairs of the LLP, the LLP liquidator shall prepare a report in Form 9 describing the manner in which the winding up has been conducted, the property has been disposed of and its debts have been discharged. The approval of the partners would be required on the said report and the final winding up accounts and explanation of the liquidator in the meeting of partners. At least two-thirds of the total number of partners shall give their consent for the approval of report and the accounts satisfied by the liquidator. The resolution for such approval shall be

passed within 30 days of the receipt of the report, winding up accounts and explanation for its dissolution.

8. **Dissolution of LLP:** After the winding up of the affairs of the LLP, the LLP liquidator shall prepare a report in Form 9 describing the manner in which the winding up has been conducted, the property has been disposed of and its debts have been discharged. Within 15 days of the passing of the resolution, the LLP liquidator shall file with the registrar a copy of the final winding up accounts, explanations and report in Form 10 and file an application with the Tribunal for passing an order of dissolution of the LLP. The tribunal on the satisfaction for the duly follow-up of the winding process passes an order for the dissolution of the LLP within 60 days of the receipt of such application. The liquidator shall file a copy of the order for the dissolution of the LLP with the registrar within 30 days in Form 11.

FOREIGN LLP

A foreign LLP can establish a place of business in India and its regulatory mechanism will be as per the rules prescribed by the central government. A foreign LLP shall, within 30 days of establishing a place of business in India, file with the registrar in Form 27:

1. A copy of the certificate of incorporation or registration and other instrument(s) constituting or defining the constitution of the LLP
2. The full address of the registered or principal office of the LLP in the country of its incorporation
3. The full address of the office of the LLP in India which is to be deemed as its principal place of business in India
4. The list of partners and designated partners, if any, and the names and addresses of two or more persons residing in India, authorized to accept on behalf of the LLP service of process and any notices or other documents required to be served on the LLP

LIQUIDATOR

A liquidator is an officer who helps to complete the liquidation proceedings by realizing the assets of the business and distributing them among the creditors in the most fairly manner. If any surplus is left, then it will be distributed between the owners of the business. For the purpose of winding up of an LLP, there shall be a 'liquidator' who may be either an official liquidator or a liquidator appointed by the court from the panel constituted by the central government. In the absence of any such order, the official liquidator shall become or act as the 'liquidator' of the LLP. The central government has appointed for each high court an official liquidator.

After receiving the winding up petition and before passing the winding up order, the court may appoint the liquidator as a 'provisional liquidator' for the time being, who shall have the same powers as a 'liquidator' unless the court limits and restricts his power by the orders appointing him or by a subsequent order. As soon as the winding up order is made, the 'provisional liquidator' shall become the 'liquidator' of the LLP.

Powers of a Liquidator

A liquidator can exercise certain powers with the sanction of court and can exercise certain powers on his own account without the sanction of the court.

Powers with the Sanction of Court

1. To institute or defend any suit, prosecution or other legal proceeding, civil or criminal, in the name and on behalf of the LLP.
2. To carry on the business of the LLP for beneficial winding up of the LLP. All liabilities incurred by the liquidator for carrying on business shall rank for payment in priority to other debts and liabilities of the company.
3. To sell the immovable and movable property and actionable claims of the LLP, either by private contract or by public auction, with power to sell whole of the undertaking of the LLP as a going concern.
4. To do all such other things as may be necessary for winding up of the LLP and distributing its assets in settling creditors and partners.
5. To disclaim an onerous property or unprofitable contract.
6. To pay any class of creditors in full or to make any compromise or arrangement with creditors.
7. To compromise partners' outstanding contributions, debts and other liabilities with partners and debtors and take any security in discharge of any such claim and give complete discharge.

Powers without the Sanction of Court

1. To do all acts in the name and on behalf of the LLP and to execute all deeds, receipts and other documents and to use the seal of the LLP when necessary.
2. To inspect records of the LLP and files with the registrar without payment of any fee.
3. To prove, rank and claim in insolvency of any partner for any balance against his estate and to receive dividends in the insolvency.
4. To draw, accept, make and endorse any negotiable instrument in the name of the LLP.
5. To take out, in his official name, letters of administration to the estate of a deceased partner and to do necessary things to obtain payment.
6. To appoint an agent to do any business which he is unable to do himself.
7. To avoid fraudulent preference done within six months before the commencement of winding up.
8. To avoid any objectionable voluntary transfers, made within one year before the commencement of winding up.

It should be noted that the exercise of all the above powers is subject to the control of the court, and any creditor or partner may apply to the court with respect to the exercise of any power. Further, to check the liquidator from abusing his power, it is provided that any person aggrieved by any act or decision of the liquidator may apply to the court to make such order as it thinks just in the circumstances.

Duties of a Liquidator

A liquidator has a fiduciary position and the following duties:

1. It is the duty of a liquidator to conduct the proceeding in winding up of an LLP and perform such duties as the court may impose. The acts of a liquidator shall be valid, notwithstanding any defect that may afterwards be discovered in his appointment or qualifications.
2. The designated partner within 21 days from the date of the winding up order or appointment of the provisional liquidator shall make out and submit a statement of affairs of the LLP to the official liquidator. After the receipt of the statement, it is the duty of the liquidator to prepare and submit a report to the court within 60 days from the date of the winding up order.
3. A liquidator must take custody and control of books, documents and assets of the LLP. The liquidator is the custodian of the LLP's property. The corporate state and the powers of LLP continue until it is dissolved.
4. It is the duty of a liquidator to give regard to the resolutions of the creditors or the partners or to any direction given by the 'committee of inspection'.
5. It is the duty of a liquidator to summon meetings of creditors and partners for the purpose of ascertaining their wishes and he shall be bound to summon such meetings, at such time, as the creditors and partners may, by resolution, direct, or request in writing by not less than one-tenth the value of the creditors or partners.
6. It is the duty of a liquidator to submit information as to pending liquidation within one year of the winding up order. In such case, the liquidator is required to file in the court and with the registrar a statement duly audited within two months of the expiry of the first year, and thereafter once every year until the winding up is concluded (Section 551 of the Companies Act, 1956).

Committee of Inspection

The court may, at the time of making an order for the winding up of an LLP or at any time thereafter, direct that there shall be appointed a 'committee of inspection' to act with the liquidator. The committee of inspection shall consist of such number of members not exceeding 12, who shall be creditors or partners of LLP as may be determined by the court.

Power of the Court after Winding Up Order

1. The court may, at any time, after making a winding up order, on the application either of the liquidator or of any creditor or partner, make an order staying the proceedings for a limited time or in full. A copy of the stay order shall forthwith be filed by the LLP with the registrar.
2. The court has the power to settle the list of partners and realize the assets of the LLP to be collected and applied in discharge of its liabilities.
3. The court has the power to require any partner, trustee, receiver, banker, agent, officer or employee of the LLP to pay, deliver, surrender or transfer to the liquidator any money, property or books and papers in his custody or under his control, to which the LLP is prima facie entitled.

4. The court may order any partner, purchaser or any other person from whom any money is due to the LLP to pay the money into the public account of the Reserve Bank of India, instead of the liquidator.
5. The court may fix a time within which the creditors will have to prove their claims. The court has the power to exclude any creditor who fails to prove its claim within the fixed time from the benefit of any distribution made immediately on the expiry of the announced date.
6. The court may summon before it any offer of the LLP or person known or suspected to have in his possession any property or books or papers of the LLP or known or suspected to be indebted to the LLP, or known or suspected to be indebted to the LLP, or any person whom the court deems capable of giving information concerning the promotion, formation, trade dealing, property, books or papers or affairs of the LLP.
7. The court has the power to order public examination of promoters, designated partners and the like on the report of the liquidator that in his opinion, a fraud has been committed by any person in the promotion or formation of the LLP, on the conduct of business of the LLP. The court has the power to direct such person or officer to appear before it on the appointed date and be publicly examined on oath.
8. If the court is of the opinion that a partner is about to quit India or to abscond or is about to remove or conceal any of his property, for evading payments of calls or avoiding examination in receipt of the affairs of LLP, it may order to arrest him and his books and papers to be seized and kept safely.
9. When the LLP has been completely wound up, the liquidator has made an application to the court and the court is of the opinion that the liquidator cannot proceed with the winding up for want of funds or for any other just and equitable reason, the court shall make an order and the LLP shall be wound up.

Test Questions

1. What are the provisions of the LLP Act, 2008, regarding winding up and dissolution of an LLP?
2. Explain the powers and duties of a liquidator under the LLP Act, 2008.
3. Explain the winding up of an LLP. Discuss the various grounds under which an LLP can be wound up by the court.
4. What is meant by the statement of account and solvency in an LLP?
5. Discuss in brief the provisions of the LLP Act, 2008, relating to voluntary winding up of an LLP.
6. Who may file a petition for winding up an LLP? Discuss the powers of court on hearing such a petition.
7. 'The court can wind up an LLP on just and equitable grounds.' Comment.
8. Write a note on a foreign LLP.

UNIT V

The Information Technology Act, 2000

22 CHAPTER

Introduction to the Information Technology Act, Digital Signature and Certifying Authorities

Learning Objectives

- To understand the meaning of e-commerce
- To understand the meaning of digital signature and electronic governance
- To understand the meaning of security of electronic records and digital signatures
- To understand the meaning of digital signature certificates
- To understand the duties of subscribers
- To understand the meaning of attribution, acknowledgement and dispatch of electronic records
- To understand the regulations of certifying authorities

INTRODUCTION

The Information Technology Act (IT Act), 2000, has been enacted for the information-based Indian society and the world. This information is consistently, effectively and efficiently acted upon, so as to take decisions. It helps in better decision-making, minimizes the response time and enables better coordination in the organization. The computer is at the core of information technology (IT) activities so much so that it is difficult to think of any aspect of life which has not been affected by the computer system. A Computer Based Information System (CBIS) is a system which uses computers and telecommunication technology to perform its intended task. The personal computers, printer, Internet and communication network are most effective when they are combined with information system.

However, this has also given an opportunity to those persons who want to take the undue advantage of developments in the IT; that is, it has resulted into crimes such as theft of data, hacking, viruses and other cybercrimes. In the case of R. vs. Governor of Brixton Prison, it was held that the operation of the keyboard by a computer operator produces a virtually instantaneous result on the magnetic disk of the computer, even though it may be thousands of miles away. It seems to us artificial to regard the act as having been done in one rather than the other place.

Electronic Commerce (E-commerce)

E-commerce means the ability to conduct business electronically or over the Internet. It describes technology-enabled communication with customers and suppliers for a business organization. Generally, people think of e-commerce as using the Internet to help the business and sell its products and services. However, e-commerce is much wider than that. There are two kinds of e-commerce:

1. **Business-to-business (B2B) e-commerce:** It refers to a company selling or buying from other companies. A company communicates with other companies by electronic means. Electronic data interchange (EDI) transactions include sending and receiving of orders, invoices and shipping notices. With the introduction of the Internet, companies, regardless of size, can communicate and do business with each other electronically and that too cheaply.
2. **Business-to-customer (B2C) e-commerce:** It refers to a company selling its products or services to the customers using the Internet as a communication medium. E-commerce is a term for an entire spectrum of activities such as EDI, electronic payment systems, inventory and order management, product support and service, information delivery and other business applications linking solutions through the use of paperless IT such as Internet bar coding, e-mail, smart cards and CD-ROMs.

When a business makes use of e-commerce, it can reduce the cost, satisfy the customers and can become a global company. However, as the use of e-commerce by public at large increases, it will present huge risk for those who do not take advantage of it. It has given birth to more frauds on smart cards, debit and credit cards and so on. It demands more laws on e-commerce so as to make it consumer- and supplier-friendly.

The IT Act, 2000

It is an Act to provide legal recognition for transactions carried out by means of EDI and other means of electronic communication, and further to amend the IPC; the Indian Evidence Act, 1872; the Bankers' Books Evidence Act, 1891; and the Reserve Bank of India Act, 1934. The IT Act, 2000, contains provisions and laws on digital signature, penalties, offences and so on. This Act also contains four Schedules incorporating consequential amendments in respect of certain other Acts.

Features of the Act

The following are the main features of this Act:

1. Electronic contracts have been made legally valid if made through secure electronic communications.
2. Legal recognition has been granted to digital signatures.
3. A security procedure for electronic records and digital signatures has been laid down.

4. A procedure for appointment of adjudicating officers for holding enquiries under the Act has been laid down.
5. A provision has been made for the establishment of Cyber Regulations Appellate Tribunal under the Act.
6. An appeal against the order of the controller or adjudicating officer can be made to Cyber Regulations Appellate Tribunal and not to any civil court.
7. Appeals against the order of the Cyber Regulations Appellate Tribunal are to be made in the high court.
8. Digital signatures are to be effected by use of asymmetric cryptosystem and hash function.
9. A provision has been made for the appointment of a Controller of Certifying Authorities (CCA) to licence and regulate the working of certifying authorities.
10. The controller is to act as a repository (a storehouse, i.e., who will maintain an authentic and complete information) of all digital signature certificates.
11. The Act is to apply to offences or contraventions committed outside India.
12. Senior police officers and other officers have been given power to enter any public place and search and arrest without warrant.
13. Provisions have been made for the constitution of a Cyber Regulations Advisory Committee to advise the central government and the controller.

Non-applicability of the Act

As provided under Section 1(4), the provisions of the IT Act, 2000, shall not apply to the following:

1. Execution of a negotiable instrument under the Negotiable Instruments Act, 1881, except cheques.
2. Execution of a power of attorney under the Powers of Attorney Act, 1882.
3. Creation of a trust under the Indian Trusts Act, 1882.
4. Execution of a 'will' under the Indian Succession Act, 1925, including any other testamentary disposition by whatever name called.
5. Entering into a contract for the sale of conveyance of immovable property or any interest in such property.
6. Any such class of documents or transactions as may be notified by the central government in the official gazette.

Important Definitions

The important definitions given in the Act are as follows:

1. **Accessibility or access:** According to Section 2(1)(a), it means 'gaining entry into, instructing or communicating with the logical, arithmetical, or memory function resources of a computer, computer system or computer network'.
2. **Electronic form:** According to Section 2(1)(r), '"electronic form" with reference to information means any information generated, sent, received or stored in media, magnetic, optical, computer memory, micro film, computer generated micro fiche or similar device'.

3. **Computer:** According to Section 2(1)(i),

   'computer' means any electronic, magnetic, optical or other high-speed data processing device or system which performs logical, arithmetic, and memory functions by manipulations of electronic, magnetic or optical impulses, and includes all input, output, processing, storage, computer software, or communication facilities which are connected or related to the computer in a computer system or computer network.

4. **Computer network:** As per Section 2(1)(j), it means 'the interconnection of one or more computers through—
   i. the use of satellite, microwave, terrestrial line or other communication media; and
   ii. terminals or a complex consisting of two or more interconnected computers whether or not the interconnection is continuously maintained'.
5. **Computer system:** According to Section 2(1)(l), it means

   a device or collection of devices, including input and output support devices and excluding calculators which are not programmable and capable of being used in conjunction with external files, which contain computer programmes, electronic instructions, input data and output data, that performs logic, arithmetic, data storage and retrieval, communication control and other functions.

6. **Data:** According to Section 2(1)(o), it means

   a representation of information, knowledge, facts, concepts or instructions which are being prepared or have been prepared in a formalised manner, and is intended to be processed, is being processed or has been processed in a computer system or computer network, and may be in any form (including computer printouts, magnetic or optical storage media, punched cards, punched tapes) or stored internally in the memory of the computer.

7. **Information:** According to Section 2(1)(v), '"information" includes data, text, images, sound, voice, codes, computer programmes, software and databases or micro film or computer generated micro fiche'.
8. **Key pair:** As per Section 2(1)(x), '"key pair", in any asymmetric crypto system, means a private key and its mathematically related public key, which are so related that the public key can verify a digital signature created by the private key'.
9. **Originator:** As per Section 2(1)(za), '"originator" means a person who sends, generates, stores or transmits any electronic message or causes any electronic message to be sent, generated, stored or transmitted to any other person but does not include an intermediary'.
10. **Private key:** As per Section 2(1)(zc), it means 'the key of a key pair used to create a digital signature'.
11. **Public key:** According to Section 2(1)(zd), it means 'the key of a key pair used to verify a digital signature and listed in the Digital Signature Certificate'.
12. **Subscriber:** As per Section 2(1)(zg), it refers to 'a person in whose name the Digital Signature Certificate is issued'.
13. **Verify:** According to Section 2(1)(zh),

    'Verify' in relation to a digital signature, electronic record or public key, with its grammatical variations and cognate expressions means to determine whether—
    (a) the initial electronic record was affixed with the digital signature by the use of private key corresponding to the public key of the subscriber;
    (b) the initial electronic record is retained intact or has been altered since such electronic record was so affixed with the digital signature.

DIGITAL SIGNATURE

Digital signatures are electronic signatures equivalent to handwritten signatures. Since in an electronic message or transaction, affixing handwritten signatures is not possible, authentication has to be achieved by some electronic or digital method. Digital signatures facilitate this authentication. Section 2(1)(p) provides that 'digital signature' means authentication of any electronic record by a subscriber, that is, a person in whose name the 'Digital Signature Certificate' is issued, by means of an electronic method or procedure in accordance with the provisions of Section 3 of the Act.

Authentication of Electronic Records

Section 3(1) provides that any subscriber may authenticate electronic records by affixing his digital signature. Further, Section 3(2) provides that the authentication of the electronic record shall be effected by the use of asymmetric cryptosystem and hash function, which envelop and transform the initial electronic record into electronic record.

Explanation: The 'hash function' means an algorithm mapping translation of one sequence of bits into another, generally smaller, set known as 'hash result' such that an electronic record yields the same hash result every time the algorithm is executed with the same electronic record as its input, making it computationally infeasible:

1. To derive or reconstruct the original electronic record from the hash result produced by the algorithm
2. Those two electronic records can produce the same hash result using the algorithm

It is provided that any person by the use of a public key of the subscriber can verify the electronic record. The private key and the public key are unique to the subscriber and constitute a functioning key pair.

Affixing Digital Signature

Section 2(1)(d) explains the provisions related to affixing digital signature, which means adoption of any methodology or procedure by a person for authenticating an electronic record by means of 'digital signature'.

ELECTRONIC GOVERNANCE

There are following provisions related to electronic governance (e-governance):

1. **Legal recognition of electronic records:** Section 4 provides,

   Where any law provides that information or any other matter shall be in writing or in the typewritten or printed from, then, notwithstanding anything contained in such law, such requirement shall be deemed to have been satisfied if such information or matter is—

(a) rendered or made available in an electronic form; and
(b) accessible so as to be usable for a subsequent reference.

2. **Legal recognition of digital signatures:** Section 5 provides,

Where any law provides that information or any other matter shall be authenticated by affixing the signature or any document shall be signed or bear the signature of any person then, notwithstanding anything contained in such law, such requirement shall be deemed to have been satisfied, if such information or matter is authenticated by means of digital signature affixed in such manner as may be prescribed by the Central Government.
Explanation.— For the purposes of this section, 'signed', with its grammatical variations and cognate expressions, shall, with reference to a person, mean affixing of his handwritten signature or any mark on any document and the expression 'signature' shall be construed accordingly.

3. **Use of electronic records and digital signatures in government and its agencies:** Section 6(1) provides for:

(a) The filing of any form application or any other document with any office, authority, body or agency owned or controlled by the appropriate Government in a particular manner;
(b) The issue or grant of any licence, permit, sanction or approval by whatever name called in a particular manner;
(c) The receipt or payment of money in a particular manner,

then, notwithstanding anything contained in any other law for time being in force, such requirement shall be deemed to have been satisfied if such filing, issue, grant receipt or payment, as the case maybe, is effected by means of such electronic form as may be prescribed by the appropriate Government.

Further, Section 6(2) provides,

The appropriate Government may, for the purposes of sub-section (1), by rules, prescribe—
(a) the manner and format in which such electronic records shall be filed, created or issued;
(b) The manner or method of payment of any fee or charges for filing, creation or issue any electronic record under clause (a).

4. **Retention of electronic records:** Section 7(1) provides,

Where any law provides that documents, records or information shall be rationed for any specific period, then, that requirement shall be deemed to have been satisfied if such documents, records or information are retained in the electronic form, if—
(a) the information contained therein remains accessible so as to be usable for a subsequent reference;
(b) the electronic record is retained in the format in which it was originally generated, sent or received or in a format which can be demonstrated to represent accurately the information originally generated, sent or received;
(c) the details which will facilitate the identification of the origin, destination, date and time of dispatch or receipt of such electronic record are available in the electronic record.

It is further to be noted that this clause does not apply to any information which is automatically generated solely for enabling an electronic record to be dispatched or received. Section 7(2) provides, 'Nothing in this section shall apply to any law that expressly provides for the retention of documents, records or information in the form of electronic records.'

5. **Publication of rules, regulation and so on in electronic gazette:** Section 8(1) provides,

> Where any law provides that any rule, regulation, order, by-law, notification or any other matter shall be published in Official Gazette, then, such requirement shall be deemed to have been satisfied if such rule, regulation, order, by-law, notification or any other matter is published in the Official Gazette or in Electronic Gazette:
>
> Provided that where any rule, regulation, order, by-law, notification or any other matter is published in the Official Gazette or Electronic Gazette, the date of publication shall be deemed to be the date of the Gazette which was first published in any form.

6. **It is not mandatory to accept the document in electronic form:** Section 9 explains that Sections 6, 7 and 8 do not confer a right to insist that a document should be accepted in electronic form. Further, it shall not confer a right upon any person to insist that any ministry or department of the central government or the state government or any authority or body established by or under any law or controlled or funded by the central or state government should accept, issue, create, retain and preserve any document in the form of electronic records or effect any monetary transaction in the electronic form.
7. **Power to make rule by central government in respect of digital signature:** As per Section 10 of the Act,

> The Central Government may, for the purposes of this Act, by rules, prescribe—
> (a) the type of digital signature;
> (b) the manner and format in which the digital signature shall be affixed;
> (c) the manner or procedure which facilitates identification of the person affixing the digital signature;
> (d) control processes and procedures to ensure adequate integrity, security and confidentiality of electronic records or payments; and
> (e) any other matter which is necessary to give legal effect to digital signatures.

Security of Electronic Records and Digital Signatures

The IT Act, 2000, lays down following legal provisions through which 'electronic records' and 'digital signatures' are deemed secure. These provisions are as follows:

1. **Secure electronic record:** Section 14 explains, 'Where any security procedure has been applied to an electronic record at a specific point of time, then such record shall be deemed to be a secure electronic record from such point of time to the time of verification.'
2. **Secure digital signature:** Section 15 provides,

> If, by application of a security procedure agreed to by the parties concerned, it can be verified that a digital signature, at the time it was affixed, was—
> (a) unique to the subscriber affixing it;
> (b) capable of identifying such subscriber;
> (c) created in a manner or using a means under the exclusive control of the subscriber and is linked to the electronic record to which it relates in such a manner that if the

electronic record was altered the digital signature would be invalidated, then such digital signature shall be deemed to be a secure digital signature.

3. **Security procedure:** Section 16 provides,

   The Central Government shall for the purposes of this Act prescribe the security procedure having regard to commercial circumstances prevailing at the time when the procedure was used, including—
   (a) the nature of the transaction;
   (b) the level of sophistication of the parties with reference to their technological capacity;
   (c) the volume of similar transactions engaged in by other parties;
   (d) the availability of alternatives offered to but rejected by any party;
   (e) the cost of alternative procedures; and
   (f) the procedures in general use for similar types of transactions or communications.

DIGITAL SIGNATURE CERTIFICATES

The purpose of a digital signature certificate is to authenticate the identity of an individual. It ensures that the purported person is in fact the person who sent the message. The certifying authority signs it digitally.

Certifying Authority to Issue Digital Signature Certificates

Section 35(1) provides, 'Any person may make an application to the Certifying Authority for the issue of a Digital Signature Certificate in such form as may be prescribed by the Central Government.' Section 35(2) further provides, 'Every such application shall be accompanied by such fee not exceeding twenty five thousand rupees as may be prescribed by the Central Government, to be paid to the Certifying Authority.' Section 35(3) further provides that a certification practice statement shall accompany every such application or where there is no such statement, then a statement containing such particulars, as may be specified by regulations.

Section 35(4) provides,

On receipt of an application under sub-section (1), the Certifying Authority may, after consideration of the certification practice statement or the other statement under sub-section (3) and after making such enquiries as it may deem fit, grant the Digital Signature Certificate or for reasons to be recorded in writing, reject the application:

Provided that no Digital Signature Certificate shall be granted unless the Certifying Authority is satisfied that—

(a) the applicant holds the private key corresponding to the public key to be listed in the Digital Signature Certificate;
(b) the applicant holds a private key, which is capable of creating a digital signature;
(c) the public key to be listed in the certificate can be used to verify a digital signature affixed by the private key held by the applicant:

Provided further that no application shall be rejected unless the applicant has been given a reasonable opportunity of showing cause against the proposed rejection.

Representations upon Issuance of Digital Signature Certificates

Section 36 of the Act provided,

> A Certifying Authority while issuing a Digital Signature Certificate, shall certify that—
>
> (a) it has complied with the provisions of this Act and the rules and regulations made thereunder;
> (b) it has published the Digital Signature Certificate or otherwise made it available to such person relying on it and the subscriber has accepted it;
> (c) the subscriber holds the private key corresponding to the public key, listed in the Digital Signature Certificate;
> (d) the subscriber's public key and private key constitute a functioning key pair;
> (e) the information contained in the Digital Signature Certificate is accurate;
> (f) it has no knowledge of any material fact, which if it had been included in the Digital Signature Certificate would adversely affect the reliability of the representations made in clauses (a) to (d).

Suspension of Digital Signature Certificates

Section 37(1) provides,

> The Certifying Authority which has issued a Digital Signature Certificate may suspend such Digital Signature Certificate—
>
> (a) On receipt of a request to that effect from—
> (i) the subscriber listed in the Digital Signature Certificate; or
> (ii) any person duly authorised to act on behalf of that subscriber,
> (b) if it is of opinion that the Digital Signature Certificate should be suspended in public interest.

Section 37(2) provides, 'A Digital Signature Certificate shall not be suspended for a period exceeding fifteen days unless the subscriber has been given an opportunity of being heard in the matter.'

Section 37(3) provides, 'On suspension of a Digital Signature Certificate under this section, the Certifying Authority shall communicate the same to the subscriber.'

Revocation of Digital Signature Certificates

Section 38(1) provides,

> A Certifying Authority may revoke a Digital Signature Certificate issued by it—
>
> (a) where the subscriber or any other person authorised by him makes a request to that effect; or
> (b) upon the death of the subscriber; or
> (c) upon the dissolution of the firm or winding up of the company where the subscriber is a firm or a company.

Section 38(2) provides,

> Without prejudice to the provisions of sub-section (1), a Certifying Authority may revoke a Digital Signature Certificate which has been issued by it at any time, if it is of the opinion that—
> (a) a material fact represented in the Digital Signature Certificate is false or has been concealed;
> (b) a requirement for issuance of the Digital Signature Certificate was not satisfied;
> (c) the Certifying Authority's private key or security system was compromised in a manner materially affecting the Digital Signature Certificate's reliability;
> (d) the subscriber has been declared insolvent or dead or where a subscriber is a firm or a company, which has been dissolved, wound-up or otherwise ceased to exist.

Section 38(3) provides, 'A Digital Signature Certificate shall not be revoked unless the subscriber has been given an opportunity of being heard in the matter.'

Section 38(4) provides, 'On revocation of a Digital Signature Certificate under this section, the Certifying Authority shall communicate the same to the subscriber.'

Notice of Suspension of Revocation

Section 39(1) provides,

> Where a Digital Signature Certificate is suspended or revoked under section 37 or section 38, the Certifying Authority shall publish a notice of such suspension or revocation, as the case may be, in the repository specified in the Digital Signature Certificate for publication of such notice.

Section 39(2) provides, 'Where one or more repositories are specified, the Certifying Authority shall publish notices of such suspension or revocation, as the case may be, in all such repositories.'

DUTIES OF SUBSCRIBERS

The IT Act, 2000, specifies the following duties of the subscribers who have obtained a digital signature certificate from the certifying authority:

1. **Generating key pair:** Section 40 states that where any subscriber has accepted any digital signature certificate, the public key of which corresponds to the private key of that subscriber, which is to be listed in the digital signature certificate, the subscriber shall generate the key pair by applying the security procedure.
2. **Acceptance of digital signature certificate:** Section 41 provides,

   > (1) A subscriber shall be deemed to have accepted a Digital Signature Certificate, if he publishes or authorises the publication of a Digital Signature Certificate—
   > (a) to one or more persons;
   > (b) in a repository.
   > (2) By accepting a Digital Signature Certificate the subscriber certifies to all who reasonably rely on the information contained in the Digital Signature Certificate that—
   > (a) the subscriber holds the private key correspondent to the public key listed in the Digital Signature Certificate and is entitled to hold the same;

(b) all representations made by the subscriber to the Certifying Authority and all material relevant to the information contained in the Digital Signature Certificate are true;

(c) all information in the Digital Signature Certificate that is within the knowledge of the subscriber is true.

3. **Control of private key:** Section 42(1) provides,

   Every subscriber shall exercise reasonable care to retain control of the private key corresponding to the public key listed in his Digital Signature Certificate and take all steps to prevent its disclosure to a person not authorised to affix the digital signature of the subscriber.

   Section 42(2) provides,

   If the private key corresponding to the public key listed in the Digital Signature Certificate has been compromised, then, the subscriber shall communicate the same without any delay to the Certifying Authority in such manner as may be specified by the regulations.

   Explanation— For the removal of doubts, it is hereby declared that the subscriber shall be liable till he has informed the Certifying Authority that the private key has been compromised.

Attribution, Acknowledgement and Dispatch of Electronic Records

Sections 11–13 of the Act contain the provisions related to the attribution, acknowledgement and dispatch of electronic records. The provisions related to the attribution, acknowledgement and dispatch of electronic records are as follows:

1. **Attribution of electronic records:** Section 11 provides,

   An electronic record shall be attributed to the originator—

   (a) if it was sent by the originator himself;

   (b) by a person who had the authority to act on behalf of the originator in respect of that electronic record; or

   (c) by an information system programmed by or on behalf of the originator to operate automatically.

2. **Acknowledgement of receipt:** Section 12(1) provides,

   Where the originator has not agreed with the addressee that the acknowledgment of receipt of electronic record be given in a particular form or by a particular method, an acknowledgment may be given by—

   (a) any communication by the addressee, automated or otherwise; or

   (b) any conduct of the addressee, sufficient to indicate to the originator that the electronic record has been received.

   Section 12(2) provide,

   Where the originator has stipulated that the electronic record shall be binding only on receipt of an acknowledgment of such electronic record by him, then unless acknowledgment has been so received, the electronic record shall be deemed to have been never sent by the originator.

Section 12(3) provides,

> Where the originator has not stipulated that the electronic record shall be binding only on receipt of such acknowledgment, and the acknowledgment has not been received by the originator within the time specified or agreed or, if no time has been specified or agreed to within a reasonable time, then the originator may give notice to the addressee stating that no acknowledgment has been received by him and specifying a reasonable time by which the acknowledgment must be received by him and if no acknowledgment is received within the aforesaid time limit he may after giving notice to the addressee treat the electronic record as though it has never been sent.

3. **Time and place of dispatch and receipt of electronic record:** Section 13(1) explains, 'Save as otherwise agreed to between the originator and the addressee, the dispatch of an electronic record occurs when it enters a computer resource outside the control of the originator.' Section 13(2) provides,

> Save as otherwise agreed between the originator and the addressee, the time of receipt of an electronic record shall be determined as follows, namely—
> (a) if the addressee has designated a computer resource for the purpose of receiving electronic records—
> (i) receipt occurs at the time when the electronic record enters the designated computer resource; or
> (ii) if the electronic record is sent to a computer resource of the addressee that is not the designated computer resource, receipt occurs at the time when the electronic record is retrieved by the addressee;
> (b) if the addressee has not designated a computer resource along with specified timings, if any, receipt occurs when the electronic record enters the computer resource of the addressee.

Section 13(3) provides,

> Save as otherwise agreed to between the originator and the addressee, an electronic record is deemed to be dispatched at the place where the originator has his place of business, and is deemed to be received at the place where the addressee has his place of business.

Section 13(4) provides, 'The place where the computer resource is located may be different from the place where the electronic record is deemed to have been received.' Section 13(5) provides:

> (a) if the originator or the addressee has more than one place of business, the principal place of business shall be the place of business;
> (b) if the originator or the addressee does not have a place of business, his usual place of residence shall be deemed to be the place of business;
> (c) 'usual place of residence', in relation to a body corporate, means the place where it is registered.

Regulation of Certifying Authorities

A certifying authority is to regulate the transactions related to electronic matters which are explained below.

Appointment of Controller and Other Officers

Section 17(1) provides, 'The Central Government may, by notification in the Official Gazette, appoint a Controller of Certifying Authorities for the purposes of this Act and may also by the same or subsequent notification appoint such number of Deputy Controllers and Assistant Controllers as it deems fit.' The other provisions are as follows:

1. 'The Controller shall discharge his functions under this Act subject to the general control and directions of the Central Government' (Section 17(2)).
2. 'The Deputy Controllers and Assistant Controllers shall perform the functions assigned to them by the Controller under the general superintendence and control of the Controller' (Section 17(3)).
3. 'The qualifications, experience and terms and conditions of service of Controller, Deputy Controllers and Assistant Controllers shall be such as may be prescribed by the Central Government' (Section 17(4)).
4. 'The Head Office and Branch Office of the office of the Controller shall be at such places as the Central Government may specify, and these may be established at such places as the Central Government may think fit' (Section 17(5)).
5. 'There shall be a seal of the Office of the Controller' (Section 17(6)).

Functions of Controller

Section 18(1) provides,

> The Controller may perform all or any of the following functions, namely—
>
> (a) exercising supervision over the activities of the Certifying Authorities;
> (b) certifying public keys of the Certifying Authorities;
> (c) laying down the standards to be maintained by the Certifying Authorities;
> (d) specifying the qualifications and experience which employees of the Certifying Authorities should possess;
> (e) specifying the conditions subject to which the Certifying Authorities shall conduct their business;
> (f) specifying the contents of written, printed or visual materials and advertisements that may be distributed or used in respect of a Digital Signature Certificate and the public key;
> (g) specifying the form and content of a Digital Signature Certificate and the key;
> (h) specifying the form and manner in which accounts shall be maintained by the Certifying Authorities;
> (i) specifying the terms and conditions subject to which auditors may be appointed and the remuneration to be paid to them;
> (j) specifying the manner in which the Certifying Authorities shall conduct their dealings with the subscribers;
> (k) resolving any conflict of interests between the Certifying Authorities and the subscribers;
> (l) laying down the duties of the Certifying Authorities;
> (m) Maintaining a data base containing the disclosure record of every Certifying Authority containing such particulars as may be specified by regulations, which shall be accessible to public.

Recognition of Foreign Certifying Authorities

Section 19(1) provides,

> Subject to such conditions and restrictions as may be specified by regulations, the Controller may with the previous approval of the Central Government, and by notification in the Official Gazette, recognise any foreign Certifying Authority as a Certifying Authority for the purposes of this Act.

Section 19(2) provides, 'Where any Certifying Authority is recognised under sub-section (1), the Digital Signature Certificate issued by such Certifying Authority shall be valid for the purposes of this Act.' Section 19(3) provides,

> The Controller may, if he is satisfied that any Certifying Authority has contravened any of the conditions and restrictions subject to which it was granted recognition under subsection (1) he may, for reasons to be recorded in writing, by notification in the Official Gazette, revoke such recognition.

Controller to Act as Repository

Section 20(1) provides, 'The Controller shall be the repository of all Digital Signature Certificates issued.' Section 20(2) provides,

> 'The Controller shall—
>
> (a) make use of hardware, software and procedures that are secure from intrusion and misuse;
> (b) observe such other standards as may be prescribed by the Central Government, to ensure that the secrecy and security of the digital signatures are assured.'

Section 20(3) provides, 'The Controller shall maintain a computerised data base of all public keys in such a manner that such data base and the public keys are available to any member of the public.'

Licence to Issue Digital Signature Certificates

Section 21(1) provides, 'Any person may make an application, to the Controller, for a licence to issue Digital Signature Certificates.' Section 21(2) provides, 'No licence shall be issued under sub-section (1), unless the applicant fulfills such requirements with respect to qualification, expertise, manpower, financial resources and other infrastructure facilities, which are necessary to issue Digital Signature Certificates as may be prescribed by the Central Government.' Section 21(3) provides,

> 'A licence granted under this section shall—
>
> (a) be valid for such period as may be prescribed-by the Central Government;
> (b) not be transferable or heritable;
> (c) be subject to such terms and conditions as may be specified by the regulations.'

Application for Licence

Section 22(1) provides, 'Every application for issue of a licence shall be in such form as may be prescribed by the Central Government.' Section 22(2) provides,

Every application for issue of a licence shall be accompanied by—

(a) a certification practice statement;
(b) a statement including the procedures with respect to identification of the applicant;
(c) payment of such fees, not exceeding twenty-five thousand rupees as may be prescribed by the Central Government;
(d) such other documents, as may be prescribed by the Central Government.

Renewal of Licence

Section 23 provides,

An application for renewal of a licence shall be—

(a) in such form;
(b) accompanied by such fees, not exceeding five thousand rupees,

as may be prescribed by the Central Government and shall be made not less than forty-five days before the date of expiry of the period of validity of the licence.

Procedure for Grant or Rejection of Licence

Section 24 provides,

The Controller may, on receipt of an application under sub-section (1) of section 21, after considering the documents accompanying the application and such other factors, as he deems fit, grant the licence or reject the application:

Provided that no application shall be rejected under this section unless the applicant has been given a reasonable opportunity of presenting his case.

Suspension of Licence

Section 25(1) provides,

The Controller may, if he is satisfied after making such inquiry, as he may think fit, that a Certifying Authority has—

(a) made a statement in, or in relation to, the application for the issue or renewal of the licence, which is incorrect or false in material particulars;
(b) failed to comply with the terms and conditions subject to which the licence was granted;
(c) failed to maintain the standards specified under clause (b) of sub-section (2) of section 20;
(d) contravened any provisions of this Act, rule, regulation or order made thereunder, revoke the licence.

Revocation of Licence

Section 25(1) provides, 'No licence shall be revoked unless the Certifying Authority has been given a reasonable opportunity of showing cause against the proposed revocation.' Section 25(2) provides,

> The Controller may, if he has reasonable cause to believe that there is any ground for revoking ... by order suspend such licence pending the completion of any inquiry ordered by him:
>
> Provided that no licence shall be suspended for a period exceeding ten days unless the Certifying Authority has been given a reasonable opportunity of showing cause against the proposed suspension.

Section 25(3) provides, 'No Certifying Authority whose licence has been suspended shall issue any Digital Signature Certificate during such suspension.'

Notice of Suspension or Revocation of Licence

According to Section 26(1), 'Where the licence of the Certifying Authority is suspended or revoked, the Controller shall publish notice of such suspension or revocation, as the case may be, in the database maintained by him.' Section 26(2) provides,

> Where one or more repositories are specified, the Controller shall publish notices of such suspension or revocation, as the case may be, in all such repositories:
>
> Provided that the data base containing the notice of such suspension or revocation, as the case may be, shall be made available through a website which shall be accessible round the clock:
>
> Provided further that the Controller may, if he considers necessary, publicise the contents of database in such electronic or other media, as he may consider appropriate.

Power to Delegate

According to Section 27, 'The Controller may, in writing, authorise the Deputy Controller, Assistant Controller or any officer to exercise any of the powers of the Controller.'

Power to Investigate Contraventions

According to Section 28(1), 'The Controller or any officer authorised by him in this behalf shall take up for investigation any contravention of the provisions of this Act, rules or regulations made thereunder.' Section 28(2) provides, 'The Controller or any officer authorised by him in this behalf shall exercise the like powers which are conferred on income-tax authorities ... shall exercise such powers, subject to such limitations laid down under that Act.'

Access to Computers and Data

According to Section 29(1),

> Without prejudice to the provisions of sub-section (1) of section 69, the Controller or any person authorised by him shall, if he has reasonable cause to suspect that any contravention of the provisions of this Act, rule or regulations made thereunder has been committed, have access to any computer system, any apparatus, data or any other material connected with such system, for the purpose of searching or causing a search to be made for obtaining any information or data contained in or available to such computer system.

Section 29(2) states,

> For the purposes of sub-section (1), the Controller or any person authorised by him may, by order, direct any person in charge of, or otherwise concerned with the operation of the computer system, data apparatus or material, to provide him with such reasonable technical and other assistance as he may consider necessary.

Certifying Authority to Follow Certain Procedures

According to Section 30,

> Every Certifying Authority shall—
>
> (a) make use of hardware, software and procedures that are secure from intrusion and misuse;
> (b) provide a reasonable level of reliability in its services which are reasonably suited to the performance of intended functions;
> (c) adhere to security procedures to ensure that the secrecy and privacy of the digital signatures are assured; and
> (d) observe such other standards as may be specified by regulations.

Certifying Authority to Ensure Compliance of the Act and so on

According to Section 31, 'Every Certifying Authority shall ensure that every person employed or otherwise engaged by it complies, in the course of his employment or engagement, with the provisions of this Act, rules, regulations and orders made thereunder.'

Section 32 provides, 'Every Certifying Authority shall display its licence at a conspicuous place of the premises in which it carries on its business.'

Surrender of Licence

Section 33(1) provides, 'Every Certifying Authority whose licence is suspended or revoked shall immediately after such suspension or revocation, surrender the licence to the Controller.' Section 33(2) provides,

> Where any Certifying Authority fails to surrender a licence ... the person in whose favour a licence is issued shall be guilty of an offence and shall be punished with imprisonment which may extend up to six months or a fine which may extend up to ten thousand rupees or with both.

Disclosure

According to Section 34(1),

> Every Certifying Authority shall disclose in the manner specified by regulations—
>
> (a) its Digital Signature Certificate which contains the public key corresponding to the private key used by that Certifying Authority to digitally sign another Digital Signature Certificate;

(b) any certification practice statement relevant thereto;
(c) notice of the revocation or suspension of its Certifying Authority Certificates, if any; and
(d) any other fact that materially and adversely affects either the reliability of a Digital Signature Certificate, which that Authority has issued, or the Authority's ability to perform its services.

Section 34(2) states,

> Where in the opinion of the Certifying Authority any event has occurred or any situation has arisen which may materially and adversely affect the integrity of its computer system or the conditions subject to which a Digital Signature Certificate was granted, then the Certifying Authority shall—
>
> (a) use reasonable efforts to notify any person who is likely to be affected by that occurrence; or
> (b) act in accordance with the procedure specified in its certification practice statement to deal with such event or situation.

Test Questions

1. What are the different features and objectives of the IT Act, 2000? 'The IT Act is not applicable to some specified documents.' Comment.
2. What are digital signatures? Explain the methods of affixing and verification of digital signatures.
3. What are digital signature certificates? State the provisions regarding digital signature certificates in the IT Act, 2000.
4. 'E-governance is smart governance.' Discuss the provisions of the IT Act, 2000, to facilitate and strengthen e-governance.
5. Explain different terms used under the IT Act, 2000.
6. Distinguish between:
   a. Digital and electronic signatures
   b. Public and private keys
7. Explain following terms:
   a. Attribution of electronic records
   b. Acknowledgement of receipt
   c. Time and place of dispatch and receipt of electronic records
   d. Role of certifying authorities under the IT Act
8. What are the duties and roles of a certifying authority? How is the CCA appointed? What are his functions?
9. Explain the meaning and creation of digital signatures. Enumerate the circumstances in which a digital signature certificate may be revoked.
10. Describe the term 'subscriber'. Explain the duties of a subscriber under the IT Act, 2000.

23

CHAPTER

Offences, Penalties and Cyber Appellate Tribunal

Learning Objectives

- To understand offences under the IT Act, 2000
- To understand penalties and adjudication
- To understand the powers and composition of Cyber Appellate Tribunal

The increasing use of IT services in the business world has given an opportunity to those persons who want to take the undue advantage of developments in IT, that is, it has resulted into crimes such as theft of data, hacking, viruses and other cybercrimes. Some of these are given as follows.

1. **Tampering with computer source documents:** According to Section 65, whosoever knowingly or intentionally conceals, destroys or alters or intentionally or knowingly causes another to conceal destroy or alter any computer source code, used for a computer programme, computer system or computer network when the computer source code is required to be kept or maintained by law for the time being in force, shall be punishable with imprisonment up to three years or with fine which may extend up to ₹2 lakh or with both. The computer source code means the listing of programmers, computer commands, design and layout and programmer analysis of computer resource in any form.
2. **Hacking with computer system:** According to Section 66, whoever with the intent to cause or knowing that he is likely to cause wrongful loss or damage to the public or any person, destroys or deletes or alters any information residing in a computer resource or diminishes its value or utility or affects it injuriously by any means, commits hacking. It further explains that whoever commits hacking shall be punished with imprisonment up to three years, or with fine, which may extend up to ₹2 lakh, or with both.
3. **Publishing of information which is obscene in electronic form:** According to Section 67, whoever publishes or transmits or causes to be published in the electronic form, any material which is lascivious or appeals to the prurient interest or if its effects such as to tend to deprave and corrupt persons who are likely having regard to all relevant circumstantial, to read, see or hear the matter contained or

embodied in it, shall be punished on first conviction with imprisonment of either description for a term which may extend to five years and with fine which may extend to ₹1 lakh and in the event of a second or subsequent conviction with imprisonment of either description for a term which may extend to 10 years and also with fine which may extend to ₹2 lakh.

Powers of the controller to give directions: According to Section 68, the controller may, by order, direct a certifying authority or any employee or such authority to take such measures or cease carrying on such activities as specified in the order, if those are necessary to ensure compliance with the provisions of this Act, rules or any regulations made thereunder. It is further provided that any person who fails to comply with any order shall be guilty of an offence and shall be liable on conviction to imprisonment for a term not exceeding three years or to a fine not exceeding ₹2 lakh or to both.

Direction of controller to a subscriber to extend facilities to decrypt information: Section 69 of the Act provides that if the controller is satisfied that it is necessary or expedient so to do in the interest of the sovereignty or integrity of India, the security of the State, friendly relations with foreign States or public order or for preventing incitement to the commission of any cognizable offence, for reasons to be recorded in writing, then he may by order direct any agency of the government to intercept any information transmitted through any computer resource.

It is further provided that the subscriber or any person incharge of the computer resource shall, when called upon by any agency, which has been directed under Sub-section (1), extend all facilities and technical assistance to decrypt the information.

According to Section 69, the subscriber or any person who fails to assist the agency referred to in Sub-section (2) shall be punished with an imprisonment for a term, which may extend to seven years.

Protected system: Section 70 provides that the appropriate government may, by notification in the official gazette, declare any computer, computer system or computer network to be a protected system. It is further provided that the appropriate government may, by order in writing, authorize the persons who are authorized to access the protected system. It is further provided that any person who secures access or attempts to secure access to a protected system in contravention of the provisions of this section shall be punished with imprisonment of either description for a term which may extend to 10 years and shall also be liable to fine.

Penalty for misrepresentation: Section 71 provides that whoever makes any misrepresentation to, or suppresses any material fact form the controller or the certifying authority for obtaining any licence or digital signature certificate, as the case may be, shall be punished with imprisonment for a term which may extend to two years or with fine which may extend to ₹1 lakh, or with both.

Breach of confidentiality and privacy: Section 72 of the Act provides that save as otherwise provided in this act or any other law for the time being in force, any person who pursuant of any of the powers conferred under this Act, rules or regulations made there under has secured access to any electronic record book, register, correspondence, information, document or other material without the consent of the person concerned, discloses such electronic record, book, register correspondence, information, document or other material to any other person, shall be punished with imprisonment for a term which may extend to two years or with a fine which may extend to ₹1 lakh, or with both.

Penalty for publishing digital signature certificate with false particulars: Section 73 of the Act provides that:

1. No person shall publish a digital signature certificate or otherwise make it available to any other person with the knowledge that:
   a. The certifying authority listed in the certificate has not issued it.
   b. The subscriber listed in the certificate has not accepted it.
   c. The certificate has been revoked or suspended, unless such publication is for verifying a digital signature created prior to such suspension or revocation.
2. Any person who contravenes the provision of Sub-section (1) shall be punished with imprisonment for a term, which may extend to two years or with fine which may extend to ₹1 lakh, or with both.

Publication for fraudulent purpose: According to Section 74, whoever knowingly creates, publishes or otherwise makes available a digital signature certificate for any fraudulent or unlawful purpose shall be punished with imprisonment for a term which may extend to two years or with a fine which may extend to ₹1 lakh, or with both.

Act to apply for offences or contraventions committed outside India: The provisions of Section 75(1) shall apply also to any offence or contravention committed outside India by any person irrespective of his nationality. It is further provided that the Act shall apply to an offence or contravention committed outside India by any person, if the act or conduct constituting the offence or contravention involves a computer, computer system or computer network situated in India.

Confiscation: According to Section 76, any computer, computer system, floppies, compact disks, tape drive or any other accessories related thereto, in respect of which any provision of this Act, rules, orders or regulations made hereunder has been or is being contravened shall be liable for confiscation. Where it is established to the satisfaction of the court, adjudicating the confiscation that the person in whose possession, power or control of any such computer system floppies, compact disks, tape derives or any other accessories relating thereto, is found is to be responsible for the contravention of the provisions of this Act rules, orders or regulations made hereunder, the court may instead of making an order for confiscation of such computer system, floppies, compact disks tape drives or any other accessories related thereto, make such other order against the person contravening the provisions of this Act, rules, orders or regulations made thereunder as it may think fit.

Penalties and Adjudication

Penalty for Damage to Computer, Computer System and So On

Section 43 provides that if any person without permission of the owner or any other person who is incharge of a computer system or computer network:

1. Accesses or secures access to such computer system or computer network
2. Downloads, copies or extracts any data, computer database or information from such computer system or computer network including information or data held or stored in any removable storage medium

3. Introduces or causes to be introduced any computer contaminant or computer virus into any computer system or computer network
4. Damages or causes to be damaged any computer system or computer network, data, computer database or any other programs residing in such computer, computer system or computer network
5. Disrupts or causes disruption of any computer, computer system or computer network
6. Denies or causes the denial of access to any person authorized to access any computer system or computer network by any means
7. Provides any assistance to any person to facilitate access to a computer, computer system or computer network, in contravention of the provisions of this Act, rules or regulations made thereunder
8. Charges the services availed of by a person to the account of another person by tampering with or manipulating any computer, computer system or computer network.

He shall be liable to any damage by way of compensation not exceeding ₹10 lakh to the person so affected.

Explanation

1. **Computer contaminant** means any set of computer instructions that are designed:
   a. To modify, destroy, record, transmit data or programs residing within a computer system or computer network
   b. To usurp, by any means, the normal operation of the computer system or computer network
2. **Computer database** means a representation, information, knowledge facts, concepts or instructions in text, image, audio or video that are being prepared or have been prepared in a formalized manner or have been produced by a computer system or computer network and are intended for use in a computer, computer system or computer network.
3. **Computer virus** means any computer instruction, information, data or programs that destroys, damages, degrades or adversely affects the performance of a computer resource or attaches itself to another computer resource and operates when a program, data or instruction is executed or some other event takes place in that computer resource.
4. **Damage** means to destroy, alter, add, modify or rearrange any computer resource by any means.

Penalty for Failure to Furnish Information, Return and so on

According to Section 44, if any person who is required under this Act or any rules or regulations made thereunder:

1. Fails to furnish any document, return or report to the controller or the certifying authority, he shall be liable to a penalty not exceeding ₹1.5 lakh for each such failure.
2. Fails to file any return or furnish any information, books or other documents within the time specified in the regulations or fails to file return or furnish the same, he shall be liable to a penalty not exceeding ₹5 thousand for every day during which such failure continues.
3. Fails to maintain book of account or records, he shall be liable to a penalty not exceeding ₹10,000 for every day during which the failure continues.

Residuary Penalty

According to the provision of Section 45, whoever contravenes any rules or regulations made under this Act, for the contravention of which no penalty has been separately provided, shall be liable to pay a compensation not exceeding ₹25,000 to the person affected by such contravention or a penalty not exceeding ₹25,000.

Adjudication and the Appellate Tribunal

Power to Adjudicate

The process for adjudicating a person under Section 46 of this Act is given as follows:

1. Section 46 provides that for the purpose of adjudging whether any person has committed a contravention of any of the provisions of this act or of any rule, regulation, direction or order made thereunder, the central government shall appoint any officer not below the rank of a director to the Government of India or an equivalent officer of a state government to be an adjudicating officer, for holding an enquiry in the manner prescribed by the central government.
2. The adjudicating officer, after giving a reasonable opportunity for making representation in the matter and if, on such enquiry, he is satisfied that the person has committed the contravention, may impose such penalty or award such compensation as he thinks fit.
3. No person shall be appointed as an adjudicating officer unless he possesses such experience in the field of IT and legal or judicial experience as may be prescribed by the central government.
4. It provides that where more than one adjudicating officers are appointed, the central government shall specify by order the matters and places with respect to the which such officers shall exercise their jurisdiction.
5. Every adjudicating officer shall have the powers of a civil court, which are conferred on the Cyber Appellate Tribunal under Sub-section (2) of Section 58 and:
   a. All proceedings before Cyber Appellate Tribunal shall be deemed to be judicial proceedings within the meaning of Sections 193 and 228 of IPC.
   b. Shall be deemed a civil court for the purposes of Sections 345 and 346 of the Code of Criminal Procedure, 1973.

Factors to Be Taken into Account by the Adjudicating Officer

According to Section 47, while adjudging the quantum of compensation, the adjudicating officer shall have due regard to the following factors:

1. The amount of gain or unfair advantage, wherever quantifiable, made as a result of the default.
2. The amount of loss caused to any person as a result of the default.
3. The repetitive nature of the default.

Cyber Appellate Tribunal

Establishment of Cyber Appellate Tribunal

According to Section 48, the central government shall, by notification, establish one or more appellate tribunals to be known as the Cyber Regulations Appellate Tribunal. It is further provided that the central government shall also specify the matters and places in relation to which the Cyber Appellate Tribunal may exercise jurisdiction. The central government shall establish a Cyber Regulations Appellate Tribunal and should specify the matters and places along with its jurisdiction.

Composition of Cyber Appellate Tribunal

Section 49 provides that the central government by notification shall appoint one person as presiding officer of Cyber Appellate Tribunal.

Qualifications for Appointment as Presiding Officer of Cyber Appellate Tribunal

Section 50 provides that a person shall not be qualified for appointment as the presiding officer of a Cyber Appellate Tribunal unless:

1. He is, or has been, or is qualified to be, a judge of High Court.
2. He is or has been a member of the Indian legal service and is holding or has held a post in Grade I of that service for at least three years.

Term of Office

According to Section 51, the presiding officer of a Cyber Appellate Tribunal shall hold office for a term of five years from the date on which he enters upon his office or until he attains the age of sixty-five years, whichever is earlier.

Section 52 provides that the salary and allowances payable to and the other terms and conditions of services including pension gratuity and other retirement benefits of the presiding officer of a Cyber Appellate Tribunal shall be such as may be prescribed. It is provided that neither the salary and allowances nor the other terms and conditions of service of the presiding officer shall be varied to his disadvantage after appointment.

Filling up of Vacancies

Section 53 provides that if for some reason other than temporary absence, any vacancy occurs in the office of the presiding officer of a Cyber Appellate Tribunal, then the central government shall appoint another person in accordance with the provisions of this Act to fill the vacancy and the proceedings may be continued as before.

Resignation and Removal

Section 54 provides that presiding officer of a Cyber Appellate Tribunal may, by notice in writing under his hand addressed to central government, resign his office. The presiding officer shall, unless he is permitted by the central government to relinquish his office sooner, continue to hold office until the expiry of three months from the date of receipt of such notice or until a person, duly appointed as his successor, enters upon his office or until the expiry of his term of office, whichever is earliest.

The presiding officer shall not be removed from his office except by an order by the central government on the ground of proved misbehaviour or incapacity, after an enquiry made by a judge of the Supreme Court, in which the presiding officer concerned has been informed of the charges against him and given a reasonable opportunity of being heard in respect of these charges. The central government may, by rules, regulate the procedure for investigation of misbehaviour or incapacity of the previously mentioned presiding officer.

Orders Constituting Appellate Tribunal to Be Final and Not to Invalidate Its Proceedings

Section 55 provides that no order of the central government appointing any person as presiding officer of a Cyber Appellate Tribunal shall be called in question in any manner and no act or proceeding before a Cyber Appellate Tribunal shall be called in question, in any manner on the ground merely of any defect in the constitution of a Cyber Appellate Tribunal.

Staff of the Cyber Appellate Tribunal

Section 56 provides that the central government shall provide the Cyber Appellate Tribunal with such officers and employees as that government may think fit. Further, the officers and employees of the Cyber Appellate Tribunal shall discharge their functions under general superintendence of the presiding officer and the salaries and allowances and other conditions of service of the officers and employees of the Cyber Appellate Tribunal shall be such as may be prescribed by the central government.

Appeal to Cyber Regulations Appellate Tribunal

Section 57(1) states that any person aggrieved by an order made by an adjudicating officer under this Act may prefer an appeal to a Cyber Appellate Tribunal having jurisdiction in the matter. It is further provided that no appeal shall lie to the Cyber Appellate Tribunal for an order made by an adjudicating officer with the consent of the parties.

It shall be filed within a period of 45 days from the date on which a copy of order is received by person aggrieved and it shall be accompanied by prescribed fee. It is further provided that on receipt of an appeal, the Cyber Appellate Tribunal may, after giving the parties to the appeal an opportunity of being heard, pass such orders thereon, as it thinks fit, confirming, modifying or setting aside the order appealed against and the Cyber Appellate Tribunal shall send a copy of every order made by it to the parties to the appeal and to the concerned adjudicating officer. Section 57 further provides that the appeal shall be filed before Cyber Appellate Tribunal and shall be dealt with as expeditiously as possible. Endeavour shall be made by it to dispose of the appeal finally within six months from the date of receipt of the appeal.

Procedure and Powers of the Cyber Appellate Tribunal

According to Section 58, the Cyber Appellate Tribunal shall not be bound by procedure laid down by Code of Civil Procedure, 1908, but shall be guided by the principles of natural justice and subject to the other provisions of this Act and of any rules, the Cyber Appellate Tribunal shall have powers to regulate its own procedure including the place at which it shall have its sittings. It is further provided that the Cyber Appellate Tribunal shall have, for the purposes of discharging their functions under this Act, the same powers as are vested in a civil court under the Code of Civil Procedure, 1908, while trying the suit, in respect of the following matters, namely:

1. Summoning and enforcing the attendance of any person and examining him on oath
2. Requiring the discovery and production of documents or other electronic records
3. Receiving evidence on affidavits
4. Issuing commissions for the examination of witnesses or documents
5. Reviewing its decisions
6. Dismissing an application for default or deciding it *ex parte*
7. Any other matter, which may be prescribed

Right to Legal Representation

According to Section 59, the appellant may either appear in person or authorize one or more legal practitioners or any of its officers in person, before the Cyber Appellate Tribunal.

Civil Court Not to Have Jurisdiction

According to Section 61, no court shall have jurisdiction to entertain any suit or proceeding in respect of any matter which an adjudicating officer appointed under this Act or the Cyber Appellate Tribunal constituted under this Act is empowered by or under this Act to determine and no injunction shall be granted by any court or other authority in respect of any action taken or to be taken in pursuance of any power conferred by or under this Act.

Appeal to High Court

According to Section 62, any person aggrieved by any decision or order of the Cyber Appellate Tribunals may file an appeal to the High court, within 60 days from the date of communication of the decision or order of the Cyber Appellate Tribunal, on any question of fact or law arising out of such order. Provided that the High Court may, if it is satisfied that the appellant was prevented by sufficient cause from filing the appeal within such period, allow it to be filed within a further period not exceeding 60 days.

Network Service Providers Not to Be Liable in Certain Cases

Section 79 of the Act states that for the removal of doubts, it is hereby declared that no person providing any service as a network service provider (network service provider means an intermediary) shall be liable under this Act, rules or regulations made thereunder, for any third-party information (third-party information means any information dealt with by a network service provider in its capacity as an intermediary) or data made available by him if he proves that the offence or contravention was committed without his knowledge or that he had exercised all due diligence to prevent the commission of such offence or contravention.

Authorities under the Act

Powers of the Central Government to Make Rules

According to Section 87, the central government may, by notification in the official gazette and in the electronic gazette, make rules to carry out the provisions of this Act and may provide for all or any of the following matters:

1. The manner in which any information or matter may be authenticated by means of digital signature.
2. The electronic form in which filing, issue, grant or payment shall be effected.
3. The manner and format in which electronic records shall be filed, created or issued and the method of payment.
4. The matters relating to the type of digital signature, manner and format in which it may be affixed.
5. The security procedure for the purpose of creating secure electronic record and secure digital signature.
6. The qualifications, experience and terms and conditions of service of controller, deputy controllers and assistant controllers.
7. Other standards to be observed by the controller.
8. The requirements which an applicant must fulfil.
9. The period of validity of licence granted within Section 21.
10. The form in which an application for licence may be made.
11. The amount of fees payable.
12. Such other documents which shall accompany an application for licence.
13. The form and the fee for renewal of a licence and the fee payable thereof.
14. The amount of late fee payable under Section 23.
15. The form in which application for issue of a digital signature certificate may be made.
16. The fee to be paid to the certifying authority for issue of a digital signature certificate.
17. The manner in which the adjudicating officer shall hold enquiry.
18. The qualification and experience which the adjudicating officer shall possess.
19. The salary, allowances and the other terms and condition of service of the presiding officer.
20. The procedure for investigation of misbehaviour or incapacity of the presiding officers and employees.
21. The salary and allowances and other conditions of service of other officers and employees.

22. The form in which appeal may be filed and the fee thereof.
23. Any other power of a civil court required to be prescribed.
24. Any other matter which is required to be, or may be prescribed.

Constitution of Advisory Committee

According to Section 88, the central government shall, as soon as may be, after the commencement of this Act, constitute a committee called the Cyber Regulations Advisory Committee. The Cyber Regulations Advisory Committee shall consist of a chairperson and such number of other official and non-official members representing the interest principally affected or having special knowledge of the subject matter as the central government may deem fit. The Cyber Regulations Advisory Committee shall advise the central government either generally as regards to any rules or for any other purpose connected with the Act and the controller in framing the regulations under this Act. The non-official members of such committee shall be paid such travelling and other allowances as the central government may fix.

Power of the Controller to Make Regulations

The controller may, after consultation with the Cyber Regulations Advisory Committee and with the previous approval of the central government, by notification in the official gazette, make regulations and the rules to carry out the purposes of this Act. In particular, and without prejudice to generality of foregoing power, such regulations may provide for all or any of the following matters:

1. The particulars relating to maintenance of database containing the disclosure record of every certifying authority.
2. The conditions and restrictions subject to which the controller may recognize any foreign certifying authority.
3. The terms and conditions subject to which a licence may be granted.
4. Other standards to be observed by a certifying authority.
5. The manner in which the certifying authority shall disclose the matters.
6. The particulars of statement which shall accompany an application.
7. The manner by which the subscriber communicate the composition of private key to the certifying authority.

As per Section 89(3), every regulation made under this Act shall be placed before each House of the Parliament within 30 days in one or more sessions to pass it with or without modifications.

Power of State Government to Make Rules

According to Section 90, the state government may, by notification in the official gazette, make rules to provide for all or any of the following matters:

1. The electronic form in which filing, issue, grant receipt or payment shall be effected
2. For matters specified in Sub-section (2) of Section 6

3. Any other matter, which is required to be provided by rules by the state government
4. Every rule made by the state government under this section shall be laid, as soon as may be after it is made, before each House of the State Legislature where it consists of two Houses, or where such Legislature consists of one House, before that House

TEST QUESTIONS

1. How the IT Act, 2000, deals with unauthorized access to computer, computer system and computer network? What are its provisions regarding 'cyber contraventions'?
2. What is 'Cyber Appellate Tribunal'? What is the procedure and powers of Cyber Appellate Tribunal under the IT Act, 2000? What is the procedure for appeal against the order of it?
3. Do you feel Orders by Cyber Appellate Tribunal to be final and not to invalidate its proceedings?
4. Distinguish between 'contraventions' and 'offences' as per the IT Act, 2000. Is 'hacking with the computer system' an offence under the Act.
5. Answer the following on the basis of your reading of the chapter:
   a. What is cyber contravention? How it is different from cyber offences?
   b. What is 'confiscation' as per the IT Act, 2000?
6. Explain the following:
   a. Hacking is an offence punishable under the IT Act, 2000.
   b. Electronic records are as authentic as the hard copies.
   c. Cyber terrorism as under the IT Act.
   d. Tampering with computer source documents.
   e. Cyber contraventions and cyber offences.
7. A person knowingly or intentionally conceals, destroys or alters any computer source, computer program, computer system or network. Is such an act is an offence? If so, what is the punishment?
8. Indicate whether the following are true or false:
   a. The IT Act, 2000, does not apply on negotiable instruments.
   b. Cryptography is a technique of writing messages in abbreviated form.
   c. A public key is one which is obtained by the user from a public authority.
   d. Recognition of electronic records as valid has made paper-based communication invalid.
   e. India's IT Act, 2000, is based on the model law proposed by UNO.
   f. The public key of sender and addressee are always the same.
   g. An electronic message is said to be received at the time when it enters the computer of the addressee.
   h. The public and private keys that form one pair are related to each other.
   i. A calculator can be called a small computer.
   j. Use of the Internet requires knowledge of programming languages.
   k. A website is merely a location on a computer to provide and receive data.
   l. A sender of an electronic message uses addressee's public key to encrypt his message.
   m. A hash function is same as an algorithm.

   Answers: a. (T), b. (F), c. (F), d. (F), e. (T), f. (F), g. (F), h. (T), i. (F), j. (F), k. (T), l. (T), m. (T)

PRACTICAL PROBLEMS

1. J sends electronic message offering to law firm to become their subscriber of an electronic journal. The offer is received in the computer resource of the firm and the programmed computer sends an automated reply to J that the subscription fee shall be ₹200 per month. J responds through his computer that he agrees to pay the fees. Is there any contract between J and the law firm?
   Hint. Yes. Even if the law firm is not aware of the communication, the firm is deemed to be the originator of the communication from the programmed computer under Section 11.
2. R sends a secure electronic offer to S to sell his building to S. S, through a secure electronic message, conveys his acceptance of the terms of the offer. When S demands execution of the deal, R backs out. Can S take action against R?
   Hint. No. Because the deals involving immovable property cannot be made electronically, see Section (4).
3. K sends an offer to C to make a contract. K has place of business in Bangalore. C sends a secure electronic message to convey his acceptance to K's computer resource. K downloads C's message on his laptop computer while he was waiting for his flight at the Kolkata airport. What would be deemed to be the place of making the contract, Kolkata or Bangalore?
   Hint. Bangalore, because under Section 13(3), the place of business of addressee is the place of receipt of a message.
4. G adopts the symmetrical crypto method using single private key to encrypt his electronic offer to Z. G sends the key to Z also but Z does not want to accept the offer. A staff member of Z has stolen the key and he conveys an electronic acceptance properly encrypted to G as if it is given by Z. Is there a contract between G and Z?
   Hint. Yes. Because the act of staff member cannot amount to forgery of signature and the acceptance shall be deemed to be sent by Z.
5. A person wants to send a message 'MEET VARUN' to a friend in coded language. The formula to convert the message is as follows: every character in the message shall be replaced by a character, which is the fifth after the character in the alphabet. The blank space in the message shall also be a character, supposed to be after Z in the alphabet. What will be coded form of the message?
   Hint. RJJYE FWZS.
6. A person received a coded message 'STEUQJFXT'. Assuming that the formula mentioned in Question 5 was used to code the message, decode the received message into the original one.
   Hint. NO PLEASE.
7. M sends to R his message through the Internet coding it into his own public key. On receiving it, R wants to decode the encoded text into original message. Advise R.
   Hint. Decoding by R is not possible without M's private key. R should give to M his own public key and obtain the message coded in that public key.

UNIT VI

The Negotiable Instruments Act, 1881

24 CHAPTER

Introduction to Negotiable Instruments Act

Learning Objectives

- To understand negotiable instruments
- To understand promissory note: elements, parties and test
- To understand bill of exchange: elements, types
- To understand parties, essentials, difference between bill of exchange and promissory notes

The negotiable instruments are the most important tools which facilitate the trade and business and the negotiable instruments law is the law of commercial world in general. Certain principles of equity, usage or trade recognize something as an instrument in commerce which has some value. The laws relating to negotiable instruments in India are contained in the Negotiable Instruments Act, 1881, which deals with promissory notes, bills of exchange and cheques. The Act does not affect the provisions of Section 31 of the Reserve Bank of India Act, 1934. The object of the Negotiable Instruments Act is to legalize the system under which the negotiable instruments pass from one hand to other hand in negotiations like ordinary goods.

Definition of Negotiable Instruments

Negotiable instrument is a piece of paper, which contains some value and is transferable by simple delivery or some time by endorsement and delivery. Section 13 provides that negotiable instrument means a promissory note, bill of exchange or cheque payable either to order or to bearer, whether the words order or bearer appear on the instrument or not. Bhashyam and Adiga define a negotiable instrument as it is the one which when transferred by delivery or endorsement and delivery passes to a transferee a good title to payment according to its tenor and irrespective of title of the transfer.

Negotiable instrument is one, which is by a legally recognized custom of trade, or law, transferable by delivery, in such circumstances that:

1. The holder of it for time being may sue on it in his own name and
2. The property in it passes free from equities, to a bonafide [*sic*] transferee for value, notwithstanding any defect of the transferor.

In the case of Khirodnath Gountia vs. Arjun Panda, the court held that a promissory note might be negotiable even if there is no indication as such in the document itself. In the absence of any bar of negotiability in the document, it shall be presumed to be negotiable. The name given to a document is not the determinative feature for deciding the nature of document. Thus, a negotiable instrument means a written document whose ownership can be transferred by one person to another by delivery alone or by delivery and endorsement.

In addition to promissory note, bill of exchange and cheques, there are some other instruments which are negotiable by the usage or customs of trade. These are as follows:

1. Hundis
2. Share warrants
3. Debentures of Bombay Port Trust
4. Railway receipts
5. Delivery orders
6. Dividend warrants
7. Banker's drafts
8. Circular notes
9. Bearer debentures

Exceptions: However, the following instruments are not regarded as negotiable instruments:

1. Money orders
2. Postal order
3. Deposit receipt
4. Share certificate
5. Dock warrants

Features of a Negotiable Instrument

According to Section 13 and some definitions, the features of a negotiable instrument are as follows:

1. Negotiability of the instrument, that is, the instrument is freely transferable either by delivery or by endorsement and delivery.
2. It confers absolute and good title to the transferee.
3. The holder can recover the money in his own name.
4. It consists of certain presumptions.

5. The holder of the bill may sue in his own name.
6. The holder has the right to transfer. The negotiability continues until maturity.

PROMISSORY NOTE

Section 4 provides that a promissory note is an instrument in writing containing an unconditional undertaking, signed by the maker, to pay certain sum of money only to or to the order of a certain person, or to the bearer of the instrument. Here, it is to be noted that the promissory note is not a bank note or a currency note. There are two parties to a promissory note:

1. The person who makes or executes and promises to pay is called the 'maker'.
2. The person to whom payment is to be made is called the 'payee'.

Example: X signs instruments in the following terms:

1. I promise to pay to Y or order ₹500.
2. I acknowledge myself indebted to B for ₹1,000 to be paid on demand for value received.

Elements of a Promissory Note

In the case of Sant Singh vs. Madandas Panika, the court held that following are the essential elements of a promissory note:

1. It must be in writing.
2. It must contain an undertaking to pay.
3. The promise to pay should be unconditional.
4. It must be signed by the maker.
5. The maker must be certain.
6. The sum payable must also be certain.
7. It must contain a promise to pay money and money only.
8. Payee must be certain.

In the case of B. B. Lohar vs. Prem Prakash Goyal, it was held that a mere receipt of cash deposits cannot be a promissory note, even though it is a promise to pay money. In the case of S. S. Namboori vs. Mathal Abraham, the court held that as the amount was payable only on the settlement of account after the litigation is over, hence it is not a promissory note as it is a precondition for a promissory note that the promise to pay must be unconditional.

Parties to a Promissory Note

Following are the partied to a promissory note:

1. The maker is the person who promises to pay the amount stated in the note. He is the debtor.

2. The payee is the person to whom the amount of the note is payable. He is the creditor.
3. Holder is either the payee or the person to whom the note might have been indorsed.
4. When the holder transfers or indorses the instrument to anyone else, the holder becomes the 'indorser' (endorser).
5. The person to whom the bill is indorsed is called an 'indorsee' (endorsee).

Test for Promissory Notes

In the case of C. N. Sankaran Namboodiripad vs. Vijayan, the court held the following test for the promissory note:

1. Is the sum to be paid certain?
2. Is the payment to be made to or to order of a person who is certain or to the bearer of the instrument?
3. Has the maker signed the document?
4. Is the promise to pay, the substance of the instrument?
5. Did the parties intend that the document should be a promissory note?

However, it should be noted that under Section 31 of the Reserve Bank of India Act, 1934, no person in India except the Reserve Bank of India or the central government could make or issue a promissory note payable to bearer. Thus, a promissory note cannot be originally made payable to a bearer. However, a promissory note payable to order, if it is endorsed in blank, becomes payable to bearer and is a valid instrument.

Specimen of a Promissory Note

1. When Promise Is Made to Pay on Demand

₹50,000 New Delhi
1 August 2018

On demand, I promise to pay to Shri Abhishek or order a sum of rupees fifty thousand, value received.

To

Abhishek Revenue Stamp

J2XX, Saket (Sd/)

New Delhi Rakesh

2. When Promise Is Made to Pay Money after a Fixed Time

₹5,000

New Delhi
1 August 2018

Three months after date, I promise to pay Shri Mohan or order a sum of rupees five thousand, value received.

To

Mohan — Revenue Stamp

H22X, Saket — (Sd/)

New Delhi — Rakesh

Bill of Exchange

According to Section 5, it is an instrument in writing, containing an unconditional order, signed by the maker, directing a certain person to pay certain sum of money only to or to the order of a certain person or to the bearer of the instrument. It means a bill of exchange is a written acknowledgement of the debts, written by the creditor and accepted by the debtor.

In a bill of exchange, one person makes an order to another person to pay a certain sum of money to someone. A bill of exchange is different from a promissory note as there is a promise to pay by the maker of promissory note, whereas a bill of exchange is an order to pay a certain sum of money.

Elements of a Bill of Exchange

Following are the elements of bill of exchange:

1. It must be in writing.
2. It must contain an order to pay.
3. The order contained in it should be unconditional.
4. It must be signed by the drawee.
5. The drawee must be certain.
6. The sum payable must also be certain.
7. The instrument must contain an order to pay money and money only.
8. The payee must be certain.

In the case of Sinha vs. Bidhu Bhasan, the Calcutta High Court held that an essential character of a bill of exchange is that it contains an order to accept or to pay and that the acceptor should accept it, in the absence of such a direction to pay, the document will not be a bill of exchange. In the case of Birbhum Central Co-Op. Bank vs. Pioneer Bank, a banker's draft was held as bill of exchange. In the case of S. N. Shukla vs. PNB, the court held that a demand draft, even if it were drawn upon another office of the same bank, is treated as bill of exchange.

Specimen of Bill of Exchange

1. A Bill Made on Demand

₹50,000	New Delhi
	18 July 2018

On demand pay to Shri Atul or order a sum of rupees fifty thousand only, value received.

To	
Atul	Revenue Stamp
Saket	(Sd/)
New Delhi	Sukesh

2. A Bill Where Payment Is after a Specified Period

₹20,000	New Delhi
	18 July 2018

Three months after date, pay Shri Atul or order a sum of rupees twenty thousand only, value received.

To	
Atul	Revenue Stamp
K-56, Saket	(Sd/)
New Delhi	Rakesh

Parties to a Bill of Exchange

Following are the parties to a bill of exchange.

1. **Drawer:** The maker of a bill of exchange or of cheque is called the drawer.
2. **Drawee:** The person who is directed to pay on the bill of exchange is called the drawee.

3. **Acceptor:** The person who gives assent to make the payment on the bill of exchange is known as the acceptor.
4. **Payee:** The person named in the instrument, to whom or to whose order the money is directed to be paid by the instrument is called the 'payee'.
5. **Indorser:** When the holder transfers or indorses the instrument to anyone else, the holder becomes the 'indorser' (endorser).
6. **Indorsee:** The person to whom the bill is indorsed is called an 'indorsee' (endorsee).
7. **Holder:** A person who is legally entitled to the possession of the negotiable instrument in his own name and to receive the amount thereof is called a 'holder'. He is either the original payee or the endorser. In case the bill is payable to the bearer, the person in possession of the negotiable instrument is called the 'holder'.
8. **Drawee in case of need:** When in the bill or in any endorsement the name of any person is given, in addition to the drawee, to be resorted to in the case of need, such a person is called 'drawee in case of need'. He is merely in the position of a drawee who has not accepted the bill. The bill cannot be presented to him for acceptance but only for payment.
9. **Acceptor for honour:** In case the original drawee refuses to accept the bill or to furnish better security when demanded by the notary, any person who is not liable on the bill can accept it with the consent of the holder for the honour of any party liable on the bill. Such an acceptor is known as 'acceptor for honour'.

Different Types of Bill of Exchange

Following are the different kinds of bill of exchanges, which may be issued.

1. **Bearer negotiable instruments:** It is a negotiable instrument which is payable to bearer of instrument, which means
   a. It is expressed to be so payable; or
   b. Explanation to Section 3 provides that only or last endorsement on the instrument is an endorsement in blank.

   Any person, who is in lawful possession of such instrument, is entitled to enforce payment due on it. When he receives money, he may be required to acknowledge receipt of money by signing on it.
2. **Order instruments:** A negotiable instrument is payable to order which is so expressed or which is expressed to be payable to a particular person and does not contain words prohibiting transfer or indicating an intention that it shall not be transferable.
3. **Inland instruments:** Section 11 provides that an inland instrument means a promissory note, bill of exchange or cheque which is both drawn and made payable in India or drawn upon any person resident in India. A bill of exchange drawn upon a resident in India is an inland bill irrespective of the place where it was drawn.
4. **Foreign bills:** Section 12 provides that an instrument which is not an inland instrument is deemed to be a foreign instrument. Further, foreign bills must be protested for dishonour if such protest is required by the law of the place where they are drawn. However, protest in case of inland bills is optional.
5. **Instrument payable on demand:** A cheque is always payable on demand and it cannot be expressed to be payable otherwise than on demand. A promissory note or bill

of exchange is payable on demand when it is expressed to be payable 'on demand', or 'at sight' or 'on presentment'.

6. **Time instruments or fixed period instrument:** A time instrument means a bill or note which is payable after a fixed period, or after sight, or on a specified day or on the happening of an event, which is certain to happen. However, if the event is probable but not certain to happen, the instrument does not become valid even if the event happens. According to Section 21, 'after sight' in a promissory note means after presentment for sight and in case of a bill of exchange means after accepting or noting for non-acceptance or protest for non-acceptance.
7. **Accommodation bill:** An accommodation bill means a bill which is drawn, accepted or endorsed without any consideration rather to help each other. It is the bill which is made to provide financial help to other party. The party lending (accommodating party) is not liable for such bill of exchange to the accommodated party. Further, there is no consideration between the parties.

   Example: X is in need of ₹50,000. He approaches Y for the amount. Y is not in a position to give but he suggests that X might draw a bill on Y, which Y would accept. If the credit of X were good, he would get the bill discounted with his banker. On the due date, X would pay ₹50,000 to Y who would meet the bill. This bill is an accommodation bill. In this case, Y is the 'accommodating party', and X is the 'accommodated party'. The accommodated party signs the 'accommodation bill' as drawer, acceptor. He is liable on the bill to the holder, and it is immaterial whether, when such holder took the bill, he knew such party to be an accommodation party or not.

   Some of the rules regarding accommodation bills are as follows:

   a. Section 43 provides that the accommodated party cannot, after he has paid the amount of the bill, recover the amount from any person who became a party to the bill for his accommodation.

      Example: X's bill is drawn and accepted for the accommodation of Y, the payee. Y endorses the bill to Z. The bill is dishonoured and Y pays the amount.

   b. Section 59 provides that an accommodation bill can be negotiated after maturity, provided the person to whom it is negotiated takes it in good faith and for consideration.
   c. Non-presentment of an accommodation bill to the acceptor for payment does not discharge the drawer.
   d. If an accommodation bill is dishonoured, failure to give notice of dishonour does not discharge the prior parties from the liability.
8. **Documentary bill and clean bill:** When documents of title to the goods and other documents, for example, invoice, marine insurance police and so on, are annexed to a bill, the bill is called a documentary bill. Such documents are delivered to the buyer only on acceptance or payment of the bill. When no documents relating to the goods represented by the bill are attached to it, the bill is termed as a clean bill.
9. **Ambiguous instruments:** Section 17 provides that where an instrument owing to its faulty drafting may be treated either as a bill of exchange or a promissory note, such instrument is known as ambiguous instrument. In such a case, the holder may treat it either as a bill or a promissory note. Once the holder elects to treat it in a particular manner, later on he cannot change and cannot treat it in a different manner.

   Example: R draws a bill on P and negotiates it away. P is a fictitious person or is a minor. The holder may treat the bill as a note made by R. In case the amount promised or ordered to be paid is written differently in figures and in words, the amount stated in words is the amount promised or ordered to be paid. In this case, it will not be an ambiguous instrument.

10. **Inchoate instruments:** Section 20 provides that an instrument which is incomplete in some respect is called an inchoate instrument. Where one person signs and delivers to another person a paper stamped in accordance with the law, relating to negotiable instruments, either wholly blank or incomplete in some respect, thereby gives prima facie authority to the holder thereof to make or complete it, for any amount not exceeding the amount covered by the stamp. To make the person liable who has signed it, it is necessary that the instrument should be delivered to another. Delivery is essential to fix up responsibility. Thus, where someone steals it and, after filling it up, delivers it to an innocent holder. Such a holder for value is not entitled to recover the amount from the person who signed the instrument because he never delivered the instrument to be used as a negotiable instrument.
    Example: X gives a promissory note, after affixing ₹1 stamp and signing, to Y but without writing the amount. The actual amount intended to be paid is ₹3,000 but Y fills up ₹5,000. However, Y can recover only ₹3,000. But if Y endorses the instrument in favour of Z, a holder in due course, then Z can recover ₹5,000 from X. However, if the amount filled up is ₹15,000, then even Z cannot recover the amount because the stamp does not cover the amount of ₹15,000.
11. **Fictitious bill:** A fictitious bill means when either the drawer or the drawee of instrument is fictitious. According to Section 42, the acceptor of such a bill is not relieved from liability to any holder in due course, provided that holder in due course could show that the signature of the drawer and the first endorsement on the bill are in the same handwriting. Thus, the liability of the acceptor of a fictitious bill is only to the holder in due course, subject to the signature of the drawer and the first endorsement being under the same hand.
12. **Escrow:** When any negotiable instrument is delivered to any person with a condition and the condition of such delivery is not negotiable, it will be called escrow. In such a case, the instrument takes effects only upon the fulfilment of the condition.
    Example: When a bill is given as collateral security for a loan, the property in the bill does not pass to the endorsee. The duty of the person receiving it is to keep the same with him as collateral security, return it when the loan is repaid or enforce payment when the loan is not repaid. Thus, there is no liability on the bill until the condition subject to which it was delivered is fulfilled. The rights of a holder in due course are not, however, affected in the case of such an instrument delivered or endorsed conditionally.
13. **Bill in sets:** Sections 132 and 133 provide that foreign bills are generally drawn in sets of three, and each set is termed as a 'via'. The practice of drawing a bill in parts is called drawing a bill 'in a set'. Each part is dispatched by a separate means of conveyance so that there may be no delay because of miscarriage in the transit. All these parts form only one bill, the stamp is affixed on one part only and on each part, there is a reference of the other two parts.
    Following are the rules that govern bills in sets:
    a. According to Section 132, bill of exchange may be drawn in parts, each part being numbered and containing a provision that it shall continue to be payable only so long as the others remain unpaid. When payment is made on one part, the other parts will become inoperative.
    b. Section 132 further provides that the drawer should sign and deliver all the parts but the acceptance to be conveyed only on one of the parts. In case a person accepts or

endorses different parts of the bill in favour of different person, he and the subsequent endorsers of each part are liable on such part as if it were a separate bill.

c. Section 133 provides that between holders in due course of the different parts of the same bill, he who first acquired title to any one part is entitled to the other parts and is also entitled to claim the money represented by the bill.

Specimen of a Bill in Sets (First Copy)

₹150,000

Kanpur
18 January 2019

Ninety days after the sight of First of Exchange (Second and third of the same tenor and date being unpaid) pay to the order of M/S Parkash & Co. Delhi, the sum of Rupee One lac Fifty thousand only, value received.

To
M/s Balram Gupta & Brothers,
Chandni Chowk
Co. Delhi

Revenue Stamp
(Sd/)
for M/S Parkash &

CHEQUE

Section 6 provides that a cheque is a bill of exchange drawn on a specified banker and not expressed to be payable otherwise then on demand and it includes the electronic image of a truncated cheque and a cheque in the electronic form. Further, the cheque satisfies all the requirements of a bill of exchange and it is intended for immediate payment but the demand by holder is necessary for payment. All the cheques are bills of exchange but all the bills of exchange are not cheques.

Explanation:

1. **Cheque in the electronic form** means a cheque drawn in electronic form by using any computer resource and signed in a secure system with digital signature (with or without biometrics signature) and asymmetric crypto system or with electronic signature, as the case may be.
2. **Truncated cheque** means a cheque which is truncated during the course of a clearing cycle, either by the clearing house or by the bank whether paying or receiving payment, immediately on generation of an electronic image for transmission, substituting the further physical movement of the cheque in writing.

   The expression 'clearing house' means clearing house managed by the Reserve Bank of India or a clearing house recognized by the Reserve Bank of India. Further, the expressions 'asymmetric crypto system', 'computer resource', 'digital signature', 'electronic form' and 'electronic signature' shall have the same meanings respectively assigned to them in the IT Act, 2000.

Parties to a Cheque

Following are the parties to a cheque.

1. **The drawer:** Drawer is the person who draws the cheques, that is, the depositor of money in the bank.
2. **The drawee:** The drawee is the bank/organization directed by the depositor to pay a certain sum of money to the payee.
3. **The payee:** Payee is the person who is entitled to receive the payment of a cheque.

Specimen of Cheque

Date............

Pay...

....Or order

The sum of Rupees..

....(₹.......................)

Account no...................

Canara Bank, District centre

Janakpuri, New Delhi 110018

IFSC:

Cheque No ------------- MICR no

Essentials of a Cheque

On the basis of the provisions of Section 6 of the Act, following are the essentials of a cheque:

1. A cheque must be in writing.
2. Cheque is an order drawn on a specified bank to pay the amount.
3. It is always payable on demand without any days of grace.
4. A cheque requires no acceptance.
5. A cheque to be valid must be made payable to, or to the order of a certain person or to the bearer of the instrument.
6. A cheque may be crossed.
7. The order to pay the amount must be an unconditional order.
8. A cheque is always drawn on a banker.
9. The drawer must sign it.
10. The amount to be paid by the bank must be certain.

DIFFERENCE BETWEEN A CHEQUE AND A BILL OF EXCHANGE

A cheque is different from a bill of exchange in the following ways.

	Cheque	*Bill of Exchange*
1.	**Drawee:** A cheque is always drawn on a specified banker only.	A bill may be drawn on any one, including a banker.
2.	**Payable on demand:** A cheque is always payable on demand.	A bill may be drawn payable on demand or on the expiry of a certain period after date or sight.
3.	**Payable to the bearer on demand:** A cheque is always payable on demand and may be made payable to bearer or order.	A bill cannot be drawn payable to the bearer or demand.
4.	**Acceptance:** A cheque requires no acceptance.	A bill must be accepted before payment can be claimed.
5.	**Days of grace:** No days of grace are allowed.	In the case of time bills, three days of grace are allowed from the due date for calculating the maturity of the bill.
6.	**Supposition:** A cheque is supposed to be drawn upon funds in the hands of the banker.	In case of a bill, there is no such presumption.
7.	**Crossing:** A cheque can be crossed either generally or specially.	A bill cannot be crossed.
8.	**Stamping:** A cheque does not require any stamp.	A bill must be properly stamped (except in the case of demand bills).
9.	**Countermanding:** The drawer can countermand the payment of a cheque.	The drawer cannot countermand the payment of a bill.
10.	**Circulation:** A cheque is not intended for circulation but for immediate payment.	A bill may be circulated by endorsing it.
11.	**Discounting:** A cheque cannot be discounted.	A bill can be discounted and rediscounted with the banks.
12.	**Failure to present:** If the cheque is not presented for payment at the due time, the drawer is not discharged from liability unless he suffers only damage by delay in presentment, for example, the liquidation of the bank.	The drawer of a bill is discharged if it is not duly presented to the acceptor for payment or else.
13.	**Primary liability:** The drawer of a cheque is primarily liable for payment.	The drawee or the acceptor of a bill is primarily liable on it.
14.	**Statutory protection:** The banker is protected if he pays a cheque under a forged endorsement.	The drawee of a bill has no such protection.
15.	**Noting and protesting:** A cheque need not be noted and protected when dishonoured.	A bill must be noted and protected when it is dishonoured.
16.	**Sets:** Cheques are not issued in sets.	Foreign bills are generally drawn in sets of three.

Difference between a Cheque and a Promissory Note

A cheque may be differentiated from a promissory note on the basis of the following points.

	Cheque	*Promissory Note*
1.	**Number of parties:** A cheque has three parties, namely drawer, drawee and payee.	A promissory note has two parties only, that is, maker and payee.
2.	**Order and promise:** A cheque contains an unconditional order to the banker to pay the money.	A pro-note contains an unconditional undertaking by the debtor to pay the money.
3.	**Drawee:** The drawee is a specified banker, that is, the drawee of a cheque is always a banker.	A promissory note many be executed either by a banker or by a non-banker.
4.	**Payable on demand:** A cheque is always payable on demand.	It must be payable either on demand or after a certain period.
5.	**Bearer or order:** A cheque may be payable to order or to bearer.	A promissory note cannot be made payable to the bearer on demand.
6.	**Crossing:** A cheque can be crossed either generally or specially.	There is no practice of crossing a promissory note.
7.	**Stamping:** A cheque does not require any stamp.	It must be properly stamped.
8.	**Days of grace:** Grace days are not allowed because it is always payable on demand.	A grace period of three days is allowed.
9.	**Discounting:** A cheque cannot be discounted.	A promissory note can be discounted and rediscounted with banks.

Difference between Promissory Note and Bill of Exchange

A bill of exchange is different from promissory note in the following ways.

	Bill of Exchange	*Promissory Note*
1.	**Drawer:** A creditor draws it.	A debtor draws/writes it.
2.	**Parties:** There are three parties: (a) drawer, (b) drawee and (c) payee.	There are two parties: (a) maker and (b) payee.
3.	**Acceptance:** A bill of exchange requires acceptance of the drawee before it is presented for the payment.	In case of promissory note, no acceptance is necessary.
4.	**Conditional:** It may be accepted conditionally by the drawee.	It cannot be made conditional by the maker.
5.	**Copies:** Foreign bills are drawn in sets, normally three copies are prepared.	Only one copy of a foreign promissory note is prepared.
6.	**Position of maker:** The drawer stands in immediate relationship with the acceptor and not the payee.	Here, the maker stands in immediate relationship with the payee.

	Bill of Exchange	*Promissory Note*
7.	**Nature of liability:** In case of bill of exchange, the liability of drawers is conditional and secondary.	In case of promissory note, the liability of makers is absolute and primary.
8.	**Notice of dishonour:** The holder must give it to the drawer and to all previous endorsers.	Notice of dishonour is not necessary to be given to the maker.
9.	**Drawer and payee—same:** In case of bill of exchange, the drawer can be the payee.	In case of promissory note, the maker cannot pay to himself.

TEST QUESTIONS

1. What is meant by a negotiable instrument? Explain its characteristics.
2. What are the presumptions as to negotiable instruments? Note down the instruments that are regarded as negotiable and the ones that are not regarded as negotiable.
3. Define a promissory note and distinguish it from a bill of exchange.
4. What is a bill of exchange? Draw a specimen of it. How does it differ from a promissory note?
5. Define a cheque and state its main characteristics. Can it be accepted like a bill of exchange? Compare it with a bill of exchange.
6. Distinguish between an inland bill and a foreign bill.
7. What is a bill in sets? State its requirements. Differentiate between bill in sets and accommodation bill.
8. Explain the following:
   a. Inchoate instruments
   b. Escrow
   c. Fictitious bill
   d. Ambiguous instruments

PRACTICAL PROBLEMS

1. Discuss whether either of the following is a promissory note:
   a. A promises to pay the bearer a sum of ₹1,500 six months after date.
   b. A promises to pay B ₹1,500 one month after C's death.
   Hint. The first one is not a promissory note as it offends Section 31 of the Reserve Bank of India Act. a promissory note cannot originally be made payable to bearer. The second one is a valid promissory note since C's death is certain.
2. Is the following a promissory note?
   The instrument is duly signed, dated and stamped. 'I promise to pay X's son ₹1,500 for value received.'
   Hint. Yes, refer Section 92, Provision 6 of the Evidence Act, if it could be proved that the amount has been lent to the maker by a particular son of X.
3. Is the following a good promissory note?
   The instrument is duly signed, dated and stamped. 'I Promise to pay B ₹500 with interest' (interest rate is not specified).

Hint. Yes, though the rate is not specified, the amount is payable with interest at the rate of 6 per cent per annum, Section 80 of the Act.

4. Can a negotiable instrument be made payable to bearer on demand? Explain.
   Hint. Yes, but only a cheque. A promissory note cannot be originally made payable to bearer on demand. Sections 31 and 32 of the Reserve Bank of India Act override the provisions of the Negotiable Instruments Act.
5. B obtains A's acceptance to a bill by fraud. B endorses it to C who takes it as a holder in due course. C endorses the bill to D, who knows of the fraud. Can D recover from A?
   Hint. Yes, D derives his title from C, who is a holder in due course. Hence, he enjoys the same rights as a holder in due course. A cannot put up the defence of fraud. (Section 53 and 58)

25

CHAPTER

Parties to Negotiable Instrument

Learning Objectives

- To understand holder and holder in due course
- To understand rights and privileges of a holder in due course
- To understand payment in due course
- To understand extent of liability of parties to negotiable instrument

In case of a negotiable instrument, there will be maker of the instrument, holder and holder in due course. The holder and holder in due course are explained as follows.

Holder

Holder is a person who is in possession of the instrument and who obtained it by delivery or by endorsement and delivery. According to Section 8, the holder of a promissory note or bill of exchange or cheques mean any person entitled in his own name to the possession thereof and to receive or recover the amount due thereon from the parties thereto. Further, Section 2 of the Act explains that to treat any person as holder, it is necessary that the holder should:

1. Be entitled in his own name to the possession of the instrument.
2. Have the right to receive or recover the amount due thereon from the parties thereto.

Rights of a Holder

The holder of a negotiable instrument has the following rights:

1. To cross open cheques either generally or specially.
2. To convert a blank endorsement into a full endorsement.
3. To negotiate the instrument to a third party.
4. To present it to the maker or drawee.
5. To use it in his own name.
6. To obtain a duplicate of a lost instrument.

Holder in Due Course

Section 9 provides that the holder in due course is 'any person who for consideration became the possessor of a promissory note, bill of exchange or cheque, if payable to bearer, or the payee or endorsee thereof, if payable to order, before the amount mentioned in it became payable and without having sufficient cause to believe that any defect existed in the title of the person from whom he derived his title.

A holder becomes the holder in due course when he satisfies the following conditions:

1. He should have received the instrument for consideration.
2. The instrument should be regular and proper.
3. He should have received the instrument before its maturity.
4. He should have received it without knowing the defective title of the transferor.

Rights and Privileges of a Holder in Due Course

Once a person becomes a holder in due course, he is entitled to enjoy the following rights and privileges.

1. **Presumptions:** Section 32 provides that every holder is deemed prima facie to be holder in due course having obtained the instrument for valuable consideration. The holder in due course obtains a better title to the instruments as the position of a holder in due course is an exception to the maxim 'nemo dat quod non habet'.
2. **Transfer of better title:** Once an instrument passes through the hands of a holder in due course, it is free of all defects. According to Section 53, a holder of a negotiable instrument who derives title from a holder in due course gets rights thereon of that of a holder in due course.
3. **Removal of prior defects:** Section 58 provides that the party (maker, acceptor or holder) liable to pay on an instrument cannot contend against a holder in due course that he had lost the instrument or obtained from him by fraud or for an unlawful consideration. Thus, the defective title of the endorsee will not affect adversely the rights of the holder in due course.
   Example: X obtained an instrument by fraud. He transfers this instrument in favour of Y in such circumstances that Y becomes the holder in due course. Y gets a better and different title, that is, the title of the transferee shall not be the same as that of the transferor. If some defect exists in the title of the transferor, the title of the transferee is not affected.
4. **Liability of prior party to holder in due course:** Section 36 provides that every prior party to a negotiable instrument is liable to a holder in due course until the instrument is duly satisfied. Prior parties include the maker or drawer, the acceptor and all intervening endorsers. The holder in due course can sue all or any of the prior parties in his own name.
   Example: X draws a bill on Y and endorses it to Z, Z endorses it to P and P to S. S is a holder in due course. S can recover the amount either from X or Y or Z or P.

5. **Right in case of inchoate instrument:** Section 20 provides that the rights of a holder in due course are not at all affected even though the instrument was originally an inchoate stamped instrument and the transferor completed the instrument for a sum greater than what was intended by the maker or drawer. The holder in due course has the right to recover the whole amount of the instrument even though the amount filled therein was more than what was authorized by the maker.
   Example: X delivers to Y a promissory note duly signed and affixed the stamps worth ₹50. The intention of X was that Y would write the amount ₹5,000. Y writes therein ₹8,000 and endorses it to Z who becomes a holder in due course. Here, Z can recover ₹8,000 from X.
6. **Rights in case of bill drawn in fictitious name:** Section 42 provides that an acceptor of a bill of exchange drawn in a fictitious name and payable to the drawer's order is not relieved from a liability to any holder in due course claiming under an endorsement by the same hand as the drawer's signature and purporting to be made by the drawer on the ground that such name is fictitious. When a bill is drawn in a fictions name and is made payable to the drawer's order, the bill is said to be a fictitious bill. Such a bill cannot be enforced at law. However, the acceptor of such a bill is not relieved from liability to any holder in due course provided he can show that the signature of the supposed drawer and the first endorsement on it are in the handwriting of the same person.
7. **Conditional delivery:** Where a negotiable instrument delivered conditionally is negotiated to the holder in due course, the other parties to the instrument cannot escape liability on the ground that the delivery of the instrument was conditional or for a special purpose only.
8. **Estoppel against denying original validity of instrument:** No maker of a promissory note, no drawer of a bill of exchange or cheque and no acceptor of a bill of exchange for the honour of the drawer shall, in a suit thereon by a holder in due course, be permitted to deny the validity of the instrument as originally made or drawn. It means that the previously mentioned parties cannot argue as against the holder in due course that the instrument is not valid. However, a holder in due course cannot recover money if the instrument is void ab initio, or where the maker of the note or drawer of bill or cheque is a person incompetent to contract.
9. **Estoppel against denying capacity of payee to endorse:** No maker of a promissory note and no acceptor of a bill of exchange payable to order shall, in a suit thereon by a holder in due course, be permitted to deny the payee's capacity at the date of the note or bill to endorse the same. The payee must be competent to endorse, otherwise the endorsee cannot recover the amount. However, if the endorsee is a holder in due course, then he can recover the amount in his own name.
10. **Estoppel against denying signature or capacity of prior party:** No endorser of a negotiable instrument shall, in suit thereon a subsequent holder, be permitted to deny the signature or capacity to contract of any prior party to the instrument.
11. **Negotiable instruments without consideration:** A negotiable instrument made, drawn, accepted without consideration does not create any obligation as between the parties to the transaction. However, if the instrument gets into the hands of a holder in due course, he can recover the amount from any of the prior parties. The plea that there was no consideration cannot be set up against a holder in due course.

Difference between Holder and Holder in Due Course

It is presumed that every holder is a holder in due course but this presumption is rebuttable. Following are the differences between a holder and a holder in due course:

1. A holder need not be in possession of the instrument and it is enough if he is entitled to the possession of the instrument. However, a holder in due course must have been in possession of the instrument.
2. A holder need not have paid the consideration but a holder in due course must have paid the consideration.
3. A person will be a holder even if he becomes entitled to the possession after the amount mentioned in it becomes payable but a holder in due course must have obtained possession of it before the amount mentioned in it becomes payable.
4. A person may still be a holder even if he takes it with notice of any defect in the instrument but a holder in due course must not have notice of any defect in the instrument.
5. A holder takes the instrument subject to all defects and equitable but a holder in due course takes the instrument free from all defects and equities.

Drawee in Case of Need

Section 7 provides that when in the bill or in any endorsement thereon the name of any person is given in addition to the drawee to be resorted to in case of need, such person is called a 'drawee in case of need'. The bill being dishonoured for non-payment or non-acceptance.

Section 115 provides that the bill is not dishonoured unless it is dishonoured by the drawee in case of need. Therefore, in case of need, it is the duty of the holder or payee to produce it to the drawee. In the English law, he is called referee in case of need.

Holder for Value

It is not defined in the Negotiable Instrument Act, however, it is defined in Section 27 of the Bill of Exchange Act of England. In India, it is a presumption. Whenever the value of the instrument is guaranteed to any holder, he is called holder for value. No consideration is needed, that is, a person who claimed to be a holder need not give value since it may be given by a prior party.

Payment in Due Course

In order to discharge all the parties from liability, the amount due on the instrument must be paid by the maker or the drawee to the right persons. So simply payment over the instrument will not discharge the parties from the liability. It will become effective payment when such payment amounts to payment in due course. According to Section 10, the payment in due course means payment in accordance with the apparent tenor of the instrument in good faith and without negligence to any person in possession thereof under circumstances which do not afford a reasonable ground for believing that he is not entitled to receive payment of the amount therein mentioned.

Conditions

Payment in due course should satisfy the following conditions.

1. **The payment should be in accordance with the apparent tenor of the instrument:** Apparent tenor means the tenor which appears on the face of the instrument and it will be the intention of the parties. If the banker makes payment of a post-dated cheque before the date mentioned therein or pays a crossed cheque at the counter, he acts against the true intentions of the drawer, and hence such payment will not be treated as payment in due course.
2. **Payment must be made to the person in possession of the instrument:** Payment must be made to the person in possession of the instrument under circumstances which do not arouse any suspicion about his right to receive payment thereof. In other words, payment should be made to the rightful holder who can give a valid discharge. If the instrument is made payable to bearer, the rightful holder is the person who has received it by delivery. Further, the payment must be made by the maker or the drawee of the instrument or on his behalf.
3. **Payment should be made in good faith and without negligence:** The maker or drawee should make the payment honestly after enquiry into the title of the possessor of instrument. Whenever doubt arises about the validity of the title of the payee, the bank should not make the payment without making proper enquiry. A payment by a bank after receiving instructions from the drawer to stop payment is not a payment in due course.

   Exceptions: Payment of a forged cheque is not a payment in due course. Since it is the duty of the banker to keep in touch with the nature of the signature of the customer, the failure to do so will make the banker responsible to his customer for the payment of the forged instruments.
4. **Payment should be made in money:** The payment of negotiable instrument shall be made in terms of money only; however, if holder agrees to accept cheque or draft, the payment can be made by cheque or draft.

Capacity of the Parties

Section 11 of the Contract Act provides that an agreement by or with a minor, with the persons of unsound mind and persons prohibited by law is void and cannot be enforced against them. The provisions of Section 11 of the Contract Act are being confirmed by Section 26 of the Negotiable Instruments Act and provide that every person capable of contracting according to the law to which he is subject may bind himself and be bound by the making, drawing, accepting, endorsing, delivery and negotiation of a promissory note, bill of exchange or cheque.

THE EXTENT OF LIABILITY OF PARTIES TO A NEGOTIABLE INSTRUMENT

1. **Minor:** Section 26 provides that a minor may draw, endorse, deliver and negotiate such instrument to bind all parties except himself. It means a minor may be a party to negotiable instrument without being liable on it. He may be the drawer, maker, acceptor or endorser, but he cannot be held liable in any of these capacities. He is not liable even if the instrument is given for the necessaries supplied to him. Further, the instrument does not become invalid merely because one of the parties is a minor. A bill drawn by a minor is perfectly valid so long as the acceptor is of the age of majority. It is only when the acceptor dishonours the bill, the same becomes void, since the holder cannot recover the money from the minor drawer. In the case of Sulochana vs. Pandiyan Bank Ltd, where a minor along with another person executed a promissory note, it was held that though no liability could be enforced against the minor executant but the other executant is also a party to the document and cannot escape his liability.
2. **Lunatics:** A lunatic or a drunken person, who for the time being is incapable to understand the effect of a contract, on his interest, at the time of making it, is on the same footing as a minor and a contract made by him during this time is void.
3. **Insolvent:** A person who has been adjudicated insolvent cannot accept or endorse a bill. However, if he endorses an instrument of which he is the payee to a holder in due course, the latter can recover from all parties, except the insolvent. An insolvent cannot sue on an instrument as his property vests in the official receiver. A negotiable instrument obtained by an insolvent after his insolvency but before discharge will also automatically vest in the official receiver.
4. **Joint stock company:** While a trading company has implied powers to draw, accept or negotiate an instrument, non-trading joint stock companies do not enjoy any such implied powers, unless such powers are conferred by the Memorandum of Association of the company. Section 26 provides that nothing herein contained shall be deemed to empower a corporation to make, endorse or accept such instruments except in cases in which, under the law for the time being in force, they are so empowered. This was upheld by the court in Oriol Industries Ltd vs. Bombay Mercantile Bank Ltd.
5. **Agents:** According to Section 27, every person capable of contracting may make, draw, accept, endorse, deliver and negotiate a bill, note or cheque either himself or through a duly authorized agent acting in his name. However, a general authority to transact business and to receive and discharge debts does not confer upon an agent the power of accepting or endorsing bill of exchange to bind his principal. However, in Hazari Lal vs. Sohan Lal, it was held that if it is known to the parties that the money was lent to the firm and not to the agent in his personal capacity, then agent will not be liable.

   An authority to draw bills of exchange does not of itself impart an authority to endorse. An agent who signs a negotiable instrument for his principal may bind his principal provided:
   a. He signs the principal's name or states on the face of the instrument that he signs as agent, for example, by using the words 'for and on behalf of' or *per pro.*
   b. He acts within the scope of his authority.

   However, he will be personally liable if he puts signature to an instrument without indicating thereon that he signs as agent. However, he is not personally liable to those who induced him to sign the instrument upon the belief that the principal only would be held liable.

Example: The director of a company borrows ₹50,000 on a promissory note. There is no indication on the face of the promissory note whether the money is borrowed for the company. Even if the company gets the benefit of the money so borrowed, the director will be liable to pay the debt. Further, he executes an instrument without or in excess of his authority.

6. **Hindu undivided family (HUF):** The *karta* of HUF represents the family in all dealings with the outside world. He has an implied authority, on behalf of family, to contract debts, pledge the credit of the family and borrow money on a note or bill where he carries on family business. Such a note or bill is binding on all the members of the joint family and can be enforced against them. The minor members are equally liable to the extent of their share, though they are not personally liable.
7. **Legal representatives:** Section 29 provides that a legal representative of a deceased person who signs his name to a promissory note, bill of exchange or cheque is liable personally thereon unless he expressly limits his liability to the extent of the assets received by him as such.
8. **Partner:** In the case of a trading partnership, every partner has implied authority to bind his co-partners by drawing, making, accepting or negotiating an instrument. In the case of a non-trading partnership, however, there is no such implied authority. Hence, a partner signing an instrument on behalf of the firm should do so in the name of the firm.

LIABILITY OF THE PARTIES

In the case of a negotiable instrument, the general rule is that no person can be sued on an instrument unless he appears as a party thereon. It is, therefore, necessary to know the provisions of the Act relating to the liability of the parties. The liability of the parties is explained as follows.

1. **Liability of drawer:** According to Section 30, the drawer of a bill of exchange or cheque is bound, in case of dishonour by the drawee or acceptor thereof, to compensate the holder, provided due notice of dishonour has been given to, or received by, the drawer. The drawer will be liable when the instrument has been dishonoured, it is necessary that due notice of dishonour must be given to him. In case of a bill of exchange, the liability of the drawer is of a secondary nature, that is, the drawer will be liable only when the drawee fails to make the payment of the bill. However, in case of dishonour of a cheque, by the bank, the holder has a right of action only against the drawer and not against the bank.
2. **Liability of drawee of a cheque:** Section 31 provide that the drawee of a cheque having sufficient funds of the drawer in his hands properly applicable to the payment of such cheque must pay the cheque when duly required so to do, and, in default of such payment, must compensate the drawer for any loss or damage caused by such default. However, it should be noted here that liability of banker is only towards its customers and not towards the holder of cheque.
3. **Liability of maker of note and acceptor of a bill:** Section 32 provides that maker of a promissory note and acceptor of bill of exchange are the persons who are primarily

liable for the amount due on the instrument according to its apparent tenor in the absence of a contract to the contrary. If payment is not made, then the maker or acceptor shall be liable to pay compensation to any party to the note or bill for any loss or damage caused by such non-payment. In case of Jagjivan Mavji vs. Ranchoddas, the Supreme Court held that a mere acknowledgement does not amount to acceptance, hence he cannot be held liable.

4. **Liability of an endorser:** Section 35 provides that in absence of contract to the contrary, the endorser who has endorsed the instrument before maturity is liable to every subsequent holder, in case of dishonour by the drawee, acceptor or maker, to compensate such holder for any loss or damage caused to him by such dishonour. The endorser will be liable if the following conditions are satisfied:
   a. There must be no contract to the contrary.
   b. The instrument should have been dishonoured.
   c. The endorsee must not have expressly excluded his liability by 'sans recourse' endorsement.
   d. Due notice of dishonour has been given to or received by such endorser.
5. **Liability of prior parties:** Section 36 provides that every prior party to a negotiable instrument is liable thereon to a holder in due course until the instrument is duly satisfied. The liability of prior parties is, therefore, joint and several. Section 38 provides that as between the parties they are liable as sureties. Each prior party is, in the absence of a contract to the contrary, also liable thereon as a principal debtor in respect of each subsequent party. It means that each prior party is liable as a principal debtor to succeeding party.

   Example: A draws a bill payable to his own order on B, who accepts it. A afterwards endorses the bill to C, C to D and D to E. As between E and B, B is the principal debtor and A, C and D are his sureties. As between E and A, A is the principal debtor and C and D are his sureties. As between E and C, C is the principal debtor and D is his surety.

TEST QUESTIONS

1. Who is a holder and holder in due course? Explain the privileges of holder in due course.
2. The defence of absence of consideration in the case of a negotiable instrument is available only between parties in immediate relationship. Comment.
3. Distinguish between 'holder' and 'holder in due course'. What are the privileges of a holder in due course?
4. Who are the important parties to a negotiable instrument? What do you know of their capacities to make, draw, accept, endorse or negotiate such instruments?
5. Explain to what extent can a minor be a party to a negotiable instrument. Discuss the liability of various parties to a negotiable instrument.
6. Write short notes on following:
   a. Drawee in case of need
   b. Payment in due course
   c. Holder for value

PRACTICAL PROBLEMS

1. A drew cheques in favour of B. A's clerk forged B's endorsement and negotiated the cheques to C, who took them in good faith and for value. C received the payment of the cheque. A claims to recover the amount form C. Will he succeed?
   Hint. Yes, C has no title to the cheques because of forgery. Only the paying banker is protected but not the person who received payment on a cheque bearing a forged endorsement.
2. A bill is drawn payable to 'A or order'. A loses the bill and B, who finds it, forges A's signature and endorses it to C, who takes it in good faith and for value. Examine the rights of C.
   Hint. Forgery being nullity in the eyes of law does not convey any title even to a holder in due course. C cannot receive payment. If he receives payment, the party liable continues to be liable to the true owner.
3. A is the payee of an order cheque. B steals the cheque and forges A's signature and endorses the cheque in his (B's) favour. B then endorses it to C who takes it in good faith and for valuable consideration. Is C a holder in due course?
   Hint. C is not a holder in due course even though he takes it in good faith and for value. He has no title to the cheque because of forged endorsement.
4. A is the payee of a bearer instrument. A misplaces the instrument in his office. It is picked up by B. B delivers it to C, who takes it in good faith and for valuable consideration. Is C a holder in due course?
   Hint. Yes. The instrument being a bearer one, title is passed by mere delivery and not endorsement and delivery. Thus, C gets an independent title to it.
5. A signs the following endorsements on different negotiable instruments payable to bearer. Point out the endorsements, if any, that exclude the right of further negotiation by B:
   a. Pay B for my use
   b. Pay B or order for the account of A
   c. Pay B
   d. Pay B value in account with South Indian Bank Ltd
   e. The amount must be credited to B within 10 days

   Hint. The instruments a, b and e cannot be further negotiated; instruments c and d can be further negotiated.

26
CHAPTER

Endorsement and Crossing of Cheque

Learning Objectives

- To understand negotiation and assignment
- To understand endorsement and its types
- To know 'once a bearer always a bearer'
- To understand crossing of cheque and types of crossings

NEGOTIABLE INSTRUMENT

A negotiable instrument is freely transferable from one person to another. It can be transferred either by negotiation or assignment.

Negotiation

Negotiation means that the instrument is transferred to a person in such a manner that the transferee of the instrument becomes its holder. As a holder, he has the right to possess the instrument in his own name and to recover the amount mentioned therein from concerned parties. Negotiation of an instrument is the process by which the ownership of the instrument is transferred by one person to another. As per Section 14, when a promissory note, bill of exchange or cheque is transferred to any person to constitute that person the holder thereof, the instrument is said to be negotiated. There are two ways given under the Negotiable Instruments Act for the transfer by negotiation, which are as follows.

1. **By payable to bearer:** According to Section 47, a promissory note, bill of exchange or cheque payable to a bearer is negotiable by delivery thereof. However, it is necessary that the delivery of the negotiable instrument must have been made with intention to transfer the ownership.

Example: X, the holder of a negotiable instrument payable to bearer, delivers it to Y's agent to keep it for Y. The instrument has been negotiated.

Negotiation by delivery: A negotiable instrument payable to bearer is negotiable by delivery thereof. The delivery may be actual or constructive. A bearer instrument does not require the signature of the transferor, that is, endorsement. The instrument should be delivered with the intention of transferring property in the instrument. The delivery must be voluntary and absolute. A person who finds or steals a bearer instrument does not become the holder of it.

Example: X, the holder of an instrument payable to bearer, delivers it to Y and Y to Z and Z to P. The instrument is negotiated to P and he becomes the holder.

2. **By payable to order:** According to Section 48, a negotiable instrument can be negotiated by order for promissory note, bill of exchange or cheque payable to order.

   Negotiation by endorsement and delivery: A negotiable instrument payable to order is negotiable by the holder by endorsement and delivery thereof. Thus, for an instrument payable to order, two things are necessary—endorsement and delivery. If an instrument is endorsed but it is not delivered, then there is no negotiation.

Assignment

The negotiable instruments may also be transferred like goods by writing a separate deed of transfer. In such a case, they can be assigned even without endorsement. The Negotiable Instruments Act does not deal with this method of transfer of negotiable instruments. Section 130 of the Transfer of Property Act provides in case of transfer by assignment, the assignee acquires the rights of an assignor only. In case of assignment, the title of the assignee shall be the same as that of the assignor. He does not get the rights of a holder in due course.

Distinction between Negotiation and Assignment

From the table given below, it is clear that negotiation is a far better method of transferring the ownership of an instrument than assignment. It is for these reasons, most of the instruments are transferred by negotiation rather than by assignment.

S. No.	*Basis of Difference*	*Negotiation*	*Assignment*
1.	Consideration	When the instrument is negotiated, consideration is always presumed, but it is not so in case of assignment.	In the case of assignment, the burden of proving consideration will always lie on the assignee.
2.	Title	The title of the transferee (i.e., the holder in due course) is better than that of the transferor.	In the case of assignment of an instrument, the assignee does not get a better title than that of the assignor. The title of the assignee is subject to the defects in the title of the assignor.

S. No.	*Basis of Difference*	*Negotiation*	*Assignment*
3.	Notice of transfer	In the case of negotiation, notice of transfer is not necessary, that is, when the instrument is negotiated, the transferee need not give any notice to the debtor about the transfer.	Notice of assignment of a debt, in order to make the assignment complete and effective, is necessary to be given to the debtor.
4.	Formalities	In case of instruments payable to bearer, negotiation is effected by mere delivery. In case of instruments payable to order, negotiation is effected by endorsement and delivery.	It requires a written document duly signed by the transferor.
5.	Right to sue	Transferee of a negotiable instrument can sue the third party in his own name.	An assignee cannot sue in his own name.
6.	Act	It is covered within the provisions of Section 14 of the Negotiable Instruments Act.	This is covered under Section 130 of the Transfer of Property Act.

Delivery in Negotiation

According to Section 46, a negotiable instrument is not made, accepted or endorsed unless it is delivered to a proper person. The instrument should be delivered with the intention of transferring the ownership of the instrument. It is for this reason that when a cheque is given to B for safekeeping, B does not become its holder. If the holder of a negotiable instrument, payable to order, dies after endorsing it but before its delivery, then his legal representatives cannot negotiate such an instrument by delivery only.

Where an instrument is delivered conditionally or for a special purpose only, the transferee does not become its owner until the condition is fulfilled. However, where an instrument is negotiated to the holder in due course, the other parties to the instrument cannot escape liability on the ground that the delivery of the instrument was conditional or for a special purpose only.

Importance of Delivery in Negotiation

Delivery of the negotiable instrument is essential whether the instrument is payable to bearer or order for effecting the negotiation. The delivery must be voluntary and it is important that the object of delivery should be to pass the property in the instrument to the person to whom it is delivered to constitute that person the holder thereof. Delivery may be actual, constructive or conditional.

1. **Actual delivery:** It takes place when the instrument changes hands physically.
2. **Constructive delivery:** It takes place when the instrument is delivered to the agent, clerk or servant of the endorsee on his behalf or when the endorser, after endorsement, holds the instrument as an agent of the endorsee.

3. **Conditional delivery:** An instrument is delivered conditionally or for a special purpose only and the property in it does not pass to the transferee, even though it is endorsed to him. However, where an instrument is negotiated to a holder in due course, the other parties to the instrument cannot escape liability on the ground that the delivery of instrument was conditional or for a special purpose only.

There are two types of negotiable instruments—bearer and ordered.

1. **Bearer instruments:** The bearer instrument does not require the signature of the transferor for negotiation. The person who has taken it is a holder, and can sue on it in his own name. Where the bearer negotiates an instrument by mere delivery without putting his signature on it, and if the instrument is dishonoured, he is not liable to any party to the instrument because the transaction is the mere sale of the instrument.
2. **Ordered instruments:** In ordered instrument, signature of the transferor and at the same time, the delivery of the instrument is essential. A person has to sign on the instrument for the purpose of negotiation. The transferor is called endorser and the transferee is called endorsee. Therefore, endorsement is a legal formality which should be followed to transfer the rights over ordered instruments.

Endorsement or Indorsement

Endorsement is defined under Section 15, where the maker or holder of a negotiable instrument signs the same, otherwise than as such maker, for the purpose of negotiation, on the back or face thereof, or on a slip of paper annexed thereto or so signs for the same purpose a stamped paper intended to be completed as a negotiable instrument, he is said to endorse the same, and is called the 'endorser'.

Object of Endorsement

Following are the objects of endorsement:

1. At the time of endorsement, the endorser has a good title to the instrument.
2. The instrument is a genuine one.
3. All prior endorsements are genuine and regular.
4. The instruments will be duly paid at maturity.

Who May Endorse?

Following persons may endorse a negotiable instrument:

1. The payee of the instrument
2. The holder of the instrument
3. The maker signing it otherwise as such maker
4. The holder in due course of the instrument

Features of Endorsement

Following are the features of endorsement:

1. There is no proper procedure to be followed.
2. Endorsement may be either on face of instrument or on backside of it or in a separate sheet.
3. It requires the signature of holder or his agent.
4. The payee or the holder must sign in their exact name.
5. Endorsement should be by pen only.
6. It need not contain any complimentary words.
7. An illiterate can also endorse by thumb impression.
8. An endorsement is presumed to have been made in the order in which it appears.
9. Endorsement should be for full value.
10. If married woman endorses, her husband's name is to be included.
11. The endorsement will be completed by delivery.
12. In the case of signing on behalf of the holder or as an agent, it should be made clear by adding 'on behalf of' or any other similar phrase.
13. It can be endorsed any number of times.

Kinds of Endorsement

Endorsement can be of the following types.

1. **General or blank endorsement:** Where payee or endorsee merely signs his name on the back of the instrument without stating the name of the endorsee, it is known as blank or general endorsement. By the blank endorsement, a negotiable instrument even though payable to order becomes a bearer instrument for all purposes of negotiation. An endorsement in blank can be converted into an endorsement in full, and then it does not remain a bearer instrument.
2. **Special or full endorsement:** When an endorser adds to his signature a direction to pay the amount mentioned in the instrument to or to the order of a specified person, the endorsement is full. Thus, when endorsement is made by writing the words pay X or order, followed by the signature of the endorser, it is an endorsement in full. The endorser may not add the words or order and may use some other words to convey his intention, it is only the endorsee that can negotiate the instrument by endorsement.
3. **Partial endorsement:** A partial endorsement purports to transfer to the endorsee a part of the amount payable under the instrument. Section 56 prohibits endorsement for a partial value of the instrument. Thus, a partial endorsement is invalid. However, where amount of instrument has been partly paid, a note to that effect may be endorsed on the instrument, which may then be negotiated for the balance.
4. **Restrictive endorsement:** Restrictive endorsement, by express words, restricts the right of further negotiation of the instrument or entitles endorsee to receive amount of instrument. Such an endorsement may either prohibit further negotiation of the instrument or constitute an endorsee the agent of endorser for a special purpose or vests the title in the endorsee in trust for the use of some other person, for example:

a. Pay B only; Sd/A
b. Pay B for my use; Sd/A
c. Pay B or order for account of C; Sd/A

Under a restrictive endorsement, the endorsee acquires all the rights of endorser except the right to negotiation.

5. **Conditional or qualified endorsement:** When the endorser inserts some condition in his endorsement, it is known as conditional endorsement. It limits liability of the endorser by putting some condition. However, it does not restrict or prohibit the negotiability of instrument as in the case of restrictive endorsement. It imposes some conditions, which restricts the liability of the endorser. A conditional endorsement may take place in any of the following ways.
   a. **Sans recourse endorsement:** If the endorser wants to avoid liability as endorser, he can do so by adding appropriate words at the time of endorsement. He may endorse like this 'pay A or order sans recourse' or 'pay A or order at his own risk'.
   b. **Facultative endorsement:** Where an endorser by express words extends his liability or waives his right to which he is entitled, the endorsement is called facultative endorsement. For example, 'pay X or order, notice of dishonour waived' is an illustration of facultative endorsement. In this case, holder has waived notice of dishonour, but will remain liable for non-payment.
   c. **Sans frais endorsement:** *Sans frais* endorsement is where the endorser does not want that endorsee or any subsequent holder should incur any expense on his account on the instrument.
   d. **Liability dependent upon a contingency:** When an endorser makes his liability dependent upon the happening of a specified event, which may or may not happen. For instance, an endorser may write 'pay A or order on his marriage' or 'pay A or order on the arrival of X ship'. Here, the endorser will not be liable to make payment until the marriage takes place or the ship arrives as the case may be.

Once a Bearer Cheque Is Always a Bearer Cheque

The word 'bearer' means the instrument can be made originally payable to the bearer or it may be made bearer subsequently by the holder making a blank endorsement. With regard to bearer cheques, the rule is 'once a bearer cheque always a bearer cheque', which is originally expressed by the drawer himself to be payable to the bearer, the paying banker is fully protected if he makes the payment to the bearer or even if there is any forged or restrictive endorsement on the cheque. However, the payment must be a payment in due course.

The banker is not required to verify endorsements on cheques drawn payable to bearer because a bearer cheque does not require endorsement for the purpose of negotiation but only delivery. However, in practice, the banks in India insist upon the presenter to sign the cheque presented over the counter before payment is made. Such a signature, besides operating as a receipt, may even perhaps help the bank later in identifying the person to whom payment was made. This principle of once a bearer always a bearer has been introduced in Section 85(2) which provides that where a cheque is originally expressed to be payable to bearer, the drawee is discharged by payment in due course to the payee thereof, notwithstanding any endorsement whether in full or blank appearing thereon, and notwithstanding that any such endorsement purports to restrict or exclude further negotiation.

The Bombay High Court held that before the amendment was passed a bearer cheque could be converted into an order cheque by endorsement and Court held that where a hundi was drawn in favour of a payee or bearer and the payee endorsed it to a named person, it ceased to be a bearer hundi and have been nullified with the introduction of Section 85(2) in Negotiable Instrument Act. Which reads as 'Where a cheque is originally expressed to be payable to bearer, the drawee is discharged by payment in due course to the bearer thereof, notwithstanding any endorsement whether in full or in blank appearing, thereon, and notwithstanding that any such endorsement purports to restrict or exclude further negotiation.'

The crossing of a cheque serves as an instruction to drawee, that is, the paying bank that the payment is not to be made at the counter but through a bank account. The basic purpose behind crossing the cheque is to make it secure. Crossing of cheque does not affect the negotiation of the cheque. A crossed cheque can be negotiated in the same way as an uncrossed cheque. The effect of crossing is that holder cannot have payment at the counter. He has to get the proceeds collected through his bank account. Cheques may be classified as open cheques and crossed cheques.

1. **Open cheque:** Section 126 provides that open cheque is the one which has no crossing and which can be presented by holder to banker upon whom it is drawn and is paid over the counter of the bank. If the holder loses it, its finder may go to bank and get the payment. A banker is discharged by payment in due course of such cheques.
2. **Crossed cheque:** It is the one which has two transverse parallel lines marked across its face with or without the words like account payee/and company or any abbreviation thereof. Crossing is an instruction from drawer to the paying banker to pay the amount of a cheque through bank only and not directly to the person presenting it at the bank counter. A crossing is a direction to the paying banker to pay the money generally to a banker or a particular banker, as the case may be, and not to pay to holder across the counter. The crossing provides a protection and safeguard to the owner of the cheque. Crossing does not affect the negotiability of a cheque, except where the words 'not negotiable' are added.

   Crossing may be handwritten, stamped, printed or perforated. A crossed cheque is negotiable by delivery in case it is payable to bearer and by endorsement and delivery where it is payable to order. A crossed cheque can only be encased through bank of which payee of a cheque is customer. The holder of a cheque who has no account can also obtain the amount by endorsing in favour of some person who has an account with the banker. Sections 123 to 131 of the Act cover the provisions related to crossing of cheques.

   There are two types of crossing—general and special.

   a. **General crossing:** A cheque is generally crossed when two parallel transverse lines are marked across its face with or without any words. According to Section 123, general crossing means where a cheque bears across its face an addition of the words 'and company' or any abbreviation thereof, between two parallel transverse lines, or two parallel transverse lines simply, with or without the words 'not negotiable'. That addition shall be deemed a crossing or the cheques shall be deemed to be crossed generally. General crossing may be done by:

      i. Two simple transverse parallel lines
      ii. Transverse parallel lines with the words 'not negotiable'
      iii. Transverse parallel lines with the addition of the words 'and company' and 'not negotiable'

iv. The words 'and company' between two transverse parallel lines.
v. Abbreviation between transverse parallel lines.

In addition,

i. The crossing should be made across the face of the cheque.
ii. No crossing should be made on any other part of the cheque.

Two parallel transverse lines on the face of the cheque are essential for general crossing and the inclusion of words 'and company' or '& Co.' is immaterial. A banker who pays a generally crossed cheque otherwise than to a banker will be liable to the true owner for the loss sustained by him.

The effect of general crossing is that the cheque must be presented to the paying banker through any other banker and not by the payee himself at the counter.

b. **Special crossing:** If a cheque bears the name of a bank in between the transverse lines or sometimes without transverse lines, then it is called specially crossed. This crossing may also follow with some other words such as not negotiable. Section 124 provides,

> [W]here a cheque bears across its face an addition of the name of the banker, either with or without the words 'not negotiable' that addition shall be deemed a crossing and the cheques shall be deemed to be crossed specially, and to be crossed to that banker.

A special crossing requires the name of banker to be written across and on the face of the cheque. The two parallel transverse lines are not necessary for a special crossing, although they are usually drawn, nor the words 'and company' or other abbreviations since special crossing itself specifies the name of the banker. A cheque crossed specially will be paid only when it is presented with the bank name between the parallel lines. The banker, to whom the cheque is specially crossed, may appoint another banker as his agent for collection of such cheques. Thus, a special crossing makes cheques safer.

The different forms of special crossing are as follows:

i. Writing the name of the banker across the face of the cheque.
ii. Writing the name of the banker in between two transverse parallel lines, or writing the name of the bank in proximity to two transverse parallel lines.
iii. Writing the name of the banker and the words 'not negotiable' in between two transverse parallel lines across the face of the cheque.
iv. Adding the words 'account payee' along with the name of the banker or merely adding the words 'account payee' and the name of the banker in proximity to transverse parallel lines.

A specially crossed cheque is payable through the banker mentioned therein. Crossing authorized under this Act is a material part of the cheque. The banker has to give due significance to the crossing. It is the direction of the holder of the cheque to the paying banker.

Other Kinds of Crossing

1. **Double crossing:** When a cheque is crossed specially in favour of two banks, it is called double crossing. Generally, double crossing is invalid as the very purpose of the special crossing is frustrated by second one. However, there is one exception to this rule. The Negotiable Instruments Act permits two special crossing on a cheque provided the special crossing is in favour of banker acting as an agent of the first banker for collection. Section 127 provides that where a cheque is crossed specially by more than one banker, except when crossed to an agent for the purpose of collection, the banker on whom it is drawn shall refuse payment thereof. The banker shall not honour a cheque bearing a double crossing, unless the words 'agent for collection' are included in the special crossing.

2. **Not negotiable crossing:** Sections 123 and 124 permit that the words 'not negotiable' can be used in general and special crossings. However, Section 130 provides that the words 'not negotiable' in the crossing does not mean that it cannot be transferred, nor confer good title to the transferee. It takes away the important feature of negotiable instrument that is an exception to 'nemo dat quod non habet' that means no person can transfer a better title than what he himself possesses. Not negotiable crossed cheque can be transferred or assigned by the payee. The transferee gets the same rights as regards the payment as the transferor had. A person taking cheque subsequent to such crossing

cannot be a holder in due course. In the case of Great Western Railway Company vs. London and County Banking Co., it was held that banker was responsible to the true owner because he paid money to Huggins, who obtained the not negotiable crossed cheque and when he was not entitled to get the money. Anyone who takes a cheque marked 'not negotiable' takes it at his own risk.

3. **Account payee crossing:** The words 'account payee' or 'account payee only' are included to the crossing, general or special, on a cheque. These words have special significance and they are intended to make the cheque safer. Although these words are not recognized by the Negotiable Instruments Act, in practice, these words are being used. Along with these words, an instruction to the paying banker that he should collect the amount of the cheque for the benefit of the payee's account only which means to credit the amount to the account of the payee only and not for anybody else is also used. The payee banker need not take any special precaution except to confirm from the collecting banker that the payment is being secured for the benefit of the payee only if the cheque bears any endorsement.
4. **Opening of crossing:** Crossing is a material part of the cheque and, therefore, a holder cannot remove it. However, if the drawer desires to cancel the crossing, he can do so by writing 'I cancel the crossing please pay cash or by putting X' within transverse lines and adding his full signature and not initials. If any person cancels the crossing, which is already done by him, it is called opening of crossing. It is nothing but cancellation of crossing. In case of any doubt, the paying banker may confirm it with the drawer. If cash is paid at the counter of the bank to a person who is not entitled to the cheque, the bank will not be protected. Therefore, banker in his or her own interest should discourage such a practice.
5. **Restrictive crossing:** This is another kind of crossing, which is used by commercial and banking usage. In this type of crossing, the words 'A/c Payee' are added to the general or special crossing. The words 'A/c Payee' on a cheque is a direction to the collecting banker that the amount collected on the cheque is to be credited to the account of the payee. If he credits the proceeds to a different account, he is prima facie guilty of negligence and will be liable to the true owner for the cheque. It should, however, be noted that 'A/c Payee' cheques are not negotiable.

Who Can Cross the Cheques?

Section 125 provides that following persons can cross the cheque.

1. **Drawer:** The drawer can draw all types of crossing, since he is the author of the cheque.
2. **Holder:** Holder can cross any type of crossing, if he receives a cheque which is not crossed. When a cheque is generally crossed, he may add the words 'not negotiable'. Where the cheque is uncrossed, the holder may cross it generally or specially. Where it is crossed generally, he may cross it specially. Where it is crossed generally or specially, he may add the words 'not negotiable'.
3. **Banker:** A banker can cross a cheque like a holder. However, banker may cross a cheque second time that is called double crossing. Generally, the crossing should be once, and there should not be two crossings, but only the banker can enjoy the privilege of double crossing. Where a cheque is crossed specially, the banker to whom it is crossed may again cross it, specially, to another banker or his agent for collection.

Types of Cheques

The cheques can be divided into following categories.

1. **Stale cheque or outdated cheque:** After an expiry of three months from the date of its issue, a cheque becomes outdated cheque or stale cheque. A banker may also accept a stale cheque, if a customer gives consent for that cheque. The cheque must be produced before expiry of three months, otherwise the person claiming money over the cheque will be losing his right to get the money. In the case of G. Balkrishna vs. the Official Assignee, Madras, the High Court held that the holder cannot have recourse to the drawer, if he failed to present the cheque within the time allowed. As per Reserve Bank of India guidelines, with effect from 1 April 2012, the validity period of cheques, demand drafts, pay orders and banker's cheques is reduced from six months to three months, from the date of issue of the instrument.
2. **Ante-dated cheque:** A drawer while drawing a cheque gives the date in cheque prior to the date on which it is drawn. It is drawn prior to the date of drawing which means on a back date. It is called ante-dated cheque. A banker can accept such a cheque, if it does not exceed three months from the date of issue on it.
3. **Mutilated cheque:** A cheque which is cut into many pieces or defaced due to any other reason is called mutilated cheque. The drawee bank should see while honouring a cheque whether it is mutilated, cancelled or torn. If the cheque is torn into two or many pieces, it should be returned with the remark 'mutilated cheque'; if the bank is satisfied that the mutilated cheque gets the original shape of the instrument, it may accept the cheque. In the case of HSBC vs. Loo Lee Shi, it was held that if a cheque is torn accidentally, either by the drawer or by the holder, the drawer must confirm it.
4. **Post-dated cheque:** When the drawer of a cheque gives the date in the cheque later or after the date on which it is drawn, it is known as post-dated cheque. The banker must accept the post-dated cheque only after the ostensible date given in the cheque. If he accepts before, then he has to face many consequences.

Consequences in Case of Post-dated Cheques

1. **Countermanding:** Customer may stop the payment of the cheques which he issued by giving a notice to the banker. It amounts to countermanding of cheque. Therefore, there is a possibility of countermanding the post-dated cheque before ostensible date.
2. **Insufficiency of funds:** By accepting the post-dated cheques, before the ostensible date, there may be a possibility of dishonouring the subsequent cheques drawn by the customer before the ostensible date. For such dishonour, the banker is answerable to the customer.
3. **Death, insanity, insolvency of the customer:** In case of death or insanity of the customer, the banker has to face many difficulties, if he accepts post-dated cheques before that ostensible date, and customer dies or becomes an insolvent or insane person after payment by the banker. Then banker will be responsible for such payment.
4. **No payment in due course:** Payment of post-dated cheque is not a payment in due course. Therefore, banker cannot get any protection.

5. **Garnishee order:** Banker has to face another problem, if he pays over post-dated cheque before the date given in the cheque. If he receives an order from the court for freezing the customer's account before the ostensible date, that order will affect the whole amount in the customer's account in spite of the payment over the post-dated cheque.

TEST QUESTIONS

1. What is meant by negotiation? How is it effected and in what way does it differ from an ordinary assignment?
2. 'Once a bearer instrument always a bearer instrument.' Comment.
3. What is endorsement and explain different types of it?
4. Explain the meaning and effect of (a) endorsement in blank, (b) special endorsement, (c) restrictive endorsement and (d) partial endorsement.
5. What is the difference between negotiation and assignment?
6. What is cheque and explain different kinds of cheques?
7. What is crossing of cheques? Give different kinds of crossing of cheques?
8. Write a note on the following:
   a. Double crossing
   b. Not negotiable crossing
   c. Account payee crossing
   d. Restrictive crossing
   e. Consequences of post-dated cheques

PRACTICAL PROBLEMS

1. A bill is drawn payable to A or order. A loses the bill and X who finds it, forges A's signature and endorses it to B, who takes it for value and in good faith. Does B acquire any title to the bill? Discuss.
   Hint. No. There is complete absence of title.
2. A draws a cheque in favour of a minor M, who endorses it in favour of C. The cheque is dishonoured by the bank when presented by C. State the position of C.
   Hint. C can sue A, the drawer, but not M, the minor.
3. A cheque is drawn payable to 'B or order' and delivered to B in payment of a debt. B's agent, without having any authority to endorse, endorses the cheque 'per pro' for B and obtains payment of money and misappropriates it. Is the banker discharged by payment in due course? State reasons.
   Hint. Yes. Section 85(1) provides protection to a banker.
4. A cheque is payable to 'M or order'. It is stolen and the thief forges M's signature and presents it to the banker, who makes the payment in due course. Can M recover the amount from the banker?
   Hint. M cannot recover the amount since it is a payment in due course.
5. X is the holder of a bill of exchange. X endorses it in blank and delivers it to Y. Y endorses it in full to Z or order. Z without endorsement transfers the bill of exchange to F. Discuss the rights of F.
   Hint. X is entitled to proceed against drawer, acceptor and F but not against Y or Z.

27
CHAPTER

Customer–Banker Relationship and Dishonour of a Negotiable Instrument

Learning Objectives

- To understand protection to a paying banker and statutory protection
- To understand protection to a collecting banker and statutory protection.
- To understand protection to dishonour of a negotiable instrument.
- To understand marking of cheques for payment
- To understand circumstances when a banker may dishonour a cheque
- To understand the meaning of material alteration
- To understand the process in case of dishonour of a cheque

The relationship between a banker and a customer depends on the contract signed by them and the different services provided by the bank. So the relationship between a banker and a customer is a transactional relationship. According to Section 3, the word 'banker' includes any person acting as a banker and any post office savings bank. The Reserve Bank of India has stipulated certain norms, 'Know Your Customer' (KYC) guidelines, for opening an account, and banks have to strictly follow them. Section 131 provides that when a banker receives payment of a crossed cheque in good faith and without negligence for a customer, the bank does not incur any liability to the true owner of the cheque by reason only of having received such payment. It obviously means that to become a customer, an account relationship is must. An account relationship is a contractual relationship. The relationship between a banker and a customer confers certain rights and obligations on the part of both the banker and the customer. However, the personal relationship between a bank and its customers is a long-lasting relationship. The banker–customer relationship can be classified as debtor–creditor, creditor–debtor, bank as a trustee, bailee–bailor, lessor–lessee, agent–principal, as a custodian and as a guarantor.

Circumstances When a Banker May Dishonour a Customer's Cheque

A banker may dishonour a customer's cheque in the following cases:

1. Where the banker does not have sufficient funds to the credit of the customer.
2. Where the cheque is not duly presented.
3. Where the cheque is post-dated. In such a case, if the bank makes payment before the date of the cheque, and the customer countermands payment, or issues another cheque bearing a prior date and it is dishonoured because the funds have depleted, the bank will be liable to the customer in damages.
4. Where the cheque has become stale (i.e., has not been presented for six months from the date of its issue).
5. Where the cheque is ambiguous or materially altered.
6. Where an account is in joint names of a few persons, but they have not all signed the cheque.
7. Where the customer's signature does not tally with his specimen signature.
8. Where the cheque is mutilated to make it imperfect.
9. Where the cheque is of doubtful legality.
10. Where the cheque is presented at a branch other than the one where the customer has the account.
11. Where the funds to the credit of the customer are not applicable to the payment of the customer's cheque, for example, when the money is held in trust.

Reasons for Dishonouring a Customer's Cheque

A banker must dishonour his customer's cheques in the following cases:

1. When the banker receives notice of the customer's insanity.
2. When a grantee receives notice of the customer's insanity.
3. When the customer or the banker gives notice to the other party to close the account.
4. When the customer gives notice of assignment (or transfer) of the credit balance of the account. When the banker suspects, or has reason to believe that the title of the person presenting the cheque is defective.
5. When the customer becomes insolvent or an order of adjudication has been made against him.
6. When the customer countermands payment (i.e., asks the bank not to honour a cheque).
7. When the banker receives notice of the customer's death, but if the banker pays a cheque before he receives notice of his customer's death, the payment is valid.
8. When the holder gives a notice of loss of cheque to the banker.

Material Alteration

Any alteration made in an instrument which affects legal validity of the instrument or which changes the rights and responsibilities of the parties to the instrument is called material alteration. Any material alteration of a negotiable instrument renders it void. Any alteration which is made by an endorsee discharges his endorser from all liability to him in respect of the consideration thereof. Material alteration is covered within the provisions of Sections 20, 49, 86 and 125 of the Negotiable Instruments Act. Examples of material alteration include alterations of date, time, place, amount, parties, interest rate, converting an order instrument into a bearer instrument, and affixing more stamps to the instrument. However, law does not consider following alterations as material alteration:

1. Filling the blanks in an inchoate instrument
2. Converting blank endorsement into special endorsement
3. Crossing of a cheque

Exceptions: The following alterations are not considered as material alteration:

1. If it is made before issuing
2. If it is done for correction
3. If it is made to carry on the intention of the drawer
4. If it is done with the consent of the parties
5. Where it is immaterial alteration

FORGERY OF A CUSTOMER'S SIGNATURE

Forgery is one where one person signs on an instrument as if the customer has signed it, in order to give effect over cheque. It is nothing but one person signing another's name on an instrument without his consent. If a forged cheque comes before a banker for acceptance and he knows that the customer's signature is forged, he must reject the payment. It is the duty of a banker to have vouched with the customer's signature and to verify the same before acceptance. Therefore, in this respect, the law expects certain responsibilities or duties from a banker. In Kepitigalla Rubber Estates vs. The National Bank of India Limited, one officer forged the signature of a director on two cheques and the banker paid the amount. It was decided that the banker was liable because he failed to detect the forgery of the customer's signature.

Further, it is the duty of a customer also not to be negligent in keeping his chequebook. His negligence should not be a proximate cause of loss of a cheque or forgery. In the case of Greenwood vs. Martin's Bank, Greenwood's wife forged the signature of her husband and the payment was made to his wife. Greenwood came to know of this fact, but after the death of his wife he claimed money from the bank. The court rejected his claim because he failed in his duty to bring forgery to the notice of the banker.

MATURITY AND DAYS OF GRACE

A promissory note or a bill of exchange may be payable on demand or a specified date, or after a specified period. Section 22 provides that the maturity of a promissory note or bill of exchange is the date on which it falls due, whereas every instrument payable otherwise than 'on demand' is entitled to three days of grace. Three days of grace were originally allowed as a gratuitous favour to the debtor. The instruments which are *not entitled* to days of grace are as follows:

1. A cheque
2. A bill or note payable 'at sight' or 'on presentment', or 'on demand'
3. A bill or note in which no time is mentioned

The above instruments are intended for on-demand delivery, which means that they are payable on demand. The instruments which are *entitled* to 'days of grace' are as follows:

1. A bill or note payable on a specified day
2. A bill or note payable 'after sight'
3. A bill or note payable at a certain period after date
4. A bill or note payable at a certain period after the happening of a certain event

In case of bills or notes entitled to days of grace, the ascertainment of date of maturity becomes important. All these instruments must be presented for payment on the last day of a grace. Where an instrument is payable by instalments, each instalment is payable three days after the day fixed for the payment of each instalment.

Example: A bill dated 1 January 2019 is made payable four months after the date. It falls due on 4 May 2019.

Protection to a Banker

Protection to a banker is classified into two categories: protection to a paying banker and protection to a collecting banker.

Paying Banker and Statutory Protection

The Negotiable Instruments Act protects a paying banker and treats it as statutory protection.

The Risk of Paying Banker

If a banker pays money analogous and of wrong instruments even in the circumstances a reasonable prudent person might have misled, the banker is not entitled to charge it to the customer's account because he failed to follow the customer's mandate. Sometimes, it amounts to the offence of conversion against the true owner. Then the banker should face double risk in this respect. So protection is provided to the paying banker. Based on the nature of the protection available to the banker, it may be divided mainly under three points:

1. **Statutory protection in case of an open instrument:** An open instrument is one which is not crossed. Some protection is provided to the banker for the payment over an open instrument. Here, the protection given to the banker may be divided into two categories:

a. **Protection in case of bearer instruments:** Section 82(c) protects the banker in case of cheques payable to the bearer or endorsement in blank (become bearer), provided the payment is made as payment in due course. The payment over the forged cheques is not a payment in due course, and there is no protection.
b. **Protection in case of order instruments:** Cheques are of two types: bearer cheques and order cheques. Transfer of order cheques requires endorsement. So a banker must observe every time the signature of the endorser and then pay the amount. The protection of the paying banker in this respect is as follows:
   i. **Where the endorsement is forged or unauthorized:** Protection is given to a paying banker for the payment over the forged enforced cheques. Section 85(1) and 85(2) protect the interest of a paying banker if that payment amounts to payment in due course. The same protection is also applicable to a bank draft under Section 85A of the Negotiable Instruments Act.
   ii. **Where the endorsement is irregular or absent:** In India, there is no statutory protection to the unendorsed or the irregular endorsed instrument. But in England, the statutory protection to the paying banker over these instruments is recognized under Section 60 of the Bills of Exchange Act.

2. **Statutory protection in case of a crossed instrument:** Sections 126 and 128 give the statutory protection. The banker's right would be protected for the payment over a crossed cheque if the payment is made strictly in accordance with the crossing. So the banker while paying a crossed instrument must follow the direction given in the crossings, otherwise the banker will not get any protection.
   Obliterating of crossing: Section 87 protects interest of a paying banker when the banker has made a payment over the instruments where crossing is obliterating. To get this protection, the banker must satisfy that obliterating of crossing should be a non-apparent one and the payment must be the payment in due course.
3. **Statutory protection in case of a materially altered instrument:** Section 89 protects the interest of a paying banker when he pays the amount over the material altered instruments. However, material alteration discharges the liability of each banker over the cheques. He can reject the payment over the instruments materially altered. If the banker pays the amount over materially altered instruments, his interest would be protected, provided the following conditions are satisfied.
   1. When such alteration is not apparent
   2. When the banker has made the payment in due course and
   3. When the banker is liable to that cheque

However, whether the instrument is altered or not is a question of law decided by the court, which depends much upon the circumstances of each case. In the case of Tanjore Permanent Bank Ltd vs. S. R. Rangachari, the statutory protection was rejected to the paying banker because of the fact that alterations were material and apparent and were not authorized by the drawer.

However, the customer must also take reasonable care over the instrument. He should not allow any person by his negligence to alter the instrument. If it is there, he has to bear the loss caused to him due to any alteration.

Collecting Banker and Statutory Protection

Even though there is no legal obligation, most of the banks collect cheques and bills as an agency service. Sir John Paget explained that the collection of cheques, whether crossed or uncrossed, is one of the functions of a banker. In this role, the banker is referred as the collecting banker. While collecting the cheques on behalf of his customer, the banker may come across with many difficulties. To overcome these difficulties, a statutory protection is given to the collecting banker in Sections 131 and 131A of the Negotiable Instruments Act.

Statutory protection: Section 131 protects a collecting banker against fraudulent endorsements on cheques collected by him. A banker who has, in good faith and without negligence, received payment for a customer of a cheque, crossed generally or especially, shall not, in case the title to the cheque proves defective, incur any liability to the true owner of the cheque by reason only of having received such payment. However, if the banker does not enjoy any protection under Section 131, he becomes liable for the conversion of the cheque or instrument. However, Section 131A extends the protection to the collection over the draft.

Explanation I: A banker receives payment of a crossed cheque for a customer within the meaning of Section 131 of the Act, notwithstanding that he credits his customer's account with the amount of the cheque before receiving the payment thereof.

Explanation II: It shall be the duty of the banker who receives payment based on an electronic image of a truncated cheque held with him, to verify the prima facie genuineness of the cheque to be truncated and any fraud, forgery or tempering apparent on the face of the instrument that can be verified with the due diligence and ordinary care.

Thus, in order to enjoy the protection under Section 131, a banker must satisfy the following conditions:

1. He must have received the payment in his capacity as an agent of the customer but not as the holder for value.
2. He must have acted in good faith and without negligence.
3. This protection is for crossed cheques only and not for open cheques.
4. The banker must have received the payment for the customer only.

NEGLIGENCE OF A COLLECTING BANKER

Section 131 provides that there should not be any negligence on the part of the collecting banker to invoke the protection. Negligence indicates lack of care, which is necessarily to be taken in any circumstance. In the case of Blyth vs. Birmingham Waterworks Co., the court held that negligence is the omission to do something which a reasonable prudent person would do or doing something which a prudent and reasonable person would not do.

Examples of negligence: A collecting banker may not be able to take the statutory protection in the following circumstances:

1. **Opening an account without proper references:** Any bank is under the obligation not to open an account for a new customer without obtaining proper references.
2. **Failure to obtain the employment particulars of the customer:** It is the duty of a banker to know the particulars of the customer, failure of which amounts negligence on his part.
3. **Failure to follow up the references where the referee is unknown:** In the case of St John's Hampstead vs. Barclays Bank Ltd, a customer opened an account in a false name. He gave his true name as reference and produced an excellent reference. The bank lost the protection because of the acceptance of reference of a stranger.

4. **Where the significance of crossing is missing:** If the cheque is crossed to some other banker other than himself, he should refuse to collect it. Further, he should not ignore the instructions appearing as part of crossing.
5. **In the case of not-negotiable crossing:** The bankers are not held negligent merely because of the collection of not-negotiable crossing instruments. In the case of Crumpling vs. London Joint Stock Bank Ltd, the court held that a 'not-negotiable' crossing is merely one factor among others to be considered to decide about banker's negligence. It was observed the mere taking of a 'not-negotiable' cheque ought not to be held to be the evidence of negligence.
6. **Where the instruction on the face of the instrument is disregarded:** This is the most important type of negligence. Sometimes the form of the instrument itself conveys the warning that the customer is either commuting a breach of trust or misappropriating money belonging to somebody else. This can happen in many ways:
   a. Collection of cheques of the principal for credit of account of the agent
   b. Collection of cheques payable to the firm for credit of partner's account
   c. Collection of cheques payable to the company for credit of account of a director or a principal officer of the company
   d. Collection of cheques payable to a public official for credit of personal account of the officer
7. **Disregarding the status of a customer's account:** In the case of Guardians of St John's Hampstead vs. Barclays Bank Ltd, it was held that the collecting banker cannot shut his eyes to the transaction concerning an account incomparable with the customer's circumstances in life known to the banker.
8. **Negligence in the collection of cheques payable to third parties:** When third-party cheques are given to a bank for collection, the banker must fully enquire where other connecting circumstances indicate the possible misuse of such cheques.

Marking of Cheques for Payment

Marking of a cheque is nothing but certifying the cheque by any authorized person in a bank by writing words 'Approved' or 'Good' for payment. It requires the signature of the certifying officer of the bank. It means that at the time of marking, the cheque has satisfied all its requirements and it is properly submitted and the customer is having sufficient amount in his account to meet this cheque. Further, the following persons may request the banker to mark the cheque:

1. Marking at the request of the customer
2. Marking at the instance of the holder
3. Marking by the banker

Dishonour of a Negotiable Instrument

Dishonour of a negotiable instrument means when the drawee of the instrument does not accept or make the payment of it. Dishonour of negotiable instruments is of two types:

1. Dishonour by non-acceptance
2. Dishonour by non-payment

Promissory notes and cheques may be dishonoured by non-payment only, whereas bills of exchange may be dishonoured by non-payment or by non-acceptance, as they require acceptance from drawees. When a promissory note or bill of exchange or cheque is rejected by the drawee for payment, then it amounts to dishonour of instrument. This means that the debtor of the instrument denies his liabilities.

Types

Dishonour by Non-acceptance

According to Section 91, a bill of exchange is said to be dishonoured by non-acceptance when the drawee or one of the several drawees not being partners makes default in accepting the bill when being duly required to accept the bill. Where the drawee is incompetent to contract, or acceptance is qualified, the bill may be treated as dishonoured. Dishonour by non-acceptance will take under following circumstances:

1. When the drawee refuses to accept
2. When the drawee becomes incompetent
3. When the drawee gives qualified acceptance
4. When the drawee's presentation is excused

Dishonour by Non-payment

According to Section 92, a promissory note, bill of exchange or cheque is said to be dishonoured by non-payment when the maker of the note, acceptor of the bill or drawee of the cheque makes default in payment upon being duly required to pay the same. It is very common in the case of every instrument that when any person who is required to pay the negotiable instrument but fails to pay the money to the person entitled, then it amounts to dishonoured by non-payment. Notice of dishonour should be served to the party responsible for payment of the instrument.

Notice by Whom and to Whom

According to Section 93, when a negotiable instrument is dishonoured by non-acceptance or non-payment, the holder of the instrument or some party thereto who remains liable thereon must give notice that the instrument has been so dishonoured to all other parties, by whom he seeks to make jointly liable thereon.

Notice by Whom

The notice of dishonour is to be given by a person who wants to make some prior party liable on the instrument. The notice may be given either by the holder or by any party to the instrument who is entitled to get the money.

Example: A is the payee of a bill of exchange which he endorses to B, B endorses to C, C to D and D to E. E is the holder of the bill, but the parties liable on the bill towards the holder are the accepter of the bill, the drawer and the endorsee, that is, A, B, C and D. If E presents the bill and on the due date bill is dishonoured, E, the holder, may give notice to all, that is, A, B, C and D.

In the case of the Union bank vs. Dinanath, court held that holder's right of enforcing the liability is only against those who are otherwise liable under the law and to whom the notice has been given. It was not intended to enlarge the holder's right so as to enable him to claim damages.

Notice to Whom

When a negotiable instrument is dishonoured by the maker, acceptor or drawee, the notice of dishonour is to be given to all the other parties who are liable towards the instrument. According to Section 94, a notice should be given to an authorized agent, the legal representative when the drawee or endorsee is dead, official assignees or receiver when the party to whom notice is required to be given has been declared as an insolvent.

Mode of Notice

Section 94 provides that a notice may be oral or in case of written, a notice must be sent to the person to whom it is given, either in express terms or by reasonable intendment, that the instrument has been dishonoured. It must be delivered at the place of business or at the place of residence of the party for whom it is intended. However, it is to be noted that miscarriage of notice when sent by post will not invalid it. In Nenu Ram vs. Shri Kishan, the court held that a notice of dishonour must be given within a reasonable time and a notice given four years after the dishonour is not covered within the reasonable time.

When a Notice of Dishonour Is Not Necessary

According to Section 98, no notice is required to be given under the following circumstances:

1. When it is dispensed with by the party entitled thereto
2. In order to charge the drawer when he has countermanded payment
3. When the party charged could not suffer damage for want of notice
4. When the party entitled to notice cannot after due search be found; or the party bound to give notice is, for any other reason, unable without any fault of his own to give it
5. To charge the drawers when the acceptor is also a drawer
6. In the case of a promissory note, which is not negotiable
7. When the party entitled to notice, knowing the facts, promises unconditionally to pay the amount due on the instrument

NOTING

Section 99 provides that when a promissory note or bill of exchange has been dishonoured by non-acceptance or non-payment, the holder may cause such dishonour to be noted by a notary public upon the instrument, or upon a paper attached thereto, or partly upon each. The holder may sue the other party for non-payment, but before he does that, he may get the fact of dishonour authenticated by noting by a notary public. In such a case, the notary makes formal demand upon the drawee or acceptor for acceptance or payment as the case may be. On refusal by the drawee or acceptor, he makes noting on the bill. 'Noting, therefore, means the recording of the fact of dishonour by a notary public on a dishonoured bill, or upon a paper attached thereto, or partly upon each.'

Noting must contain the following:

1. The fact of dishonour
2. The date of dishonour
3. The reasons, if any, assigned for such dishonour
4. If the instrument has not been expressly dishonoured, the reasons why the holder treats it as dishonoured
5. The amount notary has charged

Noting must be made by the notary within a reasonable time after dishonour. Noting is not compulsory in the case of an inland bill or note. The omission to get the instrument noted does not, in any way, affect the rights of the holder thereon.

PROTEST

The holder of a promissory note, or bill of exchange, which has been dishonoured by non-acceptance or non-payment, may, within a reasonable time, cause such dishonour to be noted and certified by a notary public according to Section 100. Such a certificate is called a protest. A protest is a formal notary certificate attesting the dishonour of a bill of exchange or promissory note. Section 101 provides that a protest must contain the following:

1. The instrument or a literal transcript of the instrument
2. The name of the person for whom and against whom the instrument has been protested
3. The fact and reasons for dishonour
4. The place and time of dishonour
5. The signature of the notary public
6. In case of acceptance for honour or of a payment for honour, the name of the person accepting or paying and the name of the person for whose honour it is accepted or paid

Protest for Better Security

Section 100 provides that when the acceptor of a bill of exchange has become insolvent, or his credit has been publicly impeached, before the maturity of the bill, the holder may, within a reasonable time, have the bill protested for better security of the acceptor through a notary public. If the acceptor refuses to give a better security, the holder may, within a reasonable time, cause such facts to be noted and certified by notary public. Such a certificate is called a protest for better security. It should, however, be noted that the acceptor is not bound to give such security.

Liability in Case of Dishonour of a Cheque

Till recently, the drawer of a dishonoured cheque was subject to civil liability only, in respect of the money due on a cheque, for whatsoever reasons. However, Sections 138–142, which have been inserted in the Negotiable Instruments Act, 1881, provide for conditions, procedure and punishment for criminal liability of the drawer:

1. Dishonour of cheque for insufficiency of funds and so on (under Section 138)
2. Presumptions in favour of the holder (under Section 139)
3. Defence which may not be allowed in any prosecution under Section 138 (under Section 140)
4. Offences by companies (under Section 141)
5. Cognizance of offence (under Section 142)

Dishonour of a Cheque for Insufficiency of Funds and so on

According to Section 138, where any cheque is drawn by a person on an account maintained by him with a banker for the payment of any amount of money to another person from that account for the discharge of any debt, either in part or in full, is returned by the bank unpaid, either because the amount of money standing to the credit of that account is insufficient to honour the cheque or it exceeds the amount arranged to be paid from that account by an agreement made with that bank, such person shall be deemed to have committed an offence and shall, without prejudice to any other provisions of this Act, be punished with imprisonment for a term which may extended to two years or a fine which may extend to twice of the amount of the cheque or both. This section further provides that it shall not apply unless:

1. The cheque has been presented to the bank within a period of three months from the date on which it is drawn or within the period of its validity, whichever is earlier
2. The payee or the holder in due course of the cheque, as the case may be, makes a demand for the payment of the said amount of money by giving a notice in writing to the drawer of the cheque within 30 days of the receipt of the information by him from the bank regarding the return of the cheque as unpaid
3. The drawer of such cheque fails to make the payment of the said amount of money to the payee or as the case may be to the holder in due course of the cheque within 15 days from the date of the receipt of the said notice

The above aspects of Section 138 for fixing the criminal liability of the drawer are explained by the court in the case of Canbank Financial Services Ltd vs. Gitanjli Motors Ltd & Ors, which held that the dishonour of the cheque in itself is not an offence under Section 138 of the Act. To come in the purview of this section, certain other requirements have to be fulfilled. These are as follows:

1. The cheque has been issued in discharge of a debt or other liability in whole or in part.
2. The cheque should be presented to the paying banker in time, that is, within three months or its specific validity period, whichever is earlier.

3. The dishonour of cheque should be because of insufficiency of funds only—the amount of money standing to the credit of the account is insufficient or that the amount of cheque exceeds the amount arranged to be paid from that account by an agreement with the bank.
4. The payee or holder in due course should have given notice in writing to the drawer demanding payment within 30 days of his receiving information of dishonour.
5. The drawer can make payment within 15 days of the receipt of the notice; if he fails to do so, prosecution can take place.
6. The complaint can be made within 1 month of the cause in action arising (i.e., expiry of 15 days' time given to the drawer to make payment).
7. No court lower to that of metropolitan magistrate or judicial magistrate of first class will try the offence.

Section 139 provides that the holder of the cheque has the right to receive the amount of the cheque for the discharge of loan or debt in full or in part.

Section 140 further provides that the drawer of a dishonoured cheque cannot defend himself on the ground that he had no reason to believe when he issued the cheque that the cheque may be dishonoured on presentation on account of insufficiency of funds.

Section 141 provides that if a dishonoured cheque is drawn on behalf of a company, firm or association of individuals, every person who was in charge of and was responsible to the company or the firm for the conduct of its business, at the time the offence was committed, and also the company, shall be deemed to be guilty of the offence. However, if any such person proves that the offence was committed without his knowledge or that he had exercised all due diligence to prevent the commission of such an offence, he will not be liable to punishment.

It is to be noted that the complaint is to be lodged with the criminal court and not with police. The cheque should pertain to the debt which is alive and not barred by limitation. The complaint is to be lodged against the person who has issued the cheque. If the cheque is issued by a company, then the person means every person who is responsible for the conduct of the business of the company.

TEST QUESTIONS

1. Is presentment of a negotiable instrument for acceptance necessary in all cases? State the circumstances under which presentment for acceptance is excused.
2. What is the effect of non-presentment for acceptance of a bill? When is presentment for acceptance not necessary?
3. Is acceptance of a bill of exchange necessary? By whom and how can a bill be accepted? Explain.
4. Explain the meaning of material alteration in a negotiable instrument. What is the effect of such alteration? Give examples.
5. How are the parties to a negotiable instrument discharged? What is meant by dishonour by non-acceptance and dishonour by non-payment?
6. Define 'acceptance for honour'. Can a drawee of a bill of exchange accept it for honour?
7. What is 'payment for honour'? State the essential conditions for a valid payment for honour.

8. Under what circumstances a banker (a) may refuse and (b) must refuse payment of a cheque?
9. Under what circumstances is a paying banker protected? Explain with hint of examples. What are the privileges of a collecting banker?
10. What do you understand by the dishonour of a cheque due to insufficiency of funds? What is the process in case of such dishonour of a cheque?

PRACTICAL PROBLEMS

1. A cheque crossed 'not negotiable' was drawn in favour of a firm. X, one of the partners, to defraud his co-partner Y, endorsed the cheque to Z, who cashed it. Can X recover the amount from Z? State reasons.
   Hint. Yes. Z's title is vitiated on account of the defective title of the transferor X.
2. A draws a bill of exchange on B for ₹15,000 payable to the order of A. B accepts the bill but subsequently dishonours it by non-payment. A sues B on the bill. B proves that it was accepted for value as to ₹5,000 and as an accommodation to the plaintiff as to the residue. Can A recover ₹10,000?
   Hint. No. Consideration is absent in part. A can recover only ₹5,000.
3. A steals B's chequebook from his drawer and then forges B's signature on a cheque and draws money from B's banker. A then disappears. Who will bear the loss, B or the banker?
   Hint. Since the drawer's signature is forged, no statutory protection can be claimed by the banker. The payment is not payment in due course. The banker has to bear this loss.
4. H is the holder in due course of a bill, of which A is the acceptor. D, the drawer of the bill, is fictitious. Can A escape his liability to H?
   Hint. A cannot escape the liability, since H is the holder in due course.
5. A cheque payable to a company was endorsed by a director to himself in his capacity as the director and he paid his personal account with the bank for collection. The bank received the money and allowed him to withdraw. Is the bank liable to the company for conversion of its cheque?
   Hint. Yes.
6. X, by means of fraud, obtained from Y a cheque crossed 'not negotiable' and got it cashed at a bank other than the drawee bank. Y sues the bank for conversion. Is the bank liable for conversion?
   Hint. The transferor had a defective title, and the cheque being crossed 'not negotiable', the bank also got a defective title. The bank is, therefore, liable for conversion.
7. A cheque is drawn payable to B or order. It is stolen and B's endorsement is forged. The banker pays the cheque in due course. (a) Is the banker discharged from liability? (b) Would it make any difference if the drawer's signature is forged?
   Hint. (a) Yes. (Section 85(1)); (b) If the drawer's signature is forged, the banker cannot debit the account of the customer. (Section 10)
8. A crossed cheque for a large amount drawn by a firm on their account with Y bank was from time to time delivered to B, a clerk of the firm, for payment to their creditors. B forged the endorsement of the payees and paid the cheque into his personal account with the same bank and drew the money out. Can Y bank debit the account of the firm?
   Hint. Yes. (Section 85)

Appendix

Important Key Words for Revision

UNITS I AND II: INDIAN CONTRACT ACT, 1872

1. **Acceptance:** Acceptance is the expression of assent for the proposal/offer.
2. **Agency:** Agency is the legal relationship which exists between an agent and his principal to bring the principal into legal relationship with third parties.
3. **Agency by ratification:** It implies the adoption or recognition by the principal of an act made by an agent on his behalf but without his authority.
4. **Agency coupled with interest:** An agency is said to be coupled with interest when it is created for the purpose of securing some benefit to the agent over and above his remuneration.
5. **Agent:** An agent is a person employed to do any act for another or to represent another in dealing with third persons.
6. **Alien enemy:** Alien enemy is the citizen of a country at war with the country in which he lives.
7. **Anticipatory breach:** A breach of contract occurring before the due date of performance is known as anticipatory breach of contract.
8. **Appropriation of payments:** Appropriation of payments means application of payments.
9. **Assignment of contract:** Assignment of contract means transfer of contractual rights or liability by a party to the contact to some other person who is not a party to the contract.
10. **Auctioneer:** An auctioneer is an agent appointed by a seller to sell his goods by public auction for a reward generally in the form of a commission.
11. **Bailment:** Bailment is a delivery of goods by one person to another for a specific purpose. The goods are delivered on a condition that they shall be returned to the owner after the fulfilment of the purpose.
12. **Bilateral mistake:** Bilateral mistake occurs when both the parties to a contract are at a mistake about the facts which are essential to the agreement.
13. **Breach of contract:** Breach of a contract means failure or refusal of a party to perform his obligations under a contact without any lawful excuse.
14. **Coercion:** It implies the use of force by one party or using a threat to compel a person to enter into a contract.

15. **Consideration:** Consideration is something in return for the promise. Both parties must give and take something.
16. **Contingent contract:** When the performance of a contract becomes due only after the happening or non-happening of some uncertain event.
17. **Continuing guarantee:** A guarantee which extends to a series of transactions and is not exhausted by or confined to a single credit transaction is called a continuing guarantee.
18. **Contract of guarantee:** A contract of guarantee is a contract to perform the promise or discharge the liability of a third person in case of his default.
19. **Contract of indemnity:** A contract of indemnity is a contract in which one person promises to protect or compensate the other for the loss suffered by him due to the conduct of the promisor or any other person.
20. **Convict:** A convict is a person who has been held guilty and convicted of an offence.
21. **Counter-offer:** Counter-offer means an offer in response to an offer.
22. **Damages:** Damages are a monetary compensation allowed to the injured party by the court for the loss or injury suffered by him.
23. **Del credere agent:** A del credere agent is an agent who assumes, for a special commission, the responsibility for ensuring that the parties with whom his principal is brought into contractual relations will pay the money on the due date.
24. **Delegatus non protest delegare:** This means that a person to whom authority has been given cannot delegate that authority to another.
25. **Discharge of contract:** The termination of contractual relationship between the parties is called the discharge of contract.
26. **Executed contracts:** These are contracts which have been completed by performance from both the sides, and nothing remains to be done by any party.
27. **Executory contracts:** These are contracts in which performance is still due either from one side or both the sides.
28. **Finder of goods:** Finder of goods is a person who finds goods belonging to another and takes them into his custody.
29. **Fraud:** The term 'fraud' includes all intentional or wilful misrepresentation of facts which are material for the formation of a contract.
30. **Free consent:** A consent is said to be free if it is not influenced by the coercion, undue influence, fraud, misrepresentation and mistake.
31. **General lien:** General lien means a right to hold the goods bailed as a security for general balance of account.
32. **General offer:** An offer is general when it is made to the world at large. It can be accepted by anyone from the public.
33. **Gratuitous bailment:** It is a bailment in which neither the bailor nor the bailee gets remuneration.
34. **Idiot:** Idiot is a person who is devoid of any faculties of thinking.
35. **Illegal agreement:** An illegal agreement is one which is against the provisions of any law prevalent in India.
36. **Injunction:** Injunction is an order of the court restraining a person from doing a particular act. Injunction may be prohibitory or mandatory.
37. **Irrevocable agency:** Irrevocable agency is the agency which cannot be revoked by the principal.
38. **Lien:** Lien is the right of any person to retain the possession of goods belonging to someone else until the charges due to the person in possession are paid.

39. **Liquidated damages:** When the amount of damages to be paid fixed by an agreement between the parties, in case of breach, is in the nature of a fair and honest pre-estimation of probable damages, it is called 'liquidated damages'.
40. **Lunatic:** Lunatic is a person whose mental power has been damaged.
41. **Minor:** A person who is below 18 years of age.
42. **Mercantile agent:** A mercantile agent is an agent who has the authority to sell the goods or to consign goods for sale, or to buy goods or to raise money on the security of goods on behalf of his principal.
43. **Misrepresentation:** An honest mis-statement of facts is called misrepresentation.
44. **Mistake:** Mistake may be defined as an erroneous belief concerning something.
45. **Nominal damages:** Nominal damages are those damages which are awarded only for namesake. They are neither compensatory nor punitive.
46. **Non-gratuitous bailment:** It is a bailment in which either the bailor or the bailee is entitled to some remuneration.
47. **Novation:** Substitution of a new contract in place of the old existing contract is known as 'novation of contract'.
48. **Ostensible authority:** Ostensible authority is the authority of an agent as it appears to others.
49. **Pardanashin woman:** Pardanashin woman is a lady who is totally isolated or secluded from the ordinary social intercourse.
50. **Pledge:** The bailment of goods as security for the payment of a debt or performance of a promise is called 'pledge'.
51. **Present consideration:** When the promisor receives consideration simultaneously with his promise, it is present consideration.
52. **Quantum meruit:** Quantum meruit means as much as is merited or as much as earned.
53. **Reciprocal promises:** Promises which form consideration or part of the consideration for each other are called reciprocal promises.
54. **Remission:** Remission means acceptance of a lesser performance than what is actually due under the contract.
55. **Rescission:** Rescission means cancellation or revocation of the term of the contract.
56. **Revocation:** Revocation means withdrawal or taking back.
57. **Right of set-off:** Set-off implies a counter claim or deduction from the amount of loan.
58. **Specific offer:** An offer is specific when it is made to a particular person and can be accepted only by him and no one else.
59. **Specific performance:** Specific performance means 'the actual carrying out of the promise by the party in contract, exactly according to the terms of the contract'.
60. **Sub-agent:** A person appointed by and acting under the control of the original agent in the business of agency is called sub-agent.
61. **Substituted agent:** A substituted agent is a person named by the agent, at the request of the principal, to act for the principal.
62. **Tender:** An offer to perform one's obligations under a contract is called 'tender'.
63. **Unenforceable contracts:** These are contracts which are not enforceable because of some technical defect in the formation of the contract such as non-registration and understamping.
64. **Unilateral mistake:** It is a mistake of fact on the part of one of the parties only to the contract as to a matter of fact.

65. **Universal agent:** A universal agent is one who is authorized to transact all the business of his principal and to do all the acts which the principal can lawfully do and can delegate.
66. **Valid contracts:** These are contracts which are enforceable by law and which satisfy all requirements as laid down in Section 10 of the Contract Act.
67. **Vindictive damages:** Vindictive or exemplary damages are those which are intended to show the court's strong disapproval of the conduct of the guilty party in committing the wrong.
68. **Void agreement:** An agreement which is not enforceable by law.
69. **Voidable agreement:** An agreement which is enforceable at the option of aggrieved party.
70. **Waiver:** Waiver means giving up or foregoing certain rights.

UNIT III: THE SALE OF GOODS ACT, 1930

1. **Agreement to sell:** Where under a contract of sale, the transfer of property in the goods is to take place at a future time or subject to the fulfilment of certain conditions, the contract is called an 'agreement to sell'.
2. **Ascertained goods:** Goods identified subsequent to the formation of the contract of sale are called ascertained goods.
3. **Auction Sale:** Auction sale is a mode of sale where different buyers come to purchase the goods and the goods are sold to the person who is ready to pay the highest price.
4. **Caveat emptor:** The term 'caveat emptor' is a Latin word which means let the buyer beware.
5. **Conditions:** A condition is a stipulation essential to the main purpose of the contract, the breach of which gives rise to a right to treat the contract as repudiated.
6. **Contingent goods:** Goods identified subsequent to the formation of the contract of sale are called 'specific goods'.
7. **Contract of sale of goods:** A contract of sale of goods is a contract whereby a seller transfers the ownership in goods to buyer or agrees to transfer it for a price.
8. **Nemo dat quod non habet:** This maxim means no one can transfer a better title than he himself has.
9. **Right of stoppage in transit:** The right of stopping the goods while they are into the possession of a carrier and resuming possession is known as the right of stoppage in transit.
10. **Specific goods:** Goods identified and agreed upon at the time a contract of sale is made are called specific goods.
11. **Symbolic delivery:** Symbolic delivery occurs by doing some act which has the effect of putting the goods in the possession of the buyer.
12. **Transfer of property in goods:** Transfer of property in goods implies transfer of ownership. Transfer of property in goods is the essence of a contract of sale.
13. **Unascertained goods:** The goods which are not identified and ascertained at the time of sale are unascertained goods.
14. **Unpaid seller:** When buyer does not pay the price of the goods, the seller is deemed to be unpaid seller.

15. **Warranties:** A warranty is a stipulation collateral to the main purpose of the contract, the breach of which gives the aggrieved party a right to sue for damages only and not to avoid the contract itself.

Unit IV: The Limited Liability Partnership Act, 2008

1. **Business:** It includes every trade, profession, service and occupation.
2. **Certificate of incorporation:** It is a legal document relating to the formation of a company or corporation. It is a licence to form a corporation issued by state government or, in some jurisdictions, by non-governmental entity/corporation.
3. **Contributions:** Partner's contributions in the form of money or property towards the capital of an LLP. The sum total of partner's contributions towards the capital forms the security for the creditors of the LLP.
4. **Designated partners:** Section 7 provides that LLP shall have at least two 'designated partners' who are individuals and at least one of them shall be 'resident in India'. Designated partners are those partners who take decisions and function in day-to-day business of the company.
5. **Designated partner identification number (DPIN):** DPIN is the identity number issued by the RoC to every designated partner. DPIN so allotted is valid for lifetime of applicants.
6. **Dissolution:** Winding up should not mean the same thing as dissolution of the LLP. On dissolution, the LLP ceases to exist, its name is actually struck off the 'registry of LLP' by the RoC and the fact is published in the official gazette.
7. **Just and equitable:** An LLP may also be ordered to be wound up, if the court is of the opinion that it is just and equitable ground that the LLP should be wound up. The meaning of 'just and equitable' will depend upon the facts of each case.
8. **Limited liability partnership:** Limited liability partnership means a partnership formed or registered under the LLP Act.
9. **Liability of partner by holding out:** If a person (not being a partner in LLP) represent to the outside world by words spoken or written or by his conduct, or knowingly permits himself to be represented that he is a partner in a certain LLP, he is then estopple from denying his being a partner, and is liable as a partner in that LLP.
10. **Liquidator:** The liquidator is an officer who helps to complete the liquidation proceedings by realizing the assets of business and distributing them among the creditors in most fairly manner. If any surplus left, then it will be distributed between the owners of business.
11. **Voluntary winding up:** Voluntary winding up may be either by members or by creditors. Foreign LLP can establish a place of business in India and its regulatory mechanism will be as per the rules prescribed by the central government. A foreign LLP shall, within 30 days of establishing a place of business in India, file with the registrar in Form 27.
12. **Whistle-blower:** Whistle blower means a person who informs in authority or the public that the company or firm they work for is doing something wrong or illegal. The partners or employees of the LLP shall be enabled to report to the management about actual or suspected dishonesty, fraud or unethical practice. A whistle-blower who helps in the convention of the guilty will thus be protected.

13. **Winding up:** LLP is an artificial entity created by law which comes to an end by law; this is called dissolution. The process of winding up involves the realization of the assets, payment of the liabilities and distribution of surplus, if any, among the partners of the LLP by the LLP liquidator.

Unit V: The Information Technology Act, 2000

1. **Accessibility:** It means gaining entry into, instructing or communicating with the logical, arithmetical or memory function resources of a computer, computer system or computer network.
2. **Computer:** Means any electronic, magnetic, optical or other high-speed data processing device or system which performs logical, arithmetic and memory functions by manipulations of electronic, magnetic or optical impulses, and includes all input, output, processing, storage, computer software or communication facilities which are connected or related to the computer in a computer system or computer network.
3. **Computer database:** It means a representation, information, knowledge facts, concepts or instructions in text, image, audio or video that are being prepared or have been prepared in a formalized manner or have been produced by a computer system or computer network and are intended for use in a computer, computer system or computer network.
4. **Computer system:** It means a device or collection of devices, including input and output support devices and excluding calculators which are not programmable and capable of being used in conjunction with external files which contain computer programs, electronic instructions, input data and output data, that performs logic, arithmetic, data storage and retrieval, communication control and other functions.
5. **Computer virus:** It means any computer instruction, information, data or programmes that destroys, damages, degrades or adversely affects the performance of a computer resource or attaches itself to another computer resource and operates when a programmed, data or instruction is executed or some other event takes place in that computer resource.
6. **Damage:** It means to destroy, alter, add, modify or rearrange any computer resource by any means.
7. **Data:** It means a representation of information, knowledge, facts, concepts or instructions which are being prepared or have been prepared in a formalized manner, and is intended to be processed, is being processed or had been processed in a computer system or computer network, and may be in any form (including computer printouts, magnetic or optical storage media, punched cards, punched tapes) or stored internally in the memory of a computer.
8. **Digital signature certificate:** The purpose of a digital signature certificate is to authenticate the identity of an individual. It ensures that the purported person is in fact the person who sent the message. The certifying authority signs it digitally.
9. **Digital signatures:** These are the electronic signatures equivalent to the handwritten signatures. Since in an electronic message or transaction, affixing handwritten signature is not possible, authentication has to be achieved by some electronic or digital method. Digital signatures facilitate this authentication.
10. **E-commerce:** It means the ability to conduct business electronically or over the Internet. It is a term to describe technology-enabled communication with customers and suppliers for a business organization.

11. **Electronic form:** Electronic form, with reference to information, means any information generated, sent, received or stored in media, magnetic, optical, computer memory, microfilm, computer generated micro fiche or similar device.
12. **Hacking with computer system:** Whoever with the intent to cause or knowing that he is likely to cause wrongful loss or damage to the public or any person, destroys or deletes or alters any information residing in a computer resource or diminishes its value or utility or affects it injuriously by any means, commits hacking.

UNIT VI: NEGOTIABLE INSTRUMENTS ACT, 1881

1. **A promissory note:** It is an instrument in writing containing an unconditional undertaking, signed by the maker, to pay certain sum of money only to or to the order of a certain person or to the bearer of the instrument.
2. **Accommodation bill:** It means a bill which is drawn, accepted or indorsed without any consideration rather to help each other. It is the bill which is made to provide financial help to other party.
3. **Ambiguous instrument:** Where an instrument owing to its faulty drafting may be treated either as a bill of exchanger or a promissory note, such instrument is known as ambiguous instrument.
4. **Bill in sets:** Foreign bills are generally drawn in sets of three, and each set is termed as a 'via'. The practice of drawing a bill in parts is called drawing a bill 'in a set'. Each part is dispatched by a separate means of conveyance so that there may be no delay because of miscarriage in the transit.
5. **Bill of exchange:** It is an instrument in writing, containing an unconditional order, signed by the maker, directing a certain person to pay certain sum of money only to or to the order of, a certain person or to the bearer of the instrument.
6. **Cheque:** It is a bill of exchange drawn on a specified banker and not expressed to be payable otherwise than on demand. The cheque satisfies all the requirements of a bill of exchange and it is always drawn on a specified banker.
7. **Conditional or qualified endorsement:** When the endorser inserts some condition in his endorsement, it is known as conditional endorsement. It limits or negatives the liability of the endorser by putting some condition.
8. **Crossed cheque:** It is one which has two transverse parallel lines, marked across its face, with or without the words 'and company' or any abbreviation thereof. Crossing is an instruction from the drawer to the paying banker to pay the amount of a cheque through bank only and not directly to the person presenting it at the counter.
9. **Escrow:** When any negotiable instrument is delivered to any person with a condition and the condition of such delivery is not negotiable, it will be called escrow.
10. **Foreign instrument:** An instrument which is not an inland instrument is deemed to be a foreign instrument.
11. **General or blank endorsement:** Where the payee or endorsee merely signs his name on the back of the instrument without stating the name of the endorsee, it is known as blank or general endorsement.
12. **Holder:** Holder is a person who is in possession of the instrument and who obtained it by delivery or by endorsement and delivery.
13. **Holder in due course:** It means any person who for consideration became the possessor of a promissory note, bill of exchange or cheque, if payable to bearer, or the payee or

endorsee thereof, if payable to order, before the amount mentioned in it became payable and without having sufficient cause to believe that any defect existed in the title of the person from whom he derived his title.

14. **Inchoate instruments:** An instrument which is incomplete in some respect is called an inchoate instrument. Where one person signs and delivers to another person a paper stamped in accordance with the law, relating to negotiable instruments, either wholly blank or incomplete in some respect, he thereby gives prima facie authority to the holder thereof to make or complete it, for any amount not exceeding the amount covered by the stamp.
15. **Inland instruments:** It means a promissory note, bill of exchange or cheque which is (a) both drawn and made payable in India or (b) drawn upon any person resident in India.
16. **Material alteration:** Any alteration made in the instrument which affects the legal validity of the instrument or which changes the rights and responsibilities of the parties to the instrument is called material alteration.
17. **Negotiable instrument:** It means a promissory note, bill of exchange or cheque payable to order or bearer whether the words order or bearer appear on the instrument or not.
18. **Negotiation:** It means that the instrument is transferred to a person in such a manner that the transferee of the instrument becomes its holder. As a holder he has the right to possess the instrument in his own name and to recover the amount mentioned therein from concerned parties.
19. **Noting:** When a promissory note or bill of exchange has been dishonoured by the non-acceptance or non-payment, the holder may cause such dishonour to be noted by a notary public upon the instrument, or upon a paper attach thereto, or partly upon each.
20. **Partial endorsement:** A partial endorsement purports to transfer to the endorsee a part of the amount payable under the instrument.
21. **Restrictive endorsement:** Restrictive endorsement, by express words, restricts the right of further negotiation of the instrument or entitles the endorsee to receive the amount of the instrument.
22. **Sans Frais endorsement:** Sans frais endorsement is where the endorser does not want that endorsee or any subsequent holder should incur any expense on his account on the instrument.
23. **Sans recourse endorsement:** If the endorser wants to avoid liability as endorser, he can do so by adding appropriate words at the time of endorsement.
24. **Special or full endorsement:** When the endorser adds to his signature a direction to pay the amount mentioned in the instrument to, or to the order of a specified person, the endorsement is said to be in full.
25. **The payment in due course:** It means payment in accordance with the apparent tenor of the instrument in good faith and without negligence to any person in possession thereof under circumstances which do not afford a reasonable ground for believing that he is not entitled to receive payment of the amount therein mentioned.

Index